Praise for *Credo*

So much is said by so many about the Catholic Faith today—some of it is confusing, some is downright erroneous—that we must be profoundly grateful to Bishop Schneider for this faithful, succinct, profound, and truly up-to-date exposition of the teaching of the Catholic Church. Utterly conscious of the duty received at his episcopal consecration, faithfully to hand on intact that which he himself has received in the living tradition of the Church, in this *Compendium* Bishop Schneider invites all men and women of good will to deepen (and even, where necessary, to correct) their knowledge of Catholic doctrine. His clear and concise questions and responses facilitate this, whilst his assiduous notation of sources encourages a deeper exploration of the riches of the Faith. While I am sure that this book will serve Bishop Schneider's aim of coming to the aid of those little ones "who are hungry for the bread of right doctrine," it will also prove to be an important tool in the essential missionary work of evangelization and apologetics, in announcing the Saving Truth of Jesus Christ in our world that so desperately needs it.

—**ROBERT CARDINAL SARAH,** Prefect Emeritus of the Congregation
for Divine Worship and Discipline of the Sacraments

I am honored to join the faithful sons and daughters of the Church who have already expressed their appreciation for Bishop Schneider's *Compendium.* As others have said, the question-and-answer format is a simple and useful approach to sharing the beautiful truths that the doctrine of our Catholic faith offers the world. We are living in a time when clear and expressive presentations of our beautiful faith in God, Father, Son and Holy Spirit are at times lacking. I know that many will come to appreciate His Excellency's contribution in the near future and for years to come. May this work prove to be a great tool for those who seek to explore the truth of Jesus Christ more deeply.

—**BISHOP JOSEPH E. STRICKLAND,** Bishop of the Diocese of Tyler, Texas

When asked, "What will be the sign of Your coming and of the end of the age?" Jesus answered, "Many false prophets will arise and lead many astray" (Mt 24:3, 11). It is highly necessary to recall these words of the Lord in view of the current wide diffusion of "profane novelties of words and false knowledge" (1 Tm 6:20*) in the life of the Church and of society. With the *Credo: Compendium of the Catholic Faith*, Bishop Athanasius Schneider gives us a sure norm for guidance, since he bases it on the constant and perennial Magisterium of the Church, which has precedence over any doctrinal ambiguity, so much spread within the Church of our day. The unambiguous language of this *Compendium* offers to the faithful and clergy an opportune help to give an explanation to anyone who asks for the reason of the Catholic Faith (see 1 Pt 3:15).

—BISHOP ELIAS NASSAR, Bishop Emeritus of the
Maronite Catholic Eparchy of Sidon, Lebanon

With the *Compendium of the Catholic Faith*, Bishop Athanasius Schneider proves not only to be a true successor to the apostles, who unswervingly defends and proclaims the *depositum fidei* entrusted to him, but also like the master of a house, "who brings out of his treasury what is new and what is old" (Mt 13:52*). The special value of this *Compendium* consists above all in the fact that numerous current questions and problems (such as: transhumanism, Pentecostalism, prohibition of traditional Catholic rites, Mother Earth worship, Asian methods of meditation, female priesthood or diaconate) are clarified in the light of the traditional teaching of the Church, offering the faithful helpful orientation in times of confusion. The combination of tradition—presenting the Faith handed down to the saints once and for all (cf. Jude 3)—with innovation—dealing with today's pertinent questions regarding this Faith—sets this *Compendium* apart as uniquely valuable, and meriting to be widely distributed in other languages.

—FR. MICHAEL FIEDROWICZ, Chair of Ancient Church History
and Patrology, Theological Faculty of Trier, Germany

Returning to a presentation in the traditional language of *lex orandi—lex credendi—lex vivendi* has today become an urgent need and a great work of pastoral charity. The new work of Bishop Athanasius Schneider, *Compendium of the Catholic Faith*, in the form of questions and answers, recovers the form by which our ancestors in the Catholic Faith have been catechized, affirming the truth and rejecting error. For this reason, we are certain of the fecundity of this work. For us, contemplative nuns inserted in the heart of the Church, this organic exposition of our Catholic Faith helps us to believe, live, and joyfully celebrate the glory of the Triune God and the work of our Redemption, expressed in an eminent way in the traditional liturgy.

—COMMUNITY OF CONTEMPLATIVE NUNS FROM
SCHOLA VERITATIS, Patagonia, Chile

Certain things are classic. They're proven. The question-and-answer format, for example, has for hundreds of years been the most effective way to pass doctrine to the next generation. But good form is not enough. It fails without excellent content. In *Credo*, Bishop Schneider has renewed the form by filling it with pure doctrine, rendered in prose that is clear and direct. In these pages, doctrines are not lists to be memorized. They're cumulative. They're integrated. Bishop Schneider gives voice to the living tradition, showing that it is not merely alive, but it has power to change our lives, to make us holy. I believe this book will do much good.

—**DR. SCOTT HAHN,** Scanlan Professor of Biblical Theology, Franciscan University of Steubenville—husband and father

Bishop Athanasius Schneider says, "A Catholic mother should transmit the Catholic Faith to her children, as it were, with the 'mother's milk.'" I gave my children milk and love, but I did not always transmit all that a Catholic mother should. I now have a better chance with my youngest, having discovered Tradition and now having this *Compendium*. The way the book is organized (believing, living, and praying) is a service to us, the "little ones," whom the author declares are his primary audience. One is left with a sense of calm (despite the current crisis), and a great desire to be better.

—**DR. CATERINA LORENZO-MOLO,** Assistant Professor, University of Asia and the Pacific—wife and mother

Credo

Credo

Compendium of the Catholic Faith

by

BISHOP ATHANASIUS SCHNEIDER

SOPHIA INSTITUTE PRESS
Manchester, New Hampshire

IMPRIMATUR
✠ Peter Libasci, Bishop of Manchester
July 7, 2023

Bible quotations indicated with an asterisk (*) are either from the Challoner version of the Douay-Rheims Bible per the imprint of John Murphy Company (Baltimore, 1899), or the author's original translations from the Latin Vulgate; all others are taken from the Revised and New Revised Standard Version Bible: Catholic Edition, copyright © 1966, 1993 National Council of the Churches of Christ in the United States of America.

Printed in the United States of America. All rights reserved.

Cover design by Perceptions Studio

Front cover art: Basilica of the Holy Cross in Jerusalem. *Christ the Pantocrator*, by Antoniazzo Romano and Marco Palmezzano (ca. 1480). (DAE-97026879) © agefotostock.com: De Agostini / G. Cargagna

Sophia Institute Press
Box 5284, Manchester, NH 03108
1-800-888-9344
www.SophiaInstitute.com

Sophia Institute Press is a registered trademark of Sophia Institute.

ISBN 978-1-64413-940-0
eBook ISBN 978-1-64413-941-7

Library of Congress Control Number: 2023942472

4th printing

Dedicated to the mothers of all times, and especially of our day,
who even among persecutions transmitted to their children
the pure and changeless Catholic Faith
with mother's milk and love.

When a flood came, the waters beat fiercely
upon that house, and could not shake it,
for it was founded upon a rock.

Luke 6:48*

The simple faith of truth is greater
than the ambitious lie of eloquence.

St. Ambrose, *De Abraham*, 1:2

CONTENTS

Contents

Contents

Contents

PREFACE

O nce a common practice among Catholic bishops, the publication of this book marks the first time in over fifty years that a Roman prelate has issued a comprehensive presentation of the Faith that is entirely his own, accessible to readers of any background, and attentive to the needs of our time.

While authors of systematic works always struggle to be both concise and comprehensive, Bishop Athanasius Schneider has faced the added challenge of voicing the changeless Deposit of Faith in the popular English form of Question–Answer. Readers will find the result almost incredible: a complete explanation of Catholicism which is both thorough *and* readable; true to the changeless Magisterium *and* captivatingly current; at once ancient and contemporary, faithful and fruitful.

Some aspects of the work deserve special mention. First, the amount and variety of quoted material has necessitated standard capitalization for certain terms (e.g., Eucharist) to avoid confusion, and endnotes have been preferred to facilitate an easier read of the body text. Second, a uniquely visual page layout has been adopted: bleed tabs track the three parts of the book, while running headers indicate each section and chapter, allowing the reader to immediately find his place in the flow of ideas. Third, two excellent indexes are included, enabling rapid reference to major subjects.

Also worth noting is the fact that the author's impressive command of Sacred Scripture plainly shows itself in hundreds of biblical references from four different Bible translations: the Catholic Editions of the Revised and New Revised Standard Versions, the John Murphy edition of Challoner's Douay-Rheims, and original translations from the Latin Vulgate. For consistency, references to the latter two are indicated in the text by an asterisk (*), and all citations have been unified under the Douay-Rheims system of notation.

As a final word to the reader, it is important to emphasize that this is a systematic work: as such, terms and themes are often defined or illustrated in multiple places, shedding further light on each concept as it is considered from the different perspectives of Faith, Morals, and Worship. Regular use of the Index of Subjects is highly recommended for those seeking a strictly topical study.

We are deeply grateful to Bishop Athanasius Schneider for this clear and articulate summary of Church teaching, in which one may readily discern the living voice of the apostles. We pray that it bears lasting testimony to all that God has taught and commanded, so that we might "know, love, and serve Him in this life, so to be happy with Him forever in the next."

AUTHOR'S
PREFACE

"Teach all nations…to observe all things whatsoever I have commanded you" (Mt 28:19-20*). This authority and mandate to instruct peoples of every time and place in divine doctrine was directly conferred by the Eternal Son of God upon St. Peter and the apostolic college. Since that time, this has remained the proper mission of the Catholic hierarchy.

"Woe to me if I do not proclaim the gospel!" (1 Cor 9:16). The Second Vatican Council recalled that each bishop, "as a member of the episcopal college and legitimate successor of the apostles, is obliged by Christ's institution and command to be solicitous for the whole Church, and this solicitude…contributes greatly to the advantage of the universal Church. For it is the duty of all bishops to promote and to safeguard the unity of faith and the discipline common to the whole Church, to instruct the faithful to love for the whole mystical body of Christ."[1]

A Catholic bishop is bound to fulfill his public oath: "To maintain the deposit of faith, entire and incorrupt, as handed down by the apostles and professed by the Church everywhere and at all times."[2] Therefore, I am compelled to respond to the requests of many sons and daughters of the Church who are perplexed by the widespread doctrinal confusion in the Church of our day. I offer this work, *Credo: Compendium of the Catholic Faith*, to strengthen them in their faith and serve as a guide to the changeless teaching of the Church. Mindful of the episcopal duty to be a "nurturer of the Catholic and apostolic Faith" (*catholicae et apostolicae fidei cultoribus*) as stated in the Canon of the Mass, I also wish to bear public witness to the continuity and integrity of the Catholic and apostolic doctrine. In preparing this text, my intended audience has been chiefly God's "little ones"—faithful Catholics who are hungry for the bread of right doctrine. It is therefore in obedience to my duty toward them, laid upon me in my episcopal consecration to preach the truth in season and out of season (see 2 Tm 4:2), that I publish this *Compendium* at the present time.

The arrangement of the work follows the classic, threefold pattern. After an introduction outlining Christian identity and doctrine, Part I relates what Catholics believe, following the articles of the Apostles' Creed (*lex credendi*, the law of rightly believing); Part II explains the principles of right moral action and their application, following the commandments (*lex vivendi*, the law of rightly living); Part III treats of grace and the means of sanctification, with a focus on prayer and the sacraments (*lex orandi,* the law of rightly praying and being). Finally, the appendices include the five major creeds—demonstrating through these famous dogmatic summaries that the Catholic Church continues to hold "one Lord, one faith, one baptism" (Eph 4:5)—and some of the more prominent prayers and liturgical items from the Catholic devotional life. As a Roman prelate, my attention is generally given to the doctrine and customs of the Latin Church, although I have included several more Eastern notions and practices that help to highlight certain points. Given the antiquity and sacrality of the traditional Roman Rite—so praised by Pope Benedict XVI, under whom I was consecrated bishop—I have further chosen to highlight its rites and ceremonies as found in the ritual books predating the liturgical changes of the 1960s, noting certain differences wherever this seemed advisable.

In preparing this text for English publication, I am especially indebted to the initiative of Mr. Aaron Seng of the Catholic educational resource company Tradivox. I also owe deep gratitude to several highly qualified theologians from different countries who made a major contribution to this text by proposing valuable suggestions and amendments. My heartfelt thanks also go to Mr. Charlie McKinney and the staff of Sophia Institute Press, who made the publication of this book possible. May the Lord with His abundant graces reward all true Catholic faithful, who labor today in an exemplary manner for the preservation, transmission, and defense of the Catholic Faith, "once delivered to the saints" (Jude 3*).

May the holy Apostles, Fathers, and Doctors of the Church intercede for all who will use this *Compendium,* so that they may receive many spiritual benefits therefrom. May the Blessed Virgin Mary, the Mother of God and our tender Mother, worthily invoked in the Church as Destroyer of All Heresies and Seat of Wisdom, protect us with her motherly mantle and pray for us that we may be made worthy of the promises of her divine Son, the Word made flesh, who is full of truth and, being at the bosom of the Father, has revealed to us all truth (see Jn 1:14, 18).

May 2, 2023, Feast of St. Athanasius

✠ Athanasius Schneider, Auxiliary Bishop of the
Archdiocese of Saint Mary in Astana

INTRODUCTION — Christian Doctrine

Christian Identity

1. **What does the word *Christian* mean?**
A Christian is a baptized person, thereby incorporated into the Mystical Body of Christ and called to be a disciple or follower of Jesus Christ.

2. **What is a *Catholic*?**
A person baptized into the one Church established by Jesus Christ, bound to believe and profess the entirety of His doctrine and remain in the unity of His Mystical Body, the Church—by receiving the sacraments He instituted and submitting to the legitimate pastors He commissioned.

3. **Why is the Christian name called a *grace of God*?**
Grace is a supernatural gift of God given to intellectual creatures (men, angels) for their eternal salvation. The glory of the Christian name is therefore a grace, a divine gift made available to us through God's own pure goodness and love for us.

4. **Does this gift bestow upon us a great dignity?**
Yes. By the wondrous gift of sanctifying grace, we become adopted children of God the Father, brethren of the Eternal Son, and living temples of the Holy Spirit.

5. **What kinds of duties do Christians have?**
We have duties to God, to ourselves, and to our neighbor.

6. **What are our duties to God?**
We must follow the first and greatest of all commandments: "You shall love the Lord your God with all your heart, and with all your soul, and with all your mind" (Mt 22:37). We must strive to know, love, and serve Him in this life, so to be happy with Him forever in the next.

7. **What are our duties to ourselves?**
We must "put on the Lord Jesus Christ" (Rom 13:14), "the new man" (Eph 4:24*), by ridding ourselves of sin, error, and disordered attachments to earthly things. We must conform ourselves to the new life of God's grace in our souls, being thereby "imitators of God" (Eph 5:1), mindful that "he who loves iniquity hates his own soul" (Ps 10:6*).

8. **What are our duties to our neighbor?**
We must observe the second of all commandments: "You shall love your neighbor as yourself" (Mt 22:39). We must act for our neighbor's good, and above all for his eternal salvation. "Love one another, as I have loved you" (Jn 13:34*).

9. **What is the symbol of the true Christian?**
   The *sign of the cross*: a symbolic gesture reminding us of our dignity and duties in Christ. "What else is the sign of Christ but the Cross of Christ? For unless that sign be applied, whether it be to the foreheads of believers, or to the very water out of which they are regenerated, or to the oil with which they receive the anointing chrism, or to the sacrifice that nourishes them, none of them is properly administered."[1]

10. **What is the power of the sign of the cross?**
    Derived from Christ's sacrifice on the Cross, this sign has power to draw down the blessing of God, cast out the devil, and banish or weaken temptation.

11. **How should we make the sign of the cross?**
    With attentive faith, gratitude, and love, we trace this sign from forehead to breast, from left shoulder to right (or, among Eastern Christians, from right to left), invoking the Blessed Trinity: "In the name of the Father, and of the Son, and of the Holy Spirit."

12. **When should we make the sign of the cross?**
    When we rise in the morning and retire at night; before and after meals; at the beginning and end of important actions; in any danger or temptation; at various moments in the sacred liturgy.

Divine Revelation

13. **What is Christian doctrine?**
    From Latin *doctrina* (teaching), it is the teaching of Jesus Christ, preserved and transmitted by the Church.

14. **Is Christian doctrine truly divine?**
    Yes. Christian doctrine is divine because Christ, its author, is God.

15. **What does the Christian doctrine contain?**
    It contains the entirety of divine revelation, as well as many natural truths that are necessary to believe.

16. **What is divine revelation?**
    Revelation is a supernatural communication that occurred publicly in human history, in which God has revealed Himself and shown what man must know, believe, and do to live well on earth and be united to God forever in the bliss of heaven. Jesus Christ, the Incarnate Word of God, Himself is the fullness of divine revelation: "The only-begotten Son who is in the bosom of the Father, He has made Him known" (Jn 1:18*).

17. **Why must we believe what God has revealed?**
    Because God is Truth itself, and He can neither deceive nor be deceived.[2]

18. **Into how many historical periods may revelation be grouped?**
Three: 1. The *primitive* period, in which a Redeemer was promised after the Fall of man; 2. The *Old Covenant* period, which prepared His way by prophecies, foreshadowings, and legal ceremonies; 3. The *New Covenant* or *evangelical* period, in which God came personally to live on earth and teach by word and example.

19. **Is divine revelation ongoing?**
No. Public revelation concluded in the first Christian century with the death of St. John, the last of Christ's apostles. It exists now as the *depositum fidei*, a fixed and stable "deposit of faith" (see 1 Tm 6:20; and 2 Tm 1:12–14) often simply called "the Faith."

Sources of Christian Doctrine

20. **Where is divine revelation contained?**
This one sacred deposit of the word of God is found in both *Sacred Scripture*, called the written word of God, and *Sacred Tradition*, called the "handed-on" or unwritten word of God.[3]

21. **What is *Sacred Scripture*?**
The word of God, written under the inspiration of the Holy Spirit, and contained in the Church-recognized books that make up what is commonly known as the Holy Bible. "All Scripture is divinely inspired and has its use for teaching the truth and refuting error, for reformation of manners and discipline in right living, so that the man who belongs to God may be efficient and equipped for good work of every kind" (2 Tm 3:16–17*).

22. **How are the books of Scripture divided?**
The Bible consists of seventy-three books, divided into two principal parts: 1. The Old Testament portion of forty-six books; 2. The New Testament portion of twenty-seven books.

23. **What is the Old Testament?**
The books of the Old Testament are the inspired word of God, containing the record of that *covenant* or "sacred oath" God made with His Chosen People, and which lasted until the coming of Christ and found its fulfillment in Him.

24. **What is the New Testament?**
The books of the New Testament are the inspired word of God, containing the record of that new and everlasting covenant God made with the whole human race through Jesus Christ, His coeternal and divine Son, which will last to the end of time.

25. **Why were the various sacred books included in the Holy Bible?**
The Church authoritatively and infallibly recognized each as inspired by God, and thus established the *canon* (rule or measure) of Scripture in the early Christian centuries.

26. **What does it mean to say that Holy Scripture is *divinely inspired*?**
"In composing the sacred books, God chose men, and, while employed by Him, they made use of their powers and abilities, so that, with Him acting in them and through them, they, as true authors, consigned to writing everything and only those things which He wanted. Therefore, since everything asserted by the inspired authors or sacred writers must be held to be asserted by the Holy Spirit, it follows that the books of Scripture must be acknowledged as teaching solidly, faithfully, and without error that truth which God wanted put into sacred writings for the sake of salvation."[4]

27. **Can we compare the divine inspiration of Holy Scripture with the mystery of the Incarnation?**
Yes. "As the substantial Word of God became like to men in all things except sin, so the words of God, expressed in human language, are made like to human speech in every respect, except error."[5]

28. **How do we know that the sacred books were written under divine inspiration?**
We know it from the witness of history (see Ez 3:1–4; 16–17; Jer 1:7–10; 2 Pt 1:21; and 2 Tm 3:16), and above all from the Church, which teaches with the inerrant authority of Christ.

29. **How did the Church identify the canon of books in Holy Scripture?**
By her own constant tradition, already present in the first centuries, as witnessed by St. Athanasius in 367,[6] Pope Damasus I in 382,[7] the Council of Carthage in 397,[8] and elsewhere. Until Martin Luther (1483–1546), the traditional canon of the biblical books was not contested. Luther rejected some New Testament books (e.g., the Epistle to James, which he called the "straw letter") and the so-called "deuterocanonical" books of the Old Testament (Tobias, Judith, Baruch, Ecclesiasticus, Wisdom, Machabees I and II, and certain portions of Esther and Daniel).

30. **When did the Church dogmatically define the canon of Holy Scripture?**
At the Council of Trent (1545–1563), to correct the errors of Martin Luther and other heretics.[9]

31. **Must all the books of Holy Scripture be equally respected and honored?**
Yes. "The Church receives and venerates with a feeling of piety and reverence all the books both of the Old and New Testaments, since one God is the author of both."[10]

32. **Why do the books of Holy Scripture hold such authority?**
"Not because, having been composed by human industry, they were afterward approved by her authority, nor merely because they contain revelation without error, but because, having been written under the inspiration of the Holy Spirit, they have God for their author, and as such were handed down to the Church herself."[11]

33. **Can reason demonstrate the historical reliability of Scripture?**
Yes. Historical, literary, and theological studies have repeatedly upheld its authenticity, integrity, and veracity.

34. **Does the Church forbid the private reading of the Bible?**
No. Indeed, it may nourish our personal spiritual life and prayer, especially the Gospels and the Psalms. Pope Benedict XV recommended that especially the Gospels and the Acts of the Apostles be so widely diffused that no Christian family go without them. [12] Well known are the words of the Doctor of the Church, St. Jerome: "Ignorance of Scripture is ignorance of Christ."[13]

35. **Have many other saints recommended private reading of the Bible?**
Yes. St. Thérèse of Lisieux, Doctor of the Church, said: "I have only to open the holy Gospels and at once I breathe the perfume of Jesus' life, and then I know which way to run. ... I feel that even had I on my conscience every crime one could commit ... my heart broken with sorrow, I would throw myself into the arms of my Savior Jesus, because I know that He loves the prodigal son who returns to Him."[14]

36. **What is the true role of the *exegete*—one who comments on Scripture?**
"Commentators of the sacred letters, mindful of the fact that here there is question of a divinely inspired text, the care and interpretation of which have been confided to the Church by God Himself, should no less diligently take into account the explanations and declarations of the teaching authority of the Church, as likewise the interpretation given by the holy Fathers, and even 'the analogy of faith.'... With special zeal should they apply themselves, not only to expounding exclusively these matters which belong to the historical, archaeological, philological, and other auxiliary sciences—as, to Our regret, is done in certain commentaries—but, having duly referred to these, insofar as they may aid the exegesis, they should set forth in particular the theological doctrine in faith and morals of the individual books or texts so that their exposition may not only aid the professors of theology in their explanations and proofs of the dogmas of faith, but may also be of assistance to priests in their presentation of Christian doctrine to the people, and in fine may help all the faithful to lead a life that is holy and worthy of a Christian."[15]

37. **What resources should Catholic exegetes regularly consult?**
"The Catholic exegete will find invaluable help in an assiduous study of those works in which the Holy Fathers, the Doctors of the Church and the renowned interpreters of past ages have explained the sacred books. For, although sometimes less instructed in profane learning and in the knowledge of languages than the scripture scholars of our time, nevertheless by reason of the office assigned to them by God in the Church, they are distinguished by a certain subtle insight into heavenly things and by a marvelous keenness of intellect, which enables them to penetrate to the very innermost meaning of the divine word and bring to light all that can help to elucidate the teaching of Christ and to promote holiness of life."[16]

38. **Is Sacred Scripture the only source of Christian doctrine?**
    No. The word of God is also contained in Sacred Tradition.

39. **What is *Sacred Tradition*?**
    The word of God not written in the Bible, but transmitted in unbroken succession from the apostles to us. *Sacred* or *dogmatic* Tradition, then, contains those truths which the apostles received from Christ or the Holy Spirit and which the Church has then propagated unadulteratedly through all ages.

40. **Did the Church Fathers hold Sacred Tradition as a source of the Faith?**
    Yes, e.g., St. Epiphanius: "Tradition must be used too, for not everything is available from the Sacred Scripture. Thus the holy apostles handed some things down in scriptures but some in traditions, as St. Paul says, 'the traditions we delivered to you' [2 Thes 2:15*]";[17] and St. Augustine: "There are customs, coming, I suppose, from apostolic tradition, like many other things which are held to have been handed down under their actual sanction, because they are preserved throughout the whole Church."[18]

41. **How do Sacred Scripture and Sacred Tradition refer to one another?**
    They support one another in bearing witness to the revealed truths. Catholic theology therefore speaks of *traditio declarativa* as Tradition clarifies and expounds the sometimes obscure words of Scripture, and of *traditio constitutiva* as it enriches the content of revelation given in Holy Scripture with its own divine truth;[19] e.g., the determination of the canon of Holy Scripture, infant baptism, the number of the sacraments, the doctrine of purgatory, Mary's Immaculate Conception and bodily Assumption, and the sacrament of orders (episcopate, presbyterate, deaconate) as being able to be received only by men.

42. **Is Tradition of equal authority with Scripture?**
    Yes, because it is equally the divine word of God, communicated in a different mode.[20]

43. **Where are the teachings of Sacred Tradition contained?**
    In the dogmatic decrees of the ecumenical councils; in the doctrinal acts of the Holy See; in the doctrinal decrees of local councils, approved by the Holy See; in liturgical rites of venerable antiquity; in constant ecclesiastical laws ("canon law"); in the writings of the Church Fathers and Doctors; and in the common, constant, and universal teaching of the entire episcopacy in union with its head, the Roman Pontiff.

44. **Who may authoritatively interpret both Scripture and Tradition?**
    Only the infallible teaching authority of the *Magisterium*, the formal teaching office of the Catholic Church, which is exercised by the pope alone or by the pope together with the bishops.

45. **Is the Magisterium also a source of divine revelation?**
    No. The Magisterium is only the servant, guardian, and expositor of God's revelation: "Not so that they might make known some new doctrine, but that, by [God's]

assistance, they might religiously guard and faithfully expound the revelation or Deposit of Faith transmitted by the apostles."[21]

46. **Can the Magisterium change the content of this Deposit of Faith?**
No. "Heaven and earth shall pass away, but My words shall never pass away" (Mt 24:35*). It is beyond the power of the Church to add to, subtract from, or alter the content of divine revelation, for she is charged strictly to teach "all those things whatsoever I have commanded you" (Mt 28:20*).

47. **What is the true meaning of the expression *living Magisterium*?**
It means that the apostolic preaching, voiced through the Church's Magisterium, will not cease until the end of the world. The voice of the apostles still lives and speaks when their successors, in an unbroken and faithful tradition, preserve and transmit the revealed truths; passing the living torch of the immutable doctrine of Faith, always *eodem dogmate, eodem sensu, eademque sententia*—"the same dogma, in the same sense, and in the same meaning."[22]

48. **What of a *development of doctrine*, subject to changing circumstances?**
The expressions "living tradition," "living Magisterium," "hermeneutic of continuity," and "development of doctrine," properly understood, can only mean that a greater clarity or precision is given to the same changeless content of divine revelation over time. Such new insights can never contradict what the Church has previously and definitively proposed, because Christ promised that the Holy Spirit would not reveal anything new, but only remind the disciples of what He told them (see Jn 14:26).

49. **What are the main errors against the fact of divine revelation?**
1. Materialism, naturalism, deism, atheism, and all systems of belief that irrationally deny the existence or even the possibility of divine revelation; 2. All heresies which reject any one of the revealed truths.

50. **What is the principal source of these errors?**
Sin. Pride and lust darken the mind and especially lead man to prefer his own judgment and personal comfort over submission to a divinely revealed body of doctrine, morals, and worship.

Study of Christian Doctrine

51. **Why is Christian doctrine, the "science" of religion, the most excellent of sciences?**
Because it is the most certain, the most beautiful, the most consoling, and the most necessary of all sciences.

52. **Why is the science of religion the most certain?**
Because it is founded on the infallible word of God: "I am the way, and the truth, and the life" (Jn 14:6).

53. **Why is the science of religion the most beautiful?**
Because it concerns realities that are most worthy of our admiration: God and His infinite perfections, the marvelous work of our Redemption, the human soul and its glorious destiny.

54. **Why is the science of religion the most consoling?**
Because it alone offers a universal and effective remedy for moral evil, and gives man strength and solace in his trials.

55. **Why is the science of religion the most necessary?**
Because it alone teaches us fully about the "one thing necessary": our divine calling, and the way to attain the eternal joys of heaven.

56. **Is doctrine the same as dogma?**
Sometimes used interchangeably, *dogma* properly refers to those particular tenets of faith that have been defined by the Church as divinely revealed truths which are to be believed with divine faith.

57. **Is ignorance in matters of religion a very great evil?**
Yes. Ignorance is the source of countless disorders in individuals and society, and culpable ignorance leads to eternal damnation.

58. **When should we begin to study Christian doctrine?**
In early childhood, for children with the use of reason are bound to know, love, and serve God, their simple souls are naturally disposed to receive the truths of religion, and virtuous habits are most easily formed and maintained from the early years, even before reason is fully operative.

59. **In studying Christian doctrine, what should our attitude be?**
Love of wisdom, humility of mind, purity of heart, desire for God, docility to God's authentic teaching, and fidelity to prayer.

60. **How may Christian doctrine be divided?**
Into three parts: faith, morals, and worship.

61. **What is contained under the category of *faith*?**
Those supernatural truths that we should believe, as summarized in the various *Creeds* or Symbols of Faith, used by the Catholic Church.

62. **What is contained under the category of *morals*?**
Those works or actions that we should perform, as summarized in the commandments of God and the moral teaching of the Church.

63. **What is contained under the category of *worship*?**
Those supernatural means that we should use to honor God and receive His grace, especially prayer and the sacraments.

PART I — Faith: Believing Truly
Lex credendi

The Creed in General

1. **What is the Christian meaning of the word *creed*?**
From the Latin *credo* (I believe), it signifies a brief summary of the Christian doctrine, promulgated by the Church.

2. **What are the principal creeds?**
The Apostles' Creed, the Niceno-Constantinopolitan Creed, the Athanasian Creed, the Tridentine Profession of Faith, and the Credo of the People of God of Pope Paul VI.[1]

3. **Which creed is the most used?**
The Apostles' Creed, because it is the briefest and most ancient summary that we have of the doctrine taught by the apostles.

4. **Why was the Apostles' Creed composed?**
1. To give Christians a clear and simple summary of Jesus' doctrine; 2. To guarantee their unity in the same faith.

5. **Do the other creeds express the same doctrine as the Apostles' Creed?**
Yes. Some of the articles are developed more fully in the other creeds, to guard against various errors that have arisen from time to time.

6. **How many articles are in the Apostles' Creed?**
There are twelve, as follows:
   1. I believe in God, the Father Almighty, Creator of heaven and earth;
   2. And in Jesus Christ, His only Son, Our Lord;
   3. Who was conceived by the Holy Spirit, born of the Virgin Mary;
   4. Suffered under Pontius Pilate, was crucified, died, and was buried;
   5. He descended into hell; on the third day He rose again from the dead;
   6. He ascended into heaven, and sits at the right hand of God, the Father Almighty;
   7. From thence He shall come to judge the living and the dead;
   8. I believe in the Holy Spirit;
   9. The holy Catholic Church, the communion of saints;
   10. The forgiveness of sins;
   11. The resurrection of the body;
   12. And life everlasting.

7. **What kinds of truths are contained in the Creed?**
Two kinds: 1. Truths of the natural order; 2. Truths of the supernatural order.

8. **What are truths of the natural order?**
Truths that human reason can discover and demonstrate without the help of grace; e.g., the existence of God, His providence, and the immortality of the soul.

9. **What are truths of the supernatural order?**
Truths that can only be known if God reveals them; e.g., His nature as a Trinity of divine Persons, and the Incarnation of the Son of God.

10. **How may the twelve articles of the Creed be divided?**
Into three groups: 1. The first article, about God the Father and Creation; 2. The following six articles, about God the Son and Redemption; 3. The last five articles, about God the Holy Spirit and Sanctification.

11. **What are a Christian's duties with respect to the Creed?**
1. To know the Creed and recite it often; 2. To recite it with lively faith and devotion; 3. To publicly profess it when required: "Whosoever shall confess Me before men, him shall the Son of Man also confess before the angels of God" (Lk 12:8*).

12. **Is it lawful to accept some articles of the Creed and reject others?**
No. "Such is the nature of faith that nothing can be more absurd than to accept some things and reject others. Faith, as the Church teaches, is 'that supernatural virtue by which, through the help of God and through the assistance of His grace, we believe what He has revealed to be true, not on account of the intrinsic truth perceived by the natural light of reason, but because of the authority of God Himself, the Revealer, who can neither deceive nor be deceived' (Council of Vatican I, Session 3, chap. 3). If then it be certain that anything is revealed by God, and this is not believed, then nothing whatsoever is believed by divine faith…. But he who dissents even in one point from divinely revealed truth absolutely rejects all faith, since he thereby refuses to honor God as the supreme truth and the formal motive of faith. 'In many things they are with me, in a few things not with me; but, in those few things in which they are not with me, the many things in which they are will not profit them' (St. Augustine, *In Psal.* 54, 19). And this indeed most deservedly; for they, who take from Christian doctrine what they please, lean on their own judgments, not on faith; and not 'bringing into captivity every understanding unto the obedience of Christ' (2 Cor 10:5*), they more truly obey themselves than God. 'You, who believe what you like, believe yourselves rather than the Gospel' (St. Augustine, *Contra Faustum Manichaeum*, bk. 17, 3)."[2]

Section 1: God the Father and Creation

FIRST ARTICLE OF THE CREED

I BELIEVE IN GOD, THE FATHER ALMIGHTY, CREATOR OF HEAVEN AND EARTH.

Chapter 1: God

Existence of God

13. What is the first truth that the Creed teaches?
The existence of God.

14. Who is God?
The one uncreated, pure, and perfect spirit, the source and master of all things, "Creator and Lord of heaven and earth, almighty, eternal, immeasurable, incomprehensible, infinite in understanding, will, and every perfection."[1]

15. What is the meaning of the words: *I believe in God?*
They mean: 1. I believe that there is one true God, the beginning and end of all things; 2. I believe in all that He has revealed; 3. I abandon myself with love and trust to Him, as He is goodness itself.

16. How do we know that God exists?
From both divine revelation and the light of natural reason: "There exists a twofold order of knowledge, distinct not only as regards their source, but also as regards their object. With regard to the source, because we know in one by natural reason, in the other by divine faith. With regard to the object, because besides those things which natural reason can attain, there are proposed for our belief mysteries hidden in God which, unless they are divinely revealed, cannot be known."[2]

17. How do we know God's existence from revelation?
Because God revealed Himself in various ways from the time of Adam, through Moses and the prophets in the Old Testament, and finally took on a human nature to live on the earth, in the divine Person of Jesus of Nazareth.

18. How do we know God's existence from reason?
By considering the order, quality, and intelligibility of created things, we can gain a certain knowledge of God's existence.

Proofs of the Existence of God

19. What are the main rational proofs for the existence of God?
1. Motion—all created beings were set into motion, God is the *unmoved mover*;
2. Efficient Causality—there is a chain of causes which requires God as *first cause*;
3. Contingency—created things rely for existence on God, as the *one necessary*

being; 4. Gradation—all creatures exist within grades of being and perfection, whereas God alone is *perfectly good, perfectly true, and perfectly beautiful*; 5. Finality and Order—all created beings have a purpose and order, given to them by God as the ultimate *intelligent cause*.[3]

20. **How does motion prove God's existence?**
Every thing that is in motion cannot move by itself, but must be moved by something else. But all matter is in motion, requiring some primary and universal mover; and this is God.

21. **How does the existence of the world prove the existence of God?**
No bodily thing exists necessarily, since it is not Being itself. But the world is not Being itself and need not exist. Therefore the world must depend for its existence on some other being that exists entirely of himself, indeed as Existence itself; and this is God.

22. **How does the order of the cosmos prove the existence of God?**
All natural things act in an orderly way to achieve their ends. But we observe constant and harmonious laws in the universe, even among creatures without intelligence. The parts as well as the whole must ultimately be under the control of a being that is intelligent, wise, and powerful; and this is God.

23. **How does the universal moral law prove the existence of God?**
All men recognize that they are bound by a law commanding certain behaviors and forbidding others. This law cannot be explained by any natural cause, but points to a supreme and universal lawgiver, the secret witness and judge of all our actions; and this is God.

24. **How does the consensus of all peoples through history give credibility to the existence of God?**
All peoples through history have acknowledged some unseen power on whom they depend and to whom they are responsible. But wishful thinking cannot explain this belief, since this unseen divine power is often opposed to human wants; therefore, God Himself must be the cause of this universal belief in the divine and the sense of objective moral responsibility.

25. **What should we conclude from these proofs?**
We should conclude that belief in God is a perfectly reasonable human act, and that to seek Him is the noblest and most necessary of all human endeavors.

26. **What do we call those who deny the existence of God?**
They are known as *atheists*, although they are seldom such in practice. When it is not due to desire for human esteem or material benefit, atheism can arise from simple ignorance, faulty reasoning, or corruption of heart.

27. **What should we think of professionals in the natural sciences who claim to disprove the existence of God?**
They have exceeded the inherent limits of all natural science, and have adopted the errors of a faulty philosophy. They are to be pitied, and it is necessary to pray for them, so that they can discover the truth by God's grace, the teaching of the Church, and the witness of the faithful.

Nature and Attributes of God

28. **What is meant by the *nature* or *essence* of a being?**
That intrinsic principle by which a thing is what it is; that without which it could not exist.

29. **Can we know the divine nature as it is in itself?**
No. We cannot fully comprehend the divine nature, for God is infinite in His essence and perfections, whereas our intelligence is always limited: but by His grace, we will be able to see God in heaven "as He is" (1 Jn 3:2).

30. **What is meant by the *attributes* of God?**
Those perfections that belong to Him as being proper to Him; for this reason they are also called divine properties or characteristics.

31. **What are some of these attributes?**
Some are proper to God considered in Himself, such as His infinity, unity, simplicity, uncreatedness, immutability, eternity, intelligence, and will.

32. **What is meant by the *infinity* of God?**
That His nature and perfections exceed all measure and are without any limit.

33. **What is meant by the *unity* of God?**
That there is only one God, for there is one divine being, and there cannot be many gods.

34. **What is meant by the *simplicity* or *spirituality* of God?**
That He has no material body, and is free from every kind of composition or division.

35. **What is meant by the *uncreatedness* of God?**
That He is entirely sufficient for Himself. He is not one being among others, but exists simply of Himself, with no need of other beings.

36. **What is meant by the *immutability* of God?**
That He is not subject to development or any other kind of change.

37. **What is meant by the *eternity* of God?**
That He exists forever outside of time, has no beginning, and can have no end.

38. **Are there other divine attributes?**
    Yes; e.g., His holiness, justice, truthfulness, mercy, wisdom, goodness, omnipresence, omniscience, and omnipotence.

39. **What is meant by the *holiness* of God?**
    That His goodness has no evil whatsoever, and that He has infinite love for what is good, and infinite hatred for what is evil.

40. **What is meant by the *goodness* of God?**
    That He is the unlimited ocean of perfection, and always acts for the good of His creatures.

41. **What is meant by the *justice* of God?**
    That He gives to each being that which is due to it.

42. **What is meant by the *truthfulness* of God?**
    That He is Truth itself, eternally expresses the truth, and can neither deceive nor be deceived.

43. **What is meant by the *mercy* of God?**
    That He communicates His goodness to us even though we do not deserve it, and generously pardons us when we repent.

44. **What is meant by the *wisdom* of God?**
    That He sees all things in the light of His own eternity, assigning to each its proper place in the divine plan.

45. **What is meant by the *omnipresence* of God?**
    That His existence is not bound by a particular place, and that He is in all actual places at once, though confined to none of them.

46. **What is meant by the *omniscience* of God?**
    That He knows all things past, present, and future, as well as those that could be.

47. **What is meant by the *omnipotence* of God?**
    That He can do all things, except what contradicts His own nature, such as to lie or to change.

48. **How has God especially demonstrated His power, wisdom, and goodness?**
    By the two orders of *creation* and of *providence*, particularly in His ability to bring good out of evil.

Providence of God

49. **What is meant by the *providence* of God?**
    That God, having created all things, now governs them according to His wisdom and goodness, especially directing His rational creatures toward their proper end.

50. What does divine providence imply?

Three simultaneous acts: 1. Prearranging the entire order of creation; 2. Sustaining all creatures in being; 3. Providing creatures with all that is necessary to attain their ends.

51. Does the providence of God extend to all created things?

Yes. It extends to the little and the great, from sand grains and supernovas to men and angels.

52. What effects should belief in God's providence produce in us?

This belief should encourage and console us; for, in the midst of all the many trials and troubles of this life, we know that we are in the hands of a loving Father, whom we can invoke with confidence.

53. How should we respond to divine providence?

We should: 1. Humbly adore God's will in our regard; 2. Trust in Him for the care of our soul and body, unto our supernatural good; 3. Strive always for the good, while accepting the various difficulties sent to us with submission and patience.

54. What objection is most often raised against divine providence?

The existence of evil, whether *physical*, such as suffering, or *moral*, such as sin and its consequences. Some claim that if God governs the world with wisdom, power, and goodness, then it is impossible to account for disasters, suffering, injustice, and crime in the world.

55. How may this objection be answered?

God is not the author of evil; but rather, suffering, sickness, and death are the consequence of our first parents' rebellion against God.

56. Why is it impossible for God to be the author of evil?

God is absolutely good and wills only good for His creatures, and therefore can only cause good. Evil comes from the free choice of His creatures and the resulting imperfections in creation, which He merely permits. "Though God has wrought the afflictions that have been in all ages, it is our offenses that are the cause of our troubles. No man can complain against our Creator; it is for Him to complain against us, who have sinned and constrained Him to be wrathful though He wills it not, and to smite though He desires it not."[4]

57. Then why does God allow any evil to occur?

God permits some evils as the natural consequence of creating rational beings. In His wisdom, He alone can turn evil into our benefit: "We know that to them that love God, all things work together unto good" (Rom 8:28*).

58. How can God turn physical evil to a good end?

By making it serve as an atonement for sin, a remedy for vice or test of virtue, and a source of merit for those who suffer well. Even the suffering of infants without the use of reason, God accepts as an atonement for sin.

59. **How can God turn moral evil—even sin itself—to a good end?**
1. In tolerating evildoers and persecutors, God gives the just an occasion to practice heroic virtue, and prompts the timid to greater zeal in His service; 2. In pardoning repentant sinners, He manifests His mercy and kindness; 3. In punishing the impenitent, He displays His eternal justice.

60. **What is the greatest answer to this "problem" of evil, raised against God's providence?**
That God does not abandon us to evil, but redeems us from evil through His Eternal Son, who, in an act of ineffable humility and compassion, came to earth and willingly suffered the greatest evil in history—the Crucifixion—out of love for us.

Chapter 2: The Blessed Trinity

Mysteries in General

61. **What is a *mystery*?**
A truth that is impossible for any creature to fully comprehend or explain. Some mysteries are natural, others are supernatural.

62. **Are there any true mysteries, or has our knowledge simply not advanced enough?**
Because every created mind is finite, there will always be limits it cannot pass and truths it can never fully comprehend.

63. **Are some things mysterious to man, even in the natural world?**
Yes, such as the union of soul and body or the irreducible complexity of cellular life.

64. **What should we therefore conclude?**
If this finite world contains so many things that we cannot fully comprehend, we should not be astonished to find mysteries in regard to God, who is infinite.

65. **What is a mystery of religion?**
A supernatural truth revealed by God that we must believe, although we can never completely understand or demonstrate it with our reason.

66. **What are the principal mysteries of religion?**
The *Blessed Trinity*, the *Incarnation*, and the *Redemption*.

Mystery of the Blessed Trinity

67. **What is the mystery of the *Blessed Trinity*?**
Meaning "the holy Three," the Blessed Trinity is the mystery of one God in three distinct but coequal Persons: Father, Son, and Holy Spirit.

68. **How do we know this mystery?**
We can only know this by divine revelation, as God has revealed Himself to man.

69. **Is each of the three Persons God?**
Yes. The Father is God, the Son is God, and the Holy Spirit is God.

70. **Are the three divine Persons three different gods?**
No. They are not three gods, but one and the same God. They are *consubstantial*, having the same divine nature and substance.

71. **Is any one of the three divine Persons older, more powerful, or more perfect?**
No. The three divine Persons are coequal in eternity, omnipotence, perfection, and in all other things, except what properly individuates each Person as such.

72. **Are the three divine Persons really distinct, and yet united?**
Yes. They are distinct only in the relations that distinguish them. "All things in God are one, where there is no opposition of relation."[5]

73. **What personal properties distinguish the three Persons from one another?**
1. The Father proceeds from no principle, but is the principle of the other two Persons; 2. The Son is begotten of the Father, and has no principle but the Father; 3. The Holy Spirit proceeds from both the Father and the Son as from one principle.

74. **Why are the three divine Persons distinguished in this way?**
Because the Father eternally begets the Son, who is His Word, His Wisdom, and His perfect Image. The Father and Son together eternally breathe forth the Holy Spirit.

75. **Are the three divine Persons separate in their external actions?**
No. They concur equally and perfectly in all their external actions, although Creation is fittingly ascribed to the Father, Redemption to the Son, and Sanctification to the Holy Spirit. Nevertheless, the Incarnation and Redemption, although Trinitarian in origin and power, are the personal work of the Son in execution, as He alone took flesh and died for us on the Cross.

76. **Is the mystery of the Holy Trinity contrary to reason?**
No. Although it is above our reason (*suprarational*), it is not contrary to reason itself (*irrational*).

77. **Is this mystery entirely unintelligible?**
No. Although it is impossible to understand or explain completely (*incomprehensible*), it is not entirely impossible to understand or explain in some way. We can form some idea of it through analogy.

78. **What analogy does St. Augustine offer for the mystery of the Holy Trinity?**
The unity of man's memory, intelligence, and will: "When we speak of them singly, even what pertains to one of them is done by all. After all, memory alone does not produce a speech which we produce from memory; rather, intelligence and will cooperate in producing it, though it pertains only to memory. It is quite easy to see this with regard to the other two as well. For whatever intelligence of itself speaks,

it does not speak without memory and will, and whatever the will of itself says or writes, it does not do without intelligence and memory."[6]

79. **What are the principal religious errors regarding the Holy Trinity?**
1. Arianism and Macedonianism, fourth-century heresies restricting true divinity to the Father and denying the eternal divinity of the Son and Holy Spirit; 2. Islam, contemporary Judaism, various Unitarian sects, and Modernism within the Catholic Church, all of which reject God's self-revelation as a Trinity of divine and consubstantial Persons; 3. Buddhism, Hinduism, pantheism, and other systems that reject the simplicity or unity of God independent of creatures.

Chapter 3: Creation

Fact of Creation

80. **What is creation?**
The act by which God freely creates beings out of nothing (*ex nihilo*), i.e., making a thing to be which previously did not exist.

81. **To whom does this creative act belong?**
To God alone, because it requires infinite being to cause something to exist that once had no being. Conversely, a creature only acts upon other things, as a sculptor needs marble to shape a statue.

82. **What of theories claiming that the universe began spontaneously, either by itself or from some preexisting matter?**
These are errors of philosophy rather than claims of empirical science, and are also impossibilities. Nothing can come from nothing, and nothing can cause itself to exist.

83. **Was God obliged to create all things?**
No. As the fullness of being itself, God is infinitely perfect, happy, and sufficient in Himself. He has no need of other beings; He already gives of Himself completely and fully within the Trinity of the divine Persons. Neither His nature nor His good will inevitably compelled Him to create; He was entirely free to create or not.

84. **Then why did God choose to create?**
To reveal His own goodness and perfection by the blessings which, in His love, He freely bestows on creatures.

85. **Then creation is really distinct from God, and subordinated to Him?**
Yes. Throughout history, various false religions and pantheistic philosophies have regarded creation as a divine manifestation, emanation, or somehow part of God (see Rom 1; and Ws 13)—but the true God is in no way dependent on creatures.

86. **In our time, what is the chief error about this distinction between God and creation?**
The personification and even deification of nature, often manifested in forms of environmental idolatry, ecological mysticism, Earth-goddess rituals, animism, and other forms of pagan worship.

87. **What is the error of so-called "transhumanism"?**
Man's attempt to negate his creatureliness and elevate himself to a higher level of existence by manipulating human nature through technology (genetic engineering, cryonics, implants with brain-computer interfaces, etc.), in order to achieve self-perfection or even an alleged immortality. Transhumanism embodies man's original sin of wanting to be like God without grace.

88. **Why is a correct understanding of creation so essential to right faith?**
Because "error with regard to the nature of creation begets a false knowledge of God."[7]

Work of Creation

89. **What has God revealed to man about His work of Creation?**
In the divinely revealed history especially contained in the book of Genesis, this work is described as God calling the universe into existence by His Almighty Word, and giving this creation a splendid order and harmony in a sequence of six days (see Gn 1:6–8, 14–19).

90. **What was the special work of the six days of Creation?**
In fashioning the material universe ("the heavens and the earth"), on the first day God made the light. On the second day, He made the firmament or material heavens. On the third day, He made the dry land and plants. On the fourth day, He adorned the heavens with sun, moon, and stars. On the fifth day, He filled the skies and seas with birds and fish. On the sixth day, He filled the earth with land animals, and finally crowned His creation by fashioning man and woman. God called all of these "very good" (Gn 1:31), having come forth as wondrous effects from a perfect cause.

91. **What did God do after these six days?**
God rested on the seventh day, blessing it and making it holy (see Gn 2:2–3).

92. **Must we interpret the days of Genesis as twenty-four-hour periods?**
The majority of Church Fathers held the six days of creation as six literal days, but there was not moral unanimity among them on this question. Some Catholic authorities (e.g., Sts. Augustine and Thomas Aquinas[8]) recognized a diversity of permissible interpretations; and in 1909, the Pontifical Biblical Commission ruled that the six days of Genesis could be taken either in the literal sense of natural days, or in the applied sense for certain periods of time.

93. **Has the Genesis account of Creation been disproven by the natural sciences?**
No. On the contrary, the ongoing discoveries of sedimentology, astrophysics, microbiology, genetics, and other disciplines continue to confirm the sacred history of

Genesis in those truths that, according to the Magisterium, this history is meant to teach us.[9]

94. **What major lessons can be gathered thus far?**
1. The universe is not eternal, but had its origin in time; 2. The existence of creation was not the result of natural processes, but the free act of God; 3. The universe is not random or accidental, but was formed after a determined plan of divine wisdom; 4. God did not create sin or evil, but all things good in their origin; 5. The natural world is not divine, but was fashioned for the proper use of man; 6. Natural processes have their own potentialities to develop, all of it dependent on God.

End of Creation

95. **What is the ultimate end of creation?**
To glorify God. Everything comes from God, "for from Him and through Him and to Him are all things" (Rom 11:36), and "all Your works shall give thanks to You, O Lord, and all Your faithful shall bless You" (Ps 145:10).

96. **Then man is not a creature that the Creator has willed for its own sake?**[10]
No. Although man should never be used as a mere means to an end, the notion that man exists simply "for his own sake" is the self-referential error of *anthropocentrism*, rooted in the unchristian philosophy of Immanuel Kant (1724–1804). Rather, "God wills things apart from Himself insofar as they are ordered to His own goodness as their end;"[11] and, "God is the only end of man."[12]

97. **What, then, is the divine order that we find inscribed in creation?**
Irrational creatures (e.g., minerals, plants, animals) are subject to rational creatures (angels and men), which are in turn subject to God: the supreme good and last end of all things.

98. **What is man's duty toward other creatures?**
1. Not to seek his ultimate fulfillment in them; 2. To respect and learn from them as works of divine wisdom; 3. To use them responsibly, as means to rise to God; 4. In all his actions to seek first the glory of God.

Chapter 4: The Angels

Angels in General

99. **What is an angel?**
Meaning "messenger," an *angel* is a pure spirit, a being of personal intelligence and will, created by God to glorify and serve Him.

100. **Are angels more perfect than humans?**
Yes. Being more like God in their nature, angels are more perfect than man in their intelligence, will, and power over matter.

101. **How do we know that angels exist?**
From Holy Scripture, the teaching of the Church, and the history of all peoples.

102. **Why are angels depicted with bodies and wings, or as children or young men?**
Being spirits, they can appear in bodily form, and are variously depicted in art. Wings symbolize their agility, unbounded by physical space and time, and their eagerness to do God's will; a childlike or youthful appearance expresses their innocence.

103. **In what state were the angels created?**
They were created in a state of innocence, with all the happiness proper to their nature.

104. **Did God intend for them to remain in this state?**
No. They were destined for supernatural happiness, which consists in seeing God face-to-face forever in the height of heaven. To attain this *Beatific Vision* they were submitted to a test, being given one irrevocable choice for or against God.

105. **Were all the angels victorious in this trial?**
No. Lucifer, one of the greatest angels, refused to obey God, and—according to the common theological meaning—a third of the heavenly host joined in his revolt. The rebel angels were then cast out of heaven, as Our Lord testified: "I saw Satan like lightning falling from heaven" (Lk 10:18*).

Good Angels

106. **Who are the good angels?**
Those angels who by grace overcame the trial and remained faithful to God.

107. **How were the good angels rewarded?**
They were rewarded with *salvation*: the perfect and eternal bliss of heaven, with the happiness of seeing and possessing God forever, without any fear of losing Him. The angels received this reward through the Incarnate God-Man Jesus Christ, the source of all graces.

108. **What worship do these angels give to God?**
Their life is a perpetual hymn of glory, adoration, praise, and thanksgiving to Him.

109. **How many good angels are there?**
Their number must be very great. Scripture records "myriads upon myriads" of angels in the service of God (see Dn 7:10; Heb 12:22; and Apoc 5:11).

110. **How are the good angels divided?**
Into three hierarchies, of three choirs each: 1. Seraphim, Cherubim, and Thrones; 2. Dominations, Virtues, and Powers; 3. Principalities, Archangels, and Angels.

111. **Which angels are named in Holy Scripture?**
There are three: St. Michael, St. Gabriel, and St. Raphael.

112. **Do angels interact with the visible universe?**
Yes. They have continual relations with the world, taking part in the government of nature and executing the orders of divine providence.

113. **What is a *guardian angel*?**
One of the good angels, whom God assigns to every man to protect him. According to ancient ecclesiastical tradition, each diocese, town, and nation also has a guardian angel, as recorded about the nation of Israel (see Dn 12:1).

114. **What good tasks do these angels perform for us?**
According to the direction of divine providence, they: 1. Protect our body, especially before we reach the age of reason; 2. Prevent demons from harming us; 3. Inspire good and holy thoughts; 4. Offer our prayers to God, and join their prayers to ours; 5. Console souls in purgatory, and conduct souls to heaven.

115. **What are our duties toward our guardian angel?**
We should have: 1. Respect for his presence; 2. Devotion, because of his great care for us; 3. Confidence in his protection, but without presumption; 4. Docility to his illumination and direction, which comes from God.

Evil Angels

116. **What do we call the bad angels?**
Lucifer, chief of the rebel angels, is now called Satan, the Devil, and the Enemy. The others are generally referred to as *devils* or *demons*.

117. **Are the devil and other demons merely figurative representations of evil?**
No. We know by revelation and reason that they are real and personal beings of pure spirit, invisible, unchangeably malicious, and constantly active in our fallen world.

118. **How many fallen angels are there?**
It is commonly held that as much as a third of the angels fell with Lucifer: "His tail drew the third part of the stars of heaven" (Apoc 12:4*).

119. **What sin did these angels commit when they rebelled against God?**
They were guilty of pride, for they refused to submit to God in loving obedience.

120. **How were the rebel angels punished?**
1. Their minds were darkened; 2. They were shut out from heaven forever; 3. They were condemned to the eternal fire of hell.

121. **Can the demons ever repent and convert back to God?**
No. As purely spiritual beings, they foresaw all the consequences of their choice and fixed their wills in evil forever.

122. Can the demons temporarily leave hell?
Yes. Until the last judgment, by God's permission, they can roam throughout the world, carrying the pain of their punishment with them. Properly speaking, however, angels do not occupy physical space — they are only locatable by their action in a material place.

123. How do the demons act toward God?
They curse and blaspheme Him, striving to rob Him of the adoration of creatures.

124. Can the demons exercise power over physical nature?
Yes. Although they cannot create something out of nothing or force another's will to choose, they still retain their natural strength of intelligence and will, and can exercise significant power over nature — but only so far as God permits.

125. How is this demonic power manifested?
By false wonders disguised as miracles, predictions masquerading as prophecies, illusions and apparitions, infestations, moving physical objects, etc., which nevertheless may be distinguished from true miracles and the works of God.

126. Why do the demons make use of these powers?
To lead men to damnation and make them messengers for the spread of diabolical lies, and to continually oppose the Church of Christ.

127. How does the devil act toward man?
Hating God and envying man, he seeks to injure man spiritually and physically and drag him to hell through temptation, obsession, and possession.

128. What is temptation?
Temptation is when the demons disturb man's senses, memory, or imagination, suggesting unholy thoughts and exciting his *passions* (feelings or emotions) to eclipse his reason and will. Temptation is common to all men, as even Christ "was tempted in all things like us, but without sin" (Heb 4:15*).

129. What is diabolical obsession and possession?
Obsession is a certain focused demonic attention, often in the form of unexplained psychological or emotional attacks, or physical attacks on man's body or property. *Possession* is when a demon gains control of man's body, and sometimes of his senses. These are less common forms of demonic activity, and the Church's rites of exorcism are given to combat them.

130. What is the final aim of Satan's seduction of men?
He aims that men adore him instead of God: "The devil, as he is the apostate angel, can only go to ... deceive and lead astray the mind of man into disobeying the commandments of God, and gradually to darken the hearts of those who would endeavor to serve Him, to the forgetting of the true God, and to the adoration of himself as God."[13]

131. **Can we overcome the devil?**

Yes. We can always overcome the assaults of the devil by the grace of God, and should therefore make use of constant vigilance, prayer, and mortification. "Resist the devil, and he will flee from you" (Jas 4:7).

132. **Why does God permit the devil to tempt and afflict men?**

1. To purify and strengthen the just, who gain merit by their combat; 2. To punish and admonish the wicked, who are made slaves of the devil by sin; 3. To justly torment the demons, whose fleeting victories are always followed by greater defeats.

Chapter 5: Man

Creation of Man

133. **What is man?**

Man is a creature composed of a rational or intellectual soul and a physical body.

134. **Why did God create man?**

God created man to know Him, love Him, and serve Him in this life, and so be happy with Him forever in heaven.

135. **How did God create the first man?**

God formed the body of the first man from "the slime of the earth; and breathed into his face the breath of life, and man became a living soul" (Gn 2:7*).

136. **What name was given to the first man?**

The first man was called *Adam* (reddish clay), evoking the humble origin of his body.

137. **What relations exist between the human soul and body?**

The soul imparts life, motion, and sensation to the body, while the body expresses the soul. Man is therefore a body-soul composite. "It is one and the same man who is conscious both that he understands and that he senses. But one cannot sense without a body, and therefore the body must be some part of man."[14]

138. **What is man's soul?**

The soul is a spiritual, active, free, and immortal substance, created directly by God and joined to the human body in a unity so profound that it serves as the intrinsic *form* of the human body,[15] while also having its own *subsistence* (unique and complete existence or reality).[16]

139. **Is the intellectual soul the only principle of man's life?**

Yes. "The opinion which posits only one principle of life in man, that is, the rational soul, from which the body also receives all movement and life and sense, is the most common in the Church of God, and according to the most approved theologians it seems to be connected in such a way with the dogma of the Church, that it is the legitimate and only true interpretation, and therefore cannot be denied without error in faith."[17]

140. **When does God create each human soul?**

There are sound anthropological, philosophical, and theological reasons to conclude that God creates and infuses a human soul ("ensoulment") at *conception*, the first instant of the existence of the human embryo.

141. **Can we deduce this from the dogma of the Incarnation and of the Immaculate Conception?**

Yes. The dogma of the Incarnation presupposes that the human soul of Christ was created at the very moment of His conception: "Hardly was our divine Redeemer conceived in the womb of the Mother of God, when He began to enjoy the Beatific Vision, and in that vision all the members of His Mystical Body were continually and unceasingly present to Him, and He embraced them with His redeeming love."[18] The dogma of the Immaculate Conception of the Blessed Virgin Mary testifies to the same truth: "In the first instance of her conception … [she] was preserved free from all stain of original sin."[19]

142. **Is the Church's condemnation of abortion premised on the moment of ensoulment?**

Yes. The Church teaches that the human embryo must be treated as if it were already ensouled from the moment of conception: "Certainly no experimental datum can be in itself sufficient to bring us to the recognition of a spiritual soul; nevertheless, the conclusions of science regarding the human embryo provide a valuable indication for discerning, by the use of reason, a personal presence at the moment of this first appearance of a human life: How could a human individual not be a human person? … Thus the fruit of human generation, from the first moment of its existence, that is to say from the moment the zygote has formed, demands the unconditional respect that is morally due to the human being."[20]

143. **Why is the soul called a *spiritual* substance?**

Because it is an immaterial and simple substance, endowed with understanding and free will, capable of continued existence even after being separated from the body at death, since the soul is self-subsistent.[21]

144. **Who denies the spirituality of the soul?**

Chiefly *materialists*, who imagine that nothing exists in the universe but matter. In addition to contradicting the very idea of knowledge, this notion inevitably gives rise to the eugenical mindset, which seeks the material control of human procreation and the tyrannical rule of the strong over the weak, as the history of the last century attests.

145. How is man *free*?
Because he has the power to compare various possible things by his intellect, and make a choice among them by his will. Man is not forced by some exterior power to choose or not to choose.

146. Who denies human freedom?
Chiefly *determinists*, who hold that human acts are determined by preexisting causes—e.g., social circumstances or other impersonal forces (fate, stars, etc.)—and that men are therefore not to be held responsible for their own actions.

147. How is the human soul *immortal*?
Because the human soul, once created, will live forever.

148. Who denies the immortality of the soul?
Chiefly atheists, materialists, and others who imagine that they are nothing but well-adapted animals; while others claim that God annihilates the human soul after death, which is likewise a grave error.[22]

149. Have all authentic philosophers maintained the spirituality, freedom, and immortality of the soul?
Yes. These are simple truths, proven by reason and found in the history of nearly all peoples.

150. How did God create the first woman?
Casting a deep sleep upon Adam, God took from him a rib, out of which He formed the first woman (see Gn 2:21–22).

151. What is the name of the first woman?
Adam gave her the name *Eve*, meaning: "mother of the living" (Gn 3:20).

152. Was the formation of Eve's body a miracle equal to the creation of Adam?
Yes. "We record what is known to all, and cannot be doubted by any; that God, on the sixth day of Creation, having made man from the slime of the earth ... gave him a companion, whom He miraculously took from the side of Adam when he was locked in sleep."[23] The soul of Eve was created directly by God and infused into the body taken from Adam's rib.

153. Why was the body of Eve formed from Adam in this wondrous manner?
To manifest the divine order, to show that man and woman share equally in human nature and the image of God, and to stand as a mystical foreshadowing: Adam was the source of the entire human race including his wife Eve, just as the Church, the Bride of Christ, was drawn from the side of Jesus, the Second Adam, as He slept the sleep of death on the Cross.[24]

154. Who denies the fundamental unity of body and soul in man?
Chiefly the ancient *Gnostics*, as well as various dualistic and neo-Gnostic ideologies of our time, e.g., transgenderism and transhumanism. All of these errors view man's

body as some kind of cage or machine, a manipulable and dispensable apparatus, controlled by some inner essence or so-called "true self."

155. Who denies that the body of man was created by God?
Chiefly Darwinists and other atheists, who claim that man's body was formed over countless ages of random and gradual development from some ancient protoplasm, in a process generally called *human evolution.*

156. Does the Church affirm the theory of evolution as certain?
No. "Some rashly transgress this liberty of discussion, when they act as if the origin of the human body from preexisting and living matter were already completely certain and proved by the facts which have been discovered up to now and by reasoning on those facts, and as if there were nothing in the sources of divine revelation which demands the greatest moderation and caution in this question."[25]

157. Why is such caution required in considering evolutionary theories?
Because such theories have yet to be scientifically proven, have no evident basis in Scripture or Tradition, and are remarkably similar to ancient Gnostic myths.[26]

158. In addition to Adam and Eve, were any other kinds of humans created by God?
No. Adam and Eve were the unique and original human pair, from whom all have descended by physical generation. The unity of the human race in this common ancestry is a truth of faith, revealed by God and repeatedly taught by the Church (see Rom 5:12–21).[27]

159. Has the Church rejected the theory of *polygenism*, the notion that men today evolved from two or more distinct ancestral types?
Yes. "The faithful cannot embrace that opinion which maintains that either after Adam there existed on this earth true men who did not take their origin through natural generation from him as from the first parent of all, or that 'Adam' represents a certain number of first parents. Now it is in no way apparent how such an opinion can be reconciled with that which the sources of revealed truth and the documents of the teaching authority of the Church propose with regard to original sin, which proceeds from a sin actually committed by an individual Adam and which, through generation, is passed on to all and is in everyone as his own."[28]

160. Is every human person created as a man or woman, male or female?
Yes. The male and female sexes are fundamental and unalterable biological realities, and the body of each person reveals whether they are a man or a woman. "Male and female [God] created them" (Gn 1:27), and "He who made man from the beginning, made them male and female" (Mt 19:4*).

161. What of the novel claim that our "gender" may not correspond to our biological sex?
This error of *gender ideology* or *gender theory* denies the reality of the two sexes and replaces it with unlimited private choice, claiming that one's inner thoughts and

29

feelings or merely social and educational conditioning constitute the "gender" of the "true self"—a kind of Gnostic and ultimately Satanic dualism that must be rejected.

162. **Why does the error of gender ideology appear more prevalent in our time?**
The abandonment of reason is the typical outcome of sins against chastity (and vice versa, see Rom 1), which are all too common today. Furthermore, fallen man is always tempted to make his own mind the source of truth, rather than conform to the external, objective laws of nature and revelation (see 2 Cor 10:5).

163. **What of the claim that our "sexual orientation" may not correspond to our biological sex?**
The notion that God creates a disordered sexual attraction in some persons, or that He wills such feelings to be acted upon in some cases, is contrary to both reason and revelation, "for God is not a God of disorder, but of peace" (1 Cor 14:33*).

Original State of Man

164. **In what state were Adam and Eve first created?**
In *justice* and *holiness*, i.e., in friendship with God, possessing sanctifying grace and all virtues and gifts of the Holy Spirit. However, their friendship with God needed to be perfected by perseverance.

165. **What benefits did this wonderful state confer upon them?**
It made them perfectly fulfilled and pleasing to God; they were His adopted children and heirs of heaven, which they were able to merit by their own good works.

166. **Was this state natural or supernatural?**
It was *supernatural*, because man's created nature cannot attain this state by its own power, nor did the mere act of creation give man a right to this state. It was the free gift of God.

167. **What other gifts did God add to these supernatural blessings?**
He added certain extraordinary privileges beyond the perfection required by human nature, which served to preserve the integrity of man's nature in the highest excellence.

168. **What were these gifts?**
In man's soul: infused knowledge and perfect order in his passions, which were wholly subjected to his reason. In man's body: incorruptibility and immortality, i.e., exemption from sickness and death.

169. **Did Adam and Eve receive these gifts for themselves alone?**
No. They received them for themselves and all their future descendants.

170. **How great was the happiness of our first parents?**
Endowed with all the gifts of nature and grace, they lived in an unspeakable bliss of innocence, joyful communion with God, and contemplation of the wonders of creation.

Temptation and Fall of Man

171. **Where did God place Adam and Eve?**
In a delightful garden located in Eden, sometimes called the *terrestrial paradise*.

172. **What command did God give to Adam, as head of the human race?**
He forbade him to eat the fruit from the tree of knowledge of good and evil: "In the day that you eat of it you shall die" (Gn 2:17).

173. **Why did God make this prohibition?**
To test Adam as He had tested the angels, enabling him to make a sincere and free gift of himself through loving obedience, and so merit the happiness of heaven.

174. **Did our first parents heed this prohibition?**
No. Tempted by the devil, they voluntarily disobeyed God in that terrible moment known as the *Fall of man*.

175. **How did the devil tempt Adam and Eve to disobey?**
In the form of a serpent, he persuaded Eve that by eating the forbidden fruit they would not die, but would become like God. Both Adam and Eve succumbed, disobeyed God, and ate of it.

176. **What was the nature of Adam and Eve's sin?**
Like Lucifer and his angels, their primary sin was disobedience, an act of pride: "By the one man's disobedience the many were made sinners" (Rom 5:19).[29]

177. **Was this "original sin" very grievous?**
Yes. It contained disobedience, unbelief, pride, and curiosity, and held disastrous consequences for all of creation.

Punishment of Man

178. **What were the immediate effects of this sin upon Adam and Eve?**
Having become enemies of God, they were deprived of all grace and supernatural gifts, lost the right to enter heaven, and became subject to ignorance, *concupiscence* (the inclination to sin), suffering, and death.

179. **What were the effects of this sin on the rest of creation?**
The peace and harmony that once existed in human relationships and throughout the physical universe was broken. Creation became strange and contentious, subject to disorder, corruption, and death (see Gn 2:17; 3:17–19; Rom 8:21; and 5:12).

180. **Did Adam and Eve recognize their fault?**
Yes. Immediately after their sin, they were seized with dread and hid themselves.

181. **How has the sin of Adam and Eve affected the rest of mankind?**
"By one man sin entered into this world, and by sin death; and so death passed upon all men, in whom all have sinned" (Rom 5:12*).[30] Adam's descendants are now born into his rebellion: estranged from God, and in the power of the devil.

182. **What is this state of privation and estrangement from God called?**
Original sin, the state of separation from God that bears secondary consequences of darkness in man's intellect, weakness of will, and disorder in the passions.

183. **Why is this sin called *original*?**
Because it is a sin of origin rather than imitation, transmitted by generation to all of Adam's children, as an impure source pollutes all the waters that flow from it.[31]

184. **How do we know that original sin really exists?**
From: 1. Holy Scripture; 2. The teaching of the Church; 3. The traditions of various peoples, possessing an innate sense of man's loss and exile; 4. The daily experience of our fallen nature.

185. **Have all children of Adam contracted original sin through his disobedience?**
All but the Blessed Virgin Mary, Mother of the Redeemer, who was preserved "by a singular grace and privilege ... free from all stain of original sin."[32]

186. **If we die in the state of original sin, can we attain the Beatific Vision in heaven?**
No. A supernatural remedy is required for fallen man to attain heaven: a miracle of grace by which we may be withdrawn from the power of Satan, and become friends of God.

187. **Does such a remedy exist?**
Yes. Immediately after the Fall, God promised to send a Redeemer, by whose merits we might recover sanctifying grace and friendship with God.

Chapter 6: The Messiah Promised

God's Mercy after the Fall

188. **Then God did not abandon man after the Fall?**
No. God's love for man prepared a way to reconcile His mercy with His justice through the mission of the Messiah—Jesus Christ—who could make a satisfaction more than equal to the offense.

189. **What is the meaning of the term *Messiah*?**
It signifies "anointed" or "specially chosen one." As His work was to save fallen humanity from sin, He is also called Savior and Redeemer.

190. **Why did God promise this Redeemer to man immediately after his Fall?**
Out of His infinite love, God wished to: 1. Console man in his remorse by giving him hope of pardon; 2. Offer an immediate means of salvation; 3. Teach about the coming Savior; 4. Renew the bond of love that once united man to God.

191. **What is the general term for this bond of relations between man and God?**
Religion, from the Latin root *ligare* (to bind together), or *re-ligare* (to reconnect).[33]

Religion

192. **What is *religion*?**
As a virtue, religion is the moral power or habit of honoring God. Because honor is always due to God, this term is also used to describe man's relations with God, which may be either natural or supernatural.

193. **What is *natural religion*?**
The sum of those truths and precepts concerning man's relations with God, which human reason is capable of achieving on its own; e.g., the existence of God, His providence, the obligation of worshipping Him, etc.

194. **Is natural religion sufficient for man?**
No. Since God has revealed Himself to man, all are obliged to seek and submit to this divine revelation, i.e., to profess supernatural religion.

195. **What is *supernatural religion*?**
The sum of those truths which God Himself has revealed, and the positive commands which He has made; e.g., the mysteries of the Incarnation and the Redemption, the proper worship that He desires, etc.

196. **Was the religion that God gave to man at the beginning complete and final?**
No. This religion was developed by degrees over time, passing through three historical phases: 1. *Patriarchal* religion (especially in Abel the Just and Abraham[34]); 2. *Mosaic* religion; and finally, 3. *Christian* religion. The first extends from the Fall of man to Moses; the second, from the Mosaic Law to Jesus Christ; the third will endure without change until the end of time.

197. **Are these phases to be regarded as three different religions?**
No. There has only ever been one true religion, successively developed and perfected over time, until its definitive establishment in the Person and mission of Jesus Christ.

198. **Can human history be understood apart from Jesus Christ?**
No. Human history would be dark, ultimately fruitless, and without complete meaning if Christ had not come.[35] He is the divine center point of time and space, shedding light on all events of human history.

199. **Why is Jesus Christ the central figure in the divine plan?**
Because: 1. By Him all things were made and continue in existence; 2. He is the head of the Church, which will continue to the end of time; 3. He is the source of all grace; 4. He is the goal of all creation as the infinite and complete good.

Religious Error

200. **Are all religions, with their respective forms of worship, equally pleasing to God?**
No. Only the religion established by God and fulfilled in Christ, with its divinely revealed worship, is supernatural, holy, and pleasing to God. All other religions are inherently false, and their forms of worship pernicious, or at least unavailing for eternal life.

201. **Why are non-Christian religions inherently false?**
"There can be no true religion other than that which is founded on the revealed word of God: which revelation, begun from the beginning and continued under the Old Law, Christ Jesus Himself perfected under the New Law."[36]

202. **Why are non-Christian forms of worship pernicious, or at least unavailing to salvation?**
God has revealed the way in which He desires to be worshipped in Christ, and "the Catholic Church is alone in keeping the true worship."[37] To practice a false worship, or neglect to discover and offer right worship, offends God and harms the soul.

203. **What about the many non-Catholic groups claiming the title of "Christian" or "Church"?**
Those that hold Jesus as Lord but do not profess the entirety of His doctrine or participate in the unity of His Church have no proper claim to such titles. While often composed of men of good will, these communities are separated from the true Church as products typically of *heresies* or *schisms*.

204. **Is Judaism a source of sanctifying grace and salvation for its adherents?**
No. Even in the time before Christ, no one was saved by works of the Old Law, but only by faith in the coming Redeemer. This Law, with its precepts and ceremonies, was fulfilled and surpassed by the New Covenant in Jesus Christ (see Rom 3:28; and Gal 2:16).

205. **What of John 4:22, where Our Lord says: "Salvation is from the Jews"?**
Jesus Christ is Himself the fulfillment of this prophecy, whereas contemporary Judaism, also called *Talmudic* or *Rabbinic Judaism*—without temple, priesthood, or sacrifice—is not the same religion that God established in the Old Testament. Rejecting the true Messiah, the Old Law has thus become "both dead and deadly."[38]

206. **What of Romans 11:29: "The gifts and the calling of God are irrevocable"?**
St. Paul speaks here of God's abiding love for the Jews, foretelling their conversion to Christ before the end of time. Until then, contemporary Judaism as a whole exists as a rejection of God's calling, since there can be no fidelity to the Old Covenant where

its fulfillment in the New is denied: "If you believed Moses, you would believe Me, for he wrote of Me" (Jn 5:46). The call of God is to believe in His Son, and those who believe are sons of Abraham, heirs of the promise (see Gal 3:29).

207. **Does the Muslim religion adore the one true God?**
No. The Muslim religion rejects God's self-revelation as a Trinity and denies the divinity of Jesus Christ. The adoration proposed in this religion cannot be true, as "every spirit that does not confess Jesus is not from God" (1 Jn 4:3). While an individual Muslim may incidentally adore God as Creator, this would only be at the natural level, according to man's capacity for natural knowledge of God.

208. **Then Muslims do not adore the one and merciful God "together with us" Catholics?**[39]
No. Catholics consciously profess and adore "one God in Trinity, and Trinity in Unity,"[40] not simply "the one God"; whereas one of the most famous and frequent Muslim prayers, the *Al-Ikhlas Ayat*, solemnly rejects this divine revelation.[41]

209. **Is it true to say that Muslims hold the faith of Abraham?**[42]
No. Abraham saw three and adored one[43] (see Gn 18:2–3) and rejoiced in the vision of the future Redeemer (see Jn 8:56), excluding neither Christ nor the Trinity in his faith. Conversely, the Muslim explicitly excludes faith in Christ and the Holy Trinity.

210. **Does Our Lord Jesus Christ warn those who pretend to adore only the one and merciful God, or only the Father, while refusing to adore Him, the Son of God?**
Yes. "Whoever believes in the Son has eternal life; whoever disobeys the Son will not see life, but must endure God's wrath" (Jn 3:36). "All may honor the Son just as they honor the Father. Anyone who does not honor the Son does not honor the Father who sent Him" (Jn 5:23).

211. **Does Hinduism include a supernatural contemplation of the divine mystery?**[44]
No. With its roots in ancient polytheism and shamanism, some forms of Hinduism adore a pantheon of spirits presiding over an imagined cycle of strife in the material cosmos, while other forms hold a pantheistic view of the world, as if all things are divine. Therefore, Hinduism does not adore the one true God. "All the gods of the Gentiles are devils" (Ps 95:5*).

212. **Is Buddhism a means to supreme illumination and liberation from evil?**[45]
No. Buddhism rejects the Incarnation and Redemption, proposing instead a path of self-extinction through meditation techniques. Such a path is contrary to God's plan for divine union with man in Christ, culminating in the illumination of the Beatific Vision in heaven. "If one turns away his ear from hearing the law, even his prayer is an abomination" (Prv 28:9).

213. **Do false religions nonetheless contain "seeds" or "fruits" of the divine Word?**
One may discern elements of God's truth and goodness in all created things. Such elements, if present in false religions, are natural gifts of God to man's reason, which some Church Fathers called "seeds of the Word" serving as *praeambula fidei* (preambles of the Faith).[46] However, this does not valorize the precepts of a false religion, nor make their rites and ceremonies sacred; rather, it implicates them as defections, diminutions, and obstacles to supernatural faith and right worship.

214. **Then God does not will the diversity of religions found in the world today?[47]**
No. God cannot be the author of religious error or any other evil, because "God is true" (Jn 3:33). "It is necessarily impossible for God, the Supreme Truth, to be the author of any error whatsoever."[48] Rather, false religions arise from the deception of the devil, sin, and ignorance—evils that God merely tolerates in our fallen world.

215. **Does the Holy Spirit use false religions to impart grace and salvation to man?[49]**
No. Although God is able to give graces to a man who practices a false religion in view of his innocent ignorance and sincere good will, such graces would in nowise be *mediated by* or *owing to* the false religion itself. Rather, grace may be given despite the man's error, and in order to lead him out of that error into the truth of right faith.[50]

216. **Is Christ merely a "privileged way" to God, among many other possible ways?**
No. Such a notion expresses *religious indifferentism*, the belief that all religions are channels of grace, holiness, and salvation, even if some are more "efficacious" than others. This rejects the unity of the divine plan, insults our Redeemer, and contradicts His most solemn words: "No man comes to the Father except through Me" (Jn 14:6*), "I am the way" (see Jn 14:6), and "there is no other name given under heaven whereby we must be saved" (Acts 4:12*).

217. **What does religious indifferentism lead to?**
1. *Relativism*, which makes each community or individual the sole determiner of truth and falsity, good and evil; 2. *Agnosticism*, which views God's existence, knowability, or salvific work as uncertain; 3. *Atheism*, which finally denies God's existence altogether. Religious indifferentism has therefore been strongly censured by the Church.[51]

218. **What is the true good of the human person with regard to religion?**
Not an unrestrained liberty to spread a false religion, but rather to be freed one day from that false religion, so that he can unimpededly practice the one true religion, which is the Catholic Faith.

219. **Do Christians have an obligation toward those living in various forms of religious error?**
Yes. We are ordered to make God's revelation clearly known to the ends of the earth, drawing all men into the one true Church established by Christ.

220. **In a word, what may the mission of declaring God's revelation be called?**
It may be called *evangelization* (the bringing of the Gospel), with the aim of making all men members of the Catholic Church.

221. **Then what is *proselytism*?**
Using unworthy means to spread the Gospel; e.g., violence, bribery, false promises, and omitting elements of the truth. In contrast, authentic evangelization is always acceptable because it spreads the fullness of truth by worthy means, and is motivated by love for God and neighbor.

222. **Is Christian evangelization therefore an expression of love and esteem for others?**
Yes. Our Lord came "to seek out and to save the lost" (Lk 19:10), and this same love compels His Church to "preach the Gospel to every creature" (Mk 16:15*).

223. **What of those who equate evangelization with proselytism, disrespect, or violence?**
They may mistake the true mission of the Church, reject the realities of sin and grace, or lack that charity that motivates every true Christian: "Woe to me if I do not proclaim the Gospel" (1 Cor 9:16).

Human Dignity and Fraternity

224. **Is the *dignity of the human person* rooted in his creation in God's image and likeness?**
This was true for Adam, but with original sin the human person lost this resemblance and dignity in the eyes of God. He recovers this dignity through baptism, and keeps it as long as he does not sin mortally.

225. **Then human dignity is not the same in all persons?**
No. The human person loses his dignity in proportion to his free choice of error or evil; e.g., the dignity of Adolph Hitler and St. Francis of Assisi are not the same.

226. **Isn't every human person a "son or daughter of the One who wants to be called 'our Father'"?**[52]
No. One becomes a child of God only through explicit faith in Jesus Christ, the Incarnate Word and Son of God, being reborn of God (see Jn 1:12–13) through the sacrament of baptism (see Jn 3:5; and 1 Pt 1:3–23). "It is not the children of the flesh who are the children of God, but the children of the promise are counted as descendants" (Rom 9:8).

227. **Does Christian humanism radically affirm the dignity of every person as a child of God, thereby establishing a basic fraternity?**[53]
No. It is the sacrament of baptism that establishes basic human fraternity, for, "there is no parity between the condition of those who have adhered to the Catholic truth by the heavenly gift of faith, and the condition of those who, led by human opinions, follow a false religion"; and, "if anyone shall say that the condition of the faithful, and of those who have not yet attained to the only true Faith is on a par, let him be anathema."[54]

228. **What is the Catholic meaning of** *human fraternity*?

There are two kinds of fraternity: that of blood, in Adam and Eve, and that of grace in Jesus Christ, given through His Church and sacraments. This distinction between fraternity based on nature (the bond of blood) and fraternity based on divine election and revelation is indispensable. Perfect human dignity and fraternity for all human beings can only have one source: Jesus Christ, since it is only through the Incarnate Son of God that human dignity has been restored even more admirably than it was created.

229. **Is a merely human fraternity sufficient for man?**

No. A fraternity of blood, limited to peaceful co-existence in kindness, implies an extraordinary spiritual poverty, a deficient life, and an illusory happiness; it lacks the most important thing in the entire world and in all of human history, namely Christ, the Incarnate God, the only-begotten Eternal Son of God, the brother, friend, and bridegroom of the soul of all those who are reborn in God.

230. **Does the promotion of a purely human fraternity easily lead toward a universal religion in the Freemasonic sense?**

Yes. A universal and naturalistic fraternity based on the bonds of blood and nature is the core of the condemned error of Freemasonry, which proposes "a universal religion, on which all men agree. It consists in being good, sincere, modest, and people of honor, by whatever denomination or particular belief that one can be distinguished."[55]

Promises of the Messiah

231. **To whom was the Messiah promised?**

The Messiah was promised to all people in general, to the nation of Israel in particular, and specifically to: 1. Adam, father of the human race; 2. Sem, son of Noah; 3. Abraham, father of God's Chosen People; 4. Isaac, chosen son of Abraham; 5. Jacob, grandson of Abraham; 6. Judah, head of the tribe of which the Messiah would be born; 7. Moses, leader of the Hebrews; 8. King David, head of the royal family from which the Messiah would come.

232. **Why did God wait so long after the Fall to send the Messiah?**

1. That man, by a long experience of his wretchedness, might be humbled and more eager for a Savior; 2. To arrange a series of miraculous events that would prove His divine origin; 3. So that the "fullness of time" (Gal 4:4) would be accomplished among the Jews and Gentiles who were to believe in Christ and His Gospel.

233. **Did the Messiah's delay prevent all who lived before Him from being saved?**

No. The grace of the Redemption can reach all men—past, present, and future.

Chapter 7: The Messiah Prepared For

Types of the Messiah

234. What is meant by *types* of the Messiah?
Persons, objects, and events which prefigured or foreshadowed the coming Messiah.

235. In what historical persons was the Messiah prefigured?
In very many, including Adam, Abel, Noah, Abraham, Melchizedek, Isaac, Jacob, Joseph, Job, Moses, Aaron, Joshua, Gideon, Samson, David, Solomon, and Jonah.

236. How did Adam prefigure the Messiah?
Adam's authority over the animals prefigured the power of Jesus Christ over all things; the union of Adam and Eve was a type of the union between Christ and the Church; Adam was father of all men according to the flesh, and Jesus Christ is the father of all men according to the spirit.

237. How did Abel prefigure the Messiah?
Abel, the shepherd, became the victim of his brothers' jealousy. Jesus Christ, the good shepherd, was put to death by His brethren, the Jews.

238. How did Noah prefigure the Messiah?
Noah, the only just man at the time of the Flood, built an ark of safety and repopulated the earth. Jesus Christ, the truly just one, established the ark of the Church, out of which there is no salvation, so that heaven and earth might be peopled with saints.

239. How did Abraham prefigure the Messiah?
Abraham was the father of God's Chosen People in the Old Covenant. Jesus Christ is their father in the New. The Lord said: "Abraham rejoiced that he would see My day" (Jn 8:56).

240. How did Melchizedek prefigure the Messiah?
Melchizedek, priest of the Most High, offered bread and wine to God (see Gn 14:18). Jesus Christ, the universal High Priest in the order of Melchizedek (see Heb 5:10; and 6:20), offers Himself under the same sacramental signs in Holy Mass.

241. How did Isaac prefigure the Messiah?
Isaac, the only son of Abraham, carried the wood of sacrifice up the mountain to be sacrificed by his father. Jesus, the only Son of God, ascended Mount Calvary with the wood of the Cross, where He offered Himself in loving agreement with the will of His Father.

242. How did Jacob prefigure the Messiah?
The meek and virtuous Jacob was persecuted by his brother and left his homeland to seek a spouse. Jesus was rejected by his Jewish brethren, having come from heaven to establish His spouse, the Church.

243. **How did Joseph prefigure the Messiah?**

Joseph, beloved son of Jacob, was sold and abandoned by his brothers, condemned despite his innocence, confined with two prisoners whose destiny he foretold, and after three years left his prison to govern Egypt, which he saved from ruin. Jesus was sold by Judas and abandoned by His followers, condemned despite His innocence, crucified between two thieves (to one of whom He promised paradise), and after three days in the tomb, He rose to rule the human race, which He saved from eternal ruin.

244. **How did Moses prefigure the Messiah?**

Moses escaped the cruel orders of Pharaoh; Jesus, the cruel orders of Herod. Both spent the first years of their life in Egypt. Moses was sent by God, worked miracles to prove his mission, freed Israel from bondage, and gave the Old Law. Jesus Christ was sent from God, proved His divinity by miracles, freed man from the slavery of sin, and gave the New Law of the Gospel.

245. **How were Job, Aaron, Samson, David, Solomon, and Jonah types of the Messiah?**

Job prefigured the Messiah by his patience; Aaron, by his priesthood; Samson, by his strength; David, by his humiliation and glory; Solomon, by his wisdom; Jonah, by his escape from death after three days.

246. **What were the principal *objects* that prefigured the Messiah?**

The tree of life, the paschal lamb, the manna, and the bronze serpent.

247. **How did the tree of life prefigure the Messiah?**

The tree of life in Eden yielded fruit that brought health and life. Jesus Christ, suspended on the tree of the Cross, is the true fruit of life that gives immortality.

248. **How did the sacrifice of the paschal lamb prefigure the Messiah?**

This lamb was offered in *atonement,* or satisfaction for sin. Jesus is the Lamb of God, sacrificed to take away the sins of the world. The blood of the lamb applied on the doorposts of the Israelite houses saved the Hebrews from the punishment of Egypt; the blood of Jesus saves all who apply its merits to themselves.

249. **How was the manna a symbol of the Messiah?**

The manna is called "bread of angels" (Ws 16:20*) and "bread of heaven" (Ps 105:40*). Jesus Christ is the true bread of angels, come down from heaven and given to us in the Holy Eucharist.

250. **How was the bronze serpent a symbol of the Messiah?**

At God's command, Moses set up a bronze serpent, the sight of which cured those who had been bitten by venomous serpents. Jesus was raised on the Cross to heal the wounds inflicted by Satan, the infernal serpent.

Prophecies of the Messiah

251. What is a prophet?
Broadly speaking, a *prophet* is a person inspired by God to make known His will; more specifically, it is one inspired to foretell future events that cannot be known otherwise.

252. Into how many classes are the Old Testament prophets divided?
Two: 1. *Major prophets*—Isaiah, Jeremiah, Ezekiel, and Daniel; 2. *Minor prophets*—Hosea, Joel, Amos, Obadiah, Jonas, Micah, Nahum, Habakkuk, Zephaniah, Haggai, Zechariah, and Malachi.

253. When did these prophets live?
They lived in the period from the ninth to the fifth century before Christ.

254. What is a prophecy?
In the strict sense, *prophecy* is a naturally impossible prediction of some future event. Every true prophecy necessarily implies a supernatural revelation and a divine mission.

255. What is a *Messianic* prophecy?
Any prophecy referring to the Messiah, announcing the events of the Gospel before they occurred.

256. What was the special object of the Messianic prophecies?
They foretold the Messiah's: 1. Genealogical and personal characteristics; 2. Time of appearance; 3. Birth and childhood; 4. Public life; 5. Passion and glorified life; 6. Rejection by the Jews and calling of the *Gentiles* (non-Jews).

257. What genealogical characteristics of the Messiah did the prophets foretell?
The Messiah was to be born from the: 1. Race of Sem; 2. Nation of Abraham; 3. Tribe of Judah; 4. Family of David.

258. What personal characteristics of the Messiah did the prophets foretell?
The Messiah was to be: 1. Son of God; 2. God and a hidden God; 3. Savior and High Priest; 4. Most Just and Holy One; 5. Doctor and Shepherd.

259. What particulars were foretold about the time of the Messiah's coming?
He was to appear: 1. When the Jews would have a stranger as king of the tribe of Judah; 2. After the construction of the second temple, which was to be sanctified by His presence; 3. Immediately after His precursor; 4. When the whole world would be at peace.

260. What did the prophets foretell about the birth and childhood of the Messiah?
1. The miraculous virginity of His Mother; 2. The place of His birth; 3. The adoration of the Magi; 4. The massacre of the Holy Innocents; 5. His flight into Egypt.

261. **What did the prophets foretell about the public life of the Messiah?**
1. The circumstances of His baptism; 2. His fast before beginning His mission; 3. His preaching to the poor and in parables; 4. His perfect virtue; 5. The persecutions He would suffer.

262. **What virtues in particular were to characterize the Messiah?**
Poverty, humility, obedience, meekness, love of peace, and compassion for the weak.

263. **What did the prophets foretell about the period just before the Passion?**
1. The Savior's triumphant entry into Jerusalem; 2. The institution of a new priesthood; 3. The state of victimhood that He would adopt; 4. The treason of Judas and price of his crime.

264. **What did the prophets foretell about the Savior's Passion?**
1. His agony; 2. His abandonment by His friends; 3. His silence before false witnesses; 4. The insult and mockery He would endure; 5. The scourging and Crucifixion; 6. The vinegar and gall offered to Him; 7. The dividing of His garments; 8. The darkness at His death.

265. **What did the prophets foretell about the Savior's death?**
1. The very words of His final prayer; 2. His death and burial; 3. His descent into hell.

266. **What did the prophets foretell about His glorified life?**
1. His glorious Resurrection; 2. His admirable Ascension; 3. His glory and power in heaven.

267. **What did the prophets foretell about the punishment of the Jews?**
1. That the Jews would be made wanderers over the face of the earth; 2. That they would be left without king, prophet, or temple worship; 3. That they would seek salvation but not find it; 4. That toward the end of time, they would recognize their error and be converted to Christ.

268. **What did the prophets foretell about the Gentiles?**
1. That the Lord would make a New Covenant to include all nations; 2. That the Gospel would be preached everywhere; 3. That even the most rebellious nations would submit to the pastors of the Church; 4. That the Messiah would reign forever over the nations.

Section 2: God the Son and Redemption

SECOND ARTICLE OF THE CREED

I believe in Jesus Christ, His only Son, Our Lord.

Chapter 8: The Incarnation

Mystery of the Incarnation

269. Who is Jesus Christ?
Jesus Christ is the eternal and only Son of God, made man for our Redemption.

270. What is this mystery called?
This mystery is called the *Incarnation*, when the Eternal Son of God united to Himself a complete human nature in the one divine Person named Jesus Christ: "True God was born in the complete and perfect nature of true man; completely human and completely divine."[1]

271. What does *Jesus* mean?
It means "God saves," i.e., *Savior*, because He came to save and redeem men: "God so loved the world that He gave His only Son, so that everyone who believes in Him may not perish but may have eternal life" (Jn 3:16).

272. What does the name *Christ* mean?
It means "anointed" or "consecrated," because Jesus was anointed by His Father as: 1. *King*, Lord and Head of humanity, Ruler of nations; 2. *High Priest*, eternal Mediator between God and man; 3. *Prophet*, teaching in the name and power of God.

273. Why is Jesus Christ called the *only Son* of God?
Because He alone is from all eternity begotten of the Father and consubstantial with Him. Those conformed to Him through the grace of adoption may also be called "sons of God."

274. Why do we call Jesus Christ *Our Lord*?
Because He is the divine Master of all, and we owe Him adoration and perfect obedience in all things.

Two Natures of Jesus Christ

275. How many natures are there in Jesus Christ?
There are two: 1. *Divine nature*, for Christ is fully God; 2. *Human nature*, for He is also fully man.

276. Is Jesus Christ true God?
Yes. He is the co-eternal Son of God, equal to His Father in all things.

277. **Did Christ Himself affirm His divinity?**
Yes. He attributed to Himself divine powers, rights, and honors, and publicly declared Himself to be God before His apostles, the crowds, and the tribunal of Caiaphas.

278. **How did Jesus Christ prove His divinity?**
1. By the holiness of His life and doctrine; 2. By His miracles, especially His Resurrection; 3. By His own prophecies and fulfillment of Old Testament prophecies; 4. By the establishment, growth, and wondrous preservation of His Church.

279. **Is Jesus Christ true man?**
Yes. He has a complete human nature, body and soul.

280. **Is the soul of Christ like ours?**
Yes. It only differs from ours in its marvelous perfections, graces, and freedom from all sin.

281. **What perfection of intellect was possessed by Christ?**
His divine intellect possessed infinite knowledge; His human intellect possessed all that a creature can know, with perfect awareness of Himself and His divine mission.

282. **What perfection of will was possessed by Christ?**
His divine will possessed the perfection of God Himself; His human will was endowed with perfect freedom, not subject to concupiscence or weakness, and conformed entirely to the divine will.

283. **What perfection of love did Christ possess?**
As God, He loved with an infinite and divine love; as man, His heart possessed the purest, most tender, most comprehensive, and most generous love that can be conceived in a creature.

284. **Was Christ's human body true and real?**
Yes. Like ours, it was not an illusion or heavenly apparition, but real flesh and blood.

285. **Were Christ's body and soul both subject to suffering?**
Yes. Christ's body was subject to hunger, thirst, fatigue, the sensible pain caused by wounds, and death; His soul was likewise subject to fear and sorrow. He was not subject to any defects of body or soul that would have interfered in any way with His salvific mission (e.g., ignorance, concupiscence, sickness, or physical handicap).

286. **How many persons are there in Christ?**
There is only one Person in Jesus Christ: the divine Person of the Son of God. He is one, not because His divinity was changed into flesh, but because His humanity was united to God; "not by a mingling of substances, but by unity of Person."[2]

287. **What follows from the fact that Jesus Christ is only one divine Person, the Son of God?**
1. His humanity is worthy of adoration; 2. All its operations are the operations of God and therefore of infinite value; 3. The Virgin Mary is truly the Mother of God.

Wonders of the Incarnation

288. **Why is the Incarnation a great mystery?**
Because it unites in a single Person two natures, the divine and the human, which differ infinitely from each other. This mystery is called the *hypostatic union*, and remains a truth beyond the reach of human reason alone.

289. **Why should we admire this mystery?**
Because it manifests the attributes of God more strikingly than any other mystery, and procures greater blessings and glory for us than we can imagine.

290. **What attributes of God are strikingly clear in the Incarnation?**
His power, wisdom, goodness, mercy, and justice.

291. **What benefits do we owe to the Incarnation?**
By the Incarnation, the Son of God has made Himself brother to every man and become our perfect model, showing us by His own example the way to life everlasting.

Errors about the Incarnation

292. **What were the main heresies about the Incarnation in the early centuries?**
Those of: 1. *Adoptionists* and *Arians*, who denied the eternal divine nature and personhood of Jesus Christ; 2. Gnostics and *Docetists*, who denied that He had a human body; 3. *Apollinarists*, who denied that He had a human soul; 4. *Nestorians*, who claimed there are two persons in Jesus Christ; 5. *Monophysites*, who claimed that His human nature was absorbed by the divine nature; 6. *Monothelites*, who denied that He had a human will.

293. **Of these errors, are any still to be found today?**
Yes. Chief among them is always Arianism, because many acknowledge Jesus as a great moral teacher or spiritual leader, but reject Him as their "Lord and God" (see Jn 20:28). Every departure from Catholic doctrine is essentially an error about the Incarnation.

294. **Why is it necessary to believe and profess the Incarnation of the Son of God?**
All life and existence hinges on the Incarnation of the Son of God. Those who deny it will have sorrow in this life, and be eternally lost in the next: "If you believe not that I am He, you shall die in your sin" (Jn 8:24*).

THIRD ARTICLE OF THE CREED

I believe in Jesus Christ, who was conceived by the Holy Spirit, born of the Virgin Mary.

Chapter 9: The Blessed Virgin

Life of the Blessed Virgin

295. **What does the third article of the Creed teach us?**
It teaches us that God became incarnate through the Blessed Virgin Mary.

296. **What is the meaning of the expression *conceived by the Holy Spirit*?**
This means that the formation of the body of Jesus Christ in the inviolate womb of the Virgin Mary is especially attributed to the Holy Spirit, although it is the work of the entire Blessed Trinity.

297. **Who is the Virgin Mary?**
She is a humble daughter of the tribe of Judah and the family of David, whom God chose to be the Mother of His Son.

298. **Who were the father and mother of the Blessed Virgin?**
Sts. Joachim and Anne, descendants of King David who lived in the city of Nazareth.

299. **What peculiar feature marks the birth of the Blessed Virgin?**
According to many Fathers of the Church, she was born to Sts. Joachim and Anne long after their childbearing years, in answer to their constant prayer.

300. **What remarkable event occurred in Mary's childhood?**
Joachim and Anne, full of gratitude to God, consecrated their daughter to His service in the Temple of Jerusalem.

301. **When did Mary leave the temple?**
On the occasion of her marriage to St. Joseph, the most worthy and just of men. It is commonly believed that she had also vowed virginity to God beforehand; otherwise, "she would not have been amazed [at Gabriel's message]. Her amazement is a sign of the vow."[3]

302. **Did St. Joseph also make a vow of virginity, similar to Mary's?**
It is commonly believed that Joseph, like his wife Mary, had previously vowed virginity to God. "It may be presumed that at the time of their betrothal there was an understanding between Joseph and Mary about the plan to live as a virgin. Moreover, the Holy Spirit, who had inspired Mary to choose virginity in view of the mystery of the Incarnation and who wanted the latter to come about in a family setting suited to the Child's growth, was quite able to instill in Joseph the ideal of virginity as well."[4]

303. **What heavenly message did Mary receive after her betrothal to Joseph?**
The *Annunciation*. God sent the archangel Gabriel to announce to her the mystery of the Incarnation and receive her consent to this wonder of grace.

304. **How did Mary respond to this message?**
She humbly embraced the will of God: "Behold the handmaid of the Lord; be it done to me according to thy word" (Lk 1:38*).

305. **What spectacular miracle then occurred within her?**
The *Incarnation*. By the all-powerful working of the Holy Spirit, "the Word was made flesh" (Jn 1:14*), as the Eternal Son of God took on a complete human nature in Mary's virginal womb.

306. **Where did Mary go after the Annunciation?**
She went quickly from Nazareth to visit her cousin Elizabeth, who was filled with the Holy Spirit at the moment of her greeting, and recognized Mary as the Mother of her Lord (see Lk 1:43), acknowledging Mary's divine maternity.

307. **In what manner did the Blessed Virgin give birth to the Messiah?**
In obedience to an edict of the emperor Augustus, Mary and Joseph journeyed to Bethlehem for a census of the Roman Empire. There, in a humble stable, the Messiah was born.

308. **What did Mary do forty days after the birth of her Son?**
She obeyed the Jewish law of purification, and presented her Son in the Temple of Jerusalem.

309. **Was this law of purification binding on her?**
No. She was the purest of virgins, and her son was the Redeemer of all mankind. Rather, Mary submitted to this law through humility.

310. **What extraordinary event happened when Jesus was presented in the temple?**
The Holy Spirit revealed to the old man Simeon and the prophetess Anna that the Messiah had come, and they came to adore Him and publicly declare Him as the Messiah. Simeon also prophesied Mary's share in the redemptive suffering of Christ.

311. **Why did the Holy Family flee into Egypt after this?**
King Herod resolved to destroy the Child Jesus, at which time an angel warned the Holy Family to flee and hide there for a time. After Herod's death, they returned to settle in Nazareth.

312. **What other event from Mary's life in Nazareth is recorded in the Gospel?**
The journey to Jerusalem for the feast of Passover, when Jesus had reached His twelfth year. After the feast and unknown to His parents, He remained in the temple, where He was found after three days.

313. **What did the Blessed Virgin do during Jesus' public ministry?**
She remained in communication with Him, although she is seldom mentioned in the Gospel during this period, as she did not wish to draw attention to herself.

314. **What became of Mary after the Resurrection and Ascension of her divine Son?**
She waited in Jerusalem with the apostles, and there received the Holy Spirit in a special manner at Pentecost. This inaugurated her mission of intercession and mediation in the Church.

315. **How did the earthly life of the Blessed Virgin conclude?**
It is commonly held that she died at Jerusalem or Ephesus, in a death not caused by weakness or corruption, but from desire to be entirely conformed to her Son. After this, she was assumed body and soul into heaven by the power of God.

Prerogatives of the Blessed Virgin

316. **What special prerogatives does the Blessed Virgin possess?**
An immaculate conception, perfect sanctity, divine maternity, perpetual virginity, assumption into heaven, and a unique role in the salvation of every man.

317. **What is the *Immaculate Conception*?**
"From the first moment of her conception, by a singular grace and privilege granted by Almighty God in view of the merits of Jesus Christ ... [Mary] was preserved free from all stain of original sin."[5]

318. **How did Jesus redeem Mary, if she lived before His saving death on the Cross?**
Jesus Christ is the Redeemer of all, and His grace transcends time and space. He uniquely redeemed His Mother by preserving her from sin and its effects in a preemptive way.

319. **Was Mary free from all personal sin, truly *perfect in sanctity*?**
Yes. By a special privilege of God, who confirmed her in grace, she never committed any sin, and continued to grow in holiness and supernatural merit for her entire life on earth.

320. **Why is Mary truly the *Mother of God*?**
Because she conceived and gave birth to Jesus Christ, who is truly *Emmanuel* (God with us), God Incarnate, and "on this account the Holy Virgin is the Mother of God."[6]

321. **What is the meaning of Mary's *perpetual virginity*?**
Mary retained the miraculous integrity of her virginity "before bringing forth, at bringing forth, and always after bringing forth" her divine Son.[7]

322. **How was Mary's virginity maintained *during* the birth of her Son?**
The Church's constant teaching and liturgy affirms that Mary gave birth to Jesus Christ in joy, without pains or physical injuries. The birth of Jesus Christ was a

miraculous one,[8] as Christ left the womb of Mary like He passed through closed doors in His risen body (see Jn 20:19).

323. **Why is such miraculous virginity especially fitting for Mary?**

"First, because the word is not only conceived in the mind without corruption, but also proceeds from the mind without corruption. Wherefore in order to show that body to be the body of the very Word of God, it was fitting that it should be born of a Virgin incorrupt.… Secondly, this is fitting as regards the effect of Christ's Incarnation: since He came for this purpose, that He might take away our corruption. Wherefore it is unfitting that in His birth He should corrupt His Mother's virginity.… Thirdly, it was fitting that He who commanded us to honor our father and mother should not in His birth lessen the honor due to His Mother."[9]

324. **What is the *Assumption*?**

The virginal body of Mary never experienced the corruption of the grave, but rather, "having completed the course of her earthly life, was assumed body and soul into heavenly glory."[10]

325. **What are Mary's special titles with regard to her care for us?**

Mary is at once our Coredemptrix, Mediatrix, Advocate, and Mother, for which reason the faithful often call her simply *Our Lady*.

326. **Why is Mary called our *Coredemptrix*?**

Because she cooperated in our salvation by agreeing to be Mother of the Redeemer, consenting to all His redeeming acts, and jointly offering His life to God on the Cross. "The Redeemer could not but associate His Mother in his work. For this reason we invoke her under the title of Coredemptrix. She gave us the Savior, she accompanied Him in the work of Redemption as far as the Cross itself, sharing with Him the sorrows of the agony and of the death in which Jesus consummated the Redemption of mankind."[11]

327. **Why is Mary called our *Mediatrix*?**

Because God, in giving us Jesus through her, has given us all graces through her. "She who had been the Cooperatrix in the sacrament of man's Redemption, would be likewise the Cooperatrix in the dispensation of graces deriving from it."[12]

328. **What is the proper meaning of the titles *Coredemptrix* and *Mediatrix*?**

These titles in no sense place Mary on a level of equality with Jesus Christ, the divine Redeemer. There is an infinite difference between the divine Person of Jesus Christ and the human person, Mary. These titles refer to the unique participation of the Mother of the Redeemer with and subordinated to her divine Son in the work of human redemption: "Through this fullness of grace and supernatural life, she was especially predisposed to cooperation with Christ, the one Mediator of human salvation. And such cooperation is precisely this mediation subordinated to the mediation of Christ. In Mary's case we have a special and exceptional mediation."[13]

329. **Are these two titles based on the parallels between Eve and the Virgin Mary?**
Yes. "It is true that the first man and the first woman did us grievous harm, but thanks be to God!—by another Man and another Woman all that has been lost has been restored to us.... It seemed more congruous that as both sexes contributed to the ruin of our race, so both should have a part in the work of reparation."[14]

330. **Why is Mary called our *Advocate* and *Patroness*?**
Because she is now interceding for us in heaven, and constantly takes care of us.

331. **Why is Mary called our *Mother*?**
Because Christ Himself, when dying on the Cross, gave her as spiritual Mother to all men in the person of St. John, when He said to him: "Behold thy mother" (Jn 19:27*).

332. **In sum, what are the grounds for our devotion to Mary?**
As Mother of God, she is beloved to and favorably heard by her divine Son. As our spiritual Mother, she is full of affection for us and devoted to our welfare. We could never love Mary more than Jesus loves her; and if we did not love her well, we would give Him offense.

333. **What are the advantages of pious devotion to Mary?**
1. Mary lavishes great favors upon her servants; 2. She strengthens them in temptation; 3. She obtains for them the grace of perseverance; 4. She assists them in their final hour; 5. She introduces them into heaven.

Chapter 10: The Life of Christ

Hidden Life of Jesus

334. **What are the principal events in the hidden life of Our Lord?**
His nativity, circumcision, presentation in the temple, flight into Egypt, time in Nazareth, and journey to Jerusalem.

335. **In what manner was Jesus born?**
At midnight, in Bethlehem, in the piercing cold, the Divine Child was born and laid in a manger, illustrating His later teaching: "Learn of Me, for I am meek and humble of heart" (Mt 11:29*).

336. **After Mary and Joseph, who were the first adorers of the Incarnate Word?**
Several shepherds, who were tending their flocks nearby. An angel appeared to tell them the news of Christ's birth, after which they saw a great multitude of angels singing: "Glory to God in the highest; and on earth peace to men of good will" (Lk 2:14*).

337. **What did the Holy Family do eight days after the birth of Jesus?**
In accordance with the Old Law, Jesus was circumcised and officially given His name by St. Joseph.

338. **Why did the Son of God submit to the law of circumcision?**
Although not bound by this law, He submitted to it: 1. To teach us obedience; 2. To show that He was true man, of the family of Abraham; 3. To take on the semblance of sin, for all forms of which He made complete atonement; 4. To begin shedding His blood for our Redemption.

339. **After the shepherds, who came to adore the Divine Child?**
The *Magi*, traditionally believed to be kings, who came from the East following a miraculous star. Arriving, they adored the Lord and gave gifts of gold, frankincense, and myrrh.

340. **Where was Jesus taken forty days after His birth?**
To the Temple of Jerusalem, to be presented to God according to the Law of Moses. There, He was recognized and publicly proclaimed as the Messiah by Sts. Simeon and Anna.

341. **How did King Herod react when the Magi refused to inform him about the Child?**
He was outraged, and ordered all boys up to two years old in Bethlehem to be killed. In this way, he thought he would surely destroy the rightful King of the Jews.

342. **How was the Lord rescued from this massacre?**
In a dream, an angel warned St. Joseph to take the Child and His Mother and flee into Egypt until the death of Herod. After this, they returned to Nazareth.

343. **What does the Gospel teach us about the life of Jesus in Nazareth?**
"Jesus increased in wisdom and in years, and in divine and human favor" (Lk 2:52), practicing the workman's trade with His foster father, and was subject to Joseph and Mary. His was a life of humility, silence, prayer, obedience, and labor.

344. **Why did Jesus humble Himself in this way?**
1. To share the lot of sinful man: "In the sweat of thy face shalt thou eat bread" (Gn 3:19*); 2. To dignify the working class, so despised by the pagans, who left manual labor to slaves; 3. To sanctify Christian home life, and give a model to families; 4. To prepare for His public ministry.

345. **What instructive event occurred when Jesus was twelve years old?**
Jesus went with His parents to Jerusalem to celebrate the Passover, but remained there when His family left to return home. They found Him in the temple after three days of searching, seated among the doctors of the Law and teaching them.

Public Life of Jesus

346. How did God immediately prepare the Jews for the mission of the Savior?
He sent St. John the Baptist as His precursor, the son of Zachary and Elizabeth, who prepared the way for Our Lord.

347. What was the mission of St. John the Baptist?
To preach prayer, mortification, and a baptism of repentance for the forgiveness of sins, to prepare people to accept the Messiah. He gained such publicity that many began to wonder if St. John was the Messiah.

348. Did the baptism of St. John have power to remit sin?
No. But it prepared souls by penance to receive the grace of the true sacrament of baptism, which Jesus Christ was about to institute.

349. How did Jesus begin His public life?
At the age of about thirty, He left Nazareth and went to the river Jordan to receive the baptism of St. John. At this, the heavens were opened and the Holy Spirit was seen in the form of a dove, as a voice from heaven said: "This is My beloved Son, in whom I am well pleased" (Mt 3:17*).

350. Since Christ was sinless, why did He receive this baptism?
1. To be near sinners through humility; 2. To give water its baptismal power, and show that Christian baptism is wrought by the Blessed Trinity; 3. To affirm the preaching of St. John about Himself; 4. To give the crowds proof of His divinity and mission.

351. Where was Jesus led after His baptism?
Into the desert, where He fasted forty days and forty nights to prepare for His public mission, and to show that the Christian life is one of prayer and combat.

352. What happened during His time in the desert?
Satan appeared and tempted Him, seeking to learn if He was the Son of God. As he tempted our first parents in Eden, he tempted Christ with sensuality, presumption, and ambition.

353. Why did Jesus permit Himself to be tempted?
1. To teach us that we cannot always escape temptation; 2. To merit for us the grace to overcome temptation; 3. To show by example how we should fight the enemy with truth and *mortification* (asceticism).

354. What did Jesus do after His fast in the desert?
He chose His apostles: Simon Peter and his brother Andrew; James the Great and John, his brother, the sons of Zebedee; Philip and Bartholomew; Matthew, the publican; Thomas surnamed Didymus; James the Less, and his brother Jude; Simon, and Judas Iscariot who became a traitor.

355. What sort of men were the apostles?
All were simple workmen except St. Matthew, who was a tax collector. The Gospel generally depicts them as slow to believe, but all were men of good will at first: virtuous, sincere, generous, simple-hearted, and much attached to their Master.

356. Why didn't Jesus choose men that were rich, learned, skillful, and powerful?
To show clearly that the conversion of the world to Christianity was a miraculous work of God.

357. How did Christ prepare the apostles for their work?
He gave them the grace of His divine presence, instructed them in His doctrine, trained them by counsel and example, and gave them certain missions to test them. Only after His Resurrection did He invest them with all divine powers and authority necessary to perpetuate the Church on earth.

Doctrine of Jesus

358. What did Jesus do after choosing His apostles?
He spent three years with them, going through Galilee and Judea and preaching the Gospel.

359. How did He go about teaching?
He taught the truth with divine authority and convicting power, proving His mission and divinity from the ancient prophecies about Him and by the miracles He performed.

360. In what form did He most often teach?
He especially used sermons or parables, particularly with the themes of the Kingdom of God, the mercy of God, and the Christian moral life.

361. What was the character of Christ's doctrine?
It was both old and new. *Old*, as it contained the substance of all the preceding revelation of God; *new*, as it illustrated the completion of this revelation in His own Person and teaching.

362. How did Jesus Christ demonstrate the perfection of His doctrine?
The moral principles He taught are the most beautiful that can be conceived, and He illustrated them by the supreme holiness of His life.

363. How was Our Lord regarded as a teacher?
His teaching possessed divine authority, and not the mere authority of human learning: "He taught them as one having authority, and not as their scribes" (Mt 7:29). As an example, he stood as a perfect and universal model of all virtues. His life, like His doctrine, was without spot or stain. Without fear of contradiction, He could say to His enemies: "Which of you shall convict Me of sin?" (Jn 8:46*).

Works of Jesus

364. How did Christ publicly confirm His doctrine?

By miracles and prophecies. A *miracle* is a sensible effect that is produced by God outside the natural order. A *prophecy* is a knowledge of hidden things, particularly the foretelling of future events sometimes with a precision impossible to human reason alone.

365. Which of Our Lord's miracles are specifically mentioned in the Gospel?

Several exorcisms,[15] miracles upon the natural world,[16] physical healings,[17] and resurrections.[18] "But there are also many other things that Jesus did; if every one of them were written down, I suppose that the world itself could not contain the books that would be written" (Jn 21:25).

366. What are the prophecies of Our Lord about?

His Person, His disciples, the Jewish people, the history of the Church, and the end times.

367. Which prophecies pertain to His Person?

Principally those of His Passion, His death on the Cross, and His Resurrection.

368. What did Christ prophesy about His disciples?

He foretold: 1. Their vocation as apostles; 2. The triple denial of St. Peter; 3. The betrayal of Judas; 4. The coming of the Holy Spirit; 5. Their mission to all nations of the earth; 6. Their many sufferings, and the victories they would gain by divine help; 7. That they would sit as judges at the last judgment.

369. What did Our Lord predict with regard to the Jewish people?

He foretold: 1. The destruction of Jerusalem; 2. The definitive ruin of the temple; 3. The dispersion of the Jews among the nations; 4. The calling of the Gentiles.

370. What did Our Lord prophesy about His Church?

He foretold: 1. The universal preaching of the Gospel; 2. His reign through the Church by His Cross; 3. The miracles worked through the saints; 4. The hatred of the world for His true disciples; 5. The help He always gives to His Church; 6. The indestructibility and indefectibility of the true Church.

FOURTH ARTICLE OF THE CREED

I BELIEVE IN JESUS CHRIST, WHO SUFFERED UNDER PONTIUS PILATE, WAS CRUCIFIED, DIED, AND WAS BURIED.

Chapter 11: The Passion

Preludes of the Passion

371. What does the fourth article of the Creed teach us?
The sorrowful Passion of Our Lord Jesus Christ, by which He lovingly redeemed man.

372. What is the *Passion*?
From *passio* (suffering), it signifies the terrible anguish and pain that Our Lord endured to save us from our sins.

373. How was Jesus' preaching received by the religious authorities of the time?
It hurt their pride, challenged their attachment to worldly comfort, and undermined their social standing. For this, and on account of His claim to divinity, they resolved to put Jesus to death.

374. When did they decide to take this extreme measure?
After the resurrection of Lazarus, because many Jews had witnessed this miracle and begun to believe in Jesus as the Messiah.

375. How did Our Lord enter Jerusalem, when He was going to perform His redemptive work on the Cross?
He entered the city in triumph, as the prophets Isaiah and Zechariah foretold. This event is commemorated every year on Palm Sunday, the beginning of Holy Week.

376. Where did He spend that Wednesday?
In Bethany, given to silence, prayer, and heavenly conversation with the apostles and the holy women devoted to His service.

377. What did He do on that Thursday evening?
He went to Jerusalem where He celebrated the Last Supper with his apostles, and instituted the sacraments of the Holy Eucharist and holy orders.

378. What followed the institution of these sacraments?
Our Lord offered a prayer to His Father, asking: 1. For Himself, the glory to which He was entitled; 2. For His apostles, preservation from sin and sanctification in truth; 3. For His entire Church, the grace of fraternal charity and unity.

Passion of Christ

379. Where did Jesus begin His sorrowful Passion?
In the Garden of Olives or Gethsemane, where He prayed and, as He contemplated the sins of all men and all time, suffered a terrible interior agony that even overflowed into a sweat of blood (see Lk 22:44).

380. What did Jesus do after His prayer in the garden?
He returned to His disciples and announced His coming betrayer. When Judas appeared with armed guards to arrest Jesus, the disciples all fled, as had been foretold.

381. Where was Our Lord brought, in the middle of that night?
He was first brought to Annas, and then to the tribunal of the high priest Caiaphas.

382. How was Jesus treated at the tribunal of Caiaphas?
False witnesses accused Him of blasphemy, and Caiaphas condemned Him to death. He then sent Jesus to the Roman governor Pontius Pilate, who reserved the right to execute criminals.

383. How did Pilate receive Jesus?
He declared Him innocent three times, but was so weak in character that he dared not rescue Jesus from the Jews, who were clamoring for His death.

384. What did Pilate do then?
After sending Him to Herod, tetrarch of Galilee, who merely questioned and mocked Our Lord, Pilate had Jesus brutally scourged with whips, and gave Him over to the Jews to be crucified.

385. Where did the Crucifixion of Christ take place?
On Mount Calvary, a barren hill outside the walls of Jerusalem, in the place of execution for condemned criminals called *Golgotha* (place of the skull).

386. Why was it fitting for Christ to be offered in sacrifice outside of Jerusalem?
To show that by this sacrifice: 1. He became the Redeemer of both Jews and Gentiles; 2. The worship of the Jewish temple was fulfilled and surpassed; 3. The true altar and sacrifice would henceforth be found in the Catholic Church, spread throughout the world.

387. How did the Crucifixion proceed?
After being stripped of His garments, Our Lord willingly stretched Himself upon a large wooden Cross, to which His hands and feet were nailed. After the Cross was raised, He was left to hang in torment until He died.

388. What shame did He endure in addition to this torture?
1. That of being placed between two thieves, as if He were a common criminal; 2. The jeering and insults of the crowd, whom He came to save; 3. The cowardice of those disciples who abandoned Him.

389. **Who was present at Calvary?**
Some who had remained faithful to Him, and consoled Him by their presence: chiefly His holy Mother, St. John the beloved disciple, Mary the wife of Cleophas, Mary Magdalene, and John's mother Salome, all of whom were filled with grief.

390. **What did the sign that was hung upon the Cross of Jesus say?**
"Jesus of Nazareth, King of the Jews." Written in Latin, Hebrew, and Greek, it was a universal confession that this was the Christ. Each of these three languages were thereafter included in the Roman Rite of Mass,[19] the extension in time of the one sacrifice of the Cross.

391. **Did the Cross of Jesus serve any purpose other than His altar of sacrifice?**
Yes. It was also the pulpit from which He continued His divine teachings, as we can see in the "Seven Last Words" spoken by Him on the Cross:
1. He declared Himself the one Mediator for mankind, in praying for His executioners: "Father, forgive them, for they know not what they do."
2. He declared Himself the Supreme Judge of souls, in promising heaven to the penitent thief: "Amen I say to thee, this day thou shalt be with Me in paradise."
3. He gave His Mother to all the faithful as His final bequest: "Woman, behold thy son," and to St. John, "Behold thy Mother."
4. He declared Himself the prophesied Savior, with the words of the messianic Psalm: "My God, My God, why hast Thou forsaken Me?"
5. He made known that spiritual ardor for souls that consumed Him: "I thirst."
6. He announced the completion of His redemptive work: "It is consummated."
7. He demonstrated perfect filial trust and obedience to God: "Father, into Thy hands I commend My spirit."

392. **What were the most important pulpits for Our Lord's divine teaching?**
"The pulpit of His first message was the mountain side; His audience, unlettered Galileans; His truth, the Beatitudes. The pulpit of His last message was the Cross; the audience: saints and sinners; the sermon was the Seven Last Words."[20]

Death and Burial of Christ

393. **What amazing things happened at the Savior's death?**
Darkness covered the face of the earth, the sun hid its light, the great veil of the temple was torn from top to bottom, the earth trembled, rocks split apart, graves opened, and several of the dead arose and roamed the city, testifying to Christ's divinity.

394. **What wound was inflicted on the body of Jesus while it hung upon the Cross?**
One of the soldiers pierced the side of His body with a lance, and blood and water flowed out.

395. Who buried the body of Our Lord?
Joseph of Arimathea, a good man of wealth and influence, went boldly to Pilate to demand the body of Jesus for burial.

396. What was the manner of Christ's burial?
His body was anointed with spices and ointments, and wrapped in linen. Then it was laid in a new tomb not far from Calvary, where it was sealed with a great stone and guarded by soldiers.

397. Why did Our Lord permit His body to be buried?
To affirm the reality of His death, render His Resurrection more glorious, fulfill numerous prophecies, and stand as a mystical symbol: as the body of Adam was drawn from the virgin earth by divine power, so Christ would rise from a virgin tomb by His own divine power, showing Himself able to raise all men from their graves at the end of time.

Mystery of the Redemption

398. What is the mystery of the Redemption?
It is the mystery of Jesus Christ, the Son of God, willingly dying on the Cross for the salvation of all men.

399. Why is this truth a mystery?
Because we cannot comprehend the depth of divine love that led Our Lord to offer Himself as a victim in atonement for our sins.

400. What is the meaning of *redemption* and *atonement*?
Redemption means to "ransom," to purchase, to set free. *Atonement* generally means the satisfaction of a demand; in the narrower sense, it is taken as the reparation of an insult, outweighing the injustice done.

401. From what has Christ freed us?
He has freed us from the slavery of sin and the eternal death that results from sin, at the price of His own precious blood. Holy Scripture says: "Having been freed from sin and enslaved to God, you derive your benefit, resulting in sanctification, and the outcome, eternal life" (Rom 6:22*).

402. How did sin *enslave* man?
Sin made man: 1. The debtor of God, whose justice demanded satisfaction; 2. The slave and property of Satan, who made him subject to evil; 3. The slave of sin and passion: "Very truly, I tell you, everyone who commits sin is a slave to sin" (Jn 8:34).

403. Could God alone have achieved the Redemption of man?
Yes. Sin has an infinite dimension, since it is an offense against the infinite God; and only God can offer an infinite satisfaction to make up for such an offense.

404. **How, then, has Christ redeemed us?**
By suffering for us as true man, and by giving an infinite value to that suffering as true God.

Satisfaction of Christ

405. **What qualities does Our Lord's satisfaction possess?**
His satisfaction was voluntary, equivalent, superabundant, and universal.

406. **How was this satisfaction *voluntary*?**
It was of His own free will that He offered Himself and gave up His life.

407. **How was this satisfaction *equivalent*?**
The sufferings and death of Jesus were those of the Son of God, and were therefore of infinite value; a reparation equal to the offense.

408. **How was this satisfaction *superabundant*?**
The very least of Jesus' actions is infinitely pleasing to God, so Our Lord could have atoned for all sin by a single tear, or by one prayer. Instead, He chose to endure all manner of suffering.

409. **Why did Our Lord choose to suffer so much?**
1. To demonstrate the inexhaustible riches of His love; 2. To teach us more forcibly about the destructive evil of sin; 3. To inspire us with horror of personal sin; 4. To incite us to offer our own sufferings to God for the expiation of our own sins and those of others; 5. To inflame our love for God, who has given Himself to us in the most generous manner.

410. **How was Our Lord's satisfaction *universal*?**
He died for all, and offered satisfaction for the sins of all.

Fruits of the Redemption

411. **What has Christ merited for all men?**
He merited that they may: 1. Be delivered from sin; 2. Be released from the power of the devil; 3. Be delivered from everlasting death; 4. Be reconciled with God; 5. Have the gates of heaven opened to them.

412. **Does this mean that all men will go to heaven?**
No. Only those who receive the fruits of this Redemption will attain heaven. God will not save free creatures without their cooperation or against their will: "God created us without us, but He did not will to save us without us."[21]

413. **Is it reasonable to hope that all men will go to heaven?**
No. The Son of God has warned us most solemnly: "The gate is narrow and the road is hard that leads to life, and there are few who find it" (Mt 7:14).

414. **What of the claim that the power of Christ's Redemption can be mediated through any religion?**
It is a condemned error to hold that "man may, in the observance of any religion whatever, find the way of eternal salvation, and arrive at eternal salvation."[22]

415. **Does Christ's infinite satisfaction dispense us from doing penance for our sins?**
No. We must also do works of penance, in union with Our Lord's divine sacrifice. When animated by divine grace, our little penances will share in the fruit of His atonement, and help repair the damage done by sin. Such efforts are rightly called acts of *reparation*.

416. **Do Our Lord's merits dispense us from acquiring any merit ourselves?**
No. We must also strive to cooperate with grace and merit heaven by our good works: "With fear and trembling work out your salvation" (Phil 2:12*). Of themselves, our good works have no value—but through the merits of Jesus Christ, they are worthy of the reward of grace.

417. **What are the main errors about the Redemption?**
The appearance of Protestantism in the sixteenth century, having fractured into thousands of different sects since then, was founded on a false notion of the Redemption and the application of its fruits—i.e., *justification*—apart from our active cooperation with grace.

418. **Of these errors, are any of them especially common today?**
Yes, these three grave errors: 1. Man can be saved apart from faith in Jesus Christ; 2. Faith in Jesus alone is sufficient for salvation, such that man is not also obliged to observe the commandments of God and His Church; 3. Man is unable to fulfill these commandments, such that God demands the impossible.[23]

419. **What do these errors have in common?**
Each may imply an acknowledgment of Christ as Redeemer, but refuses to adore and obey Him as King and Lawgiver. Christ is either the Lord of all, or He is not the Lord at all.

FIFTH ARTICLE OF THE CREED

HE DESCENDED INTO HELL;
ON THE THIRD DAY HE ROSE AGAIN FROM THE DEAD.

Chapter 12: The Resurrection

Descent of Jesus into Hell

420. **What happened to Christ's body and soul after He died on the Cross?**
His body was placed in the tomb, while His soul descended into hell.

421. **Did Our Lord's body and soul both remain united to His divine nature?**
Yes, Our Lord's body and soul remained always hypostatically united to His divinity. Even in their separation at death, they were always the body and soul of the Son of God.

422. **What is the meaning of the word *hell*?**
It signifies a low, inferior, or subterranean place separated from heaven. "When it says, 'He ascended,' what does it mean but that He had also descended into the lower parts of the earth?" (Eph 4:9).

423. **Into which part of hell did Our Lord's soul descend substantially?**
Into what theologians call the *limbo of the Fathers*: the waiting place of those souls who were purified from their faults, united to God by faith and charity, but still awaiting the Redemption of Christ. "Being put to death in the flesh but made alive in the spirit ... He went and proclaimed to the spirits in prison" (1 Pt 3:18–19*). This place is also called the "bosom of Abraham" (see Lk 16:22–23).

424. **What was the mission of the Redeemer in the limbo of the Fathers?**
1. To announce the Redemption to the souls detained there; 2. To gladden them by His presence; 3. To assure them that they would soon accompany Him in His triumphal entry into heaven.

Resurrection of Jesus

425. **What is the most glorious mystery of Our Lord's life?**
The mystery of His Resurrection from the dead.

426. **On what day did He rise again?**
At dawn on the third day after His death, i.e., on the first day of the week: Sunday, or *Dies Dominica* (the Lord's Day).

427. **How was Jesus raised to life?**
By a unique act of His divine omnipotence (in union with the Father and the Holy Spirit), He reunited His own soul to His body, and came forth living from the tomb.

428. **What qualities did Christ's body possess when it came out of the tomb?**
It had the qualities of glorified bodies: brightness, impassibility, agility, and subtlety.

429. **What is *brightness*?**
A brilliance capable of greater radiance than the sun, such as Our Lord revealed on Mount Tabor (see Mk 9:2–13; Mt 17:1–13; and Lk 9:28–36).

430. **What is *impassibility*?**
Exemption from all suffering and enjoying perpetual youth, generally thought to be around the age of thirty-three years, as when Our Lord carried out the principal acts of our Redemption (see Lk 3:23).

431. **What is *agility*?**
The ability to move from place to place with the rapidity of thought, as Our Lord demonstrated to the disciples at Emmaus (see Lk 24:13–35).

432. **What is *subtlety*?**
The property of the body being entirely submissive to the soul and expressive of it, as shown by the glorified wounds of Our Lord (see Jn 20:27).

433. **Why is Our Lord's Resurrection of such great importance?**
It is of first importance because it is: 1. The foundation of our faith (see 1 Cor 15:14–17); 2. The means whereby the fruits of the Redemption are applied to us (see 1 Pt 1:3); 3. The model of our spiritual life (see Rom 6:4–11); 4. The cause of our future resurrection (see Rom 6:5).

The Risen Jesus

434. **To whom did Jesus first show Himself after His Resurrection?**
Most probably and appropriately to His Blessed Mother, although this is not recorded in Scripture. "[We may] think that Jesus showed Himself first to His Mother, who had been the most faithful and had kept her faith intact when put to the test. Lastly, the unique and special character of the Blessed Virgin's presence at Calvary and her perfect union with the Son in His suffering on the Cross seem to postulate a very particular sharing on her part in the mystery of the Resurrection."[24]

435. **To whom does Scripture record Our Lord appearing after His Resurrection?**
He appeared to: 1. Mary Magdalen and the holy women; 2. Simon Peter and other disciples at the Sea of Tiberias; 3. Two disciples on the way to Emmaus; 4. Disciples assembled in Jerusalem without St. Thomas.

436. **When did He appear to St. Thomas?**
Eight days after His Resurrection, to offer all future Christians the lesson: "Blessed are they that have not seen, and have believed" (Jn 20:29*).

437. **Were there other appearances of Christ?**
Yes. He also appeared on a mountain of Galilee, and likely many other times not mentioned in the Gospel. St. Paul attests that He once appeared to an assembly of more than five hundred, and was again seen by St. James (see 1 Cor 15:6).

438. **Of what value is the testimony of the apostles?**
It is incontestably certain, for: 1. The apostles themselves were incredulous at first (see Mk 16:14); 2. The apostles could not have been deceived; 3. They did not wish to deceive others, nor would it have benefited them; 4. Others could not have been fooled by such a deception.

439. **What about claims of hysteria, hypnotism, ignorance, etc. to explain this testimony?**
They give too much credit to the apostles, who were simple men incapable of such a vast deception, and who ultimately purchased it at the cost of their own tortures and death.

440. **What manifest fact especially confirms the testimony of the apostles?**
The rapid conversion of the known world to Christianity, despite obstacles that mere nature could not overcome and the complete absence of sufficient human means to achieve it.

441. **Why has God given such striking proofs of Christ's Resurrection?**
Because this mystery is the very foundation of Christianity. If Christ has not risen, His religion is an imposture. If He has risen, then He is God, His religion is divine, and all must profess it. "If Christ has not been raised, then our proclamation has been in vain and your faith has been in vain. We are even found to be misrepresenting God, because we testified of God that He raised Christ—whom He did not raise if it is true that the dead are not raised.... If Christ has not been raised, your faith is futile and you are still in your sins.... If for this life only we have hoped in Christ, we are of all people most to be pitied" (1 Cor 15:14–15, 17, 19).

SIXTH ARTICLE OF THE CREED

He ascended into heaven, and sits at the right hand of God the Father Almighty.

Chapter 13: The Ascension

Preparation for the Ascension

442. **How long did Christ remain on earth after His Resurrection?**
Forty days.

443. **Why did Our Lord remain on earth forty days after His Resurrection?**
1. To give His apostles clear proof of His Resurrection; 2. To complete their instruction for the work of preaching; 3. To train them in offering Mass and the sacraments; 4. To formally commission the ministers of His Church.

444. **What particular instructions did Christ give to His apostles at this time?**
He taught them about the meaning of the Scriptures, the mysteries of His life, and to await the coming of the Holy Spirit in Jerusalem, after which they would be sent to the ends of the earth to be His witnesses.

The Ascension

445. Where did Jesus bring His disciples, when the forty days were completed?
He led them to Mt. Olivet, the scene of His sufferings on the night before He died, and ascended into heaven.

446. How did Jesus enter into heaven?
Victorious, escorted by the angelic host and bringing with Him all the just of the Old Law, the souls in the limbo of the Fathers whom He had redeemed with His blood.

447. Why did Christ ascend into heaven in this way?
For His own glory: 1. To enjoy the triumph He had merited; 2. To take possession of heaven, the true home of His glorified body; 3. To diffuse the brightness of His glory throughout heaven.

448. Why else did Christ ascend into heaven?
For our benefit: 1. To open to all men the gates of heaven which Adam's sin had closed; 2. To send us the Holy Spirit; 3. To intercede forever with His Father for us; 4. To give greater merit to those who have faith without seeing Him in the flesh.

449. In ascending into heaven, did Christ cease to be present on earth?
No. In fulfillment of His promise, He is at the same time in heaven and on earth in different modes, having fixed His presence here through the *Eucharist*, the Most Holy Sacrament of the Altar.

Jesus at the Right Hand of the Father

450. How does Scripture express the glory that Jesus Christ acquired as man?
In these terms, which it puts into the mouth of God the Father: "Sit at My right hand" (Ps 110:1).

451. What does it mean to say that Christ *sits*?
1. After the work of our Redemption, our Savior now enjoys an unending repose in heaven; 2. He is both King of Kings and Supreme Judge of the living and the dead, for a king sits upon his throne, and a judge sits upon his tribunal.

452. Why do we say that Christ sits at the *right hand* of God?
In recognition that Christ is God, equal to the Father in all things, enjoying infinitely greater power and glory than any mere creature, and that He reigns in both heaven and earth.

The Kingship of Christ

453. How is Christ a king?
He is the Chief Executor of God's perfect will, the primary Lawgiver and Supreme Judge, omnipotent in executing His own perfect will. "All power is given to Me in heaven and in earth" (Mt 28:18*).

454. Must the Kingship of Christ be recognized by all men?
Yes. Whether considered as individuals or in the societies of families and nations, "the empire of our Redeemer embraces all men."[25]

455. How must the Kingship of Christ be acknowledged?
1. *Individually,* by our choice to believe His doctrine and obey His commands; 2. *Collectively,* by families and nations living in accord with the same doctrine and moral precepts; 3. *Privately,* by progressing in the interior life of holiness; 4. *Publicly,* by imitating, obeying, and adoring our King in all external actions.

456. Must Christ be King and rule not only over individuals, but also over nations?
Yes. In this there is no difference "between the individual and the family or the state; for all men, whether collectively or individually, are under the dominion of Christ. In Him is the salvation of the individual, in Him is the salvation of society."[26]

457. Does Christ's royal empire extend only to Catholic nations?
No. "Christ's empire includes not only Catholic nations, not only baptized persons who, though of right belonging to the Church, have been led astray by error, or have been cut off from her by schism, but also all those who are outside the Christian faith; so that truly the whole of mankind is subject to the power of Jesus Christ."[27]

458. Are there disastrous consequences if Christ is excluded from political life?
Yes. "With God and Jesus Christ excluded from political life, with authority derived not from God but from man, the very basis of that authority has been taken away. … The result is that human society is tottering to its fall, because it no longer has a secure and solid foundation."[28]

459. What means did Christ establish to realize His reign on earth, until He returns?
The Catholic Church. Despite the imperfections of its members, this Church is therefore a divine institution, and already the visible realization of the Kingdom of God on earth.

SEVENTH ARTICLE OF THE CREED

FROM THENCE HE SHALL COME TO JUDGE THE LIVING AND THE DEAD.

Chapter 14: The Second Coming

Return of Christ in Glory

460. **What does the seventh article of the Creed teach us?**
It teaches us that the Savior has been appointed Judge of all the living and the dead.

461. **When will Christ judge all men?**
He judges every man at his death (the *particular* judgment) and will publicly confirm this sentence in His Second Coming at the end of the world (the *general* judgment).

462. **How will Christ come at the end of the world?**
Not as He did the first time, in humility and weakness; rather, He will come in all the splendor of His power and glory.

463. **Why will Christ appear in all the splendor of His glory?**
1. To glorify His sacred humanity before all men, which had been so despised and rejected; 2. To gladden and console His servants, who adored His humanity; 3. To confound the wicked, who blasphemed and denied His humanity; 4. To publicly establish His eternal kingdom in union with the angels and saints.

Signs of the Second Coming

464. **When will the general judgment take place?**
At the end of time. Our Lord has deemed it better for us not to know "the day or the hour" (cf. Mt 25:13*; and Acts 1:7), but He has told us the signs that will precede that day of judgment.

465. **What are the remote signs of Our Lord's Second Coming?**
1. The preaching of the Gospel to all nations; 2. A general weakening of faith and universal corruption in morals, like that which provoked the Flood; 3. The appearance of *Antichrist*, the most wicked and impious of men.

466. **How will God intervene in this final struggle?**
He will raise up great saints, whose miracles will far surpass the wonders of the Antichrist. Enoch and Elijah, whom God mysteriously removed from the world, will be sent back to sustain the Church in this terrible trial.[29]

467. **What will be the proximate signs of the last judgment?**
"Signs in the sun, the moon, and the stars, and on the earth distress among nations confused by the roaring of the sea and the waves. People will faint from fear and foreboding of what is coming upon the world, for the powers of the heavens will be shaken" (Lk 21:25–26).

468. **How will the dead be gathered together for judgment?**
"He will send out His angels with a loud trumpet call, and they will gather His elect from the four winds, from one end of heaven to the other" (Mt 24:31).

The General Judgment

469. **What will Our Lord do before judging all men?**
"He will separate people one from another as a shepherd separates the sheep from the goats, and He will put the sheep at His right hand and the goats at the left" (Mt 25:32–33).

470. **How will the case proceed?**
The consciences of all men will be exposed before the eyes of all like open books, and all the acts of a lifetime will be made publicly known in an instant.

471. **What sentence will the sovereign Judge pronounce?**
He will say to the good: "Come, you that are blessed by My Father, inherit the kingdom prepared for you from the foundation of the world;" and to the wicked: "You that are accursed, depart from Me into the eternal fire prepared for the devil and his angels" (Mt 25:34, 41).

472. **On what will this sentence be based?**
On our faith and our thoughts, words, deeds, and omissions, particularly those done in relation to the poor and suffering of this world (see Mt 25).

473. **What does Our Lord wish to teach us by pointing out the reason of His sentence?**
That the spiritual and corporal *works of mercy* hold the first rank in His eyes.

474. **What will then happen to the universe?**
It will be dissolved by a purifying fire, and renewed.

475. **What glory is reserved for Our Lord after the last judgment?**
The final victory: Satan, the host of demons, and all the damned will be cast into the pool of eternal fire and brimstone, and all things will be openly subject to the God-Man, Jesus Christ.

Section 3: God the Holy Spirit and Sanctification

EIGHTH ARTICLE OF THE CREED

I believe in the Holy Spirit.

Chapter 15: The Holy Spirit

Divinity of the Holy Spirit

476. **Who is the Holy Spirit?**
The Holy Spirit is the third Person of the Blessed Trinity.

477. **What is meant by *believing in* the Holy Spirit?**
That we believe in a third divine Person, called the Holy Spirit, who proceeds from the Father and the Son, and possesses the same divine nature and substance with them.

478. **Is the Holy Spirit truly God, just as the Father and the Son are God?**
Yes. Therefore, the Holy Spirit is adored and glorified together with the Father and the Son.

479. **What major heresy denies the divinity of the Holy Spirit?**
Macedonianism, condemned by the Council of Constantinople in 381. It is likewise heretical to affirm that the Holy Spirit proceeds from the Father alone, as condemned by the Ecumenical Council of Lyons II in 1274.

480. **What major heresy confuses emotions for the movements of the Holy Spirit?**
Montanism, condemned by the third century, as St. Paul had already warned the early Christians to beware of confusing falsehoods and emotions for the teachings of the Holy Spirit; for "God is not a God of confusion" (1 Cor 14:33), and we should not accept "another Christ" or "a different spirit" from that received through the apostles (2 Cor 11:4*).

481. **Why is the term *Spirit* or *Ghost* applied to the third Person of the Holy Trinity?**
These terms are derived from various Western root words signifying "breath," as the Holy Spirit is regarded as the breath of love of both the Father and the Son (see Gn 2:7; Ps 33:6; Jb 33:4; and Jn 20:22).

482. **Why is this Spirit called *Holy*?**
Because He is holiness itself, as are also the Father and the Son, and because the sanctification of souls is specially attributed to Him. "Though the Father is a spirit, and the Son a spirit, and the Father holy, and the Son holy, yet the third Person is distinctively called the Holy Spirit, as if He were the substantial holiness consubstantial with the other two."[1]

Mission of the Holy Spirit

483. **What is meant by saying that the Holy Spirit was sent by the Father and the Son?**
In union with the Father, the mission of the Holy Spirit was to reveal, confirm, and further the works of the Son of God Incarnate.

484. **When did the Holy Spirit first descend on earth?**
He was present at the Creation of the world, "moving over the face of the waters" (Gn 1:2*), but first descended in His specific mission at the moment of the Incarnation of the Son of God in the womb of the Blessed Virgin Mary: "The Holy Spirit will come upon you, and the power of the Most High will overshadow you" (Lk 1:35).

485. **At what other moments was the Holy Spirit sent to earth?**
1. At Christ's baptism in the Jordan: "When all the people were baptized, and when Jesus also had been baptized and was praying, the heaven was opened, and the Holy Spirit descended upon Him in bodily form like a dove" (Lk 3:21–22); 2. At the redeeming death of Jesus Christ on the Cross: "When Jesus had received the wine, He said, 'It is finished.' Then he bowed His head and gave up His spirit" (Jn 19:30); 3. On the day of His Resurrection: "He breathed on them and said to them, 'Receive the Holy Spirit'" (Jn 20:22).

486. **When did the Holy Spirit show Himself visibly?**
1. At the baptism of Our Lord, in the form of a dove; 2. On the day of Pentecost, in the form of tongues of fire.

487. **What did the tongues of fire signify?**
1. The miraculous gift of speaking the many languages of the nations, to whom the apostles would later preach; 2. The action of the Holy Spirit in enlightening and purifying the apostles, and inflaming them with divine charity.

488. **How did the Holy Spirit change the apostles?**
1. They were ignorant of complete revelation, but the Holy Spirit taught them all truth; 2. They were sinners, but the Holy Spirit purified their hearts; 3. They were weak and timid, but the Holy Spirit empowered them and filled them with the zeal of martyrs.

489. **What did the apostles do after receiving the Holy Spirit?**
They dispersed throughout the world, preached the Gospel, baptized many thousands, and in a few years founded a large number of local churches.

490. **What works had the Holy Spirit already achieved in the world, prior to Pentecost?**
He: 1. Cocreated the world, together with the Father and the Son; 2. Sanctified all those who held true faith and love for God; 3. Prompted the prophets to speak in preparation for Christ; 4. Inspired the sacred writers to compose the books of the Old Testament without any error.

491. **What is the invisible mission of the Holy Spirit in the Church?**
He: 1. Unifies and governs the Church as a soul governs a body; 2. Makes the Church infallible in its definitive teaching; 3. Gives the faithful an inerrant sense for right doctrine; 4. Distributes *charisms*, or unique spiritual gifts, throughout the Church; 5. Makes the Church indestructible against the attacks of all her enemies.

492. **Why is the Holy Spirit the soul of the Church?**
"As Christ is the Head of the Church, so is the Holy Ghost her soul. 'What the soul is in our body, that is the Holy Ghost in Christ's body, the Church' (St. Augustine, *Serm.* 187, *de temp.*). This being so, no further and fuller 'manifestation and revelation of the divine Spirit' may be imagined or expected; for that which now takes place in the Church is the most perfect possible."[2]

493. **What is the mission of the Holy Spirit in the soul of the individual Christian?**
He is the principle of supernatural life in the soul, and is therefore called *Vivificans* in the Creed, or "life-giving Spirit."

494. **How does the Holy Spirit give a supernatural life to the soul?**
By conferring upon it *sanctifying grace*, which cleanses it from sin, makes it holy and pleasing to God, and enables it to live a divine life—something impossible for human nature by itself. The Christian living this supernatural life of the soul is said to live in the *state of grace.*

495. **Then what is a Christian in the state of grace?**
The Christian in the state of grace is a creature who lives two different lives, marvelously united at once. One is a natural and visible life, consisting in the union of soul and body; the other is an invisible and interior life, consisting in the union of the soul with the Holy Spirit.

496. **How do Christians experience and live this interior union on earth?**
Principally through the life of the sacraments, Christian prayer, and acts of supernatural faith, hope, and love for God, which is the beginning of the life of heaven.

497. **Is this state of grace even more important than our earthly life?**
Yes. It is a greater miracle than the creation of the universe,[3] and infinitely more valuable than our earthly lives. For this reason, the true Christian is always ready to suffer death rather than commit sin. "The sufferings of this present time are not worthy to be compared with the glory which shall be revealed in us" (Rom 8:18*).

Gifts and Fruits of the Holy Spirit

498. **What does the Holy Spirit give to the soul, together with sanctifying grace?**
He communicates His seven gifts to the soul.

499. What is a *gift* of the Holy Spirit?
A gift of the Holy Spirit is a supernatural habit infused directly by God into the soul; a stable disposition that perfects the soul and inclines it to respond to God, and to act promptly regarding all affairs of salvation.

500. What are the gifts of the Holy Spirit?
Wisdom, understanding, counsel, knowledge, piety, fortitude, and fear of the Lord (see Is 11:2–3*).

501. What is the gift of *wisdom*?
The gift that enables us to judge all things in light of God, their final end, and to become detached from the world.

502. What is the gift of *understanding*?
The gift that enables us to better comprehend the truths of faith.

503. What is the gift of *counsel*?
The gift that enables us to discern the counsels of God and to choose what is most consonant with God's glory and our own salvation.

504. What is the gift of *knowledge*?
The gift that enables us to discern things rightly in themselves, especially the truth about God.

505. What is the gift of *piety*?
The gift that makes us honor God as our Father with filial affection, and to love all men insofar as they are creatures of God.

506. What is the gift of *fortitude*?
The gift that leads us to brave all obstacles and dangers like valiant soldiers of Jesus Christ, for the sake of the glory of God.

507. What is the gift of *fear of the Lord*?
The gift that leads us to avoid whatever might displease God and separate us from Him, out of filial fear or loving reverence.

508. Are the seven gifts of the Holy Spirit inseparable?
Yes. Because they are all bound together in charity, we lose them all with one mortal sin, and recover them all together with the return of sanctifying grace.

509. What does the Holy Spirit produce in our souls through these various gifts?
He produces the twelve *fruits* of the Holy Spirit: charity, joy, peace, patience, benignity, goodness, longanimity, mildness, fidelity, modesty, continency, and chastity (see Gal 5:22–23*).

510. Which fruits of the Holy Spirit perfect us especially interiorly?
For the doing of good: charity, joy, and peace. For strength against evil: patience and longanimity.

511. Which fruits of the Holy Spirit perfect us especially exteriorly?
With reference to our neighbor: goodness, benignity, mildness, and fidelity. With reference to ourselves: modesty, continence, and chastity.

512. Why are these virtues called *fruits*?
Because the just soul, being united to Our Lord by the Holy Spirit like a branch is joined to a vine, produces these virtues as naturally as a good tree will produce good fruit.

513. What are our duties to the Holy Spirit?
1. To worship Him; 2. To love the Father and the Son with the "love of the Holy Spirit" that has been poured into our hearts (see Rom 5:5); 3. To invoke the Holy Spirit's light and help before our important actions; 4. To accept all the truths that He transmits through definitive Church teaching; 5. To be docile to His inspirations, striving daily to grow in holiness; 6. To respect our body by keeping it as His temple; 7. To carry ourselves with the modesty and dignity proper to this great Guest of the soul.

NINTH ARTICLE OF THE CREED

I BELIEVE IN THE HOLY CATHOLIC CHURCH, THE COMMUNION OF SAINTS.

Chapter 16: The Church and the Communion of Saints

The Catholic Church in General

514. What is the Catholic Church?
The Catholic Church is the divinely founded society of all those who profess the true Faith of Christ, united by the sacraments He instituted and governed by the pastors He established under one visible earthly head, the pope.

515. What does the word *Catholic* mean?
Meaning "universal," this word may describe: 1. The one true religion instituted by Christ; 2. The society in which that religion is retained and practiced, under the earthly headship of the pope; 3. Any individual or group belonging to that Church.

516. What does the word *Church* signify?
From *kyriake* (the Lord's), this term may describe: 1. The entire society of Catholics, referred to as the *universal* Church; 2. The society of Catholics in one province or city, called the *particular* or *local church*; 3. The physical building in which Catholics assemble for worship.

517. Who founded the Catholic Church?
Jesus Christ Himself founded it, when He gave His religion the form of a visible society and established the papacy as its principle of unity (see Mt 16:18–19). "The Church ... was established immediately and directly by the true and historic Christ, while He lived among us."[4]

518. Why did Christ found the Church?
To preserve His true worship and doctrine on earth for all time, so to sanctify men in this life and make the glory of heaven accessible to them in the next.

519. Why is the Catholic Church called the *Body of Christ*?
Jesus Christ Himself affirms that as the branches and the vine form one living being (see Jn 15:4–5), so Christ and His disciples constitute a certain living body. "Just as the body is one and has many members, and all the members of the body, though many, are one body, so it is with Christ.... You are the body of Christ and individually members of it" (1 Cor 12:12, 27).[5]

520. Why is the Catholic Church properly called the *Mystical Body* of Christ?
By this term, "we may distinguish the Body of the Church, which is a Society whose Head and Ruler is Christ, from His physical body, which, born of the Virgin Mother of God, now sits at the right hand of the Father and is hidden under the Eucharistic veils; and, that which is of greater importance in view of modern errors, this name enables us to distinguish it from any other body, whether in the physical or the moral order."[6]

521. Is the Church therefore superior to all other human societies?
Yes. "The Church is a perfect society of its kind, and is not made up of merely moral and juridical elements and principles. It surpasses all other human societies as grace surpasses nature, as things immortal are above all those that perish."[7]

522. Then Christ and His Church are one, and yet distinct?
Yes. "The divine Redeemer and the society which is His Body form but one mystical person, that is to say, to quote St. Augustine, *the whole Christ* (see *Enar. in Psalm 17*, no. 51). Christ and His Mystical Body are in a wonderfully intimate union. Nevertheless, they are distinguished one from the other as Bridegroom from Bride."[8]

523. How can we describe the relationship of Christ to His Church?
"Christ espoused His Church as a *wife*, He loves her as a *daughter*, He provides for her as a *handmaid*, He guards her as a *virgin*, He fences her around like a *garden*, and cherishes her like a part of His *own body*. As a *head* He provides for her, as a *root* He causes her to grow, as a *shepherd* He feeds her, as a *bridegroom* He weds her, as a *propitiation* He pardons her, as a *sheep* He is sacrificed, as a *bridegroom* He preserves her in her beauty, as a *husband* He provides for her support."[9]

524. **When was the Church born?**
"The Church was born from the side of our Savior on the Cross like a new Eve, mother of all the living."[10]

525. **When did the Church first show herself before the eyes of men?**
"The Church, which, already conceived, came forth from the side of the Second Adam in His sleep on the Cross, first showed herself before the eyes of men on the great day of Pentecost."[11]

526. **What were the three moments in which Christ built up His Church?**
"The divine Redeemer began the building of the mystical temple of the Church when by His preaching He made known His precepts; He completed it when He hung glorified on the Cross; and He manifested and proclaimed it when He sent the Holy Ghost as Paraclete in visible form on His disciples."[12]

527. **Whom does Christ wish to be members of this Church?**
All men, of all times and places, until He comes again in glory.

528. **How does one become a member of this Church?**
Through reception of the sacrament of baptism.

529. **How are men able to recognize this Church?**
Through its constant and visible existence in the world, under the mission of His chosen apostles and their successors in every age who faithfully transmit His sacraments and teachings to the world.

Mission of the Church

530. **What is the mission of the Church on earth?**
The Catholic Church alone bears the divine authority and mandate to teach, govern, and sanctify all men in Jesus Christ until He returns in glory.

531. **Are there widespread errors about the mission of the Church today?**
Yes. Many mistakenly believe the Church's mission to be one of improving the temporal welfare of man, as if the Son of God became incarnate to establish a humanitarian service organization for combatting poverty, disease, or environmental pollution. Others mistakenly look for a "new humanity" in which "a real and lasting peace will only be possible on the basis of a global ethic of solidarity and … shared responsibility in the whole human family," where the Church merely "works for the advancement of humanity and of universal fraternity."[13]

532. **Can human solidarity be put at the same level with divine charity and life in the Holy Spirit?[14]**
No. Divine charity is supernatural and therefore belongs to life in the Holy Spirit, whereas human solidarity is only a natural virtue and therefore belongs to natural life.

533. How is the authentic mission of the Church carried out?

By a threefold power which Jesus Christ conferred upon the apostles during His public ministry: 1. To *teach* revealed truth; 2. To *sanctify* souls, above all through the administration of the sacraments; 3. To *govern* the faithful by promulgating good laws for them.

534. To what higher authority did Our Lord make the apostles themselves subject?

To Simon Peter, whom He placed at their head as the first Supreme Pontiff, or pope.

535. Why was the authority given to Peter and the apostles not to end with them?

Because it was not conferred for them personally, but for the Church which was to endure through all ages. Apostolic and divine authority is therefore transmitted to the bishops as successors of the apostles, and to the pope as Successor of St. Peter.

536. Which prerogatives of the apostles were intransmissible to their successors, the bishops?

Their immediate divine inspiration and miraculous assistance; for, "they knew the whole plenitude of the Faith distinctly in one intuitive glance. They proclaimed new revealed truths. In so doing, whether by word of mouth or in writing, they were divinely assisted. They could thus augment the treasure of Tradition and of Holy Scripture. They founded the Church wherever they went, whether free or in chains. They confirmed everything with miracles."[15]

537. What are the three parts, or states, of the Church?

1. The *Church Militant*, composed of its members on earth; 2. The *Church Suffering*, composed of all the souls in purgatory; 3. The *Church Triumphant*, composed of those in heaven.

538. What are the two aspects of the Church Militant, divided as a society?

1. The *Ecclesia Docens* or "teaching Church," composed of the pope and bishops in union with him, teaching authoritatively as representatives of Jesus Christ on earth; 2. The *Ecclesia Docta* or "taught Church," made up of all the faithful, who receive and live according to the teaching of Christ.

539. Must the "teaching Church" be the most obedient and docile of all toward the revealed word of God?

Yes. The Church's teaching office "is not above the word of God, but serves it, teaching only what has been handed on, listening to it devoutly, guarding it scrupulously, and explaining it faithfully."[16] "The First Vatican Council had in no way defined the pope as an absolute monarch. On the contrary, it presented him as the guarantor of obedience to the revealed Word."[17]

540. Must this obedience and docility also extend to the perennial sense of the Church's tradition?

Yes. "The pope's authority is bound to the tradition of faith, and that also applies to the liturgy."[18] St. Augustine thus characterizes true Catholic bishops: "What they found in the Church they held; what they learned they taught; what they received from the fathers they handed down to the sons."[19]

541. What are the two elements of the Church, when considered as a living body?
1. An internal element or soul, which consists of sanctifying grace and the infused virtues and gifts of the Holy Spirit; 2. An external element or body, consisting of the visible society of those who outwardly profess the Faith of Christ, partake of His sacraments, and remain in communion with the pastors established by Him.

542. Can either of these elements exist independently of the other?
No. They are as inseparable as the soul and body of the risen Christ, who is the divine Head of the Church, His Mystical Body.[20]

543. What are the main characteristics of the mission of the Church?
Universality and supernatural charity, as St. Augustine so admirably formulated it: "O Catholic Church, true mother of Christians! You not only teach that God alone, to find whom is the happiest life, must be worshipped in perfect purity and chastity,... you also contain love and charity to our neighbor in such a way, that for all kinds of diseases with which souls are afflicted for their sins, there is found with you a medicine of prevailing efficacy.... You bind brother to brother in a religious tie stronger and closer than that of blood.... You join citizen to citizen, nation to nation, yea, all men, in a union not of companionship only, but of brotherhood, reminding them of their common origin."[21]

Necessity of the Church

544. Is it necessary to belong to the Catholic Church to be saved?
Yes. This is the meaning of the affirmation often repeated by the Church Fathers, popes, and councils: *extra Ecclesiam nulla salus*, "outside the Church there is no salvation."[22] "The Church, now sojourning on earth as an exile, is necessary for salvation.... Whosoever, therefore, knowing that the Catholic Church was made necessary by Christ, would refuse to enter or to remain in it, could not be saved."[23]

545. Why is there no salvation outside the Church?
Because there is no salvation except in Jesus Christ, who "is the head of the body, the Church" (Col 1:18). Salvation outside the Church is as impossible as salvation without Christ: "Whoever listens to you listens to Me, and whoever rejects you rejects Me" (Lk 10:16).

546. Has this been the changeless teaching of the Church since apostolic times?
Yes. It is found in the New Testament, the creeds of the early centuries, the writings of countless saints and theologians, the solemn teaching of popes and councils, and the ordinary teaching of bishops spread throughout the world.

547. What have the Church Fathers taught about those outside the Church?

"Outside the Catholic Church you can find everything except salvation. One can have honor, one can have the sacraments, one can sing *alleluia*, one can answer *amen*, one can have faith in the name of the Father and of the Son and of the Holy Ghost, and preach it too, but never can one find salvation except in the Catholic Church."[24]

548. Doesn't God want all men to be saved?

Yes. As a loving Father, God "desires everyone to be saved and to come to the knowledge of the truth" (1 Tm 2:4). This is why He established His Church as the ordinary and universal means of salvation. "He cannot have God for his Father, who does not have the Church for his mother."[25]

549. Can a man be saved who does not know God's revelation, or the Church He founded?

One who neglects to pray for insight or earnestly seek the true religion is ignorant by his own fault, and so cannot be saved. Likewise, one who refuses to enter the Church once he has discovered it is refusing the known invitation of God, and thus cannot be saved.

550. What of those who die in guiltless (*inculpable* or *invincible*) ignorance of God's revelation?

If a man has not deliberately rejected grace offered to him, including divine revelation, and has the proper added dispositions, it is possible for God to join him to the Church in an extraordinary way. "Those who are affected by ignorance of the true religion, if it is invincible ignorance, are not subject to any guilt in this matter before the eyes of the Lord,"[26] and, "They who labor in invincible ignorance of our most holy religion and who live an honest and upright life, can, by the operating power of divine light and grace, attain eternal life, since God will by no means suffer anyone to be punished with eternal torment who has not the guilt of deliberate sin."[27]

551. What is this extraordinary way of being joined to the Church?

Because God is omnipotent, it is possible that He can communicate the effect of baptism independent of its ordinary sacramental sign.

552. What preconditions would be necessary for a soul to be saved in this extraordinary way?

1. Belief that God exists and is a Rewarder of those who seek Him (see Heb 11:6); 2. Sincere effort to know and do God's will as He makes it known; 3. True repentance for sin and hope for pardon.

553. What are the further preconditions for "baptism of desire"?[28]

1. Perfect conversion; 2. Sincere belief in and love for Jesus Christ and the Blessed Trinity; 3. Firm intent to enter the Church.

554. **Should we suppose that such an extraordinary way of entering the Church occurs often?**

No, it would be rash to presume so. "The gate is wide and the road is easy that leads to destruction, and there are many who take it. For the gate is narrow and the road is hard that leads to life, and there are few who find it" (Mt 7:13–14).

555. **What of martyrs like St. Felicity, who were not baptized, yet attained heaven?**

When one is put to death out of hatred for the true Faith which he professes, he perfectly imitates Christ and so attains heaven through a kind of "baptism of blood."[29]

556. **May a baptized non-Catholic who is killed for confessing Christ be saved as a martyr?**

Yes. "If anyone confesses that Jesus is the Son of God, God abides in him, and he in God" (1 Jn 4:15*). If a man is killed for confessing Christ as God and the only Savior, dying because he rejects idolatry or other crimes against the commandments of God while remaining inculpably ignorant of the true Church, God may accept the sacrifice of his life, because God alone searches hearts (see Rom 8:27). Yet he cannot be formally declared a martyr by the Catholic Church, since this would promote doctrinal relativism.

557. **Should a baptized non-Catholic who is killed for defending heresy or idolatry be regarded as a martyr?**

No. In professing heresy or idolatry, he is rejecting the revealed truth of God and thus opposing himself to God. In cases of truly invincible ignorance, God alone can judge; but he should not be regarded as a martyr, since this would imply a denial of objective truth.

Those Outside the Church

558. **Who are not members of the Catholic Church?**

All the non-baptized, including Jews, Muslims, and pagans.

559. **Who else does not belong to the unity of the Catholic Church?**

All the baptized whose crimes and sins have impeded the efficacy of their baptismal character, separating them from the spiritual goods of the Church. These include heretics, schismatics, excommunicates, and apostates.

560. **Who are *Jews*?**

Those who continue to observe certain aspects of the Mosaic Law, while rejecting its fulfillment in the revelation of the true Messiah, Jesus Christ, the Incarnate Son of God.

561. **Who are *Muslims*?**

Those professing the religion of Islam, founded by Mohammed (ca. 622), who gave himself out to be a prophet of the one true God, promised sensual joys after death, allowed polygamy, taught fatalism, and propagated his new religion mainly by fire and sword. Islam explicitly rejects the revealed truths of the Incarnation, the divinity of Christ, His redeeming sacrifice on the Cross, and the Holy Trinity. They view Christ as a mere prophet, and venerate the Virgin Mary merely as a holy woman, not the Mother of God.

562. **Who are *pagans*?**
Those who have never accepted the Christian Faith or received sacramental baptism, although they may belong to some other organized religion (e.g., Buddhists, Hindus).

563. **Who are *heretics*?**
Those who have received baptism, yet obstinately deny some article of Faith which must be held (e.g., Protestants, Modernists).

564. **Who are *schismatics*?**
Those who received baptism, yet have been separated from the unity of the Catholic Church by refusing to recognize the Supreme Pontiff or have canonical communion with him and the other members of the Church (e.g., the Orthodox).

565. **Are so-called "sedevacantists" in schism?**
Yes, inasmuch as one who obstinately refuses to recognize a lawfully reigning pope is a schismatic.

566. **Is any act of disobedience to a command of the pope by itself schismatic?**
No. One is not schismatic if he resists a pope or refuses to obey a particular teaching or command of his that is manifestly contrary to natural or divine law, or that would harm or undermine the integrity of the Catholic Faith or the sacredness of the liturgy. In such cases, disobedience and resistance to the pope is permissible and sometimes obligatory.[30]

567. **Who are *excommunicates*?**
Catholics who, for some grave crime, have been cut off from the visible communion of the Church and deprived of its spiritual blessings.

568. **Can a public sentence of excommunication ever be null and void?**
Yes. As in the case of St. Joan of Arc, the legal penalty of excommunication may be levied unjustly, and so be without judicial standing or effect.

569. **Who are *apostates*?**
Those who, after having professed the Catholic Faith, have now totally repudiated it.

570. **If a baptized Catholic commits mortal sin, is he still a member of the Church?**
Yes. Unless one sins gravely and obstinately against faith itself (e.g., by the sin of heresy), he remains a member of the Church, albeit one that is spiritually dead; like a dead limb that is still attached to a living tree.

571. **Is mere membership in the Church sufficient for salvation?**
No. To be saved, one must also be a *living* member, i.e., in the state of grace: "All the Church's children should remember that their exalted status is to be attributed not to their own merits but to the special grace of Christ. If they fail moreover to respond to that grace in thought, word, and deed, not only shall they not be saved, but they will be the more severely judged."[31]

572. **How is the divine life of grace ordinarily restored to a dead member of the Church?**
Through the sacrament of penance, in which a person repents, confesses his sin, and is absolved by an ordained minister of God.

Attributes of the Church

573. **What are the principal attributes of the Church?**
Visibility, perpetuity, indefectibility, and infallibility.

574. **What is the *visibility* of the Church?**
The fact that the Church is publicly manifest to men as a society historically established by Christ.

575. **Who err regarding the visibility of the Church?**
Those who believe that the Church is merely an invisible association of men united by shared beliefs and interior dispositions, as is commonly held among Protestants.

576. **What is the *perpetuity* of the Church?**
The fact that the Church will endure, without interruption, until the end of the world.

577. **Who err regarding the perpetuity of the Church?**
Those who believe that the true Church once ceased to exist or was essentially corrupted, as held by Mormons; or that it could give way to some new form in the future, as held by Modernists.

578. **What is the *indefectibility* of the Church?**
The fact that the Church preserves all that it once received from its divine Founder, remaining unchanged and unchangeable in its dogmas, morals, sacraments, and essential organization.

579. **Who err regarding the indefectibility of the Church?**
Those who believe that the constant Magisterium of the Church has or could definitively promulgate false doctrines, command heretical worship, or give false sacraments, contrary to the promise of her divine Founder that the gates of hell will not prevail against it (see Mt 16:18).

580. **Then the Church can never be defeated by heresies?**
No. "The one Church, the true Church, the Catholic Church, is fighting against all heresies: fight, it can; be fought down, it cannot. As for heresies, they all went out

of it, like unprofitable branches pruned from the vine; but it still abides in its root, in its Vine, in its charity. The gates of hell shall not prevail against it."[32]

581. What is the *infallibility* of the Church?

The fact that it is preserved free from error throughout time, both in definitive teaching and universal belief. "He that heareth you, heareth Me" (Lk 10:16*); "When the Spirit of truth comes, He will guide you into all the truth" (Jn 16:13).

582. Who err regarding the infallibility of the Church?

Those who believe that the Church can definitively and formally hold or teach doctrinal error, or that past definitive teaching may be superseded in a process of doctrinal evolution, or who construe the charism of infallibility too broadly, as if individual members of the Church were entirely incapable of error.

583. Why is it dangerous to misconstrue the Church's infallibility too broadly?

Because one risks being scandalized by heretical clergy, and it is a painful fact that the most pernicious errors in history have sprung from the ranks of the ordained. Christ warns us to beware of such ravening wolves and false shepherds (see Mt 7:15; 23:13; 18:6; and Acts 20:29).

584. What truths fall within the sphere of the Church's infallibility?

All revealed truths contained in Scripture and Tradition are its primary object: "This infallibility with which the divine Redeemer willed His Church to be endowed in defining doctrine of faith and morals extends as far as the deposit of revelation extends, which must be religiously guarded and faithfully expounded."[33]

585. What are some examples of this *primary object* of the Church's infallibility?

"If it is explicitly revealed that Jesus is true God and true Man, then it is already revealed, but this time implicitly, that in Jesus there are two intellects, one divine and one human, and two wills, one divine and one human. If it is revealed that Christ declared that what He offered under the appearance of bread was His body, then it is already revealed, but implicitly, that in that upper room there took place an extraordinary change of one substance into another, a transubstantiation. The Church, divinely assisted, can therefore define as revealed by the Gospel itself, that in Jesus are two intelligences and two wills, [and] that the real presence of Christ in the Eucharist presupposes transubstantiation."[34]

586. What is the *secondary object* of the Church's infallibility?

Those truths not formally revealed, but "necessarily required in order that the deposit of revelation may be preserved intact; truths without which the Deposit of Faith could not be protected and explained."[35]

587. What are some examples of this secondary object of the Church's infallibility?

The knowability of God, the power of man's mind to know truth, the spirituality of the soul, the freedom of man's will, or the philosophical concepts and terms with which dogmas are promulgated, such as "person," "substance," "transubstantiation," etc.

588. **Is the Church infallible in the purely natural order?**
No. Conclusions of the natural sciences are beyond the Church's sphere of infallibility. However, it is the Church's right and duty to condemn any theories that oppose divine revelation, since truth cannot contradict itself.

589. **Where does the infallibility of the Church reside?**
There are several organs of infallibility in the Church, the chief of which are: 1. The universal and ordinary Magisterium; 2. The solemn definitions (including anathema-affirmations) of ecumenical councils; 3. The pope's *ex cathedra* pronouncements; 4. The *sensus fidei* of the Church's living members.

590. **What is meant by the *universal and ordinary Magisterium*?**
It means the constant and unchanging teaching of the Roman Pontiffs together with the bishops spread over the world and outside an ecumenical council; that doctrine taught always (*semper*), everywhere (*ubique*), and by all (*ab omnibus*).[36]

591. **Is each teaching act of a pope or ecumenical council automatically infallible?**
No. The Church's fundamental principle says: "No doctrine is understood to be infallibly defined unless this is manifestly demonstrated."[37]

592. **Do the words *solemn* or *extraordinary Magisterium* mean automatically infallible?**
No. "Solemn" can refer to the exterior form: "The supreme power in the universal Church, which this college [of bishops] enjoys, is exercised in a solemn way in an ecumenical council."[38] Sometimes the term *solemn* is used to indicate a dogmatic definition itself: "By divine and catholic faith all those things are to be believed which are contained in the word of God as found in Scripture and Tradition, and which are proposed by the Church as matters to be believed as divinely revealed, whether by her solemn judgment or in her ordinary and universal Magisterium."[39] The term *extraordinary* may also indicate the exterior aspect or exceptional character, yet it was not used by Vatican I or Vatican II.

593. **Can a pope also proclaim a dogma of faith without any exterior solemnity?**
Yes. The pope can proclaim a dogma of faith simply by a letter addressed to the entire Church.

594. **What is the *sensus fidei*?**
It is an innate "sense of the Faith" present in every soul in the state of grace: a capacity to intuitively perceive whether or not a certain teaching is in accord with the authentic doctrine of Christ, retained in His Church. This perception acts and grows in proportion to our fidelity to perennial Catholic teaching, resistance against heresies and doctrinal ambiguities, repeated acts of faith, and the holiness of our life.

595. **How is the *sensus fidei* of the Church's living members infallible?**
"The whole body of the faithful who have an anointing that comes from the Holy One (see 1 Jn 2:20, 27) cannot err in matters of belief. This characteristic is shown in the supernatural appreciation of the faith (*sensus fidei*) of the whole people, when,

'from the bishops to the last of the faithful' they manifest a universal consent in matters of faith and morals."[40]

596. **What is a Christian's duty with respect to the truths infallibly taught by the Church?**
He must accept them without reserve, believing in them as the teachings of Christ that they are.

Marks of the Church

597. **How many churches did Christ found?**
Christ founded only one true Church: the Catholic Church. Established upon St. Peter, whose See was in Rome and whose successors still reign there, it is also called the Roman Catholic Church.

598. **Do any other religious communities claim to be the true Church of Christ?**
Yes. However, none but the Catholic Church can prove its claim.

599. **Why is it necessary to know which of these groups is the true Church?**
Because only in and through the true Church are men sanctified and finally saved.

600. **Are these groups simply branches, extensions, or partial sharings in the one true Church?**
No. "Jesus Christ did not, in point of fact, institute a Church to embrace several communities similar in nature, but in themselves distinct, and lacking those bonds which render the Church unique and indivisible."[41]

601. **Then how may the one true Church be identified?**
It may be known especially by those four *marks* or distinctive notes that Christ gave to it, which we profess in the Niceno-Constantinopolitan Creed: the Church is "one, holy, catholic, and apostolic."

602. **Must the true Church exist with all of these marks in an indestructible totality?**
Yes. 1. If the Church were not *one*, it would not be true, for unity is an essential aspect of truth; 2. If the Church were not *holy*, it could not sanctify souls; 3. If the Church were not *catholic*, it could not offer salvation to all people in all times and places; 4. If the Church were not *apostolic*, it would not have its doctrine, mission, and authority from Christ, but would instead be a merely human institution.

603. **Is there another mark that seems to accompany the Church throughout history?**
Yes, that of *persecution*. In imitation of their divine Head, faithful Catholics will be persecuted in every age: "If they persecuted Me, they will persecute you" (Jn 15:20).

UNITY

604. Why is the Catholic Church one?
Because all its faithful members worship the one true God, profess the same doctrine and morals, partake of the same sacraments, and obey the same pastors.

605. If the Church is one, how can doctrinal disputes arise in the hierarchy from time to time?
The Church is a perfect and divine society by nature, but its individual members on earth may violate this unity. Those who reject the Church's perennial teaching demonstrate that there is a unified and stable body of doctrine which they reject.

606. What is *ecumenism*, as the term is sometimes used today?
It is a general term used to describe efforts toward achieving unity among various religious communities that all claim Jesus Christ as their Lord.

607. How is ecumenism to be rightly understood by Catholics?
True ecumenism cannot be the search for a Christian unity that does not yet exist, since Christ has already conferred this perfect unity upon His true Church. Rather, it must express the intention that all should enter that unity which the Catholic Church already indestructibly possesses, "by promoting the return to the one true Church of Christ of those who are separated from it, for in the past they have unhappily left it. To the one true Church of Christ, we say, which is visible to all, and which is to remain, according to the will of its Author, exactly the same as He instituted it."[42]

608. Does ecumenism require a decrease in zeal to draw others to the Catholic Church?
No. The constant Magisterium condemns such an attitude: "Whoever, by divine grace, represents in the world Jesus Christ, the Prince of Shepherds, not only should not be satisfied with defending and preserving the flock of the Lord already entrusted to him, but would fail in one of his most serious obligations if he did not seek with every effort to win and attract to Christ the sheep still separated from Him."[43]

609. Is it proper to affirm that the Spirit of Christ uses separated Christian communities as "means of salvation which derive their efficacy from the very fullness of grace and truth entrusted to the Church"?[44]
No. This insinuates a quasi-legitimacy for separated Christian communities, undermining the unicity of the Catholic Church and promoting doctrinal relativism. In truth, God willed and established the Catholic Church as His unique Church and possessor of the means of salvation. The diversity of separated Christian communities is therefore contrary to Christ's intention, as is the diversity of world religions.

610. **Don't some separated Christian communities retain some true teachings, and administer some valid sacraments?**

Yes; but insofar as these are true and pleasing to God, such teachings or rites belong to the Catholic Church, and not to the heretical or schismatic communities. According to St. Augustine, Christians who leave the Church have made their own property out of what they have stolen from the Catholic Church.[45] "There is but one Church, who alone is called Catholic, and it is she who begets by virtue of that which remains her property in those sects who are separated from her unity, no matter who possesses them."[46]

611. **Is it dangerous to affirm: "That which unites Catholics to separated Christian communities is greater than that which separates them"?**

Yes, because the spiritual harm of their being separated — through heresy or schism — from the unique Church of God, which is the Catholic Church, is objectively greater than any partial sharing in some truths and means of salvation which properly belong to the Catholic Church. Such sharings could, of course, serve as a good base for clarification of misunderstanding and errors, in view of bringing them back into unity with the Church.[47]

HOLINESS

612. **Why is the Catholic Church holy?**

Because: 1. Its founder is the Son of God; 2. It is animated by the Holy Spirit; 3. Its dogmas, morals, worship, and discipline withdraw man from evil and lead to virtue; 4. All who have kept her commands have been good and virtuous, and all who have followed her counsels perfectly have become great saints; 5. Innumerable miracles have occurred in her fold.

613. **Then why are scandalous sinners sometimes found within the Church?**

The Church is holy, "though she has sinners in her bosom, because she herself has no other life but that of grace: it is by living by her life that her members are sanctified; it is by removing themselves from her life that they fall into sins and disorders that prevent the radiation of her sanctity."[48]

614. **Why does God permit scandals in His Church?**

In His mysterious providence, God permits the scandal of evildoers in His Church, as part of His design to sanctify and perfect the living members of the Church in every age. "For it must needs be that scandals come: but nevertheless woe to that man by whom the scandal comes" (Mt 18:7*). "Indeed, there have to be factions among you, for only so will it become clear who among you are genuine" (1 Cor 11:19).

615. **Why is the Catholic Church called *catholic*?**
Because it is: 1. Always perfectly suited to all men of all times and places; 2. Radically capable of spreading throughout the world; 3. Animated by a divine impulse to extend itself universally; 4. Filled with all supernatural truths. The Church was catholic on the day of Pentecost and will always be so until the day of the Second Coming of Christ.

616. **Then why doesn't the greater part of humanity currently belong to the Church?**
Christ's commission to "go therefore and make disciples of all nations" (Mt 28:19) remains a standing order until He comes again in glory. Until then, the Church still has work to do.

617. **Are other Christian communities with a worldwide scope also "catholic"?**
No. They all lack some essential element of catholicity, none possess all supernatural truths, and many are inventions expedient only for some people of a limited time or place.

APOSTOLICITY

618. **Why is the Catholic Church apostolic?**
Because her doctrine is that of the apostles, and her mission and authority come from Christ through the apostles. All of her bishops trace their office from man to man in unbroken succession from the twelve apostles.

619. **How can there be weak, worldly, or corrupt bishops in the Church?**
The office of bishop does not guarantee sanctity, but only apostolic authority. If a bishop is unfaithful to his vocation, the snare is often pride, vanity, or love of comfort. Although God's grace is never lacking for the fulfillment of their divine mission on earth, bishops must still choose to correspond with the grace of their calling or else they will fall away. They are always in need of prayer, and are held to severe account before God (see 1 Tm 2:1–2; and Mt 18:6).

620. **What should we conclude from these four marks of the Church?**
That the Catholic Church is the one and only true Church on earth, founded by Jesus Christ and bearing within itself a truly divine mission and authority.

621. **What else shows the Catholic Church to be a divine institution?**
Two powerful motives of credibility: its nonviolent and wondrous *propagation* despite countless obstacles, and its unchangeable *stability* through time, even as nations rise and fall. This stability in doctrine, essential institutions (papacy and hierarchy), sacraments, and prayer is especially unique in human history, and truly admirable.

622. **Is there any other religion whose overall characteristics are on a par with the Catholic Church?**
No. "What religion has there been in the world that thinks more highly and magnificently about God, that proposes better laws, that teaches more salutary advice, that has such sacraments and spiritual medicines, that so favors virtue, promising it such great benefits, and so disfavors vice, threatening such terrible punishments? Which has such holy Scriptures, full of so many mysteries and such salutary sentences, and such effective impulses to move men to the love and fear of God, to the hatred of sin and contempt of the world? What religion has there been in the world from which came so many martyrs, confessors, holy bishops and doctors of faith, virgins and innumerable monks, who turned deserts into shrines and lived more like angels than men? In what religion, in what time, in what place was found such strength as that of our martyrs, such purity, such abstinence, such heartfelt mercy, such contempt for the world, such zeal for prayer and contemplation as there was in all our saints?"[49]

623. **Then why is the true Church so bitterly persecuted, rather than universally loved?**
Like Our Lord, the Catholic Church is not of this earth. It is attacked by the worldly in every age because it condemns sin and promotes virtue and discipline for the passions, preparing man for the supernatural life of heaven.[50]

Structure of the Church

624. **Of what elements is the body or structure of the Church composed?**
It is composed of the *clergy* (those sacramentally ordained and given a ministry), *laity* (those who are ministered to), and *consecrated religious* who may be ordained or non-ordained, and belong to a separate state that is neither clerical nor lay.[51]

The Pope

625. **Who is the supreme pastor of the Church on earth?**
The Roman Pontiff, also commonly called the Pope, the Vicar of Christ, the Successor of Peter, and the visible head of the Church upon earth.

626. **Who is the invisible head of the Church?**
Our Lord Jesus Christ, who is always present in the Church to guide and assist it.

627. **Why is the pope called the *Vicar of Christ*?**
Because he is appointed to represent Christ upon earth, to act in His name, and to bring Him to the nations in a special way by reason of his position.

628. **Why is he called the *Successor of St. Peter*?**
Because he has inherited the authority of St. Peter, who was Prince of the Apostles and the first head of the universal Church, by the appointment of Jesus Christ.

629. **Why is he called the *Roman Pontiff*?**
Because Peter established his see in Rome, where he died in AD 64–68. The term *pontiff* (in Latin *pontifex*) originally means "bridge-builder," spiritually understood to mean that the pope should help bridge the gap between Christ's invisible presence and His visible Body, the Church.

630. **From whom does the pope hold his spiritual powers?**
He holds them directly from Christ, who gives them to an elected pope upon his acceptance of the office.

THE CARDINALS AND BISHOPS

631. **Who cooperates with the pope in governing the Church?**
All the bishops, and principally the cardinals known collectively as the Sacred College.

632. **What powers do cardinals possess?**
1. They form the ordinary council of the pope; 2. They preside over the various Congregations[52] performing special work at the pope's direction in the government of the Church; 3. During a vacancy in the Holy See (from *sedes* [chair] of the pope), they conduct urgent business; 4. They alone have the right to elect a new pope when the See is vacant.

633. **Who are the pastors of the first order in the Church?**
All bishops who have been canonically instituted, having received from the Roman Pontiff a diocese (territory) or another form of particular church to govern. Such a bishop is called a *local ordinary*.

634. **What is a bishop?**
Bishops are true successors of the apostles through the sacramental episcopal ordination and the canonical mission given to them by the pope. They are charged by the Holy Spirit with the spiritual government of particular dioceses, or to fulfill a special mission in the Church (e.g., apostolic administrator, auxiliary bishop, apostolic nuncio, apostolic delegate).

635. **How are the bishops true successors of the apostles?**
Because the mission which the apostles received had to pass from their hands to other men, clothed with their same apostolic authority to teach all nations to the end of time.

636. **In what respect are all bishops equal?**
All bishops possess the perfection of the priesthood, although certain episcopal sees retain titles that may include a more extended jurisdiction, e.g., patriarchs, primates, metropolitans, archbishops. In the Latin Church, *primate* and *patriarch* are only titles of honor without further jurisdiction as such, while Eastern Catholic Patriarchs and Major Archbishops do have a more extended jurisdiction.

The Other Pastors

637. Who are the pastors of the second order?

Men ordained as priests who govern parishes under the authority of their bishops, often simply called *pastors*, and any other priests who are charged with the salvation of souls, such as *rectors, chaplains,* or *religious superiors* in monasteries.

638. From whom do these pastors hold their powers directly?

Priests hold them directly from the bishops, the local ordinaries. According to canon law, superiors of clerical religious institutes of pontifical right and of clerical societies of apostolic life of pontifical right hold ordinary executive power for their own members.[53]

639. May a pastor have auxiliary clergy assisting him?

Yes. When a parish is very large, he may have other priests as auxiliaries, called *vicars, curates,* or *assistants,* and he may also be assisted by deacons.

640. To be a lawful pastor, is it enough to simply be ordained as a bishop or priest?

Normally, a bishop is also sent into a diocese by the pope, and a priest is sent into a parish by the bishop. In other words, a pastor must have both the power of order, and the power of jurisdiction.

641. What is the *power of order*?

The power of order is conferred on a bishop by his episcopal consecration and on a priest by his priestly ordination. It gives a bishop the divine power to ordain priests, and a priest the divine power to consecrate the Eucharist, absolve sins, etc.

642. What is the *power of jurisdiction*?

This refers to the office of governing (*munus regendi*) and is conferred by a superior to a subject, giving him a legal and moral right to exercise a hierarchical function in the Church—a kind of "official permission."

643. What does the power of jurisdiction determine?

It determines precisely where, upon what, and to whom bishops and priests are called to exercise their particular ministry in the Church.

644. How is the power of jurisdiction communicated?

Priests receive their jurisdiction from the bishop of the diocese or the local ordinary; bishops receive theirs by their unity with the pope; and the pope holds jurisdiction from Jesus Christ. In cases of emergency, the Church automatically supplies any bishop or priest with the necessary jurisdiction to exercise his ministry for the good of souls; otherwise, one who acts without proper jurisdiction from his lawful superior would be an impostor or a schismatic.

645. **Is it lawful to receive the sacraments from a schismatic priest or one who is in an irregular canonical situation?**
According to the constant tradition of the Church this is lawful only in the case of approaching death, when it is impossible to have an approved Catholic minister; and even then, only when no scandal is thereby given to others.

646. **Are there other ranks of clergy that serve in the Church?**
Yes. According to the constant tradition of the Church, "there are other orders, both major and minor,... a hierarchy by divine ordinance, which consists of bishops, priests, and ministers."[54]

647. **Whom are these other ministers in the Church?**
They are the deacon, subdeacon, and four minor orders of acolyte, exorcist, lector, and porter; roles of (especially liturgical) service in the Church that have existed from the earliest centuries.[55]

THE LAY FAITHFUL

648. **What do we call those Christians who are ministered to in the Church?**
They are called the *laity, laymen,* or *the lay faithful.*

649. **Are *consecrated religious* (e.g., monks and nuns) members of the laity?**
To the extent that they are not ordained, they may be understood as "laity"; however, these men and women make public vows of poverty, chastity, and obedience in service of Christ and His Church, which withdraws them from the ranks of the ordinary faithful, and sets them apart in a unique and sacred station in the life of the Church.

650. **How may the faithful support the governing of the Church by the clergy?**
By rendering it more effective through donating their time, treasure, and talents; especially by helping pastors in the maintenance of a parish or diocese, by supporting various apostolic works, or by defending the rights of Christ and the Church against the attacks of the impious.

651. **How should the faithful fulfill the mission of the Church on earth?**
They are called to order their own lives in holiness and justice before God, govern their families in charity and truth, and act practically in society to shape it according to the doctrine of Jesus Christ, in recognition of His divine Kingship on earth.

Authority in the Church

652. **What authority has Christ given to the teaching Church?**
He has invested the Church with His own triple authority in teaching, sanctifying, and governing. The pastors of His Church must therefore *instruct* the faithful in right doctrine, *sanctify* them by properly administering the sacraments and dispensing blessings, and *direct* them by good laws fostering upright moral lives.

653. **To whom does this authority in the Church belong?**
It belongs to the pope principally and universally, and to the other bishops within their dioceses. It is to these alone, in the person of St. Peter and the other apostles, that Christ said: "Go therefore and make disciples of all nations" (Mt 28:19).

654. **What are the most common errors about authority in the Church?**
1. Various forms of *conciliarism*, limiting papal authority by the authority of bishops gathered in council; 2. *Gallicanism* or *Statism*, subjecting the authority of pope and bishops to the civil power; 3. *Magisterial positivism*, receiving every word of a living pope or bishop as inherently true, good, infallible, and necessary to obey; 4. *Protestantism*, viewing private judgment as an infallible authority in matters of faith and morals.

655. **Are there different levels of the Church's Magisterium (teaching office)?**
Yes. Each level of magisterial authority requires a correspondingly different level of assent from the faithful.

656. **What teachings of the Magisterium require the highest level of assent: that of *divine faith*?**
Those truths "which are contained in the word of God as it has been written or handed down by Tradition, that is, in the single Deposit of Faith entrusted to the Church, and which are at the same time proposed as divinely revealed."[56]

657. **What specific kinds of teachings require this assent of divine faith?**
Truths taught infallibly by: 1. Papal teaching *ex cathedra*; 2. Formal dogmatic definition of an ecumenical council with the approval of the pope; 3. The pope together with the bishops spread over the world and outside an ecumenical council.[57]

658. **What teachings of the Magisterium require a *definitive assent*?**
Those truths that are definitively proposed by the Magisterium, though not yet formally defined;[58] e.g., the declaration of Pope John Paul II that the Church has no authority whatsoever to confer priestly ordination on women.[59]

659. **What teachings of the Magisterium require only a respectful religious compliance (*obsequium religiosum*)?**
All acts of the so-called *authentic*—or simply the ordinary, daily—magisterium of the pope, and all non-definitive or pastoral teachings of Church councils. Even though teachings at this level could have a universal dimension, they are non-definitive and reformable when there is no express intention to define something infallibly or propose it as definitive teaching.

660. **Can non-infallible and non-definitive teachings or commands of a pope or council be later reformulated for greater clarity, or even corrected?**
Yes. Such teachings can be reformed later by an infallible act of the Magisterium. Commands issued on a prudential level—as the Fourth Lateran Council's recommendation of a Crusade, or the command that Jews in Catholic territories wear

distinctive clothing—may be corrected by a change of laws, or by the refusal to implement such measures. Such reformable acts are especially noticeable among affirmations of the Second Vatican Council that are in themselves ambiguous and can lead to an erroneous understanding.[60]

661. **Why is Vatican II the clearest example of an ecumenical council emitting non-infallible teachings?**

Because it was not convoked to infallibly pronounce new dogmas or propose definitive teachings, but to offer a pastoral explanation of the truths of the Faith, as asserted by Pope John XXIII: "[This Council's] magisterium is predominantly pastoral in character,"[61] and "the salient point of this Council is not a discussion of one article or another of the fundamental doctrine of the Church."[62] Pope Paul VI was also very clear in stating: "Given the Council's pastoral character, it avoided pronouncing, in an extraordinary manner, dogmas endowed with the note of infallibility."[63]

662. **What was the key difference between Vatican II and all previous ecumenical councils?**

The previous ecumenical councils formulated the doctrine of faith and morals in articles with the clearest possible assertions, and in concise canons with anathemas, to guarantee an unambiguous understanding of the true doctrine and protect the faithful from heretical influences within or outside the Church. Vatican II, however, chose not to do this.

663. **What does *anathema* mean in Scripture?**

In the Old Testament, it means "to cut off" or separate (*haram* in Hebrew), indicating a person or thing condemned to be exterminated or forbidden to make use of. In the New Testament, *anathema* (from Greek) entails the loss of goods or exclusion from the society of the faithful, e.g.: "If anyone preach to you a gospel besides that which you have received, let him be anathema" (Gal 1:9*).

664. **What does *anathema* mean in the Church's dogmatic pronouncements?**

Every ecumenical council from Nicaea I to Vatican I has worded its dogmatic canons: "If anyone says ... let him be anathema," to clearly proscribe grave errors in faith.

665. **Is the menace of the *anathema* an act of charity both toward the erring and the rest of the faithful?**

Yes. "It is an act of the greatest charity toward all the faithful, comparable to preventing a dangerous disease from infecting innumerable people. By isolating the bearer of infection, we protect the bodily health of others; by the anathema, we protect their spiritual health.... And more: a rupture of communion with the heretic in no way implies that our obligation of charity toward him ceases. No, the Church prays also for heretics; the true Catholic who knows a heretic personally prays ardently for him and would never cease to impart all kinds of help to him."[64]

666. What was the approach of the Second Vatican Council?
This Council's basic approach was partly determined by a shift from primacy being given to the content of the Faith to the methods of its explanation or proclamation. Such priority given to method, history (which is mutable), and the so-called "pastoral approach" resulted in certain doctrinally unclear or ambiguous affirmations in the Council's documents.

667. Does this "pastoral approach" require ambiguity, uncertainty, or vagueness?
No. According to the perennial sense of the Church, the truly pastoral approach consists in spiritual care for the eternal salvation of souls, and therefore in leading them with utmost clarity to the eternal truths.

668. May Catholics propose emendations or corrections of evidently ambiguous or erroneous statements or commands of a pope or ecumenical council?
Yes. The faithful "have the right, indeed at times the duty, in keeping with their knowledge, competence, and position, to manifest to the sacred pastors their views on matters which concern the good of the Church. They have the right also to make their views known to others of Christ's faithful, but in doing so they must always respect the integrity of faith and morals, show due reverence to the pastors, and take into account both the common good and the dignity of individuals."[65]

669. How has the Holy See implemented the abovementioned Canon 212, §3?
The Holy See itself allows and at times invites theologians to propose objections regarding some affirmations of the Magisterium in specific difficult cases: "Objections could contribute to real progress and provide a stimulus to the Magisterium to propose the teaching of the Church in greater depth and with a clearer presentation of the arguments."[66]

AUTHORITY OF THE ROMAN PONTIFF

670. Why does the Roman Pontiff alone possess supreme authority in the Church?
Because, as Successor of St. Peter, he has the primacy which Our Lord conferred on Peter, the Prince of the Apostles (see Mt 16:17–19; and Jn 21:15–17).

671. What is this primacy of the pope with regard to doctrine?
He is the principal teacher, guardian, and defender of the revealed truths. It belongs to him to: 1. Uphold what God has revealed to be believed, done, and avoided; 2. Condemn errors contrary to this divine revelation, contained in the apostolic doctrine he has received; 3. Be the visible sign and principle of the unity of faith and communion of the episcopate and the faithful.[67]

672. Is the pope infallible—that is, unable to teach error?
The pope is assisted by manifold graces for teaching the truth of Christ in his daily ministry, which is usually not infallible. When he teaches *ex cathedra* (from the

Chair), he exercises the Church's charism of infallibility and is preserved free from error in that teaching.[68]

673. **How does infallibility differ from impeccability?**

Infallibility is the impossibility of deceiving the Church by definitively binding it to a false doctrine, whereas *impeccability* is the impossibility of offending God and harming others by personal sin. The pope is infallible under limited conditions, but not impeccable.

674. **Is papal infallibility a license to introduce new teachings?**

No. The pope is bound scrupulously to obey the Catholic Faith transmitted to him by the perennial teaching of the Church, to keep this Faith intact, and to defend it. "The Holy Spirit was promised to the Successors of Peter not so that they might, by His revelation, make known some new doctrine, but that, by His assistance, they might religiously guard and faithfully expound the revelation or Deposit of Faith transmitted by the apostles."[69]

675. **What makes a particular papal teaching *ex cathedra* and thus infallible?**

The teaching must be: 1. Concerning a matter of faith or morals; 2. Addressed to the universal Church; 3. Proposed in virtue of the pope's supreme apostolic office; 4. Formulated as a final and binding definition.

676. **Are canonizations of saints undoubtedly infallible *ex cathedra* statements?**

No. Acts of canonization guarantee that devotion to a saint is not contrary to the Faith and can be for the spiritual good of the believer. However, the Church has not infallibly proclaimed or formally taught that canonizations of saints are infallible acts. A widespread theological opinion is that canonizations are infallible, while other serious theologians have strong reasons for holding otherwise. This discussion has not been settled conclusively.

677. **Have individuals ever been removed from the *Roman Martyrology*, the Church's official list of Saints?**

Yes. The best-known case is that of St. Philomena, who was given a proper Mass and Office by Pope Pius IX in 1855, with devotion to her being showered with papal favors by Popes Leo XIII and Pius X. Pope John XXIII later removed her from every liturgical calendar, and Pope John Paul II removed her from the Roman Martyrology altogether, thereby suppressing the veneration of a very popular saint. This does not mean, of course, that the faithful may not continue to be privately devoted to St. Philomena.

678. **What of those popes that have taught errors in the past?**

No pope has ever taught—or could ever teach—an error by *ex cathedra* pronouncement. However, like any bishop, a pope may resist the grace of his office and possibly teach doctrinal errors in his daily, ordinary, and non-definitive assertions, i.e., outside of *ex cathedra* pronouncements.

679. **Have there been cases in history of popes teaching or promoting doctrinal errors?**
Yes. Although such cases have been very rare, they include: Honorius I (+638), who wrote letters with erroneous statements about the two wills of Jesus Christ, and was posthumously condemned as a heretic by the Council of Constantinople III. John XXII (+1334), who taught that the Beatific Vision of God is granted to saints only after the Last Judgement, and was widely condemned by theologians outside the papal court before recanting on his deathbed; his position was corrected posthumously by his successor, Benedict XII. In our own time, Pope Francis has publicly signed a document affirming: "The pluralism and the diversity of religions, color, sex, race, and language are willed by God in His wisdom, through which He created human beings,"[70] and taught that the death penalty "is *per se* contrary to the Gospel."[71]

680. **Have there been cases of popes promoting doctrinally ambiguous prayers in the liturgy of the Mass?**
Yes. In 1969 Pope Paul VI approved a New Order of Mass with novel Offertory Prayers modeled after Jewish Sabbath meal blessings (*Berekoth*).[72] Because these prayers emphasize the aspect of a *meal* while seriously obscuring the propitiatory nature of the *sacrifice*, these Offertory Prayers are very close to a Protestant understanding of Holy Mass as a mere banquet.[73]

681. **Have there been cases of popes promoting doctrinally erroneous and morally problematic sacramental practices?**
Yes. In 2016 Pope Francis approved the norms of the Buenos Aires bishops that granted Communion to unrepentant public adulterers: "When it is not possible to obtain a declaration of nullity, [living in continence] may not, in fact, be feasible. ... If one arrives at the recognition that, in a particular case, there are limitations that diminish responsibility and culpability, particularly when a person judges that he would fall into a subsequent fault by damaging the children of the new union [by living in continence], *Amoris Laetitia* opens up the possibility of access to the sacraments of reconciliation and the Eucharist."[74]

682. **Did the past erring popes thereby lose their papal office?**
No. In the history of the Church, no pope who taught errors thereby lost his office, or was posthumously declared an invalid pope.

683. **Then a pope is not infallible in all that he teaches or commands at every moment?**
No. A pope is guaranteed to be free from all possibility of error only when he restates prior infallible teaching, or makes an *ex cathedra* pronouncement.

684. **Why has Christ made the pope infallible only in clearly determined circumstances, rather than continuously?**
So that Christians would not divinize popes and give them the same credence and obedience that is owed only to the God-Man Jesus Christ, who is "head over all" (Eph 1:22*).

685. **What is the primacy of the pope in regard to administration?**
It consists in the full power of jurisdiction in all things pertaining to the discipline and government of the Church.

686. **Does papal power in teaching or governing depend on the ratification of bishops?**
No. The Roman Pontiff alone possesses full and immediate power of teaching and government in the universal Church, independent of the recommendation or ratification of other bishops.[75]

687. **Which heresies deny the pope's full and immediate power of teaching and government in the universal Church?**
Conciliarism maintained that an ecumenical council is above the pope.[76] Similar heresies include the Orthodox Church's concept of synodality (*sobornost* in Russian), as well as episcopalism and Gallicanism, all of which claim that the college of bishops has universal jurisdiction and teaching power over the Church, with the pope being only "first among equals."

688. **Has the Church infallibly condemned the substantial error of these theories?**
Yes. "If anyone says that the Roman Pontiff has merely an office of supervision and guidance, and not the full and supreme power of jurisdiction over the whole Church, and this not only in matters of faith and morals, but also in those which concern the discipline and government of the Church dispersed throughout the whole world; or that he has only the principal part, but not the absolute fullness, of this supreme power; or that this power of his is not ordinary and immediate both over all and each of the churches and over all and each of the pastors and faithful: let him be anathema."[77]

689. **Is there only one permanent subject of the supreme, full, and universal power of teaching and governing the entire Church?**
Yes. It is the pope, as the visible head of the Church and supreme pastor of the whole flock of Christ, according to His words: "Feed my lambs.... Feed my sheep" (Jn 21:15, 17). In her divinely established structure, the Church is not a diarchy, but a *sacred monarchy*, both at the universal level (pope) and at the local level (diocesan bishop).

690. **Are there two distinct ways of exercising this supreme and universal power?**
Yes. 1. Acts of the pope alone, which have an individual and permanent character; 2. Acts of the college (body, order)[78] of bishops which have a collegial character, although "it does not act in a strictly collegial way permanently."[79]

691. **How may the college of bishops exercise the supreme power in the Church?**
1. When the bishops dispersed throughout the world exercise the ordinary and universal teaching office in union with the pope; 2. When the pope at his discretion and freely, according to the needs of the Church, lets the college exercise supreme universal power by an extraordinary or strictly collegial act (comprising teaching

and governing), usually by means of a general or ecumenical council, although it could also be done through other means.[80]

692. **Is the pope bound by divine law to act collegially?**
No. This would nullify any act of his primacy apart from collegial deliberation or confirmation. All that the Supreme Pontiffs did in the past by their own (non-collegial) deliberation, especially in matters of great importance, would therefore be invalid by divine law.[81]

693. **Is the pope necessarily bound to convoke a general council or synods?**
No. He can use other means for letting the bishops participate in the exercise of his supreme universal power, but need not necessarily do so.[82]

AUTHORITY OF BISHOPS AND COUNCILS

694. **Do bishops have the power to teach and govern the faithful?**
Yes. They are successors of the apostles by divine right, just as the pope is the Successor of St. Peter, chief of the apostles.

695. **What powers do bishops have in their own dioceses?**
They hold full legislative, administrative, and judiciary power; i.e., they have, within their respective dioceses, the same direct, complete, and personal power that the pope exercises over the whole Church, although they cannot eliminate, omit, or change what has been promulgated for the universal Church. "Bishops, as successors of the apostles, receive from the Lord, to whom was given all power in heaven and on earth, the mission to teach all nations and to preach the Gospel to every creature, so that all men may attain to salvation by faith, baptism, and the fulfillment of the commandments."[83]

696. **How do the bishops receive their canonical mission in the Church?**
"By legitimate customs that have not been revoked by the supreme and universal authority of the Church, or by laws made or recognized by that authority, or directly through the Successor of Peter himself; and if the latter refuses or denies apostolic communion, such bishops cannot assume any office."[84]

697. **Is the bishop a vicar of the pope, likened to a branch manager of a multinational corporation?**
No. "The power of the Supreme Pontiff by no means detracts from that ordinary and immediate power of episcopal jurisdiction by which bishops, who have succeeded to the place of the apostles by appointment of the Holy Spirit, tend and govern individually the particular flocks which have been assigned to them."[85]

698. **Then a bishop is not a mere representative of the pope?**
No. "Although bishops do not receive plenary, universal, or supreme authority, they are not to be looked upon as mere representatives of the Roman Pontiffs. They

exercise a power truly their own and are the ordinary pastors of the people whom they govern."[86]

699. **What is a *Church council*?**
A formal assembly of bishops, convened for the purpose of using their apostolic authority to treat matters pertaining to faith, morals, and the discipline of the Church.

700. **How many kinds of council are there?**
Two: 1. *General* or *ecumenical* councils, which represent the universal Church; 2. *Particular* or *local* councils or *synods*, which may represent one or several ecclesiastical provinces.

701. **What is a general or ecumenical council?**
One presided over by the pope or his legates, or at least approved by a pope, and in which the bishops of the entire world assemble, either personally or through their representatives, to deliberate and pronounce solemn judgment on matters of doctrine or discipline for the universal Church.[87]

702. **What authority does an ecumenical council have?**
When properly constituted and approved by the pope, it has the same authority as the Church herself in all matters of faith and morals, because it speaks in the name of the universal Church.

703. **Are the teachings of an ecumenical council infallible?**
Like the Supreme Pontiff's *ex cathedra* statements, an ecumenical council is infallible in its approved and solemn dogmatic definitions. Its other statements, disciplinary norms, pastoral provisions, etc. are beyond the scope of infallibility, and subject to possible future revision.

704. **What is a particular or local council?**
One in which the bishops of a particular region assemble to deliberate and pronounce judgment on matters of doctrine or discipline within their territory. These include the *plenary council* constituted for all the particular churches of the same conference of bishops,[88] and the *provincial council* constituted for various particular churches of the same ecclesiastical province.[89]

705. **What is a diocesan synod?**
"An assembly of selected priests and other members of Christ's faithful of a particular church," gathered "for the good of the whole diocesan community.... Only the diocesan bishop can convene a diocesan synod," and "presides over it."[90]

706. **What authority does the bishop have in a diocesan synod?**
"The diocesan bishop is the sole legislator in the diocesan synod. Other members of the synod have only a consultative vote. The diocesan bishop alone signs the synodal declarations and decrees, and only by his authority may these be published."[91]

707. **Is a particular council infallible in its teaching?**
No. However, its decrees could be made universally binding by the express declaration of the pope.

708. **Is it strictly necessary for bishops to gather and govern as collective bodies?**
No. As true pastors, each bishop is charged by God to feed and govern the particular flock entrusted to him. Although collaboration among bishops is helpful at times, by divine law each bishop is the shepherd in his own diocese, he is the teacher of the Faith and a loving father in Christ to his own people (see 1 Cor 4:15).

709. **What is "collegiality"?**
Collegiality is a general term for collaboration between bishops, especially when they are gathered in an ecumenical council or in other councils.

710. **Does a false understanding of collegiality pose a danger for the Church?**
Yes. It can lead to viewing Church governance as a democratic or egalitarian parliament, rather than the monarchical hierarchy established by Christ the King. It would diminish the supreme authority of the pope over the entire Church, and the local authority of each bishop in his own see.

711. **How should collegiality be rightly exercised in the Church?**
A *moral* collegiality of charity and mutual cooperation aids in the apostolic work of bishops, whereas a *juridical* or *bureaucratic* collegiality as found in today's Bishops's Conferences—one of endless meetings and collective policy-making—has already tended to diminish the bishop's sense of personal responsibility and ministry to his particular flock.

712. **What is "synodality"?**
Synodality is a novel pastoral model in which bishops are encouraged to gather regularly for dialogue with each other, their priests and faithful, and various interest groups from inside and outside the Church, about ecclesiastical or humanitarian matters.

713. **Is synodality a positive development for the mission of the Church?**
At present, it has borne no fruit in apostolic commitment of preaching the Catholic Faith to all nations or the conversion of non-Catholics, and has generally consumed significant time and resources that could be better spent for prayer and preaching, as St. Peter advised: "We will give ourselves continually to prayer, and to the ministry of the word" (Acts 6:4*).

Spiritual and Temporal Powers

714. **Are there two distinct powers, exercised by the Church and the state?**
Yes. As Christ taught, "Render therefore to Caesar the things that are Caesar's, and to God the things that are God's" (Mk 12:17*), showing that the *temporal power* and the *spiritual power* differ in origin, authority, object, and end.

715. **How do the Church and civil society differ in *origin*?**
The civil power ultimately comes from God as author of nature (see Rom 13:1), since each human community arises from the natural needs and tendencies of man; whereas the spiritual power comes from God as author of grace, since the Church was founded by His direct intervention in human history.

716. **How do they differ in *authority*?**
According to the will of Christ, the Church is governed with divine authority by the successors of the apostles; whereas the civil power exercises natural authority by various governors, depending on time and place.

717. **How do they differ in *object*?**
The Church has for its object divine truth and virtue which are immediately directed toward man's supernatural end; whereas civil society looks to temporal and earthly interests which are remotely directed toward man's end.

718. **How do they differ in their *end*?**
The end or goal of the Church is to lead man to eternal happiness; whereas the proximate end of civil society is to secure the temporal goods and wellbeing of its members — the common good (*bonum commune*) — so that they might more easily fulfill their supernatural end.

719. **Does the human person represent "the ultimate end of society"?**
No. Man is only the second cause (*causa secunda*) and penultimate end (*finis proximus*) of society; the ultimate cause and absolute goal of civil society is only God.

720. **How is the good of the individual person related to the common good?**
Man as an individual, as a part of the whole, is subordinate to the state; but as a person, a spiritual being with an eternal end, he is superior to the state. The common good is only a good if it helps the members of society achieve their legitimate temporal goods and eternal end.

721. **What is therefore the proper meaning of the *common good*?**
"The implementation of normal and stable public conditions, so that both individuals and families, with the correct use of their powers, can easily lead a worthy and happy life, a life according to God's law — [This] is the goal and the norm of the state and its organs."[92]

722. **Is the power of the civil authority unlimited?**
No. "It is not an oppressive omnipotence of any legitimate autonomy.... Neither the individual nor the family should be absorbed by the state."[93]

723. **Does national sovereignty have limits?**
Yes. "Sovereignty is not the deification or omnipotence of the state, almost in the sense of Hegel or in the manner of an absolute juridical positivism."[94]

724. **What are the consequences of a deification of the state?**
It is totalitarianism: "It gives civil power an undue extension, determines and fixes in content and form all fields of activity, and in this way compresses all legitimate proper life—personal, local, and professional—into a mechanical unity or collectivity, under the imprint of nation, race, or class."[95]

725. **What is the relationship between the civil authority and the family?**
The family is "the 'society' of a man's house—a society very small, one must admit, but nonetheless a true society, and one *older* than any state. Consequently, it has rights and duties peculiar to itself which are quite independent of the state."[96]

726. **Does the family have rights proper to a civil or political community?**
Yes. "The family has at least equal rights with the state in the choice and pursuit of the things needful to its preservation and its just liberty.... Inasmuch as the domestic household is antecedent, as well in idea as in fact, to the gathering of men into a community, the family must necessarily have rights and duties which are prior to those of the community, and founded more immediately in nature."[97]

727. **What are the limits of civil authority regarding the family?**
Governments may not "intrude into and exercise intimate control over the family and the household.... Paternal authority can be neither abolished nor absorbed by the state; for it has the same source as human life itself."[98]

728. **What individual rights must the civil authority protect?**
"There are certain rights and freedoms of individuals ... or of the family, which the state must always protect and which it cannot violate or sacrifice to a so-called common good, ... [including] the right to honor and good reputation, the right and freedom to venerate the *true God*, [and] the original right of parents over children and their education."[99]

729. **Does the distinction between the spiritual and the temporal powers mean that they should be entirely separate?**
No. Although distinct, they are intended by God to act in perfect concord and harmonious order. "That the state must be separated from the Church is a thesis absolutely false, a most pernicious error.... As the present order of things is temporary and subordinated to the attainment of man's supreme and absolute welfare, it follows that the civil power must not only place no obstacle in the way of this attainment, but must aid us in effecting it."[100]

730. **Is the spiritual power objectively superior to the temporal power?**
Yes. The Church is a supernatural society: universal, immutable, and immortal. States are merely natural societies that are particular, variable, and temporal. "To wish the Church to be subject to the civil power in the exercise of her duty is a great folly and a sheer injustice. Whenever this is the case, order is disturbed, for things natural are put above things supernatural."[101]

731. **In what way is the temporal power subordinate to the spiritual power?**
It is subordinate in all that refers to the spiritual order. "Between the two powers there should be some such union as there is between the body and soul in man."[102] The civil authorities must therefore respect the full rights and liberty of the Church, never hindering the true religion or seeking to regulate its public worship.[103]

732. **Should states do more than merely respect the rights and liberty of the Church?**
Yes. All nations are obliged to defend and aid the Church in the fulfillment of her divine mission.

733. **Why is the state obligated to help the Church in this way?**
Civil society, no less than human nature and each individual man, depends on its Creator, and all authority to govern comes ultimately from Him. Therefore, every state owes God the same obedience and worship that is owed to Him by individuals.

734. **Then states have an obligation to publicly venerate the true God and protect the true religion, which is the Catholic Church?**
Yes. "Since the chief duty of all men is to cling to religion in both its teaching and practice—not such religion as they may have a preference for, but the religion which God enjoins, and which certain and most clear marks show to be the only one true religion—it is a public crime to act as though there were no God. So, too, is it a sin for the state not to have care for religion, as something beyond its scope or of no practical benefit; or out of many forms of religion to adopt that one which chimes in with the fancy; for we are bound absolutely to worship God in that way which He has shown to be His will. All who rule, therefore, would hold in honor the holy name of God, and one of their chief duties must be to favor religion, to protect it, to shield it under the credit and sanction of the laws, and neither to organize nor enact any measure that may compromise its safety.... It is evident that the only true religion is the one established by Jesus Christ Himself, and which He committed to His Church to protect and to propagate."[104]

735. **How does the civil authority's public profession of Catholicism affect historically Catholic nations?**
It has a decisive influence on the maintenance and development of the Catholic culture of the nation, contributing mainly to the continuity of its history, imbued with Catholic principles. Therefore, the common good of that nation will especially require that the representatives of civil authority publicly profess and venerate the true Catholic Faith.[105]

736. **Should states also work to limit and even proscribe heresy or schism?**
Yes, to the extent that this is prudent. In this they serve the good of all citizens, for religious unity is the foundation of social unity. "The nation and kingdom that will not serve you shall perish" (Is 60:12).

737. Does this mean that the civil power must coerce citizens to become Catholic?

No. "It is absolutely necessary that conversion should come about by free choice, since no man can believe unless he be willing."[106] The civil power may tolerate non-Catholic religions when prudence foresees a greater harm in their prohibition.

738. What right and duty do the members of the Church have in relation to the civil power?

The right to publicly oppose any act of government that injures the salvation of souls or attacks the natural rights of citizens, along with the duty to promote and shape public policy in conformity with the immutable law of the Gospel.

739. Should states separate themselves from the Church, or declare themselves entirely secular?

Complete national secularity is inadmissible. No government can withdraw from the supreme rule of Christ, and the "religiously neutral" state is an illusion; all societies are founded on values and principles of some transcendent character, and enforce them to various degrees.

740. What error affirms the radical principle of "separation of Church and state"?

It is generally called *Liberalism*. Because of its fundamental inability to recognize the true goal of human life in virtue and beatitude, Liberalism cannot build a society that serves this goal. Instead, it promotes individualism to the harm of the common good, foments unrestricted license in speech and press, and results in attacks on the one true religion.

741. What is the worst kind of Liberalism?

"To reject the supreme authority of God, and to cast off all obedience to Him in public matters, or even in private and domestic affairs, is the greatest perversion of liberty and the worst kind of liberalism."[107]

742. Why must Liberalism be rejected by Catholics and all people of good will?

Because: 1. It asserts unlimited personal freedom as an unrestricted right, which is contrary to natural law and divine revelation; 2. It denies the rightful subordination of the state to the Church; 3. It despises the social Kingship of Christ, and rejects the benefits derived therefrom; 4. It inculcates indifferentism to the moral law, and leads to hedonistic anarchy.

743. What of Catholics who find themselves in liberal societies of this kind?

They must continue to live under the Kingship of Jesus Christ themselves, affirming His reign in their families and spheres of influence, and working for its wider acknowledgment. "Be blameless and innocent, children of God without blemish in the midst of a crooked and perverse generation, in which you shine like stars in the world" (Phil 2:15).

744. **What is the principal obligation of those in public offices of civil government?**
To faithfully practice the Catholic religion themselves, to govern in accord with Catholic teaching, to promote virtue and restrain vice, and to protect the Church in their territories.

745. **What of Catholics in public office who act contrary to Church teaching?**
This is at least a sin of negligence and scandal, for which they should be corrected by their pastors with a view to repentance and redressing the scandal caused. If they continue such acts, they must be publicly admonished for the sake of the salvation of their souls, and if still unrepentant and obstinate, be excluded from the reception of the sacraments.[108] The words of St. Ambrose apply to Catholics in any rank of public office: "The emperor is within the Church, not over the Church; a good emperor seeks the aid of the Church, he does not reject it."[109]

Religious Liberty

746. **What distinction must be made when speaking of religious freedom?**
Man enjoys a *psychological freedom*, such that he is able to reject belief in God who reveals Himself. However, man is bound by the most serious commandment to embrace divine revelation; therefore, he has the *moral duty* to obey God and so is deprived of *moral freedom* in this regard. Indeed, man has the *physical ability* to sin, but he has the gravest *moral duty* to abstain from sin.

747. **But isn't "religious liberty" a fundamental and inalienable human right?**
No. Every *right*, or moral ability to do something according to law, is given to man only for true actions. But error and falsehood, especially in matters of religion, is evil in itself, and therefore does not establish the title of lawful right.[110] While everyone has the natural right to not be coerced to practice a religion, no man has the right—even a merely civil right—to offend God by choosing a moral evil, or by practicing or promoting religious error.[111] God has given all men the natural right to choose only the good and the true, which is the only proper use of their freedom.

748. **Is there any legitimate civil right to immunity in exercising and spreading a false religion?**
No. Although such affirmations have been made even by Church authorities in our time,[112] no one has a universal, positive, and natural right to practice whatever he perceives as "religion." Any civil rights to the same are likewise a grave error, as all ethically valid civil laws must be in harmony with the positive divine will, expressed in divine revelation and in the natural law. Civil laws promoting the liberty to offend God through the propagation of false religions cannot be a valid expression of or rooted in human nature.

749. **What harm may come if states permit the propagation of false religions?**
In addition to violating divine law and fostering religious indifferentism, such permission often paves the way for false religious practices that contradict natural law:

e.g., polygamy, divorce, contraception, immoral worship, magic practices, fetishism, human sacrifice, or racial hatred.

750. **What does the perennial Magisterium of the Church teach us in this regard?**
"Right is a moral power which—as We have before said and must again and again repeat—it is absurd to suppose that nature has accorded indifferently to truth and falsehood, to justice and injustice. Men have a right freely and prudently to propagate throughout the state what things soever are true and honorable, so that as many as possible may possess them; but lying opinions, than which no mental plague is greater, and vices which corrupt the heart and moral life should be diligently repressed by public authority, lest they insidiously work the ruin of the state."[113]

751. **Does an invincibly erroneous conscience in matters of religion establish a lawful right?**
No. An invincibly erroneous conscience excuses from sin when one violates divine law as a result of such an error, but can never establish a right to such violations. Rights are established according to strictly objective criteria, not in the subjective order; therefore, he who, out of an erroneous conscience, acts contrary to the divine law and does not embrace the Catholic Faith, does not acquire the right to propagate doctrines contrary to revealed truth.[114]

752. **Does a false notion of religious freedom easily make the individual conscience a source of rights and duties in religious matters?**
Yes, as it subordinates the objective to the subjective order. In truth, the dictates of the subjective conscience must submit to the objective truths and morals established by God and sufficiently manifested to man either by nature or revelation.[115]

753. **Should civil law sanction the spread of false religions out of respect for invincibly erroneous conscience?**
No. Especially in the case of minors, no one is obliged to suffer the consequences of a wrong religious opinion or action under the pretext that everyone has an alleged natural right to spread his own religion, and all the more so if such religious practices are offensive or dangerous to their religious and moral life.[116] The rights of a true and well-formed conscience are superior to the rights of an invincibly erroneous conscience.

754. **What is the true dignity of the human person regarding religion?**
The dignity of man consists in the right use of freedom. Therefore, no true and proper right can be given to the human person that contradicts divine truth in the natural or positive law of God.

755. **Has the Church condemned the theory of unlimited private choice in religion?**
Yes. Pope Pius IX formally condemned the following opinions: "Every man is free to embrace and profess that religion which, guided by the light of reason, he shall

consider true,"[117] and, "Men may, in the observance of any religion whatever, find the way of eternal salvation, and arrive at eternal salvation."[118]

756. What has the Magisterium called this theory of absolute liberty of conscience and religion?

It has been called "liberty of perdition." Pope Pius IX condemned the opinion "that liberty of conscience and worship is each man's personal right, which ought to be legally proclaimed and asserted in every rightly constituted society; and that a right resides in the citizens to an absolute liberty, which should be restrained by no authority whether ecclesiastical or civil, whereby they may be able openly and publicly to manifest and declare any of their ideas whatever, either by word of mouth, by the press, or in any other way.... [This is] preaching 'liberty of perdition' (St. Augustine, *Ep. 105 ad Donatistas*)."[119]

757. Does Catholicism alone have a natural and supernatural right to be freely exercised and spread?

Yes. Catholicism possesses the only genuine right to religious freedom in both the *subjective* and *objective order*, because it is founded not only on natural law, but also on those rights which descend from divine revelation.[120]

758. Then is there a basic difference between the "liberty" of false religions, and that of the Catholic Church?

Yes. False religions are constituted by the free will of persons. But the Catholic Church, established by divine institution, is the original and supreme religious society, whose liberty is based on the mandate given to the Church by her divine Founder to teach, govern, and sanctify all nations (see Mt 28:18–20), and therefore has the absolute right to practice, promulgate, and promote its faith in all times and places.[121]

Union among the Members of the Church

759. What is the *communion of saints*?

It is the spiritual union, relationship, and sharing of spiritual goods among the members of the Church on earth, of the souls in purgatory, and of the saints in heaven.

760. Who shares in this communion of the Church?

All those who are united in the one Mystical Body, together under their common head, Jesus Christ. These are members either of the Church Militant, the Church Suffering, or the Church Triumphant.

761. How are the members of the Church united throughout these three states?

They are united by charity and grace as adopted children of the same family, citizens of the same society, subjects of the same government (in the case of the Church Militant), stones of the same building, members of the same Mystical Body.

762. **What are the spiritual goods of the Church shared among these members?**
This treasury of the Church consists of the supernatural merits of Christ Our Lord, which are supremely located in the Holy Sacrifice of the Mass, as well as the superabundant merits of the Blessed Virgin and the saints, together with the prayers and good works of all the faithful.

763. **How great are the riches contained in this treasury of the Church?**
They are priceless, for the merits of Christ are infinite, and those of the Blessed Virgin are beyond comparison. Moreover, with these are joined the superabundant merits of all the saints in heaven and the just on earth.

764. **What is meant by the *superabundant* merits of the saints?**
The value of all their good works, in excess of what the saints owed to the divine justice.

765. **How do the faithful on earth commune with the saints in heaven?**
The faithful honor the saints, follow their example, and seek their prayers. The saints in turn intercede for the faithful with God, and obtain for them abundant graces through the merits of Christ and their own merits.

766. **How do the faithful on earth commune with the souls in purgatory?**
The faithful on earth intercede for the souls in purgatory and beg God to relieve them and mercifully receive them into heaven. Such prayer for the dead was practiced long before Christ (see 2 Mc 12:46*), and it is a pious belief that the souls in purgatory in turn pray for the faithful on earth, especially those who interceded for their deliverance.

767. **How do the saints in heaven commune with the souls in purgatory?**
By inspiring the faithful on earth to make satisfaction for them, while the souls in purgatory honor the saints and thus increase their joy and happiness.

768. **How do the faithful on earth commune with one another?**
They intercede for one another, begging God for the conversion of sinners and perseverance of the just, the exaltation of holy Church, and an end to the various scourges that afflict mankind. The graces that each one receives and the good works that he performs are profitable to all.

769. **Do we know the extent to which the members of the Church share in its spiritual treasures?**
No. God has not revealed how, in His wisdom, He applies them to those in need; but this application must depend greatly on the dispositions of each.

770. **What share do sinners have in the spiritual treasures of the Church?**
Those in a state of mortal sin have no share in the spiritual treasures of the Church, for they have cut themselves off from Christ. Those in a state of venial sins remain united to the Mystical Body of Christ and therefore share in the communion of

saints; and through the merits of Christ, to which are united the merits of their brethren, they may receive the grace of conversion and other actual graces: "When your brethren shed tears over you, it is Christ who suffers, Christ who prays the Father for mercy."[122]

771. **Who have no share in the communion of saints?**
Pagans, heretics, schismatics, and apostates. Since these are separated from the Church, they have no share in the spiritual goods of her communion. However, the inculpably separated "can, by a desire to belong to the Church (*votum Ecclesiae*), belong spiritually to the Church, and through this achieve justification and salvation."[123]

TENTH ARTICLE OF THE CREED
I BELIEVE IN THE FORGIVENESS OF SINS.

Chapter 17: The Forgiveness of Sins

Power to Forgive

772. **What is meant by *believing in* the forgiveness of sins?**
Believing that Christ gave His Church a share in His own divine power to forgive all sins.

773. **What is meant by *forgiving* sins?**
To pardon them, to blot them out, to destroy guilt in the soul as utterly as if sin had never been committed. However, even when sins are forgiven, sometimes the obligation to make reparation remains, along with the temporal punishment due to them.

774. **Who alone has the power of forgiving sins?**
This power properly belongs to God alone. All sin is an offense against God, and only the offended party may pardon an offense, just as only a creditor can release a debtor from his debts.

775. **Why does Jesus Christ have this power of forgiving sins?**
1. He is equal to His Father as God; 2. He has received this power from His Father also in His human nature because of His mission as Redeemer; 3. The precious blood of His Passion has divine power to forgive sins, since His flesh is the instrument of His divinity.[124]

776. **To whom did Christ communicate this power of forgiving sins?**
To the apostles, when He said to them on the first Easter day: "Receive the Holy Spirit. If you forgive the sins of any, they are forgiven them; if you retain the sins of any, they are retained" (Jn 20:22–23*).

777. Was it only to His apostles that Christ gave the power of forgiving sins?

No. In the person of the apostles, He gave this power to the priests of His Church for all time, so that man might always have an external and sensible means of reconciliation with God.

778. How far does this power of forgiveness extend?

There is no sin, however grave, that cannot be forgiven by the power of God acting in and through His priests in the sacrament of penance.

779. Does God place any conditions on the forgiveness of sins?

Yes. God is master of His gifts, and He grants forgiveness of sins only on those conditions which His wisdom has determined.

780. Then a mere confidence in the mercy of God is not enough to remit sin?

No. The sinner must also have the dispositions expected of him by God.

781. Why are certain dispositions required from the sinner?

Reason demands suitable preparation, so that forgiveness of sins remains a process befitting the rational and free human being. Forgiveness without repentance would violate the natural order, corresponding neither to divine wisdom nor to human freedom. "God moves everything in its own manner.... Hence He moves man to justice according to the condition of his human nature. But it is man's proper nature to have free will.... God so infuses the gift of justifying grace that at the same time He moves the free will to accept the gift of grace, in such as are capable of being moved thus."[125]

782. Is cooperation with God's grace necessary for the forgiveness of sins?

Yes. Without the grace of God, the sinner is unable to move himself to repentance and faith by his own free will. Rather, he must freely assent to and cooperate with God's helping grace, which calls him to conversion. Hence, "Turn ye to Me, ... and I will turn to you" (Zac 1:3*) reminds us of our liberty; and when we reply, "Convert us, O Lord, to Thee, and we shall be converted" (Lam 5:21*), we confess that we need the grace of God.[126]

783. On the part of the sinner, what concrete acts are necessary to be forgiven?

The first and most important disposition is *objective faith*, the assent to the truths revealed by God; there must also be an act of *obedience* toward God; then comes a *salutary fear* of God's justice, by which the sinner is prompted to consider the mercy of God; then there is the act of *hope*, trusting that God will be propitious to the sinner for Christ's sake; hatred and *detestation of sin* follows, through acts of true *repentance*, sincere *confession* of all sins, and the firm *resolution* to avoid sin in the future and do penance for sins committed.[127]

784. How does God ordinarily forgive sins?

By the sacraments of baptism and penance; and in exceptional cases, by extreme unction.

785. **What sins are we bound to confess?**
All mortal sins committed after baptism, even those that may have been effaced by perfect contrition on our part. Venial sins may also be confessed, but can also be forgiven by other means.

786. **What punishment does God always remit when the Church absolves the sinner?**
The *eternal* punishment due to mortal sin; i.e., the eternal damnation that is earned by grave sin: "The wages of sin is death" (Rom 6:23).

787. **What other punishment is incurred by each and every sin?**
Temporal punishment, which is the just penalty incurred by every knowing violation of God's law. Penitents may be forgiven, but they still must do reparation and expiation for the damage caused by their sin.

788. **Why are we obliged to this reparation and expiation?**
"We are holden to the duty of reparation and expiation by a certain more valid title of justice and of love: of justice indeed, in order that the offense offered to God by our sins may be expiated and that the violated order may be repaired by penance; and of love too, so that we may suffer together with Christ suffering and 'filled with reproaches' (Lam 3:30*), and for all our poverty may offer Him some little solace. For since we are all sinners and laden with many faults, our God must be honored by us not only by that worship wherewith we adore His infinite Majesty with due homage, or acknowledge His supreme dominion by praying, or praise His boundless bounty by thanksgiving; but besides this we must need make satisfaction to God the just avenger, 'for our numberless sins and offenses and negligences.'"[128]

789. **Does the Church also have power to remit this temporal punishment due to sin?**
Yes. The temporal punishment due to sin can be lessened or even removed within the sacrament of penance by performing the penances enjoined on us by the priest, or by indulgences.

790. **What is this power of indulgences based on?**
The words of Christ: "Whatever you loose on earth will be loosed in heaven" (Mt 18:18).

791. **What are the chief errors about the forgiveness of sins?**
1. The despairing notion that some sins are too great to be forgiven by a loving God; 2. Denial of the Church's power to forgive sins; 3. Belief that man is incapable of truly committing sin; 4. Denial of all sin; 5. The heresy that claims forgiveness of sins is given by the sole imputation of Christ's justice, or that sins are merely covered up; 6. The heresy that in order to obtain forgiveness of sins, man must necessarily believe with certainty that his sins are forgiven; 7. The heresy that man, once forgiven, can sin no more, nor lose grace.[129]

ELEVENTH ARTICLE OF THE CREED

I BELIEVE IN THE RESURRECTION OF THE BODY.

Chapter 18: The Resurrection of the Body

Bodily Resurrection

792. What does the eleventh article of the Creed teach us?

That at the end of the world, before the last judgment, the soul of every man will resume his proper body, never more to be separated from it. This is called the *general resurrection.*

793. Why do we say, the resurrection *of the body*?

Because the body, and not the soul, will be reconstituted and return to life in this final union.

794. How is the dogma of the resurrection demonstrated?

1. By the constant teaching of the Church, as found in her creeds; 2. By Scripture, which expresses this truth in many passages; 3. By reason, which tells us that human nature (constituted by the union of soul and body) should not remain permanently incomplete after death, and that the body should share in the reward or punishment of the soul in the next life, since it is the instrument of good or evil in this life.

795. May images of the resurrection be found in the natural world?

Yes. The tree seems to die in winter but revives in spring; the grain of wheat disintegrates in the ground but yields the golden ear; the caterpillar liquifies in the tomb of a chrysalis but emerges a butterfly.

796. How is the general resurrection possible, since bodies corrupt over time?

This poses no difficulty to the omnipotent God, who formed all matter from nothing and can refashion the same body from the same material as it once was. Even so, the resurrection at the end of time remains a mystery and the subject of wonder.

797. Does this doctrine reinforce the inherent value of the human body?

Yes. It shows that every human person is a unique being of both soul and body, in which he will receive his final reward or punishment. God desires that man's body should be a temple of the Holy Spirit on earth, and a glorified vessel of honor in heaven (see 1 Cor 6:19; and 15:42–44). This is why even human corpses should be treated with dignity and given a proper burial.

State of the Risen Body

798. **In what state will God raise up our bodies?**

In the state of integrity and complete physical development or *perfect age*, according to common theological opinion. This was the state in which Adam and Eve were created, and in which Christ died on the Cross and rose again.

799. **Will there be a difference between the bodies of the just and those of the damned?**

Yes, as great a difference as exists between the two eternal destinations of heaven and hell.

800. **What qualities will the risen bodies of the just have?**

Brightness, impassibility, agility, and subtlety, as possessed by the risen body of Christ.

801. **What will be the condition of the bodies of the damned?**

Although immortal like those of the blessed, they will be objects of supreme horror, deprived of all beauty and the supernatural qualities of glorified bodies.

802. **Why must they be deprived of these qualities?**

Because a soul that has been eternally separated from God by rejecting Him cannot fail to make the body that is united to it a sharer in its everlasting misery.

TWELFTH ARTICLE OF THE CREED

I BELIEVE IN LIFE EVERLASTING.

Chapter 19: The Life Everlasting

The Last Things

803. **What is *life everlasting*?**

It is a life that will follow this present life, and will have no end. It is a life of eternal happiness in heaven for the just, in which they participate in the beatitude of God; or it is eternal condemnation in hell for the wicked, also called "the second death" (Apoc 21:8).

804. **What truth does the dogma of everlasting life include?**

This dogma supposes the truths called the *four last things* or the *last ends of man*: death, judgment, heaven, and hell.

805. **Why are these truths called the four *last* things?**

Because death is the last instant of man's present life on earth; judgment is the last sentence that determines his lot for eternity; heaven is the last reward of the just, who are then called the *blessed*; and hell is the last punishment of the wicked, who are then called the *reprobate* or the *damned*.

806. **What other truth completes these four truths?**
The dogma of *purgatory*, which is the abode of souls who are bound for heaven, but still have something to expiate before entering into the finality of everlasting life with God; for, "nothing impure shall enter" the city of God, the heavenly Jerusalem (see Apoc 21:27*).

807. **What are the main errors about the last things in our own time?**
1. The refusal to acknowledge any life after death, as in *atheism* or *materialism*; 2. The rejection of the doctrine of purgatory, as in *Protestantism*; 3. The denial of an objective moral law with eternal reward for good and evil, as in *relativism*; 4. The claim that wicked souls are destroyed after death, as in *annihilationism*; 5. The claim that all men will ultimately be saved and attain heaven independently of their deeds, as in *universalism*; 6. The claim that the human soul begins a new life in a different physical form or body after death, as the notions of *reincarnation, rebirth*, or *transmigration*; 7. The claim that hell may be empty of human souls, as in the theory of *Hans Urs von Balthasar*; 8. The claim that in the end of time all men and even Satan and the demons will be saved, as in the heresy of *apokatastasis*.

808. **May one rightly affirm that "no one can be condemned for ever, because that is not the logic of the Gospel"?**[130]
No. This affirmation involves a tacit denial of the eternity of hell. A person can indeed refuse the Holy Spirit's grace of repentance for mortal sin, and therefore be in a state of condemnation, which becomes eternal upon death—called by Christ "the unquenchable fire" (Mk 9:43) and "eternal punishment" (Mt 25:46).

809. **Is it useful to think often of the four last things?**
Yes. This leads us to more effectively abandon sin and practice virtue. "In all thy works remember thy last end, and thou shalt never sin" (Ecclus 7:40*). "The devil's worst and most fatal preparation for the coming of Antichrist is the weakening of men's belief in eternal punishment. Were they the last words I might ever say to you, nothing should I wish to say to you with more emphasis than this, that next to the thought of the precious blood there is no thought in all your faith more precious or more needful for you than the thought of eternal punishment."[131]

810. **Why are the words *life everlasting* placed at the end of the Creed?**
So that this truth "would be more and more deeply impressed on the memory. To this life everlasting may the Lord Jesus Christ, blessed God forever, bring us!"[132]

Death

811. **What is death?**
The separation of the soul from the body.

812. **Why is death a *separation*?**
Because death disunites, but does not destroy, the essential parts of which man is composed. Although the body decomposes, its elements are not annihilated; and although the soul departs, it is immortal by nature.

813. **What does faith teach us concerning death?**
That death is inevitable, that it is a punishment of sin, that it will befall each of us only once, and that it will irrevocably fix our choices and our eternal destination.

814. **Is this separation of soul and body merely temporary?**
Yes. On the day of the general resurrection, the soul will again be united to its own body, miraculously recomposed by the divine power.

815. **How should the bodies of the deceased be treated?**
Sharing in some way in the image of God, every person's body must be treated with honor and respect, even in death. Burial of the dead is therefore a work of mercy.

816. **Is cremation of the dead ever permitted for Catholics?**
In imitation of Christ, bodily burial remains the norm. The Church has traditionally tolerated cremation only in cases of dire poverty or public emergency, provided that it is not chosen "for reasons which are contrary to Christian teaching,"[133] e.g., denial of the bodily resurrection.

817. **Are the medical criteria for "brain death" sufficient to determine if someone is truly dead?**
No. The body-soul union of the human person is not reducible to the level of brain function or cerebral cortex activity; if it were, the unborn or severely disabled could not be considered living human persons, contrary to what God has clearly affirmed (see Ps 139:15–16; Jer 1:5; Is 49:1; and Gal 1:15). As long as any vital functions continue, the rational soul is present, and therefore a person is present, with all his personal rights.

818. **Do we know the future time or manner of our own death?**
No. Except in limited cases of private revelation, God does not make known the time and place of our death, nor what the state of our soul will be in that decisive moment.

819. **Why does God leave us in ignorance of the hour of our death?**
To teach us that we must always be ready to appear before Him at any moment.

820. **Will death be the same for all?**
No. The death of the just is precious in the sight of the Lord, but the end of the wicked is dreadful (see Ps 116 and 37).

821. **Why is the death of the just man precious?**
Because it concludes his exile on earth, prevents him from falling into sin, fixes his will in good, and admits him to the abode of endless light, happiness, and peace.

822. **Why is the death of the wicked so dreadful?**
Because it separates him forever from everything that he has loved, prevents him from repentance, fixes his will in evil, and casts him into the everlasting fire of hell.

823. **Since death will determine our lot for all eternity, what should we do?**
We should: 1. Use the ancient monastic practice of *memento mori*, remembering that we at any moment could and soon will die; 2. Put our conscience in order without delay, and be always ready to appear before God, for death will come as a thief; 3. Desire ardently to die the death of the just; 4. Pray that the Blessed Virgin Mary will help us "at the hour of our death," along with St. Joseph, the patron of the dying.

Judgment

824. **What is judgment?**
It is the sentence by which God, the Supreme Judge, perfectly combines His justice with His mercy in determining the final reward or punishment of every man for all eternity.

825. **How many judgments will there be?**
Two: 1. The *particular* judgment, which is pronounced at the moment of each man's death; 2. The *general* judgment, which will be declared publicly for all men, at the end of time.

826. **On what is the soul judged at the moment of its particular judgment?**
On the good and the evil man has done on earth: "He that seeth into the heart, He understandeth, and nothing deceiveth the keeper of thy soul, and He shall render to a man according to his works" (Prov 24:12*).

827. **Where does the soul go after this judgment?**
It goes immediately either to purgatory, if something yet remains to be purified; or to heaven, if it is absolutely pure and perfectly united to God; or to hell, if it is stained with mortal sin and not in the state of supernatural friendship with God.

828. **What is the general judgment?**
It is that judgment which will take place at the end of time, and in which all men will be judged, not only as individuals, but as members of the human race. "The general judgment will regard more directly the generality of men than each individual to be judged. Wherefore although before that judgment each one will be certain of his

condemnation or reward, he will not be cognizant of the condemnation or reward of everyone else. Hence the necessity of the general judgment."[134]

829. **Why should there be a general judgment?**
1. It will take place so that God's wisdom and justice may be made manifest to all creatures whether just or sinners; 2. Since we sin and perform virtuous acts as a body-soul composite, it is fitting that we also be judged as a body-soul composite; 3. Each man is both an individual person and a part of the whole human race: wherefore a twofold judgment is due to him, both particular and public; 4. Christ must be Judge, so that the honor of which He was robbed may be restored to Him in the sight of all creation.

830. **Will the sentence pronounced at the general judgment differ from that of the particular judgment?**
No, it will only be its solemn confirmation. However, since it will occur after the resurrection of the body, it will be pronounced upon the whole man, body and soul. The general judgment might also be called a repetition of the world's history, for each event will be represented to the eyes of the assembled multitude: "And books were opened.... And the dead were judged according to their works, as recorded in the books" (Apoc 20:12).

831. **How should we prepare for the general judgment?**
By living daily as though we were about to appear before the judgment seat of God.

Purgatory

832. **What is *purgatory*?**
The place of final preparation for heaven, where souls suffer what remains of any punishment due to their personal sins, being purified of all remaining imperfections.

833. **How do we know that there is a purgatory?**
From Holy Scripture (see 2 Mc 12:42–46*; and 1 Cor 3:12–15), the formal teaching and constant practice of the Church,[135] by reason itself, and by the traditions of the various peoples of the earth, who have long believed in some final purgation after death.

834. **Do we know the precise intensity and duration of the pains of purgatory?**
No. We only know that these pains are proportional to the number and gravity of the faults to be atoned for, and that souls are delivered only when they have "paid the last penny" (Mt 5:26).

835. **Do the pains of purgatory surpass the sufferings of earth?**
Yes. "The fire of purgatory," says St. Augustine, "is more terrible than all that man can suffer in this life,"[136] and they cannot be alleviated by any effort of the souls themselves. The souls in purgatory are therefore often referred to as the *poor souls*. They are nevertheless also full of the surpassing eagerness of love for God, since

they know they are being prepared to enter the eternal wedding feast, to which they are guaranteed admission.[137]

836. **Can the members of the Church on earth help the poor souls in their suffering?**
Yes. The Church Militant can help the Church Suffering by: 1. The three eminent good works of prayer, fasting, and almsdeeds; 2. Indulgences gained for their relief; 3. Devout assistance at the Holy Sacrifice of the Mass; 4. Worthy reception of Holy Communion.

837. **What should we do to avoid purgatory?**
We should: 1. Guard against the slightest deliberate faults; 2. Atone for the sins we have committed while on earth, even after their guilt has been forgiven in the sacrament of penance; 3. Perform frequent acts of perfect love of God; 4. Benefit from the Church's generous dispensation of indulgences.

838. **What is the *heroic act of charity* for the poor souls?**
It consists of offering to God the satisfactory merit of every good work done in life and also to the suffrages that one can receive after death for the benefit of the souls in purgatory. One may make this act mentally, and it may be later annulled or withdrawn without being guilty of sin. No special formula is required to make this act, but one may use this or a similar formula:

My God, I place in Your hands and those of Our Lady all the meritorious works that I will do in life and those that others will do for me after my death, so that they may serve the souls in purgatory. I entrust myself to Your mercy. Amen.

Heaven

839. **What is heaven?**
Heaven is a supernatural place and condition where the angels and saints enjoy perfect and everlasting happiness, freedom from all evil, and blissful possession of all good, consisting primarily in the Beatific Vision and union with God.

840. **What is this *Beatific Vision* enjoyed by the just?**
They "see the divine essence with an intuitive vision and even face-to-face, without the mediation of any creature by way of object of vision; rather the divine essence immediately manifests itself to them, plainly, clearly, and openly, and in this vision they enjoy the divine essence," and "by this vision and enjoyment the souls of those who have already died are truly blessed."[138]

841. **Do rational creatures need a special divine grace called *lumen gloriae*, to be elevated to the Beatific Vision?**
Yes. The Church has solemnly condemned the error that "any intellectual nature in its own self is naturally blessed, and the soul does not need the *light of glory* raising it to see God and to enjoy Him beatifically."[139]

842. **How is the existence of heaven proved?**
By: 1. Scripture, which often speaks of the happiness of heaven; 2. The Church, which affirms this truth in all her creeds and liturgy; 3. Reason itself, which shows the necessity of a life in which virtue will be perfectly rewarded; 4. The unanimous desire of all men for some infinite good, unattainable on earth.

843. **Does man have a *right* to the Beatific Vision in heaven?**
No. The Beatific Vision is not due to man's nature as such, but remains a divine gift. Pope Pius V condemned the heresy of Michael Baius, that "the exaltation of human nature into the partnership of the divine nature was due to the integrity of the first condition, and hence it must be called nature, and not super-nature."[140] Pope Pius XII likewise taught: "Others destroy the gratuity of the supernatural order, since God, they say, cannot create intellectual beings without ordering and calling them to the Beatific Vision."[141]

844. **Is there any possibility of evil in heaven?**
No. The presence of the all-holy God permits no defect, deficiency, or moral evil, and "He will wipe every tear from their eyes" (Apoc 21:4).

845. **Why is heaven the possession of all good?**
Because the blessed finally possess God, the supreme good.

846. **What is the effect of seeing God face-to-face, and possessing Him forever?**
It causes the blessed to rejoice in the Lord with such unspeakable joy, that "eye hath not seen, nor ear heard, neither hath it entered into the heart of man, what things God hath prepared for them that love Him" (1 Cor 2:9*).

847. **Why is it impossible for us, while on earth, to fully conceive the happiness of heaven?**
Because eternal happiness is far above and beyond all our experience, and the good things of this earth are only dim shadows and anticipations of those to be found in heaven.

848. **Is the happiness of heaven the same for all the blessed?**
Because all souls behold the same God, all are perfectly fulfilled and happy: "In Your presence there is fullness of joy" (Ps 16:11). Nevertheless, this happiness differs in degree, according to the merits of the blessed; just as all stars shine, but not all with equal color or brightness (see 1 Cor 15:41). "All alike have that penny [see Mt 20:9*] which the householder orders to be given to all that have wrought in the vineyard. ... by which penny, of course, is signified eternal life.... But the many mansions [see Jn 14:2*] point to the different grades of merit in that one eternal life."[142]

849. **How is this happiness perfect in all the blessed, if it exists in different degrees?**
"An influence so mighty joins us together in that peace, that what any has failed to receive in himself, he rejoices to have received in another."[143]

850. **Who goes to heaven?**
Those who die in the state of grace and free from even venial sin, with heroic virtue, and who have already paid on earth whatever temporal penalty is due to the divine justice for their sins are admitted to heaven immediately. Others who die in a state of grace are admitted to heaven after their purification in purgatory.

851. **What should we do to merit heaven?**
We should: 1. Often think of it, and desire it with all the ardor of our soul; 2. Shun sin and practice virtue; 3. Suffer with patience the trials of this life, hoping for heaven as our reward; 4. Use the means of salvation and grace.

Hell

852. **What is hell?**
Hell is the place and condition in which the reprobate are condemned to suffer eternally away from the presence of God, with the demons.

853. **Has the Church's Magisterium infallibly defined hell as being eternal?**
Yes. "If anyone says or holds that the punishment of demons and impious human beings is temporary and that it will have an end at some time, and that there will be a restoration of demons and impious human beings, let him be anathema."[144]

854. **Is hell freely chosen?**
Yes. God respects those who have freely chosen the obstinate rejection of Him, and does not force them to be with Him for all eternity.

855. **How is the existence of hell proved?**
By: 1. Holy Scripture, where this truth is proclaimed in several passages; 2. The teaching of the Church, which has declared this dogma in several councils;[145] 3. Reason itself, which demands that unpunished evils in this life be revisited in another; 4. The common tradition of all peoples, describing a place of torment for obstinate evildoers.

856. **What are the essential pains of the reprobate?**
The pain of loss, and the pain of sense experience (see Mk 9:43). The essence of hell is the pain of loss of the presence of God, a natural consequence of one's free decision against Him; the pain of sense is secondary.

857. **What is the pain of loss?**
Called the *poena damni* (pain of the damned), it is the primary punishment of the evil spirits and the souls who die rejecting God. It is an everlasting separation from the vision of God, with its attendant remorse and despair. This punishment is *damnation* properly so-called, and is the greatest of the torments endured by the reprobate: "Those who do not obey the Gospel of our Lord Jesus ... will suffer the punishment of eternal destruction, separated from the presence of the Lord" (2 Thes 1:8–9).

858. What is the pain of sense?
Called the *poena sensus*, it is a suffering in all senses of both soul and body, caused principally by a consuming fire. "The fire of hell cannot be identical with material fire, but must be something at the same time physical and supra-physical, a punishment ... of which we know nothing except that it exists and torments the damned."[146]

859. Besides these pains, what other pains do the damned suffer?
The horrible society of the devils and the other damned, as well as those particular punishments corresponding to the different kinds of sins of which they are guilty.

860. Then the pains of hell are not the same for all the damned?
Hell is the greatest possible evil for each of the damned, just as heaven is the sum of all good for each of the blessed. Nevertheless, the suffering of the damned is also proportionate to the nature and number of each one's sins, "for He will repay according to each one's deeds" (Rom 2:6).

861. Why are these sufferings also called "the second death"?
Because the wicked "will be in eternal death suffering pain and punishment as great as will be the happiness and glory of the good.... They shall be ever dying, and yet never die; hence it is called eternal death, for as dying is the bitterest of pains, such will be the lot of those in hell.... We thus see the difference between doing good and doing evil. Good works lead to life, evil drags us to death."[147]

862. Who goes to hell?
All those who die with the guilt of even one unrepented mortal sin on their soul, refusing to accept the mercy of God and His forgiveness.

863. What should we do to avoid hell?
We should: 1. With firm determination of will, daily renounce every mortal sin, the devil, and all his works; 2. Act as friends of the angels and saints in this life, to deserve their eternal friendship in the next; 3. Pray that God mercifully save us from the torments of hell; 4. Cooperate with all graces and occasions of grace that God offers us.

864. What else should we do to maintain a horror of hell?
Reflect on the frightful reality of hell, e.g., through the report of Sr. Lucia of Fatima's vision: "Our Lady opened her hands once more, as she had done the two previous months. The rays [of light] appeared to penetrate the earth, and we saw, as it were, a vast sea of fire. Plunged in this fire, we saw the demons and the souls [of the damned]. The latter were like transparent burning embers, all blackened or burnished bronze, having human forms. They were floating about in that conflagration, now raised into the air by the flames which issued from within themselves, together with great clouds of smoke. Now they fell back on every side like sparks in huge fires, without weight or equilibrium, amid shrieks and groans of pain and despair,

which horrified us and made us tremble with fright (it must have been this sight which caused me to cry out, as people say they heard me). The demons were distinguished [from the souls of the damned] by their terrifying and repellent likeness to frightful and unknown animals, black and transparent like burning coals. That vision only lasted for a moment, thanks to our good heavenly Mother, who at the first apparition had promised to take us to heaven. Without that, I think that we would have died of terror and fear."[148]

865. **How are we to act as friends of the angels and saints in this life?**

By a true *lex vivendi* (rule of life): fulfilling God's holy will as we discover it written in our hearts, inscribed in nature, revealed in history, and taught by His Church.

PART II – Morals: Acting Rightly
Lex vivendi
Christian Morality in General

1. **To obtain eternal life, is it sufficient to believe all the truths of the Creed?**
   No. We must also have supernatural charity and perform the duties enjoined by Christian morality.

2. **What is *natural* morality?**
   A practical science that regulates our conduct by the principles of right reason, to choose what is good and avoid what is evil.

3. **What is *Christian* morality?**
   A practical science that regulates our actions by the principles of both right reason and revealed truth, so that we may attain our last end: the Beatific Vision of God in heaven.

4. **Is natural morality sufficient for man?**
   No, because it does not embrace all the duties which man must fulfill, and does not lead him to his supernatural end. "It is not enough to do good works; they need to be done well. For our works to be good and perfect, they must be done for the sole purpose of pleasing God."[1]

5. **Why is Christian morality the most excellent rule of human conduct?**
   1. It is *divine*, having God for its beginning and end, and teaching us to act righteously as He desires; 2. It is *complete*, addressing the whole person and all people, and including all precepts of reason and revelation; 3. It is *immutable*, pure and unchanging, guarded by the teaching authority of the Church.

6. **What are the subjects to be addressed in Christian morality?**
   1. The general principles of morality; 2. Virtue and sin; 3. The commandments of God and the Church; 4. The evangelical counsels and Beatitudes.

Section 1: General Principles of Morality

Chapter 1: Human Acts

Nature of Human Acts

1. **What is a merely *natural* act?**
   An action produced by our natural powers without the aid of grace, such as helping a neighbor out of common human courtesy.

2. **What is a *supernatural* act?**
   One that is done with the assistance of grace, such as helping a neighbor for the love of God and for love of his soul's salvation.

3. **What can diminish a person's freedom in acting?**
   Four causes: 1. Ignorance; 2. Concupiscence; 3. Fear; 4. Violence.

4. **What is *ignorance*?**
   A lack of knowledge about moral matters that ought to be known.

5. **What is *invincible* ignorance?**
   Also called *inculpable* or *guiltless* ignorance, this is a state that cannot be overcome by ordinary means, such as study or inquiry.

6. **What is *vincible* ignorance?**
   Also called *culpable* ignorance, this is a state of ignorance that can and should be overcome by the exercise of ordinary diligence, especially in matters of great importance or obligation.

7. **How can ignorance affect the moral value of an action?**
   A man who does something wrong that he invincibly believes to be good, commits no sin. Conversely, doing wrong in the state of culpable ignorance adds to the malice of sin.

8. **What is *concupiscence*?**
   A disordered interior inclination toward evil, existing in all men as a consequence of original sin. It is not sin formally and in the proper sense, but it sprang from sin and incites to sin.[1]

Moral Responsibility

9. **What is necessary to make a person morally responsible for his action?**
   Two essential conditions: 1. Knowledge of the goodness or evil of an action; 2. Freedom to do it or not do it.

10. **What causes diminish or remove moral responsibility?**
    1. Those already mentioned: ignorance, concupiscence, fear, and violence; 2. Certain physical states such as insanity, delirium, or sleepwalking; 3. Habit.

11. **How is responsibility lessened by the influence of habit?**
    Assuming the *agent* (the person acting) is striving to get rid of a bad habit, acts of that habit which are done reflexively and without deliberation may be considered involuntary. Nevertheless, a person should strive against disordered inclinations that arise from habit.

Moral Action

12. **What are the three sources of morality in a human act?**
    1. The object of the act; 2. The circumstances that surround the act; 3. The end of the act to which the act is directed.

13. **What is the *object* of a moral act?**
    The thing that is done, considered in itself. This is the most important aspect of any moral action, for if the object of the act is not good in itself or at least morally neutral, no intention or circumstance can render that action good.

14. **Are some actions therefore *objectively* evil, i.e., always and absolutely evil?**
    Yes. Also called *intrinsically* evil, such acts "are not capable of being ordered to God and to the good of the person."[2] Examples include all direct violations of divine worship (e.g., idolatry, blasphemy), truth (e.g., lying, perjury), innocent human life (e.g., murder, abortion, euthanasia), and marriage (e.g., fornication, contraception).

15. **What are the *circumstances* of an act?**
    The factors that surround the act itself: the particular persons, places, times, and things involved. Circumstances may change the character of an action, or make it more or less good or evil.

16. **What is the *end* of a human act?**
    The intention, or desired purpose to which the agent directs his action. The end is good when the desired outcome is a true good; it is evil when our purpose is opposed to the moral law.

17. **What makes the end of an act natural or supernatural?**
    The end is *natural* when our intention is within the natural order, as a man walking merely for exercise seeks a natural end. The end is *supernatural* when our intention is beyond the natural order, as a man walking on pilgrimage to honor God. These ends are not mutually exclusive (one may walk to honor God and engage in healthy activity), but the natural is always to be subordinated to the supernatural.

18. **To whom should we commend and direct all our actions?**
"Do everything for the glory of God" (1 Cor 10:31). "Whatever you do, in word or deed, do everything in the name of the Lord Jesus, giving thanks to God the Father through Him" (Col 3:17).

19. **What are the essential conditions of every morally good act?**
It must be *entirely* good: in its object, circumstances, and end. If any one of these aspects is defective, the entire act becomes morally evil.

20. **In order to be good, do our acts need to be performed in the state of grace?**
No. Even the wicked "know how to give good gifts" (Mt 7:11). However, we must be in the state of grace to perform supernaturally good acts, which alone merit the reward of grace.

21. **What false moral systems are most common today?**
1. *Determinism*, which denies the fact that man has free will, and so dissolves all moral responsibility; 2. *Consequentialism*, which declares all actions to be good if their intention is good or outcome desirable; 3. *Relativism*, which rejects all moral absolutes.

22. **What new errors about morality are beginning to emerge?**
The related notions that: 1. Man can never have sufficient knowledge to commit sin, or at least any grave sin; 2. A person who performs grave evils can still have a good "character" and even enter heaven, so long as his overall intention in life is good;[3] 3. God does not offer sufficient grace for a person to perform a good act or avoid moral evil; 4. God may command evils in some situations, in view of some social or familial good.[4]

Conscience

23. **What is *conscience*?**
A practical judgment of reason, whereby we perceive the goodness or evil of a particular action. It is the internal rule of moral action.

24. **How is the practical judgment of conscience applied to what we do?**
When "we recognize that we have done or not done something, ... conscience is said *to witness*.... [When] we judge that something should be done or not done, ... conscience is said *to incite* or *to bind*.... [When] we judge that something done is well done or ill done, ... conscience is said *to excuse, accuse,* or *torment*."[5]

25. **Is it possible for an individual's conscience to be in error about good or evil?**
Yes. The conscience must first be properly formed, according to the law of God as found in both nature and revelation.

26. **What are the most important general rules of conscience?**
    We must: 1. Not act against our conscience, even if it is in error; 2. Always seek to better inform our conscience; 3. Choose a safe course of action in matters of doubt.

27. **What if we are uncertain about the safest course of action, or struggle with scrupulosity?**
    Scrupulosity is a disordered fear that something is sinful which, in fact, is not. In all cases, if we submit to the objective moral law, seek good counsel, and pray to know and accomplish God's will in our lives, trusting in His superabundant love and mercy, we may be assured of acting in a way pleasing to Him.

28. **What are the means of properly forming our conscience?**
    1. Adequate study of morality and its laws; 2. Self-discipline of the passions; 3. Imitation of good example, especially the saints; 4. Prayer to God for direction; 5. Recourse to wise and prudent counselors.

29. **What is the general modern error about conscience?**
    "When men advocate the rights of conscience, they in no sense mean the rights of the Creator, nor the duty to Him, in thought and deed, of the creature; but the right of thinking, speaking, writing, and acting, according to their judgment or their humor, without any thought of God at all.... Conscience is a stern monitor, but in this century it has been superseded by a counterfeit: ... It is the right of self-will."[6]

Chapter 2: The Moral Law

Eternal Law

30. **What is the *eternal law*?**
    It is God Himself. "His law is not distinct from Himself,"[7] for God is divine Wisdom and the Order by which all things are measured and guided. This ordering of divine Wisdom directs the actions and movements of all things to their due end.[8]

31. **Are all true laws therefore derived from the eternal law?**
    Yes. 1. *Natural law* stems from it as God's wisdom laid into the natural order of creation, the very order of being, and is known by the intermediary of reason; 2. *Divine law* stems from it by an external revelation which God Himself has made; 3. *Human law* stems from it by the authority that God has communicated to man.

Natural Law

32. **What is the natural law?**
    Natural law is the eternal law as imprinted within rational creatures; it is a special manifestation of the eternal law and the rational creature's participation in it, inclining man to the end and actions that are suitable to his nature.[9]

33. **What are the marks of the natural law?**
It is *universal*, because it applies to all human beings; *immutable*, because it is unchangeable and no human power can dispense from it; *absolute*, because it must be observed at all costs.

34. **Do all men have an equal knowledge of the natural law?**
No. Our knowledge is more or less perfect according to our intelligence, education, and awareness; whereas ignorance, error, unruly passions, or bad habits can prevent us from seeing the truth with full clarity.

35. **How do we know the natural law?**
We can learn the natural law by reason alone. Nevertheless, God has also revealed it in history, so that we may know it more easily and perfectly. This revelation is found throughout Sacred Scripture, particularly in the Ten Commandments.

Positive Divine Law

36. **What is the positive divine law?**
That which God has directly revealed to humanity, to help us achieve our supernatural end of happiness with Him in heaven.

37. **How is the positive divine law divided?**
It is usually divided into the Old Law and the New Law; i.e., the Mosaic Law and the Christian Law. The Old Law may be said to comprise all that was revealed prior to Christ, whereas Christ inaugurated the perfect New Law which will remain forever.[10]

38. **How does the Old Law differ from the New Law?**
1. The Old Law was binding only on the Jews, and only for a time; the New Law is intended for all men, and for all ages; 2. The Old Law was the shadow of the New; the New Law is the perfection of the Old; 3. The Old Law could not justify man; the New Law has this power in itself. The New Law is nothing other than the grace of God, infused into the soul at justification, giving man the power to live according to the natural law and divine law.

39. **When did the Old Law cease to be binding?**
The Old Law contained three kinds of precepts: moral, ceremonial, and judicial. The first, founded on the natural law, are immutable; but the ceremonial and judicial precepts ceased to be binding with the coming of Jesus Christ, our divine King and Lawgiver.

40. **What are the chief errors with regard to the divine law today?**
1. *Rabbinic Judaism*, which holds fidelity to the Mosaic Law as sufficient for salvation; 2. *Judaizing*, whereby Christians adopt Jewish ceremonies that have already been fulfilled and superseded by the coming of Christ, e.g., "seder meals" and ritual circumcision; 3. *Antinomianism*, which maintains that Christians are exempt from

some or all obligations of the moral law; 4. *Moral liberalism*, which asserts that divine law in its immutable aspect of the Ten Commandments is an abstract ideal, impossible or harmful to observe in some concrete circumstances; 5. *Gradualism*, which asserts that people can be in right relationship with God and the state of grace by gradually becoming more "ethical," even while knowingly continuing in mortal sin.

41. **What does Holy Scripture say about the divine law?**

"It is said: 'The law of the Lord is unspotted,' i.e., allowing no foulness of sin; 'converting souls,' because it directs not only exterior, but also interior acts; 'the testimony of the Lord is faithful,' because of the certainty of what is true and right; 'giving wisdom to little ones,' by directing man to an end supernatural and divine."[11]

Human Law

42. **What is *human law*?**

An ordinance of reason for the common good, promulgated by one who has legitimate authority over the community for which the law was created.[12]

43. **How does human law come from God?**

It comes from God indirectly, inasmuch as He makes legitimate governing authorities share in His authority (see Rom 13:1).

44. **How does human law differ from natural law?**

Human law is not universal, but differs according to those subject to it and the power of the legislator; it is not immutable, but admits of exceptions, dispensations, and abrogations; it is not absolute, and is generally not regarded as binding when gravely inconvenient.

45. **What is *ecclesiastical law*?**

That which has been established by the Church for the spiritual welfare of the faithful. Universal ecclesial law applies to all the baptized who have the use of reason. The *Code of Canon Law* is a main compendium of this law.

46. **Are there cases where a human law should not be followed?**

Yes. If a law is made that exceeds the jurisdiction of the legislator, gravely threatens the common good, or contradicts natural law or divine law, it is an act of violence rather than a true law. It is null and void, and need not be followed.[13]

47. **What should we do when two laws appear to conflict?**

The higher law takes precedence; e.g., natural law takes precedence over positive law, divine law takes precedence over human law, and ecclesiastical law takes precedence over civil law.

48. **What should we do when an ecclesiastical law is manifestly harmful?**
    Any law or command of an ecclesiastical superior—even the pope—that under-mines or evidently harms the clarity or integrity of the Church's constant law of faith (*lex credendi*), morals (*lex vivendi*), or liturgy (*lex orandi*) must not be obeyed.

49. **Aren't Catholics bound to obey the pope and other ecclesiastical superiors in all things?**
    No. Although the pope has universal and immediate jurisdiction over every Catholic, no one must obey him in all things without qualification: "Man is subject to God simply as regards all things, both internal and external, wherefore he is bound to obey Him in all things. On the other hand, inferiors are not subject to their superiors in all things, but only in certain things and in a particular way, in respect of which the superior stands between God and his subjects, whereas in respect of other matters the subject is immediately under God, by whom he is taught either by the natural or by the written law."[14]

50. **What is the chief reason for such disobedience to ecclesiastical laws or commands?**
    "If the Faith were endangered, a subject ought to rebuke his prelate even publicly. Hence Paul, who was Peter's subject, rebuked him in public, on account of the imminent danger of scandal concerning faith."[15] St. Paul relates in Galatians 2:11: "When Cephas [Peter] came to Antioch I opposed him to his face, because he was to be blamed."

Section 2: Virtue and Sin

Chapter 3: Virtue

Virtue in General

51. **What is *virtue*?**
In the fullest sense, virtue is the habit of goodness; it is a firm and stable inclination to do what is right, enabling us to choose the good with greater ease, skill, and enjoyment.

52. **What is a *theological virtue*?**
From the Greek *theos* (God), these are habits having God as their *object*, known by revelation; as their *principle*, being infused and operating by His grace; as their *motive*, which is His truthfulness, fidelity, and goodness; and their *end*, which is the Beatific Vision. There are three such virtues: faith, hope, and charity.

53. **What is a *moral virtue*?**
Habits having as their object some created thing that can serve as a means of arriving at God. There are many such virtues: prudence, chastity, fortitude, piety, magnanimity, etc.

54. **When are virtues infused, and when are they acquired?**
Infused virtues are those which God produces immediately in us by His grace. *Acquired* virtues result from the effort of repeated similar acts. Theological virtues are infused, whereas moral virtues can be infused or acquired.

55. **When are virtues supernatural, and when are they natural?**
Virtues are *supernatural* when they belong to the order of grace, and *natural* when they belong to the order of nature. Theological virtues are supernatural, whereas moral virtues can be natural or supernatural.

56. **When are virtues *heroic*, and when are they *ordinary*?**
Virtues are heroic or ordinary based on the ordinary standard of human goodness. To give out of our abundance to the poor is an act of ordinary charity; to give all of our possessions to the poor is an act of heroic charity.

Growth in Virtue

57. **Can virtue increase in the soul?**
Yes. All the virtues, of whatever kind, can be continuously increased in the soul.

58. **How are the natural moral virtues increased?**
By frequent repetition of the acts which produce them, e.g., repeated acts of bravery to grow in the virtue of fortitude.

59. **How are the theological and infused moral virtues increased?**
    By an increase of divine grace in the soul. Whatever increases grace (e.g., sacraments, prayers, good works) also increases the infused virtues.

Chapter 4: Faith

Faith in General

60. **What is faith?**
    Faith is a supernatural virtue by which we firmly believe all the truths which God has revealed to us, and which He teaches through the unchanging and perennial Magisterium of His Church, because He is truth itself.

61. **How is faith a *supernatural* virtue?**
    It possesses the following characteristics, which are above nature: 1. It is infused into the soul by God; 2. It has revealed truth as its object; 3. It has our eternal salvation as its end.

62. **What is *living* faith?**
    Faith that is accompanied by the observance of the commandments; it is faith working by supernatural charity.

63. **What is *dead* faith?**
    Faith without supernatural charity, i.e., faith in a soul with at least one unrepented mortal sin.

64. **What is the motive of faith?**
    The reason we should believe what God has revealed is the truthfulness of God Himself, "who can neither deceive nor be deceived."[1]

65. **Can we know with certainty what God has revealed?**
    Yes. He has given us external signs of credibility of the revelation which He has made, in order to show the reasonableness of our obedience of faith.

66. **What are these external signs of credibility?**
    1. The fulfillment in Jesus Christ of the prophecies of the Old Testament; 2. His holiness, miracles, and prophecies; 3. The excellence of His doctrine; 4. The marvelous effects of His doctrine in the world; 5. The astonishing conversion of so many nations to Christianity; 6. The testimony of countless martyrs; 7. The heroic virtues and miracles of many saints; 8. The astounding preservation of the Church, in spite of endless attempts to destroy it from within and without.

67. **How does the Church propose revealed truths to the belief of the faithful?**
    In two ways: 1. The unanimous and constant preaching of the pastors of the Church throughout the world and throughout all ages, called the ordinary and universal Magisterium, which has the charism of infallibility; 2. Solemn

judgments, such as the infallible pronouncements of ecumenical councils or *ex cathedra* teachings of sovereign pontiffs.

68. **Can someone be a true Catholic while rejecting even one revealed truth?**
No. "Such is the nature of Catholicism that it does not admit of more or less, but must be held as a whole or as a whole rejected: 'This is the Catholic Faith, which unless a man believe faithfully and firmly; he cannot be saved' (Athanasian Creed). There is no need of adding any qualifying terms to the profession of Catholicism: it is quite enough for each one to proclaim, 'Christian is my name and Catholic my surname,' only let him endeavor to be in reality what he calls himself."[2]

69. **What qualifying term best connotes the true *Christian* and *Catholic*?**
The term *traditional*, because it does not distract from, but rather articulates and resolutely defends, the glory of our Christian name and Catholic surname.

70. **Why is the qualifying term *traditional* so essential for Catholics?**
Because the Catholic's entire law of faith and prayer must be characterized by fidelity to Sacred Tradition. The holy apostles commanded: "If anyone preach to you a gospel besides that which you have received (*quod accepistis*), let him be anathema" (Gal 1:9*); "I delivered that which I also received (*tradidi quod et accepi*)" (1 Cor 15:3*); "Hold the traditions (*tenete traditiones*) which you have learned" (2 Thes 2:14*); and, "Contend for the Faith (*semel traditae*) once delivered to the saints" (Jude 3*). The Roman Church has always followed this as the surest way: "Let nothing new be introduced, but only what has been handed down (*nihil innovetur nisi quod traditum est*)."[3]

71. **By what certain criteria may we recognize the authentic Catholic tradition?**
The criteria formulated by St. Vincent of Lerins: "What has been taught always, everywhere, and by all (*quod semper, quod ubique, quod ab omnibus*)."[4]

72. **How does the Catholic Church follow the apostolic principle of tradition?**
"The Church of Christ, the careful and watchful guardian of the doctrines deposited in her charge, never changes anything in them, never diminishes, never adds, does not cut off what is necessary, does not add what is superfluous, does not lose her own, does not appropriate what is another's, but, while dealing faithfully and judiciously with ancient doctrine, keeps this one object carefully in view—if there be anything which antiquity has left shapeless and rudimentary, to fashion and polish it, if anything already reduced to shape and developed, to consolidate and strengthen it, if any already ratified and defined, to keep and guard it."[5]

73. **Is this principle of fidelity to Sacred Tradition essential for right faith?**
Yes. "That meaning of the sacred dogmas is ever to be maintained which has once been declared by holy mother Church, and there must never be any abandonment of this sense under the pretext or in the name of a more profound understanding. May understanding, knowledge, and wisdom increase as ages and centuries roll along, and greatly and vigorously flourish, in each and all, in the individual and the whole

Church: but this only in its own proper kind, that is to say, in the same doctrine, the same sense, and the same understanding (*eodem sensu eademque sententia*)."[6]

74. **Did the Second Vatican Council stress the same principle of fidelity?**
Yes: "This teaching office is not above the word of God, but serves it, teaching only what has been handed on (*quod traditum est*), listening to it devoutly, guarding it scrupulously and explaining it faithfully."[7]

75. **In our day, what is the most insidious enemy of the Church's constant Tradition?**
It is *Modernism*, against which the Magisterium of the Church has warned: "The monstrous errors of 'Modernism'... Our Predecessor rightly declared to be 'the synthesis of all heresies,' and solemnly condemned.... As the plague is not yet entirely stamped out, but lurks here and there in hidden places, We exhort all to be carefully on their guard against any contagion of the evil.... Nor do We merely desire that Catholics should shrink from the errors of Modernism, but also from the tendencies or what is called the 'spirit' of Modernism. Those who are infected by that spirit develop a keen dislike for all that savors of antiquity and become eager searchers after novelties in everything: in the way in which they carry out religious functions, in the ruling of Catholic institutions, and even in private exercises of piety. Therefore, it is Our will that the law of our forefathers should still be held sacred: 'Let there be no innovation; keep to what has been handed down.'"[8]

76. **Can a layman's *sensus fidei* ever lead him to reject a teaching of the clergy?**
Yes. Alerted by his *sensus fidei*, the lay faithful may deny assent even to the teachings of legitimate pastors when these appear evidently contrary to right faith or morals, or undermine their integrity. St. Paul warned even of bishops who would teach error as "ravening wolves" (Acts 20:29*), formulating this principle for both clergy and lay faithful: "Even if we or an angel from heaven should proclaim to you a Gospel contrary to what we proclaimed to you, let that one be accursed! As we have said before, so now I repeat, if anyone proclaims to you a Gospel contrary to what you received, let that one be accursed [*anathema sit*]!" (Gal 1:8–9).

77. **Isn't this sinful disobedience, dissent from the Magisterium, and a form of Protestantism?**
No. Rather than treat oneself as the ultimate criterion of truth (which *is* a form of Protestantism), the faithful Catholic faced with a disturbing yet "authorized" teaching merely defers to the superior authority of the universal, perennial, traditional teachings of the Church, rejecting what departs from it.

78. **When and how may clergy or laity legitimately resist or admonish their superiors—even a pope?**
"Just as it is licit to resist the pontiff that aggresses the body, it is also licit to resist the one who aggresses souls or who disturbs civil order, or, above all, who attempts to destroy the Church. I say that it is licit to resist him by not doing what he orders

and by preventing his will from being executed; it is not licit, however, to judge, punish, or depose him, since these acts are proper to a superior."[9]

79. **Are there historical examples of such lawful resistance to ambiguous and erroneous teachings of the Church's legitimate pastors?**
Yes. Providence has given a clear example in the Arian crisis of the fourth century, when heresy infected almost the entire episcopate and yet the lay people remained faithful to the traditional Catholic Faith. "In that time of immense confusion, the divine dogma of Our Lord's divinity was proclaimed, enforced, maintained, and (humanly speaking) preserved, far more by the *Ecclesia docta* [laity] than by the *Ecclesia docens* [hierarchy].… The body of the episcopate was unfaithful to its commission, while the body of the laity was faithful to its baptism.… At one time the pope, at other times the patriarchal, metropolitan, and other great sees, at other times general councils, said what they should not have said, or did what obscured and compromised revealed truth; while, on the other hand, it was the Christian people who, under providence, were the ecclesiastical strength of Athanasius, Hilary, Eusebius of Vercellae, and other great solitary confessors, who would have failed without them."[10]

Necessity of Faith

80. **Is faith a necessary virtue for salvation?**
Yes. "The one who does not believe will be condemned" (Mk 16:16). Faith is an absolutely necessary condition for the reception of sanctifying grace, without which no one can be saved.

81. **Is habitual faith sufficient for salvation?**
Habitual faith, an interior disposition communicated by baptism, is sufficient for those who do not have the use of reason; but those who have use of their reason must have *actual* faith to be saved, meaning that we must submit our intellect and will to God by our own personal choice.

82. **To be saved, what truths must we believe with explicit faith?**
We must at least believe and profess: 1. The existence of one God, who is a Rewarder of our works in eternity; 2. The mystery of the Blessed Trinity; 3. The Incarnation of the Son of God for our salvation.[11]

83. **What obligation do we have with regard to the other revealed truths?**
It is sufficient to believe these implicitly; however, each is obliged to acquire a deeper understanding and faith in accord with his own ability and state in life.

84. **When are we obliged to make interior acts of faith?**
1. As soon as we have sufficient knowledge of revealed truth; 2. Often through life; 3. At the moment of death; 4. Under certain special circumstances, e.g., when facing violent temptation, especially against the Faith.

85. **What are we bound to do with regard to exterior acts of faith?**
We must: 1. Never deny our faith whether privately or publicly, or simulate a false faith; 2. Openly profess our faith whenever silence might be regarded as apostasy, or would give grave scandal to others.

Sins against Faith

86. **In how many ways may we sin against faith?**
We may sin against faith in two ways: by excess and by defect.

87. **How may we sin against faith by *excess*?**
Through *rash credulity*, accepting as truths of faith things that are not (e.g., various private revelations); and forms of *superstition* by which we believe to be supernatural that which is merely natural. Both errors run the danger that we may lose our faith.

88. **What are *private revelations*?**
"Throughout the ages, there have been so-called 'private' revelations, some of which have been recognized by the authority of the Church. They do not belong, however, to the Deposit of Faith. It is not their role to improve or complete Christ's definitive revelation, but to help live more fully by it in a certain period of history.... Christian faith cannot accept 'revelations' that claim to surpass or correct the revelation of which Christ is the fulfillment, as is the case in certain non-Christian religions and also in certain recent sects which base themselves on such 'revelations.'"[12] These are not binding in faith, and must be discerned carefully: "Test the spirits" (1 Jn 4:1).

89. **May rash credulity regarding presumed apparitions or revelations harm the virtue of faith?**
Yes. As faith must be strong and meritorious even without seeing proofs, those who seek apparitions and revelations often weaken their faith by desiring proofs of extraordinary phenomena. The phenomena of apparitions or revelations can be mixed with auto-suggestion and self-deception and sometimes produced by the evil spirits, to lead people to error and deceit in attributing to a merely human authority a supernatural or divine authority.

90. **What extraordinary things can demons cause in such false apparitions or revelations?**
Whatever nature or science can cause, the devils too are able to cause, according to what God may permit; e.g., the magicians and sorcerers of Pharaoh accomplished some of the same miracles worked by Moses and Aaron.[13] Demons can: 1. Produce corporeal or imaginative visions; 2. Falsify ecstasy; 3. Instantaneously cure sicknesses caused by their own influence; 4. Produce false stigmata; 5. Simulate miracles and levitation; 6. Make people or objects move or seem to disappear; 7. Cause a person to hear sounds or voices; 8. Cause a person to speak in tongues; 9. Declare a fact which is hidden or distant; 10. Heal or temporarily calm emotional distress, psychological difficulties, and other natural maladies.

91. **What are the signs of the diabolical spirit?**
1. Spirit of falsity, instilling half-truths and pseudo-mystical phenomena; 2. Morbid curiosity; 3. Confusion, anxiety, and deep depression; 4. Obstinacy; 5. Constant indiscretion and a restless spirit; 6. Neglect of one's primary duties and state of life; 7. Spirit of pride and vanity; 8. False humility; 9. Lack of confidence, and discouragement; 10. Impatience in suffering and stubborn resentment; 11. Uncontrolled passions and strong inclination to sensuality, usually under the guise of mystical union; 12. Hypocrisy, simulation, and duplicity; 13. Excessive attachment to sensible consolations.[14]

92. **What are some norms for discerning apparitions or private revelations?**
1. A revelation contrary to dogma or morals must be rejected as false, as God does not contradict Himself; 2. A revelation contrary to the common teaching of theologians or purporting to settle an argument among schools of theology is gravely suspect; 3. If some detail in a revelation is false, the remainder may still be authentic; 4. The fact that a prophecy is fulfilled is not itself a conclusive proof that the revelation is from God; 5. Revelations concerning merely curious or useless matters, or that are detailed, lengthy, and filled with a superfluity of proofs and explanations should be considered false, as divine revelations are generally brief, clear, and precise; 6. The recipient of the revelation should be examined carefully, especially in temperament and character, and if he is humble, well-balanced, discreet, evidently advanced in virtue, and enjoys good mental and physical health, one may proceed further to examine the revelation itself; 7. If the individual suffers from nervous affliction, periods of great exhaustion or depression, or is eager to divulge the revelation, there is cause for serious doubt.[15]

93. **Can the devil produce a false revelation encouraging people to pray, fast, and do penance?**
Yes. The devil is willing to lose much if he can gain souls in the long run. "Even Satan disguises himself as an angel of light" (2 Cor 11:14), and St. John warns us: "Do not believe every spirit, but test the spirits to see whether they are from God" (1 Jn 4:1). Demons may produce false revelations to: 1. Distract us from genuine private revelations; 2. Lead us to spiritual exercises not blessed as such by God; 3. Bring all private revelations into complete disrepute; 4. Cause disappointment and even crises of faith when a seer is later plainly seen to be false; 5. Lead us to reject the tried and true means of spiritual growth in chasing after the extraordinary and unapproved; 6. Subtly lead us out of the Church altogether.[16]

94. **What have the Church's great saints and Doctors said about presumed apparitions or revelations?**
St. Theresa of Avila warned: "When you learn or hear that God is granting souls these graces, you must never beg or desire Him to lead you by this road. Even if you think it is a very good one ... there are certain reasons why such a course is not wise."[17] St. John of the Cross taught: "Any person questioning God or desiring

some vision or revelation would not only be guilty of foolish behavior but also of offending Him, by not fixing his eyes entirely upon Christ and by living with the desire for some other novelty."[18] In declaring these saints Doctors of the Church and quoting from their writings in her liturgy and official documents, the Church recognizes this doctrine as her own.

95. **How do we sin against faith by** *defect?*
The baptized may do so through sins of *omission* or *denial*; the unbaptized may do so through sins of *unbelief.*

96. **How do we sin against faith by** *omission?*
1. By neglecting to learn the truths that we are bound to know; 2. By not performing acts of faith when they are necessary; 3. By religious indifferentism.

97. **How do we sin against faith by** *denial?*
Through heresy, apostasy, and false or idolatrous worship.

98. **Who is guilty of the sin of** *heresy?*
Those who obstinately deny or willfully doubt a revealed truth. One who errs in good faith and is ready to submit to Church teaching as soon as he recognizes the truth (a merely "material" heretic), is not guilty of the sin of heresy.

99. **Is willful doubt the same as hesitation, or seeking greater understanding?**
No. Merely being puzzled by a revealed truth, perplexed by its implications, or desirous of studying further to overcome objections, is not sinful doubt.

100. **Who is guilty of the sin of** *apostasy?*
Those who completely abandon the Christian Faith. The principal causes of apostasy are intellectual pride, ignorance, desire for temporal benefits, and slavery to the passions.

101. **Who is guilty of the sin of** *false* **or** *idolatrous worship?*
Those who actively participate in non-Catholic religious services, which worship God not as He desires; those who actively participate in syncretistic worship honoring pagan deities; those who worship inanimate objects or tokens of pagan mythology (e.g., symbols of the pagan Incan earth goddess Pachamama); Yoga and Reiki practitioners; those who worship nature itself, e.g., in the New Age movement or Gaianism (from the pagan Greek earth goddess Gaia), with terms like *Mother Nature* and *Mother Earth.*

102. **Has the Church warned against Gaianism and "Mother Earth" worship?**
Yes. The Holy See identified their basic ideological principles as "the generalization of ecology as a fascination with nature and resacralization of the earth, Mother Earth or Gaia, with the missionary zeal characteristic of Green politics. The Earth's executive agent is the human race as a whole, and the harmony and understanding required for responsible governance is increasingly understood to be a global

government, with a global ethical framework. The warmth of Mother Earth, whose divinity pervades the whole of creation, is held to bridge the gap between creation and the transcendent Father-God of Judaism and Christianity, and removes the prospect of being judged by such a Being."[19]

103. **Why must Catholics be warned against Yoga and similar practices?**
Yoga and similar practices (e.g., Zen meditation) are body and mind training derived from Hindu and/or Buddhist religions. "In their own context, the postures and exercises are determined by their specific religious purpose: they are, in themselves, steps that guide the practitioner toward an impersonal absolute. Even when they are carried out in a Christian environment, the intrinsic meaning of the gestures remains intact. Non-Christian forms of meditation are actually practices of deep concentration and not prayer. Through the relaxation exercises and the repetition of a *mantra* (sacred word) it is about plunging into the depth of one's own self in search of the anonymous absolute."[20]

104. **Has the Church also warned against Reiki practices?**
Yes. As a Japanese form of a so-called "energy healing," Reiki practitioners claim to transfer a "universal energy" through their palms to the patient, in order to encourage emotional or physical healing. "Without justification either from Christian faith or natural science, however, a Catholic who puts his or her trust in Reiki would be operating in the realm of superstition, the no-man's-land that is neither faith nor science. Superstition corrupts one's worship of God by turning one's religious feeling and practice in a false direction."[21] Some forms of Reiki also appeal for the assistance of angelic beings or "spirit guides," introducing further danger of exposure to the demonic.

105. **Is the New Age movement merely a novel form of Gnosticism?**
Yes. "We cannot delude ourselves that [New Age practice] will lead toward a renewal of religion. It is only a new way of practicing Gnosticism—that attitude of the spirit that, in the name of a profound knowledge of God, results in distorting His Word and replacing it with purely human words. Gnosticism never completely abandoned the realm of Christianity. Instead, it has always existed side by side with Christianity, sometimes taking the shape of a philosophical movement, but more often assuming the characteristics of a religion or a para-religion in distinct, if not declared, conflict with all that is essentially Christian."[22]

106. **Why are all neo-pagan globalist movements mortal enemies of the Catholic Church?**
Because they maintain that "the New Age which is dawning will be peopled by perfect, androgynous beings who are totally in command of the cosmic laws of nature. In this scenario, Christianity has to be eliminated and give way to a global religion and a new world order."[23]

107. **How do unbelievers sin against faith through *unbelief*?**
When they: 1. Remain culpably ignorant of the truths they are bound to believe; 2. Know the existence of the truths of faith, but refuse to accept them.

Freemasonry

108. **What form of false worship has been repeatedly condemned by the Church?**
Freemasonry. First explicitly condemned by Pope Clement XII in 1738, this pernicious error remains under the strongest censure.

109. **What is the fundamental reason for the Church's negative judgment on Masonic associations?**
"Because their [Masonic] principles have always been considered irreconcilable with the doctrine of the Church."[24]

110. **Why do Freemasonic associations represent a false worship?**
In its lower grades, Freemasonry is a "naturalistic religion"—a mixture of pantheism, gnosis, and "self-salvation." Masons of higher grades seem to worship the devil more directly, with a "religion" that is only apparently tolerant; for, they maintain that they alone are the "initiated," the "perfect" and "illuminated" people, while the rest of humanity is for them profane, imperfect, and darkened.

111. **What is the essence of Freemasonry?**
The essence of the Masonic religion consists of the perversion, that is, of the subversion of the divine order of creation and of the transgression of the laws given by God. Higher-degree Masons see in this perversion the "true progress" of humanity, the mental building of the "temple of humanity." Instead of God's revelation, there stands the "Masonic secret," and the human being ultimately makes himself a god.

112. **Can we say that Freemasonry is the Anti-Church?**
Yes. Freemasonry is a complete Anti-Church, where all the theological and moral foundations of the Catholic Church are turned into their opposite! With the rejection of divine revelation, Freemasonry also rejects the natural law—the exact point which leads to all political and ideological totalitarian systems.

113. **What shows that Freemasonry is truly a religious sect?**
"One becomes a Freemason through initiation. The initiation is a constitutive act through which the human being is given a dimension, which he did not have before. An analogy we find in baptism. One is not born a Christian, one becomes a Christian through baptism. In the same manner, one becomes a Freemason through initiation. That means that one remains a Freemason for the whole life; even if someone later rejects Freemasonry, he remains nevertheless a Freemason. Even if one is sleeping, if one is an enemy of Freemasonry, one remains a Freemason, because one has received the initiation. And the initiation is a holy act."[25]

114. **What shows Freemasonry to be a Gnostic and ultimately Satanic sect?**
The multi-volume *Great Encyclopedic Dictionary of Freemasonry and Symbology*, published by the Freemason Nicolas Aslan, a scholar of Masonic historiography,[26] affirms: 1. The Antichrist as the "negative pole" necessary for all Manifestation and for Progress;[27] 2. The bisexuality of the supreme Deity;[28] 3. The Serpent as a symbol of universal energy, harmony of opposites, and the great magical agent;[29] 4. The Fire-Principle in the Masonic High Degrees, called "the universal power of regeneration" and "Lucifer."[30] Such explicit self-testimonies entirely warrant the Church's description of Freemasonry as "a Satanic sect, which has the devil as its god."[31]

115. **How has the Magisterium described the actions of Freemasonry?**
Pope Leo XIII thus summarized the essence, principles, and actions of Freemasonry: "Wherever it has set its foot, it penetrates into all ranks and departments of the commonwealth, in the hope of obtaining at last supreme control. Under the pretense of vindicating the rights of man and of reconstituting society, it attacks Christianity; it rejects revealed doctrine, denounces practices of piety, the divine sacraments, and every sacred thing as superstition; it strives to eliminate the Christian character from marriage and the family and the education of youth, and from every form of instruction, whether public or private, and to root out from the minds of men all respect for authority, whether human or divine. On its own part, it preaches the worship of nature, and maintains that, by the principles of nature, truth and probity and justice are to be measured and regulated. In this way, as is quite evident, man is being driven to adopt customs and habits of life akin to those of the heathen, only more corrupt in proportion as the incentives to sin are more numerous."[32]

116. **To what extent has Freemasonry influenced social and political life?**
Freemasonry represents a contagion, called the "Masonic virus,"[33] which has invaded almost all spheres of the social and political order of many countries and international organizations. Already by 1884, Pope Leo XIII could make the following fitting observation: "The sect of Freemasons grew with a rapidity beyond conception in the course of a century and a half, until it came to be able, by means of fraud or of audacity, to gain such entrance into every rank of the state as to seem to be almost its ruling power. This swift and formidable advance has brought upon the Church, upon the power of princes, upon the public well-being, precisely that grievous harm which Our predecessors had long before foreseen."[34]

117. **What are the consequences of this Masonic predominance in society?**
One can deduce that many modern states are permeated with Freemasonry. Thanks to the immense resources that journalism offers today, Freemasonry can arrive at such a monopoly of social functions and public opinion that someone who does not submit to its dominion cannot be socially and politically influential.

118. **What is the most common disguise with which Freemasonry camouflages itself?**
Beneficence and philanthropy, making it appear convenient and likeable.

119. **What was the most recent judgment of the Church on Freemasonry?**
The *Declaration on Masonic Associations*, approved by Pope John Paul II in 1983. It maintains the Church's condemnation of Masonic associations, despite the fact that the new Code of Canon Law does not mention them expressly, unlike the previous Code of 1917.[35]

120. **Are Catholics ever permitted to be members of Masonic associations?**
No. "The faithful who enroll in Masonic associations are in a state of grave sin and may not receive Holy Communion."[36]

121. **Can individual cardinals or bishops approve of Freemasonry?**
No. "It is not within the competence of local ecclesiastical authorities to give a judgment on the nature of Masonic associations which would imply a derogation from what has been decided [in the 1983 Declaration]."[37]

Preserving Faith

122. **Is faith a precious gift?**
Yes. It is among the most precious of God's gifts, since it is the seed of man's salvation, the foundation and root of all justification.

123. **Can faith be lost?**
Yes. The supernatural virtue of faith is lost by every grave sin of unbelief.

124. **What are the means of preserving faith?**
1. Fidelity to grace, particularly the grace of prayer; 2. Combatting pride, avarice, and sensuality; 3. Careful study of Christian doctrine; 4. Avoiding the familiar company of heretics and unbelievers; 5. Care to avoid impious books and other media.

125. **What is a suitable formula for the act of faith?**
O my God, I firmly believe that You are one God in three divine Persons, Father, Son, and Holy Spirit. I believe that Your divine Son became man and died for our sins and that He will come to judge the living and the dead. I believe these and all the truths which the holy Catholic Church teaches, because You have revealed them who are Eternal Truth and Wisdom, who can neither deceive nor be deceived. In this faith, I intend to live and die. Amen.

Chapter 5: Hope

Hope in General

126. **What is hope?**
Hope is a supernatural virtue by which we firmly desire and trust that God will give us eternal life and the necessary means to obtain it, because He is a loving Father who keeps His promises.

127. **Why is hope a supernatural virtue?**
Because it is given to us by God's grace, so that we may look for a divine reward to which we have no right by nature: eternal happiness in heaven.

128. **What is the object of hope?**
The *principal* object of hope is everlasting happiness: God Himself, in heaven. The *secondary* object of hope is the necessary means of gaining eternal happiness: sanctifying grace, actual grace, and those temporal goods that help us in the way of salvation.

129. **What are the reasons for our hope?**
1. God's fidelity to His promises; 2. His infinite goodness to man; 3. His almighty power; 4. The merits of Jesus Christ; 5. The intercession of the Blessed Virgin and all the saints; 6. Past manifestations of God's mercy in our lives, such as our possession of the Faith, reception of the sacraments, etc.

Necessity of Hope

130. **Is the virtue of hope necessary?**
Yes. It is as necessary as faith, for without it there is no justification.

131. **Is habitual hope sufficient for salvation?**
It is sufficient for those who do not have the use of reason; but those who are capable must make explicit acts of hope.

132. **When are we obliged to make acts of hope?**
1. When we arrive at the age of reason and sufficiently understand the happiness God has promised us; 2. Often through life, just as with acts of faith; 3. At the point of death; 4. Under certain circumstances, such as when we are tempted to despair.

Sins against Hope

133. **How may we sin against hope?**
Whenever we sin against the *desire* of everlasting happiness in heaven, or the *confidence* of obtaining it with the assistance of God's grace.

134. **Who sins against the desire of everlasting happiness?**
Those who are so strongly attached to worldly goods that they would prefer to live forever in this world, or would prefer non-existence after this life if it were possible. Such wishes imply a renunciation of heaven as our final end, and are therefore gravely sinful.

135. **How may we sin against the confidence of obtaining eternal life?**
Either by defect or by excess; that is, either by despair or presumption.

136. **When do we sin by *despair*?**
When we abandon the hope of obtaining eternal bliss or the necessary means to secure it, such as the forgiveness of our sins, the grace of overcoming evil habits, etc.

137. **Is despair a grave sin in itself?**
Yes. It implies a fundamental rejection of the supreme goodness of God.

138. **What are the principal remedies for despair?**
1. Meditation on the infinite goodness and mercy of God; 2. Confidence in Christ, who died on the Cross for our salvation; 3. Devotion to the Blessed Virgin, refuge of sinners; 4. Gratitude for the many gifts already given to us by the loving God; 5. Remembrance of the wonderful conversions wrought by grace, e.g., Sts. Paul and Augustine.

139. **How do we sin by *presumption*?**
If we: 1. Expect to be saved by our own efforts without the help of God's grace, as the heresy of *Pelagianism*; 2. Expect to be saved by faith alone and without works of penance or charity, as the heresy of *Martin Luther*; 3. Remain in sin and delay our conversion, trusting the divine mercy to be always available at our pleasure; 4. Willfully expose ourselves to near occasions of sin, confident in our strength to resist temptation.

140. **Is presumption a grave sin in itself?**
Yes. It implies a contempt for God's justice and the order established by divine Wisdom.

141. **What are the principal remedies for presumption?**
1. Exercises of humility; 2. Frequent meditation on the justice and judgments of God.

142. **What is a suitable formula for making an act of hope?**
O my God, relying on Your infinite goodness and promises, I hope to obtain pardon of my sins, the help of Your grace, and life everlasting, through the merits of Jesus Christ, my Lord and Redeemer. Amen.

Chapter 6: Charity

Charity in General

143. **What is *charity*?**
The supernatural virtue by which we love God above all things for His own sake, and our neighbor as ourselves for the love of God.

144. **What is *love*?**
"To love is to will the good of another."[38] Only God and rational creatures (angels and men) are able to love in this way, as the intellect is required to know the good, and free will is required to choose it.

145. **Why is charity called a supernatural virtue?**
1. God Himself is love, he who abides in charity abides in God, and God abides in him (see 1 Jn 4:16); 2. It has the grace of God as its source, and without it we can only love God as Creator and Master, but not as a Father; 3. It has God as its primary object, with others loved from the standpoint of faith; 4. It has our eternal salvation as its end, which consists in seeing and loving God infinitely and eternally; 5. It is the infused habit or disposition of love, "poured into our hearts through the Holy Spirit that has been given to us" (Rom 5:5).

146. **Is charity the most excellent of the theological virtues?**
Yes. Charity is the queen of virtues. "There remain faith, hope, and charity, these three: but the greatest of these is charity" (1 Cor 13:13*).

147. **Why is charity the most excellent of virtues?**
1. It establishes a true and supernatural friendship between God and man; 2. It justifies the sinner, and is sufficient to wipe out all sin in the souls of the faithful even before confession and absolution, if it includes a desire for these; 3. Without it, all other virtues are imperfect and dead; 4. It makes everything contribute to our salvation; 5. It is eternal.

148. **What is the object of charity?**
Its principal object is God; its secondary object is ourselves and our neighbor.

149. **What is the motive of charity?**
God Himself, considered as infinitely good and worthy of all our love; with everything else being loved on His account.

Charity toward God

150. **What is the love of God through charity?**
An interior inclination of the heart that leads us to attach ourselves to God as our divine Friend, whom we love above ourselves, and whose interests we prefer to our own.

151. **Through what two motives may we love God?**
1. For His own sake, because He is infinitely true, good, beautiful, and worthy of all our love — this is *perfect charity*; 2. For our sake, on account of the blessings we receive from Him.

152. **Is charity toward God necessary for salvation?**
Yes. *Habitual* charity is necessary for all, since it is inseparable from sanctifying grace, which is the principle of eternal life.

153. **When are we obliged to make acts of charity?**
As often as we are bound to make acts of faith and hope, and under the same circumstances; especially when we are bound to have contrition for our sins, and there is no priest present to absolve us from our sins.

154. **By what unmistakable mark may we know that we love God above all things?**
By the careful observance of all His commandments. "Those who love Me will keep My word" (Jn 14:23).

155. **How may we sin against charity toward God?**
1. By omitting an act of charity when it is required; 2. By inordinate love of created things, which makes us prefer them to God; 3. By willful disgust or contempt for the things of God; 4. By every mortal sin and deliberate venial sin.

Charity toward Ourselves

156. **How should we love ourselves?**
1. With a *holy* love, loving ourselves for God's sake; 2. With a *well-ordered* love, loving ourselves within the strict limits of what is right and proper; 3. With a *true* love, not for self-interest or worldly pleasure, but solely with a view to a real, virtuous good.

157. **Should we love our bodies?**
Yes. The body is created good by God, is an intrinsic part of our nature, shares in the dignity of the image of God, serves as an instrument for good works, and will be raised by divine power in imitation of the risen Christ. However, the love of any bodily good (health, nutrition, exercise, pleasure) must always be subordinated to the good of the soul, and never contrary to God's law, the order of nature, or the demands of virtue.

158. **What is the remedy for an inordinate love of self?**
Our Lord says: "Let him deny himself, and take up his cross daily, and follow Me" (Lk 9:23*); for, "those who love their life lose it" (Jn 12:25).

Charity toward Others

159. **What is *fraternal charity*?**
The love of our neighbor, for the love of God.

160. **Who is our neighbor?**
All those who are capable of attaining heaven, or who are already there; it includes all men who live now on earth, the souls in purgatory, and the angels and saints.

161. **Are we obliged to love our neighbor?**
Yes. God binds us to do so by a special command, connected to our love of Him: "If any man say, I love God, and hateth his brother; he is a liar" (1 Jn 4:20*).

162. **How should we love our neighbor?**
We should love our neighbor as we love ourselves, for the love of God.

163. **What is meant by loving our neighbor *as ourselves*?**
Charity toward our neighbor ought to be like charity toward ourselves; but not equal to or greater than the love we have for ourselves. We can never abandon the good of our own soul, or sin, on account of a love of neighbor.

164. **What is meant by loving our neighbor *for the love of God*?**
We should love our neighbor because he is created to the image of God, redeemed by the blood of Christ, and called to eternal happiness.

165. **What duties do we owe to our neighbor?**
We are bound not to harm him, but rather to love him, in the same way that we should wish him to do for us.

166. **How is fraternal charity put into practice?**
1. By *interior* acts, consisting chiefly in wishing our neighbor well for the love of God, and praying for him; 2. By *exterior* acts, known as the spiritual and corporal *works of mercy*.

Works of Mercy

167. **What are the spiritual works of mercy?**
1. Admonish the sinner; 2. Instruct the ignorant; 3. Counsel the doubtful; 4. Comfort the sorrowful; 5. Bear wrongs patiently; 6. Forgive all injuries; 7. Pray for the living and the dead.

168. **What are the corporal works of mercy?**
1. Feed the hungry; 2. Give drink to the thirsty; 3. Clothe the naked; 4. Visit the prisoner; 5. Shelter the homeless; 6. Visit the sick; 7. Bury the dead.

169. **How should we perform these works of mercy?**
Our works of mercy should be well-ordered, discreet, and unselfish. "When you give alms, do not let your left hand know what your right hand is doing" (Mt 6:3).

170. **What order should be followed in practicing charity toward others?**
Charity should first be shown to ourselves and our relatives; next, to those bound to us by friendship, gratitude, obedience, country, and religion; finally, to strangers, heretics, and unbelievers. Spiritual goods should be preferred to temporal goods, life to reputation, and reputation to wealth.

171. **Has God imposed on us the precept of also loving our enemies?**
Yes. Jesus Christ has formally commanded us: "Love your enemies and pray for those who persecute you" (Mt 5:44).

172. **How should we love our enemies?**
1. Forgive from our heart the wrong which they have done; 2. Help them in their need when we can do so without great inconvenience; 3. Pray for them; 4. Show them the ordinary good will that we would show to any other, unless this would result in foreseeable harm or abuse.

173. **Does this love of enemies require that we submit to injustice?**
No. We may waive our rights for some greater good in imitation of Christ, but this is not a requirement of the Christian moral life. On the contrary, it is often a violation of charity or other moral duties to willingly submit to known evils.

Sins against Fraternal Charity

174. **What are the chief interior sins against fraternal charity?**
Hatred of our neighbor is wishing him harm, either because he opposes us, or because we dislike him for some reason; *Envy* is sadness upon seeing the prosperity of others, regarding it as our own loss; *Discord* is antagonism of will, when people are violently or bitterly opposed to one another in some matter.

175. **What are the chief exterior sins against fraternal charity?**
They are curse words, gossip, calumny, strife, scandal, and cooperation in evil.

176. **What is *strife*?**
An open conflict of opinion or desire, characterized by obstinacy, bitterness, and injurious language.

177. **What is *scandal*?**
Any word, act, or omission, evil in itself or only in appearance, that leads another to sin.

178. **Is scandal a grave sin in itself?**
Yes. As it is a serious violation of charity to lead another to sin, scandal only becomes a venial sin when the matter is trifling.

179. **What are the worst scandals?**
1. Blasphemy or sacrilege; 2. False and heretical teachings; 3. Creation or distribution of media that oppose religion or morality; 4. Public exposition of obscenity and perversion in art; 5. Gossip, which often breeds hatred, desire for revenge, and lasting enmities; 6. Lustful and immodest speech, attire, or behavior.

180. **How may scandal be repaired?**
1. By doing everything possible to limit its fatal effects, such as retracting statements, withdrawing bad books or opinions from circulation, etc.; 2. By bearing a legitimate and public punishment with submission and gratitude; 3. By amending our life and giving good example in its place.

181. **What is *cooperation in evil*?**
Sometimes called "moral cooperation," this is when a man engages in some level of agreement or participation in the evil act of someone else. This cooperation may be either formal or material.

182. **What is *formal* cooperation in evil?**
Sometimes called "being accessory in sin," this is when we agree with the sinful action of another, and perform some act of our own in support. Such cooperation is always evil in itself, and makes us equally guilty in the other's sin.

183. **What are the nine ways of being accessory in sin?**
1. By counsel; 2. By command; 3. By consent; 4. By provocation; 5. By praise or flattery; 6. By concealment; 7. By partaking; 8. By silence; 9. By defense of the evil done.

184. **What is *material* cooperation in evil?**
When we do not agree with the sinful act of another, but nonetheless contribute to the sinful act in some unintentional way.

185. **Is material cooperation in evil ever morally permissible?**
Yes, provided that: 1. We do not share the sinner's intention; 2. Our own action is morally good or neutral; 3. We have a grave reason for acting; 4. Scandal is excluded, so that our cooperation will not give de facto support to a grievously sinful situation. An example of proximate material cooperation in evil: The hostage forced at gunpoint to open a bank vault cooperates materially in theft, but his culpability is greatly lessened or removed.

186. **What is a suitable formula for making an act of love?**
O my God, I love You above all things, with my whole heart and soul, because You are all good and worthy of all my love. I love my neighbor as myself for love of You. I forgive all who have injured me, and ask pardon of all whom I have injured. Amen.

Chapter 7: The Moral Virtues

Moral Virtues in General

187. **What is a moral virtue?**
Any virtue that regulates the appetites and free actions of man according to reason, ordering them to the good.

188. **How do they differ from the theological virtues?**
1. They do not have God for their immediate object; 2. They are not necessarily infused and supernatural, since they may be acquired and natural.

189. **What are the principal moral virtues?**
Prudence, justice, fortitude, and temperance, which are also called the *cardinal virtues*.

Prudence

190. What is prudence?

The moral virtue that perfects the practical intellect, enabling us to choose the right and proper means to a good end in a particular case. "The prudent man looks where he is going" (Prv 14:15*).

191. What is the function of prudence?

1. It *deliberates* on the means and circumstances necessary to make our action good; 2. It *judges* whether these are as good and suitable as they should be; 3. It *commands* the will to carry out the action it has deemed correct.

192. What faults are opposed to prudence by defect?

1. *Precipitation*, whereby we undertake a work without sufficient deliberation on the means to achieve it; 2. *Inconsiderateness*, which judges these means before having sufficiently examined them; 3. *Inconstancy*, which makes us change opinion for no reason, or without sufficient justification; 4. *Negligence*, whereby we fail to take sufficient counsel before deciding a course of action.

193. What faults are opposed to prudence by excess?

1. *Worldly prudence*, which limits deliberation to merely temporal concerns; 2. *Cunning*, which employs tortuous and perverse means to achieve an end; 3. *Excessive solicitude*, or an inordinate attachment to temporal goods; 4. *Worry about the future*, implying a certain distrust of divine providence.

Justice

194. What is justice?

The moral virtue that disposes the will to give to each what is his proper due. "Do not judge by appearances, but judge with right judgment" (Jn 7:24).

195. What are the principal virtues under justice?

1. *Religion*, or obedience to and right worship of God; 2. *Filial piety*, or devotion to our parents and lawful superiors; 3. *Truthfulness*, which avoids speaking lies; 4. *Gratitude* for benefits received; 5. *Zeal* in opposing evil and repairing injuries.

196. How may we sin against justice?

If we violate: 1. *Commutative justice*, by harming the life, liberty, honor, reputation, or property of others, by not repaying debts, by cheating and usury, by theft and robbery; 2. *Distributive justice*, by undue partiality and wasting common property as an authority, by tax evasion and avoiding our duty to authority as a subordinate; 3. *Social justice*, by forming and enforcing unjust laws, violating just laws, or acting exclusively for private interests over the common good.

197. **What vices are opposed to the virtues allied to justice?**
1. Irreligion, neglect of duties to our parents or country, irreverence toward superiors, and disobedience to just orders; 2. Lying, breaking good vows, hypocrisy, ingratitude, cruelty, and overindulgence of others' faults; 3. Greed, wastefulness, hardness of heart toward the poor, bitterness of speech, flattery, inconstancy, disloyalty to friends, and lack of kindness.

Fortitude

198. **What is fortitude?**
The moral virtue that enables us to undertake great and difficult works or suffer great evils in pursuit of a good. "I will trust, and will not be afraid, for the Lord God is my strength" (Is 12:2).

199. **What virtues should accompany fortitude?**
1. *Magnanimity* or greatness of soul, which inclines us to heroic acts of every kind of virtue; 2. *Magnificence*, which inclines us to do great things at great expense; 3. *Patience*, which makes us keep our souls in peace; 4. *Perseverance*, which pursues a good cause to the very end, despite obstacles and setbacks; 5. *Confidence* in the assistance we can receive from God or others to accomplish difficult goals.

200. **How may we sin against the virtue of fortitude?**
The sin by excess is *rashness,* whereby we go into danger when, where, or in a way that is unreasonable or unnecessary. The sin by defect is *cowardice,* whereby we flee from a danger that we ought to confront.

201. **Where is the virtue of fortitude most manifest?**
In Christ's willingness to suffer even unto death on the Cross, and in the witness of the martyrs who died for the Faith, following Christ's example: "Blessed are those who are persecuted for righteousness' sake, for theirs is the kingdom of heaven" (Mt 5:10).

Temperance

202. **What is temperance?**
The moral virtue that enables us to use pleasurable things reasonably, and in appropriate measure. "Do not follow your base desires, but restrain your appetites" (Ecclus 18:30).

203. **What are some of the virtues connected to temperance?**
1. *Abstinence*, which moderates eating and drinking for the sake of our spiritual welfare; 2. *Sobriety*, which especially regulates the desire for and use of intoxicants; 3. *Chastity*, which subjects sexual desire to the law of reason; 4. *Studiousness*, which regulates the desire for knowledge or information so that we seek what is necessary or serviceable in our Christian life; 5. *Humility*, which moderates our self-love with

a reasonable measure; 6. *Modesty*, which regulates our clothing and behavior to befit our state of life and the manifestation of virtue.

204. **What major vices are opposed to the different kinds of temperance?**
1. *Gluttony*, which opposes abstinence; 2. *Drunkenness*, which opposes sobriety; 3. *Lust*, which opposes chastity; 4. *Curiosity*, which opposes studiousness; 5. *Pride*, which opposes humility; 6. *Immodesty* or *shamelessness*, which opposes modesty.

205. **Which of these vices poses the greatest danger to man's salvation today?**
As Our Lady of Fatima disclosed to St. Jacinta of Fatima, "the sins which cause most souls to go to hell are the sins of the flesh," or sins of lust.[39]

206. **What can especially engender the vice of curiosity in our time?**
The unguarded and immoderate use of various information and communication technologies, especially through personal computers and mobile devices.

207. **Is modesty a particularly necessary virtue today?**
Yes. Evil forces in our time are everywhere seeking to undermine customary manners, attire, and speech, to make men live like beasts.

208. **Then modesty is more than simply covering the body?**
Yes. Modesty is the virtue of regulating our entire outward appearance and actions according to the dignity and decorum proper to beings made in the image of God and heirs to eternal life by His grace.

209. **Are many current fashions a danger to Christian modesty and chastity?**
Yes. Our Lady warned St. Jacinta that many fashions would come that offend Our Lord very much. Those who serve God should not follow the fashions.[40]

210. **When does a merely natural temperance become *Christian mortification*?**
When we freely perform actions painful to human nature through a desire to imitate the humiliations and sufferings of Jesus Christ, and to satisfy the divine justice in union with Him.

211. **What vice is opposed to Christian mortification?**
Overindulgence is the vice of the "enemies of the Cross of Christ ... their god is the belly; and their glory is in their shame; their minds are set on earthly things" (Phil 3:18–19).

Chapter 8: Sin

Sin in General

212. What is sin?

Sin is any voluntary violation of the law of God in thought, word, deed, or omission; whereby we fail to do what we ought or go beyond the just limits of our moral freedom, and commit evil.

213. How is sin divided?

Sin is divided by cause as original or personal; divided by gravity, it is either mortal or venial. *Original sin* is the state of estrangement from God inherited from the disobedience of Adam and transmitted to all his posterity. *Personal sin* has its source in the individual will of each and every person.

214. What are the general errors about original sin?

Two extremes: 1. Those who deny original sin, as the Pelagians; 2. Those who overstate the condition or effects of original sin, as Luther, Calvin, Baius, and the Jansenists.

215. Did the sin of Adam injure him alone?

No. It affected all his descendants (excepting the Blessed Virgin Mary and Our Lord Jesus Christ). The Church condemned the errors of the Pelagians: "If anyone asserts that Adam's transgression injured him alone and not his descendants, or declares that certainly death of the body only, which is the punishment of sin, but not sin also, which is the death of the soul, passed through one man into the whole human race, he will do an injustice to God, contradicting the Apostle who says: 'Through one man sin entered in the world, and through sin death, and thus death passed into all men, in whom all have sinned' (Rom 5:12*)."[41]

216. What was the main error of Martin Luther regarding original sin?

Luther asserted the following heresy: "The nature of man is corrupted through and through by original sin and is damned within and without, in body and soul, and flees from God.... Spiritual powers are not only corrupted, but even totally destroyed in both men and devils, and nothing remains but a corrupted intellect and a will which is hostile and opposed to God at every point, which thinks and desires nothing but that alone which is contrary and opposed to God."[42]

217. What are the Lutheran and Jansenist errors about the effects of original sin?

That sanctifying grace being an essential part of human nature, original sin must have the following consequences: 1. Man's absolute powerlessness in doing any good; 2. The necessity for him always to do evil, unless God intervenes to help. Man thus becomes no more than a lifeless object, devoid of natural goodness, that God moves at His will.

218. **In the Lutheran and Jansenist theories, how can the "totally corrupted" nevertheless do good works?**

They erroneously affirm that God's grace frees man from his powerlessness to do good by imposing itself on him, so that man can do a good work. The Church condemned this error: "If anyone saith, that man's free will moved and excited by God, by assenting to God exciting and calling, nowise cooperates toward disposing and preparing itself for obtaining the grace of justification; that it cannot refuse its consent, if it would, but that, as something inanimate, it does nothing whatever and is merely passive; let him be anathema."[43]

Causes and Effects of Sin

219. **What are the main causes of sin?**

The chief *interior* causes are ignorance, concupiscence, bad habits, and malice. The chief *external* causes are the world and the devil.

220. **What is an *occasion of sin*?**

Any situation that can directly lead us to sin, such as bad company, bad books and media, etc.

221. **Are we absolutely obliged to avoid every possible occasion of sin?**

No. We are obliged to avoid the *near occasion* of sin, when the danger of committing grave sin is nearly certain or likely. "Whoever loves danger will perish in it" (Ecclus 3:26).

222. **How does sin affect man's relationship with God?**

Every sin implies some preference of the creature to the Creator. It is a wrong done to the infinitely good God, and an insult to His divine Majesty—an offense greater than any other harm that could befall a creature.

223. **Should we therefore avoid sin even at great personal cost?**

Yes, for, one mortal sin is a more dreadful calamity than the death of all mankind. "What shall it profit a man, if he gain the whole world, and suffer the loss of his soul?" (Mk 8:36*). We must "resist unto blood," striving against sin (see Heb 12:4*).

224. **How does sin affect the sinner in himself?**

Every sin is followed by two effects in the sinner: 1. *Guilt*, which is the blameworthiness incurred by the sinner, and the obligation to make reparation to God; 2. *Punishment*, by which the sinner is forcibly deprived of some good, and consequently suffers.

225. **Is all sin fully punished in this life?**

No. Although the loss of God's friendship and grace is the immediate punishment and the natural consequence of every mortal sin, many particular punishments are withheld by divine mercy until the next life, allowing time for repentance and, in the case of venial sins, purification in purgatory (see 2 Pt 3:9).

226. **Are all sins equally grievous?**
No. As their gravity differs, sins are divided into: 1. *Mortal* sins, which are grave enough to extinguish charity and destroy the life of grace in the soul; 2. *Venial* sins, which weaken charity and further incline man toward evildoing.

Mortal and Venial Sin

227. **What is *mortal* sin?**
A grave offense against God, which causes us to lose His friendship and merit everlasting punishment.

228. **Why is it called *mortal*?**
From the Latin *mors* (death), it deprives the soul of its spiritual life, which is supernatural charity and sanctifying grace, and makes us deserving of everlasting death.

229. **What are the three conditions that render a sin mortal?**
1. Grave matter; 2. Full knowledge of one's action; 3. Full consent of the will.

230. **What is *grave matter*?**
When the act itself is an objective and serious violation of a law of great importance, such as one of the Ten Commandments.

231. **When may circumstances change a normally venial sin into a mortal sin?**
Whenever we: 1. Erroneously believe that it is a mortal sin; 2. Commit it with an extremely evil end in view; 3. Commit it in explicit contempt of the law and lawmaker; 4. Knowingly cause serious scandal; 5. Consciously run the probable risk of mortal sin.

232. **What is *knowledge of one's action*?**
When we know the moral value of an action we undertake, i.e., if it is good or evil.

233. **What is *consent of the will*?**
When we have freely chosen the action.

234. **What are the effects of mortal sin?**
1. It gives an offense to God that is so grievous, that no created being can make atonement for it on his own efforts; 2. It disfigures and tarnishes the soul so that it resemble the demons; 3. It inflicts spiritual death on man by depriving him of sanctifying grace; 4. It deprives the soul of any past merits and the ability to acquire more; 5. It closes the doors of heaven to man; 6. It merits everlasting punishment.

235. **Are the effects of mortal sin completely irreparable?**
No. True repentance and the reception of grace can restore a soul to friendship with God.

236. **What is** *venial* **sin?**
Venial sin is an offense against God which does not deprive the soul of His friendship, but does merit some temporal punishment.

237. **Why is this sin called** *venial?*
From Latin *venia* (pardon), it is a less grievous offense; it does not remove us from the path to heaven, but only makes us stumble on the way. It is therefore more easily pardoned than mortal sin.

238. **What causes a sin to become venial?**
Either the action is not a grave wrong in itself, or else it is not fully consented to, as is often the case with the first movements of sinful thoughts.

239. **Can a large number of venial sins render a person as guilty as one mortal sin?**
No. Mortal sin alone makes us lose the friendship of God, by which we turn completely away from Him. One mortal sin surpasses all venial sins in gravity, no matter how numerous.

240. **Is venial sin nevertheless an evil to be shunned?**
Yes, because every venial sin, however trifling it may seem, is a wrong done to the divine Majesty. It would be better for the whole universe to be destroyed, than to attempt to save it by committing even one venial sin: "It were better for sun and moon to drop from heaven, for the earth to fail, and for all the many millions who are upon it to die of starvation in extremest agony, so far as temporal affliction goes, than that one soul, I will not say, should be lost, but should commit one single venial sin, should tell one willful untruth, though it harmed no one."[44]

241. **What harm does venial sin do to us?**
1. It dims the light of our intellect and weakens the strength of our will; 2. It tarnishes the beauty of our soul, and renders our works less pleasing to God; 3. It robs us of degrees of grace and glory that we might have gained; 4. It disposes and leads to mortal sin; 5. It brings punishments in this life, and if not expiated before death, consigns us to the pains of purgatory in the next.

Sins of Malice

242. **What sins are especially regarded as sins of malice?**
1. Sins that cry to heaven for vengeance; 2. Sins against the Holy Spirit.

243. **What are the** *sins that cry to heaven for vengeance?*
1. *Willful murder*, as homicide, murder, and abortion—the innocent blood of Abel cried from the earth to God (see Gn 4:10); 2. *Sodomitical sin*: sexual acts against nature, as man with man, woman with woman, or man with animal—the cry of this sin came to God from the earth, and God poured down fire and brimstone to destroy its perpetrators, the Sodomites (see Gn 18:20; 19:13; and Jude 7); 3. *Oppression of the poor, orphans, and widows*, as when God punished Pharaoh and the Egyptians

for oppressing the Israelites (see Ex 3:7–10; and 20:20–22); 4. *Defrauding workers of just wages* when they have done their service or work (see Dt 24:14–15; and Jas 5:4).

244. **Why are these sins said to *cry to heaven* for vengeance?**
Because their depravity is so manifest, that it provokes the fullness of divine justice more than other sins.

245. **What are the *sins against the Holy Spirit*?**
1. Despair of salvation; 2. Presumption; 3. Rejecting the known truth; 4. Envy of another's spiritual good; 5. Obstinacy in sin; 6. Final impenitence.

246. **Why are these called sins *against the Holy Spirit*?**
Because they imply a stubborn resistance to His inspirations and contempt for His gifts, and, "the mortal sin wherein a man perseveres until death will not be forgiven in the life to come, since it was not remitted by repentance in this life."[45]

247. **Are sins against the Holy Spirit unpardonable?**
No sin is absolutely unpardonable—but those who sin against the Holy Spirit stubbornly resist His grace, and do not wish to repent, and no unrepented sin can be forgiven. "People will be forgiven for every sin and blasphemy, but blasphemy against the Spirit will not be forgiven" (Mt 12:31).

Committing Sin

248. **In how many ways may we commit sin?**
By thought, word, deed, and omission.

249. **How do we sin by *thought*?**
Although a passing thought or feeling is not sinful in itself, voluntarily allowing our mind to be occupied with something forbidden is sinful. "Everyone who looks at a woman with lust has already committed adultery with her in his heart" (Mt 5:28).

250. **Why does God forbid evil thoughts?**
Because: 1. The mind is the natural repository of truth, but evil thoughts attach it to what is false; 2. Wrong in themselves, they are offensive in His sight; 3. They defile the soul, which is His temple; 4. Evil thoughts lead to other evil actions.

251. **How do we sin by *word*?**
When we speak against faith, religion, charity, purity, truth, etc. "On the day of judgment you will have to give an account for every careless word you utter; for by your words you will be justified, and by your words you will be condemned" (Mt 12:36–37).

252. **How do we sin by *deed* and by *omission*?**
When we do what is forbidden, or voluntarily fail to do what is required of us. God "will repay according to each one's deeds" (Rom 2:6).

253. **Is it also possible to participate in the sins of others?**
Yes, through *moral cooperation*, or being accessory in sin.

Chapter 9: The Capital Sins

Capital Sins in General

254. **What are capital sins?**
From the Latin *caput* (head), these are the perverse inclinations which form the basis of all other evil actions, as the head and source of all sins. Also called *deadly* sins, they either are mortal sins in themselves or naturally give rise to mortal sins, which cause spiritual death.

255. **Why are these also called capital *vices*?**
Because when these sins are repeated, they create the habit or tendency to commit sin as a result.

256. **Do the deadly sins have a common origin?**
Yes: inordinate love of self. To desire and seek our personal welfare is right and good when governed by reason and faith; but if we go beyond these proper bounds, we violate the principles of order.

257. **What are the seven deadly or capital sins?**
1. Pride; 2. Avarice; 3. Lust; 4. Wrath; 5. Gluttony; 6. Envy; 7. Sloth.

Pride

258. **What is *pride*?**
An excessive love of ourselves, especially our own greatness or excellence.

259. **Was pride the original and most dangerous vice?**
Yes. It was the first sin of a rational creature, the fallen angels: "Satan was not thrown out of heaven because of fornication or adultery or theft, but rather pride has thrown him out of heaven into the deepest depths of hell."[46]

260. **Why is pride an *excessive* self-love?**
Because a well-regulated and legitimate love of self, based on truth in the sight of God, is commendable; only its excess is sinful.

261. **What vices spring from pride?**
Pride begets: 1. *Presumption*, whereby we undertake tasks beyond our capacity; 2. *Ambition*, an inordinate longing for positions of dignity and honor; 3. *Vainglory*, an inordinate love of human praise.

262. **Is human respect also connected to pride?**
Yes. Especially common today, *human respect* is excessive regard for public opinion, and fear of man as opposed to fear of God. To avoid the contempt and ridicule of others, one might pridefully hide his faith or neglect his rightful Christian duty; but, "whoever denies Me before men," says Our Lord, "I will also deny him before My Father" (Mt 10:33*).

263. **What are the principal remedies for pride?**
1. Accurate self-knowledge; 2. Meditation on the vanity and passing nature of our achievements; 3. Imitation of Jesus Christ, the model of perfect humility; 4. Amiably accepting little humiliations, e.g., performing the humblest tasks with cheer; 5. Increasing our love for God and neighbor.

Avarice

264. **What is *avarice*?**
Also called *covetousness* or *greed*, it is an excessive love of and attachment to earthly goods.

265. **Why is avarice said to be an *excessive* love?**
Because there is a proper and legitimate love of earthly goods; as we may seek, acquire, and carefully preserve them for a good end.

266. **When does the love of earthly goods become sinful?**
When we make amassing, handling, or manipulating riches our chief aim in life, hoard our goods without measure or limit, or begin to covet our neighbor's property.

267. **What vices does avarice give rise to?**
Covetousness leads to: 1. *Greed*, which is the love of money and wealth above all other things; 2. *Preoccupation*, which leads to neglect of duty; 3. *Hardness of heart*, which stifles empathy and care for the poor; 4. *Theft*, unjustly appropriating the goods of others; 5. *Fraud*, which deceives our neighbor by an unjust act; 6. *Guile*, or the regular practice of deceit, particularly for the sake of profit; 7. *Perjury*, or deceiving our neighbor by means of a false oath.

268. **What are the principal remedies for avarice?**
Above all, *almsgiving* and *detachment* from worldly goods. Also, *meditation* on these subjects: 1. With death we must give up everything on earth (see Lk 12:20); 2. It is difficult for lovers of riches to be saved (see Lk 18:25); 3. The Eternal Son of God became poor for our sake (see 2 Cor 8:9).

Lust

269. **What is *lust*?**
The disordered desire for or enjoyment of sexual pleasure.

270. **Why is lust said to be a *disordered* love of sexual pleasure?**
Because sexual pleasure is not evil in itself; it becomes disordered only when sought outside of a valid marriage, or, within marriage, in the deliberate exclusion of its unitive or procreative dimensions.

271. **What vices can result from lust?**
Lust leads to: 1. *Blindness of mind*, dulling and clouding our reason; 2. *Inconstancy*, especially in our good resolutions; 3. *Self-love*, unto the hatred of God; 4. *Attachment* to the things of this world; 5. *Irreligion* and *atheism*, as justifications for immoral behavior; 6. *Despair*.

272. **Is the public normalization of sexual sin a clear mark of a decaying civilization?**
Yes. As demonstrated many times throughout history, the society that normalizes any sexual sin—especially sodomy—is on the way to collective destruction.

273. **What of those who habitually experience same-sex attractions?**
One must distinguish between same-sex attraction, and homosexual behavior or acts. Involuntary sexual feelings, even if they are against nature, are not sinful unless one consents to them. Those who merely experience such attractions are to be treated with compassion, and are called to chastity and personal holiness no less than others.

274. **Are sins of lust between persons of the same sex very grave?**
Yes. Two persons of the same sex sin gravely when they seek venereal pleasure from each other, because homosexual acts are contrary to nature, reason, and divine law (see Lv 18:22; 20:13; Rom 1:24–28; 1 Cor 6:9–10; 1 Tm 1:10; and Jude 7).

275. **What are the principal remedies for lust?**
1. Intense prayer; 2. Frequent reception of the sacraments of penance and Eucharist; 3. Filial devotion to the Blessed Virgin Mary, e.g., the Total Consecration prescribed by St. Louis de Montfort; 4. Regular use of sacramentals like the Cord of Purity of the Angelic Warfare Confraternity, the Cord of St. Philomena, or St. Joseph's Cincture; 5. Corporal mortifications, e.g., hard bed, fasting, cold shower, the discipline, i.e., self-flagellation; 6. To shun idleness, physical dissipation, bad company, and all sexually explicit media; 7. Meditation on the heroic chastity of so many saints, especially the martyrs of chastity; 8. Remembrance that sins of lust exclude man from eternal salvation (see 1 Cor 6:9–10); 9. An increase of love for God and holy things.

Wrath

276. What is *wrath*?

An excessive anger that wills evil toward someone out of desire for revenge, or an excessive reaction against something contrary to our will or desire.

277. Is all anger therefore sinful?

No. On the contrary, it is virtuous to be angry for a just cause and in right measure, as Jesus did when He drove the profaners out of the temple (see Jn 2:13–16). Indeed, "he who is not angry, whereas he has cause to be, sins. For unreasonable patience is the hotbed of many vices, it fosters negligence, and incites not only the wicked but even the good to do wrong."[47]

278. When does anger become sinful wrath?

Whenever we inflict or desire punishment on someone who has not deserved it, or in excess of what is due, or without lawful authority to do so, or only to gratify spiteful feelings. "Whosoever is angry with his brother, shall be in danger of the judgment" (Mt 5:22*).

279. What are the principal remedies for wrath?

1. Meditation on the righteous anger of our Savior, coupled with His perfect meekness; 2. Consideration of how many murders and wars have arisen from wrath; 3. The habit of never doing anything serious while angry; 4. The practice of virtues opposed to anger, especially patience, humility, meekness; 5. Recognition of our own imperfections, faults, and failures; 6. Meditation on how God's justice will be accomplished at the end of time, for all people.

Gluttony

280. What is *gluttony*?

A disordered love of eating and drinking.

281. Why is it called a *disordered* love?

Because there is a good and wholesome way to enjoy the proper nourishment of the body. For this reason the Church commands certain feast days throughout the year. Whether we eat or drink, we do it "for the glory of God" (1 Cor 10:31).

282. How do we commit the sin of gluttony?

We may eat sinfully by: 1. Quantity, in eating or drinking to excess, taking more than nature requires; 2. Quality, in choosing exceedingly fine or costly foods relative to our state in life; 3. Mode, in eating or drinking too eagerly, or merely for the pleasure of consumption.

283. **When does gluttony become gravely sinful?**
Chiefly when man: 1. Makes eating and drinking the great object of his life; 2. Seriously injures his health; 3. Is deprived of the use of reason or rendered unable to fulfill his duties; 4. Is led to break the Church's laws of fast and abstinence.

284. **Is substance abuse also included under the vice of gluttony?**
Yes. Any intoxicating substance may be used improperly: alcohol, tobacco, certain medicines, etc. Whenever these needlessly deprive a person of the use of his reason or endanger his health and life, such use is sinful.

285. **How can debilitating drugs or substances be used licitly?**
When used for a recognized medical purpose, such as the alleviation of extreme physical pain, or as preparation for surgery, etc., in professionally-recommended doses.

286. **Is the recreational use of marijuana a sin of intoxication?**
Yes. Due to its swift and immediate effect of impairing the intellect, marijuana may only be licitly used for genuine medicinal reasons under the supervision of a healthcare professional.

287. **Is a person responsible for sins he commits while intoxicated?**
Yes. If one foresees, even in a confused way, that he might commit them, then they are voluntary in cause, for which the intoxicated person is culpable.

288. **What are the effects of gluttony?**
It: 1. Brutalizes the mind; 2. Entails neglect of religious duties; 3. Fosters impurity and sloth; 4. Produces quarrels and dissension; 5. Destroys health and wealth, and shortens life; 6. Promotes attachment to pleasures; 7. Leads to hastiness and ravenousness in our eating and general manner.

289. **What are the principal remedies for gluttony?**
1. Consideration of its fatal consequences from the intellectual, moral, and physical points of view; 2. Avoidance of the near occasion of gluttony; 3. Temperance, especially by regular fasting and abstinence; 4. Acceptance of simplicity, with a focus on higher things, in our forms of recreation.

Envy

290. **What is *envy*?**
A selfish sadness at the prosperity of others, sometimes united with a desire to destroy it.

291. **How is envy a *selfish* sadness?**
Because the envious man views the prosperity of another as a loss to himself; he would prefer that the other be deprived of his goods, and would rejoice at the misfortune.

292. Why is envy a particularly harmful sin?

Whereas the object of other sins involves the enjoyment of some good—e.g., intemperance fixates on goods of taste or touch—the object of envy is to prevent or diminish another's good; harming both our neighbor and ourselves, with no gain of good whatsoever.

293. What sins spring from envy?

1. Hatred of our neighbor; 2. Joy over his misfortunes; 3. Regret at his success; 4. Backbiting, calumny, and complaints against superiors; 5. Rivalry and discord among equals.

294. What are the principal remedies for envy?

Chiefly the practice of Christian gratitude, blessing God for whatever gifts He sends, and striving to share in the joys and sorrows of our brethren: "Rejoice with those who rejoice, weep with those who weep" (Rom 12:15).

Sloth

295. What is *sloth*?

Also called *acedia*, it is a kind of sorrow and weariness about or distaste for spiritual goods, tending to an inordinate love of rest and neglect of duties.

296. Is an involuntary distaste for duty always sinful?

No. Distaste for work is an effect of the original sin of Adam and Eve (see Gn 3:19), and can be an occasion of merit if we courageously overcome such involuntary feelings, acting rightly despite obstacles.

297. What vices spring from sloth?

1. Torpor, or laziness in doing our duty; 2. Voluntary distraction from prayer and other necessary goods; 3. Cowardice, which draws us away from difficult goods; 4. Bitterness toward those who prompt us to good deeds; 5. Resentment toward those who perform good deeds well; 6. Easy discouragement in the face of difficulties; 7. Indignation and even hatred toward religious acts, and eventually spiritual goods altogether.

298. What are the principal remedies for sloth?

1. The conviction that we cannot be saved without good works; 2. Meditation on the great labors and sufferings of Jesus Christ and the saints; 3. The thought of the eternal repose awaiting those who strain toward heaven, which can only be attained by great personal effort—"The kingdom of heaven suffereth violence, and the violent take it by force" (Mt 11:12*); 4. Accomplishing our duties with love and gratitude; 5. Steadfast perseverance in prayer and the sacramental life, even when consolations are lacking.

Chapter 10: Temptation

Temptation in General

299. What is *temptation*?
A provocation to evil, arising from internal or external causes.

300. Is temptation itself a sin?
No. On the contrary, Christ Himself was tempted, but without sin (see Heb 4:15). Whenever one experiences temptation but bravely resists and overcomes it, the temptation has become an occasion of greater merit.

301. What are the three sources of temptation?
They are classically referred to as: the world, the flesh, and the devil (see 1 Jn 2:16).

302. What is *the world*, and how does it tempt us?
"The world" includes all earthly influences that draw us away from our heavenly calling, leading us to prefer temporal goods over the life of grace. It tempts us especially through *worldlings*, or other people who live primarily for this life, and through *human respect*.

303. What is *the flesh*, and how does it tempt us?
"The flesh" refers to our own concupiscence, that interior disorder arising from original sin that inclines our will to evil. It especially tempts us to sins of sensual pleasure.

304. What is *the devil*, and how does he tempt us?
As a keen and cunning liar (see Gn 3:1; and Jn 8:44), the devil principally tempts us by acting on the imagination and sense appetites, to give evil the appearance of good and prompt us to sin.

305. What are the three different phases of all temptation?
1. *Suggestion*, when a thought occurs, presenting what is evil as attractive, or what is good as repulsive; 2. *Delectation*, when pleasure arises from the suggestion; 3. *Consent*, when the will accepts the suggestion and delectation in the mind.

306. When does mere temptation become a sinful thought?
It is *consent* alone that can make a person responsible and guilty of a sinful thought.

307. Can we always withhold our consent to sinful suggestion and delectation?
Yes. Our will is essentially free and can always implore the divine assistance, which will always be given: "God is faithful, and He will not let you be tested beyond your strength" (1 Cor 10:13).

308. Is temptation unavoidable?
Yes. As long as we live in a fallen world, we will never be entirely free from temptation. "The life of man upon earth is a warfare" (Job 7:1*). However, we should never willingly expose ourselves to dangerous temptations through near occasions of sin.

309. **Then why does God allow us to be tempted?**
We pray, "lead us not into temptation," to show our firm will against the allure of sin; but at times God allows temptation for His own glory, and for our sanctification.

310. **How does temptation promote the glory of God?**
When by God's grace we overcome temptation, it manifests His power in overcoming evil, His wisdom in arranging a way for us to escape evil, and His goodness in giving us grace to overcome evil.

311. **How does temptation contribute to our sanctification?**
Temptation can: 1. Teach us to depend on God rather than our own strength; 2. Purify us from our faults; 3. Strengthen our virtues; 4. Trains us to greater spiritual combat, even on behalf of others; 5. Increase our merits and future glory, if we persevere; 6. Contribute to our self-knowledge; 7. Keep us spiritually vigilant, especially by constant awareness of God's presence.

Combatting Temptation

312. **How can we combat temptation?**
We can: 1. Distrust ourselves, placing all our confidence in God; 2. Lead a life of prayer and union with God; 3. Avoid idleness; 4. Know our weak side and our ruling passion; 5. Guard against temptations that present themselves as virtues; 6. Avoid situations where our outer senses may be overwhelmed.

313. **What should we do during temptation?**
First remove the cause, if possible, and divert our minds from evil thoughts. Then offer calm but firm resistance, imploring the help of God and the Blessed Virgin. As necessary, we should flee the place or change the scene and busy ourselves with some occupation.

314. **What should we do if temptation persists?**
Then it is best to take no heed of it, but to treat it with contempt instead. This is especially the rule to follow when tempted against faith, charity, and chastity.

315. **What should we do after having been tempted?**
If the battle has been won, we should humbly thank God. If the battle has been lost, we should humble ourselves, extricate ourselves from the consequences, and repent as children of a merciful Father.

316. **What if we are in doubt as to whether or not we have sinned?**
If the victory remains in doubt, we should not go back to consider it at all. If we continued to have a certain repugnance for the temptation and implored the help of grace during the battle, we should rather be fully persuaded that we have not sinned.

317. **What rule should we follow in difficult cases?**
We should follow the advice of a prudent confessor or spiritual director.

Section 3: The Commandments

Chapter 11: Commandments in General

Commandments of God

318. What is the Decalogue?

From the Greek *deca* (ten), the Decalogue is that code of Ten Commandments, or commandments of God, which sum up all of man's natural duties and rights.

319. Are all men able to know these commandments of God?

Yes, in principle; for, they are a summary of the natural law. However, because knowing them could take much time and effort, God took pity on the darkness of intellect that came upon man as a result of original sin, and also revealed these commandments in an extraordinary and explicit way.

320. Is everyone able to fulfill these commandments of God?

Yes. God's grace is available to all, and with the assistance of divine grace, "I can do all things through Him who strengthens me" (Phil 4:13). The Church teaches infallibly: "If anyone says that the commandments of God are, even for one that is justified and constituted in grace, impossible to observe, let him be anathema."[1]

321. How did God reveal the Ten Commandments?

Fifty days after the Exodus, God ordered Moses to gather the people of Israel at Mount Sinai. There, amid wondrous thunder and fire, God promulgated the Decalogue (see Ex 20:1–18; and Dt 5:4–22).

322. What are the Ten Commandments?

1. I am the Lord thy God; thou shalt not have strange gods before Me.
2. Thou shalt not take the name of the Lord thy God in vain.
3. Remember to keep holy the Sabbath day.
4. Honor thy father and thy mother.
5. Thou shalt not kill.
6. Thou shalt not commit adultery.
7. Thou shalt not steal.
8. Thou shalt not bear false witness against thy neighbor.
9. Thou shalt not covet thy neighbor's wife.
10. Thou shalt not covet thy neighbor's goods.

323. Did God limit Himself to merely declaring His law?

No. He also engraved it on two tablets of stone, which He delivered to Moses; and with the coming of the Son of God to earth, He promulgated it anew and perfected it, by bestowing the grace that enables man to follow God's law in righteousness.

324. **How did Our Lord sum up the Decalogue?**
By reducing it to two fundamental principles: love of God and love of neighbor. "'You shall love the Lord your God with all your heart, and with all your soul, and with all your mind.' This is the greatest and first commandment. And a second is like it: 'You shall love your neighbor as yourself.' On these two commandments hang all the law and the prophets" (Mt 22:37–40).

325. **Which commandments relate to love of God, and which to love of neighbor?**
The first three, written on the first stone tablet, regulate our relations with God. The following seven, written on the second tablet, concern our relations with each other.

326. **Is it necessary to keep all the commandments of God?**
Yes. To willfully break any one of them in a grave matter is to commit a mortal sin.

Precepts of the Church

327. **Are we obliged to keep only the commandments of God?**
No. We must also keep the precepts of that Church He established, because the Church exercises His legislative power: "Whoever listens to you listens to Me" (Lk 10:16), and, "I will give you the keys of the kingdom of heaven, and whatever you bind on earth will be bound in heaven, and whatever you loose on earth will be loosed in heaven" (Mt 16:19).

328. **Why has the Church made these precepts?**
To strengthen and encourage the faithful to keep the commandments of God, practice the maxims of the Gospel, and establish the reign of supernatural charity in their souls.

329. **What is the difference between the commandments of God and the precepts of the Church?**
The precepts of the Church fix the time and manner of keeping the commandments of God. They differ from the latter in three ways: 1. They are human and mutable, whereas the commandments of God are infallible and immutable; 2. They bind only the members of the Church, whereas the commandments of God are binding on everyone; 3. They cease to bind when a grave difficulty stands in the way of observing them, whereas there is no dispensation from the commandments of God.

330. **What are the precepts of the Church?**
    1. To assist at Mass on Sundays and holy days of obligation.
    2. To fast and abstain on the days appointed.
    3. To confess at least once a year.
    4. To receive the Holy Eucharist at least once a year, at Easter time.
    5. To contribute to the support of the Church's pastors.
    6. To observe the marriage laws of the Church.

Chapter 12: First Commandment

*I AM THE LORD THY GOD; THOU SHALT NOT
HAVE STRANGE GODS BEFORE ME.*

331. What does the first commandment require of us?
It requires *right worship*, whereby we make acts of faith, hope, charity, and religion. "Let us offer to God acceptable worship, with reverence and awe, for our God is a consuming fire" (Heb 12:28–29).

332. What is the virtue of religion?
Foremost of the moral virtues, *religion* disposes us to give God the worship that is His due as Creator and sovereign King of the universe.

333. What is Christian worship?
The proper homage paid to God (including the honor of His angels, saints, and holy places and things), and in the way that He desires.

334. How may Christian worship be divided?
1. Into *internal* and *external* worship; 2. Into *public* and *private* worship; 3. Into *latria*, *dulia*, and *hyperdulia*.

335. What is *internal* worship?
Acts of worship that are accomplished in the soul, without any outward sign or external manifestation. These include offerings of interior adoration, mental prayer, acts of faith, hope, and charity, etc.

336. Is internal worship necessary?
Yes. Without it, all external acts of worship are an empty show: "This people honors Me with their lips, but their hearts are far from Me" (Mt 15:8).

337. What is *external* worship?
Acts of worship that are accomplished with the body. These include vocal prayer and singing, gestures of homage like bowing or kneeling, processions, and above all, participation in the public worship of the Church.

338. Is external worship necessary?
Yes. As creatures of both body and soul, our worship is deficient and insincere if we refuse to honor God with external worship. "Therefore glorify God in your body" (1 Cor 6:20).

339. What is *public* worship?
Also called *liturgy*, this comprises all acts of worship offered in the name of the entire Church, by her ministers, and in the manner prescribed by her received and approved *rites*, or official ceremonies. These include especially Holy Mass and the Divine Office.

340. **Is this public worship necessary?**
Yes. It is of greater importance than the preservation of the entire universe, because it is the reason for its creation and redemption in Christ Jesus, who shed His blood to establish this true worship in His Church: "Christ Jesus, high priest of the New and Eternal Covenant, taking human nature, introduced into this earthly exile that hymn which is sung throughout all ages in the halls of heaven."[2]

341. **What is *private* worship?**
Acts of worship offered by individuals or groups that lack any of the conditions required for liturgical worship, e.g., personal pilgrimages, family Rosary, Stations of the Cross, etc.

342. **What is *social* worship?**
The formal acknowledgement of God's providence and supreme dominion over a given state, expressed in its official acts, laws, and customs. These include public prayers for divine assistance in government affairs, for an end of wars or famine, etc.

343. **Should civil governments take part in public worship?**
Yes. Like the family and the individual, all societies owe to God the homage of public worship, which may only be offered in accord with the rites that He has prescribed in His Church. As the government represents a society, it should take part in such worship of the one true God, the most Holy Trinity.

344. **What is *latria*?**
It is *adoration*, given to God alone, on account of His infinite perfection and supreme dominion over all of creation.

345. **What is *dulia*?**
It is *veneration*, given to the angels and saints, on account of their perfections and excellence in grace and glory.

346. **What is *hyperdulia*?**
It is *highest veneration*, given to the Blessed Virgin Mary, on account of her unique and extraordinary elevation above all other creatures.

Worship of God

347. **What are the principal acts of interior and exterior worship of God?**
Acts that are chiefly interior include *prayer* and *devotion*. Acts that are chiefly exterior include *adoration, sacrifice, vows, oaths,* and *tithes.*

348. **What is *prayer*?**
The lifting of the heart and mind to God—to adore Him, to thank Him, to ask His pardon, and to beg for His graces.

349. What is *devotion*?

The efficacious desire to give ourselves promptly to all that pertains to the worship and service of God.

350. What is *adoration*?

The honor given to God on account of His sovereign perfection, while professing our absolute dependence upon Him. It is due to the Blessed Trinity, and to Jesus Christ Our Lord in the Holy Eucharist. Adoration may be outwardly expressed by kneeling, genuflecting, bowing, or prostration.

351. What is *sacrifice*?

The external offering of a sensible thing to God, by a lawful minister who either destroys or changes it according to a sacred ceremony, in order to acknowledge God's sovereign dominion over man in a special way.

352. Must the visible sacrifice be sustained by an interior, invisible sacrifice?

Yes. "The visible sacrifices are signs of the invisible, as the words we utter are the signs of things. And therefore, as in prayer or praise we direct intelligible words to Him to whom in our heart we offer the very feelings we are expressing, so we are to understand that in sacrifice we offer visible sacrifice only to Him to whom in our heart we ought to present ourselves an invisible sacrifice."[3]

353. What is a *vow*?

Considered as an act of religion, it is a promise of some future and greater good, including one's very self, made to God alone after due deliberation.

354. What is an *oath*?

An act of calling upon God as a witness that we are telling the truth.

355. What is *tithing*?

The regular offering of some portion of our material goods for the support of God's ministers or His holy people, in order to honor God and thank Him for His gifts. Originally it was to be a tenth of all one's income, which remains a commendable practice even if no longer strictly required.

Prayer to Saints

356. What is a saint?

One who is in the enjoyment of the Beatific Vision; those who are *canonized* have furthermore been presented by the Church for the public veneration of the faithful in her liturgy, on account of their outstanding likeness to Christ in the exercise of heroic virtue and fidelity to the duties of their state in life.

357. **What is the veneration of saints founded upon?**
1. The constant teaching and practice of the Church;[4] 2. Holy Scripture;[5] 3. Tradition;[6] 4. Reason; 5. The witness of innumerable miracles wrought through their intercession.

358. **What kind of veneration do we give the saints?**
Dulia, or a veneration of respect and honor, rather than *latria*, or adoration due to God alone. When we pray to God, we ask Him to have mercy and grant us His grace; when we pray to saints, we ask them to intercede for us with God.

359. **What are our duties toward the saints?**
We should praise, admire, and imitate them, asking them to intercede for us. We should especially honor St. Joseph, St. John the Baptist, the apostles, the patrons of our parish and diocese, and the saints we are named after.

360. **Should we also venerate the angels?**
Yes; just as we do for the saints, and for similar reasons. We should especially honor St. Michael, St. Gabriel, St. Raphael, and our own guardian angel.

361. **What is the veneration owed to the Blessed Virgin Mary?**
Hyperdulia, or highest veneration, because she is full of grace, immaculate, the most perfect of creatures, Mother of God and spiritual Mother of all humanity, Queen of heaven and earth, and Mediatrix of all graces.

362. **What must we do to serve Mary worthily?**
We must be especially devoted to her and fulfill her command regarding her divine Son: "Do whatever He tells you" (Jn 2:5).

Relics and Images

363. **What are *relics*?**
Relics of the first class are the remains of the body of a saint, whereas a saint's clothing or treasured belongings are regarded as relics of the second class. Items touched to a saint's body are often referred to as relics of the third class.

364. **Is it lawful to venerate relics of the saints?**
Yes. This veneration is an extension of our honor of God and His saints, approved in Scripture, Tradition, and numerous miracles by which God has rewarded the veneration of relics.

365. **What are *sacred images*?**
Artistic depictions that remind us of the blessings we have received from God and His saints, and excite us to acts of devotion and the leading of holy lives.

366. **Isn't the veneration of images a form of idolatry?**
No. As defined against the iconoclast and Protestant heresies, this is only a *relative veneration*, offered to the person to whom these sacred items refer. It is good to keep

and honor images of Our Lord, the Blessed Virgin, and the saints in our churches and homes.[7] "The honor which is paid to the image passes on to that which the image represents, and he who reveres the image reveres in it the subject represented."[8]

Superstition

367. In how many ways may we sin against the first commandment?
1. By excess, through acts of *superstition*; 2. By defect, through acts of *irreligion*.

368. What is superstition?
Acts of worship that are sinful in either their *object* or *mode*; i.e., the worship of a false god, or the worship of the true God in an undue manner. "Superstition is a vice contrary to religion by excess, not that it offers more to the divine worship than true religion, but because it offers divine worship either to whom it ought not, or in a manner it ought not."[9]

369. Are sins of superstition very grave?
Yes. They are the most serious sins that man can commit, because right worship of the true God is our highest moral obligation. "True worshippers will worship the Father in spirit and truth, for the Father seeks such as these to worship Him. God is spirit, and those who worship Him must worship in spirit and truth" (Jn 4:23–24).

370. What kinds of superstition involve the worship of a false god?
Chiefly *idolatry*, which gives divine honor to any real or imagined creature, as in various forms of nature worship, e.g., the so-called Pachamama or Mother Earth ceremonies; all *divination*, *magic*, and *sorcery*, which seek the aid of demons or occult powers to learn what is hidden or exercise control, as in various forms of witchcraft, Wicca, and New Age practice.

371. Is the worship of false gods increasingly prevalent today?
Yes. As men abandon the only true worship of God in Christ, they increasingly revert to the errors of ancient paganism, or worship bodily health, power, nature, the Earth, and pleasure as their gods.

372. What kinds of superstition involve undue worship of the true God?
False worship, which contains something contrary to natural truth or divine revelation, as when false revelations are maintained; *impious worship*, as when a man-centered worship is established in violation of the Church's constant liturgical tradition.

373. Is it sinful for Catholics to actively participate in the worship services of heretical sects or other false religions?
Yes. Any non-Catholic prayer service, whose content contradicts the Catholic Faith, constitutes *false worship*. By actively participating in such worship, we: 1. Refuse to worship God in the manner He desires; 2. Assent to the errors proclaimed there; 3. Fail in charity toward the erring; 4. Scandalize the faithful; 5. Endanger our own faith.

374. **May we attend a non-Catholic religious service for reasons other than joining their prayer?**
Even passive attendance at such services (e.g., weddings, funerals) is generally discouraged, but may be permitted if: 1. There is a very serious reason to attend; 2. We do not engage in the prayer or rite itself; 3. Any potential scandal is mitigated; 4. All danger to our faith is precluded.

375. **Why do man-centered forms of worship violate the Church's constant liturgical tradition?**
Because only "the received and approved rites of the Church"[10] offer to God the worship that He has prescribed, and only her constant liturgical custom best safeguards the truly God-centered form of worship.

376. **What is the most common form of man-centered worship today?**
Drastic liturgical innovations and abuses, by which one introduces into the worship of the Church something contrary to her traditional doctrine or custom, e.g., a Protestant and banquet-style celebration of the Mass as in a closed circle, dances, show performances, tokens of secular organizations or pagan religions, etc.

377. **Why are such innovations reprehensible within Catholic worship?**
Even if they contain no objective falsehood, such innovations undermine the constant Tradition of the Church, and violate the sacred rites themselves: "He is unworthy who celebrates the mystery otherwise than Christ delivered it."[11]

378. **Should we avoid a Mass in which liturgical abuses will foreseeably occur?**
Yes. The presence of a valid Eucharist notwithstanding, ceremonies with liturgical abuses are objectively contrary to the divine and apostolic tradition, displeasing to God, scandalous, and often dangerous to faith.

379. **Should we attend a Mass with liturgical abuses to fulfill our Sunday obligation?**
This depends on the gravity of such abuses in each place. If a Sunday Mass would include practices like dances, heresies in preaching, or other serious liturgical abuses, we may not be obliged to attend such a Mass, even if it were the only one available in our vicinity, because we cannot be obliged to place ourselves or our families in a near occasion of danger to faith.

380. **In this specific case, would we violate the third commandment?**
No. The obligation to attend Sunday Mass is an ecclesiastical and not a divine law, and therefore subject to exemption and dispensation. If a Sunday Mass with liturgical abuses were the only available option, we should sanctify the Sunday in some other way; and in this way we are keeping the third commandment.

Irreligion

381. What is irreligion?
Any attack made on the proper honor that is due to God—whether *directly*, by tempting God, blasphemy, perjury, and breaking vows, or *indirectly*, by sacrilege and simony.

382. What is *tempting God*?
Any word or act which defiantly challenges God to prove some attribute of His, rashly awaiting some extraordinary or miraculous effect.

383. Is it permitted to ask extraordinary things of God?
Yes. If we have already used the means available to us, have a just reason for asking, pray humbly, and submit to His will, we do not tempt God, but rather honor Him through an act of filial confidence.

384. What is *sacrilege*?
The profanation of the sacred; it is the unworthy or irreverent use of something or someone consecrated to divine worship.

385. How do we learn the proper treatment of sacred things?
God Himself has revealed it, and the Catholic and apostolic tradition of the Church has retained it. Even natural reason instructs us here, as "it belongs to the dictate of natural reason that man should do something through reverence for God."[12]

386. What is *simony*?
The deliberate wish to buy or sell spiritual goods for a temporal price, as did Simon Magus (see Acts 8:9–24).

Chapter 13: Second Commandment

THOU SHALT NOT TAKE THE NAME OF THE LORD THY GOD IN VAIN.

387. What does the second commandment forbid?
It forbids us to profane God's holy name by careless use of it, blasphemy, false or unjust oaths, indiscreet vows, and the breaking of vows.

Blasphemy and Cursing

388. What is blasphemy?
An expression that is insulting to God, religion, or the saints.

389. What are the kinds of blasphemy?
Blasphemy is *heretical* when it contains something contrary to faith, as the denial of God's existence, goodness, or justice, or the perpetual virginity of Our Lady; it is *execratory* when evil is wished upon God, the saints, or any of His works, as to speak

ill of the Church or her sacraments; it is *injurious* when God, the saints, or religion is spoken of in a careless or joking manner.

390. **What is a *curse*?**
An expression of anger or hatred by which we intend some evil to ourselves or our neighbor. Willing and praying for justice, or predicting the coming of evil, are not curses, as seen in the Psalms and prophetic books of Scripture.

Oaths and Vows

391. **Is it permissible to take an oath, i.e., to *swear*?**
Yes. While Our Lord condemns all unnecessary or incautious swearing (see Mt 5:34–37), the act of calling God to witness our sincerity gives honor to His truthfulness and places us under a solemn obligation.

392. **What conditions render an oath lawful and good?**
1. *Truth*, swearing only what we know to be true or morally certain; 2. *Justice*, swearing only what we are allowed to; 3. *Discretion*, swearing only in cases of great utility or necessity.

393. **What do we call an oath that contradicts truth?**
A *false* oath or *perjury*, whereby we sin gravely in calling God as witness to a lie.

394. **What do we call an oath that contradicts justice?**
An *unjust* oath, whereby we sin gravely in taking God as security for our sin, or on account of the great wrong which the oath does to our neighbor.

395. **What do we call an oath that contradicts discretion?**
An *indiscreet* or *rash* oath, whereby we run the risk of perjury and scandal.

396. **When is an oath useful or necessary?**
When an important truth is cast into doubt and we must convince someone of it, or when civil or ecclesiastical authority requires it, e.g., in an oath of conversion to the Catholic Church (abjuration of heresy), or assuming an ecclesiastical office (oath of fidelity).

397. **Has the Church ever prescribed a general oath for all clergy?**
Yes. The very useful and timely *Oath against Modernism* was in force from 1910–1967, required of all clergy, pastors, confessors, preachers, religious superiors, and seminary professors.

398. **What were the main reasons for the *Oath against Modernism*?**
Pope Pius X prescribed it because: 1. Modernist churchmen were "ceaselessly injecting the poison of their pernicious teachings into the veins" of the Christian people; 2. Modernism contains the "summary of all errors"; 3. Unless the Church took clear and vigorous action, clergy and faithful might mistakenly believe that the Church "at least tacitly tolerated the doctrinal deviations of the Modernists."[13]

399. **When are we not obliged to keep an oath?**
Whenever the oath: 1. Aims at something unlawful, unjust, or impossible; 2. Has been taken by mistake, or in consequence of some fraud affecting its substance or motive.

400. **Is it permissible to take vows, as acts of religion?**
Yes. Such are oaths made to God Himself, to perform some good act. "Make vows to the Lord your God and perform them" (Ps 76:11).

401. **What conditions make a vow lawful and good?**
1. He that vows must act freely, with knowledge and deliberation; 2. The thing he promises must be possible, morally good, and better than the contrary; 3. His motives must be good.

402. **When does the obligation of a vow cease?**
Whenever: 1. The reason for the vow ceases to exist; 2. There has been such a change in its matter that its fulfillment has become unlawful or impossible; 3. Its obligation ceases by annulment, dispensation, or commutation by one with lawful authority.

Chapter 14: Third Commandment
REMEMBER TO KEEP HOLY THE SABBATH DAY.

403. **Has God determined a particular sacred time in each week?**
Yes. Every seventh day is to be spent for the glory of God and welfare of man.

404. **What day was reserved for God under the Old Law?**
Saturday or the *Sabbath*, a word signifying repose: "On the seventh day God finished the work that He had done, and He rested" (Gn 2:2).

405. **What day is reserved for God under the New Law?**
The first day of the week, Sunday, is "the Lord's day"—in Latin *Dominica*, as Sunday was called from apostolic times.[14]

406. **Who made this substitution of Sunday for the Sabbath?**
The apostles, by virtue of the authority which God had given them.

407. **Why was the first day of the week substituted for the last?**
Because of the great works of the Blessed Trinity on that day: Sunday was the first day of Creation, the day of Christ's Resurrection, and the day of the Holy Spirit's descent at Pentecost.

408. **Why is the first day of the week also called the "eighth day"?**
The eighth day, transcending the entire week, is like a door to eternity: "An image of the age which we expect, wherefore, though it is the beginning of days, it is not called by Moses *first*, but *one*. For he says: 'There was evening, and there was morning, one day,' as though the same day often recurred. Now one and eighth are

the same day ... [signifying] the state which follows after this present time: the day which knows no waning or eventide, and no successor, that age which ends not, nor grows old."[15]

409. **What does the third commandment require of us?**
It obliges us to sanctify every Sunday, by abstaining from unnecessary servile works and transactions (buying and selling), in order to devote our whole being, soul and body, to the religious veneration of God.

410. **To sanctify Sunday, what must we especially avoid?**
We should carefully avoid all occasions of sin, by which we profane the Sunday.

411. **Is the profanation of Sunday a great evil?**
Yes. Like blasphemy, the profanation of Sunday is a direct attack upon the holiness of God, which often provokes His just punishments.

Prohibition of Servile Work

412. **What kind of work is prohibited on Sunday?**
Servile work, in which the body has a larger share than the mind, and which are chiefly intended for the advantage of the body; such as field labor, mechanical and industrial operations, manual trades, judiciary works, commercial works, and excessive or burdensome academic or mental work.

413. **Why is this kind of work forbidden?**
Because it tends to draw man away from affairs of the spirit, making him forgetful of God and his eternal calling, and preventing him from enjoying needful rest of mind and body.

414. **Is Sunday rest detrimental to society?**
No. God cannot give harmful laws, and the law of rest is given for His glory as well as the prosperity of society, since human nature itself requires periodic rest and refreshment. Experience also shows that work on Sunday is harmful to workers and the welfare of society.

415. **What kind of works may anyone do on Sunday?**
Provided that they do not exhaust us or hinder proper worship, we may perform: 1. *Ennobling* works, e.g., reading, writing, teaching, fine arts; 2. *Common* works, e.g., traveling, hunting, fishing; 3. *Household maintenance* works, e.g., cooking, light cleaning, care of animals; 4. *Leisure* activities, e.g., sports and other pastimes that relax and refresh the body and mind.

416. **What works on Sunday are permitted by *piety*?**
Any works related to divine service or maintenance of the sanctuary that could not be performed in advance, such as cleaning the church, adorning altars, etc.

417. **What works on Sunday are permitted by *charity*?**
Any of the works of mercy, such as care for the sick or burying the dead.

418. **May necessity sometimes permit servile works on Sunday?**
Yes. Public or private necessity may permit such work when it cannot be deferred without risk of some harm. "The Sabbath was made for man, and not man for the Sabbath" (Mk 2:27*).

419. **What servile works are permitted by public necessity?**
1. *Public safety* works, e.g., policing, soldiering, and disaster relief; 2. *Public health* works, e.g., hospitals and pharmacies; 3. *Public transit* works, e.g., maintenance of roads, bridges, and mail.

420. **What servile works are permitted by private necessity?**
1. Food production and distribution in large urban centers; 2. Private transactions between individuals; 3. Works necessary to avoid impoverishment.

421. **Do employers sin by requiring needless servile work on Sunday?**
Yes. They sin as much as if they did such work themselves, and are further responsible for the sin of each man working at their insistence.

422. **Should societies guard against circumstances that would necessitate work on Sunday?**
Yes. All private and social life should be ordered toward Sunday rest and divine worship. "Let the working man be urged and led to the worship of God, to the earnest practice of religion."[16] "Work is for man and not man for work."[17]

Requirement of Worship

423. **What works of religion should Christians perform on Sunday?**
1. Worship of God, from which no cause excuses and no authority can dispense; 2. Assisting at Holy Mass, if we are able to observe this precept; 3. Other pious works.

424. **Is everyone bound to perform all of these works on every Sunday?**
No. The law of Sunday worship binds universally; the precept of attending Mass only binds Christians with the use of reason, and additional pious works are merely encouraged.

425. **What is required to satisfy the precept of attending Mass?**
1. Our bodily presence in the place where Mass is offered, at least from the Offertory to the priest's reception of Communion; 2. Our active participation in the rite itself.

426. **What constitutes *active participation* in Holy Mass?**
1. *Interior* engagement, consisting of having the intention to assist at Mass, and lifting the soul to God through prayer; 2. *Exterior* engagement, consisting of devout attention and not disturbing the rite, and possibly joining in responses, singing,

silence,[18] and sacramental Communion when we are properly disposed. The worthy, pious, and fruitful reception of Holy Communion is the highest form of this active participation.

427. **What is the best means of interior participation at Mass?**
To attentively follow the action of the priest in the sanctuary, striving to reverently unite our prayer to his. Further study and understanding of the rite itself are helpful to this end.

428. **Are we required to risk our life to fulfill the obligation of attending Mass?**
No. Physical dangers like extreme weather, plague, or war automatically suspend this obligation, until we may do so without grave danger. Even so, it is praiseworthy to go to great lengths to attend Holy Mass.

429. **What other causes automatically suspend the obligation to attend Mass?**
1. *Physical impossibility*, as with the homebound, sick, prisoners, or those with no available priest; 2. *Moral impossibility* and *charity*, as with caretakers of small children or those treating the ill or disaster victims; 3. *Danger to reverence or faith*, as when a Mass is celebrated in an unworthy or heretical manner, being the only available Mass in the wider area.

430. **If we have a legitimate reason not to attend Mass, what should we do instead?**
The obligation of Sunday worship always remains, and may be fulfilled through other forms of private, family, or communal prayer, to which other works of piety may also be added.

431. **What works of piety are recommended to help us sanctify Sunday?**
Attending Sunday Vespers, Benediction of the Blessed Sacrament, and catechetical instruction, as well as reading devotional books and performing works of charity.

432. **May a bishop ever suspend the obligation to attend Sunday Mass in his diocese?**
No. He may remind the faithful of those circumstances in which the obligation ceases to bind, but because this is a universal law for Catholics based on divine law, it is beyond his authority (and spiritually and pastorally detrimental for his flock) to suspend the obligation itself.

433. **May a pope or bishop prohibit the public offering of Mass for any cause?**
No. As a divine institution and the common good of the entire Church, Holy Mass may only be prohibited in a particular place and time as an extreme measure of canonical punishment through *interdict*, and only for the most serious ecclesiastical crimes.

434. **May the clergy ever prohibit rites of public worship due to concerns about public health?**
No. The prohibition of divine worship or the sacraments in the name of public health is a violation of the rights of God and the faithful, as well as a subordination of the Church's supreme law—the salvation of souls[19]—to the care of bodies.

Chapter 15: Fourth Commandment

HONOR THY FATHER AND THY MOTHER.

435. Whom does this commandment oblige us to honor?
All those who have legitimate authority over us, including parents, teachers, civic leaders, and pastors of the Church.

436. Are only subordinates required to keep this commandment?
No; it also entails the duties of superiors to their subordinates. As superiors have the right to exact obedience, they also hold the duty to command properly and in accord with the precepts of the Gospel.

437. Where does the authority of every legitimate earthly superior come from?
From God Himself. "Whoever resists authority," says St. Paul, "resists what God has appointed" (Rom 13:2).

438. Are we bound to obey even incompetent or wicked superiors?
Yes, except in orders that manifestly contradict natural or divine law. We express our love and submission to God by obeying even deficient earthly leaders, for it is to Him that all earthly obedience is ultimately directed.

Duties in the Family

439. What does *honor* mean, with regard to children and parents?
This word embraces all duties of *filial piety*: love, respect, obedience, and assistance.

440. How do we *love* our parents?
By truly willing their good, praying for them, and being interested in their well-being and helpful in their sufferings.

441. Who sins against the love we owe to our parents?
Those who: 1. Show them neglect or hostility; 2. Neglect their needs and legitimate interests; 3. Reveal their defects or calumniate them; 4. Provoke them or cause them undue sorrow; 5. Wish them evil.

442. How do we *respect* our parents?
By venerating them, showing outward signs of respect to their person and also to their will, to the extent that it is in conformity with right reason.

443. Who sins against the respect due to our parents?
Those who: 1. Threaten or strike them; 2. Insult or ridicule them; 3. Are ashamed of their misfortune or sickness; 4. Contradict or undermine them with scorn or bitterness.

444. How do children *obey* their parents?

By promptly and cheerfully doing all that they command; provided that this be lawful, honorable, consonant with good morals, in service of our salvation and the good government of the family.

445. Who sins against the obedience due to parents?

Those who: 1. Contemn and refuse to obey their legitimate orders; 2. Do not serve the good government and peace of the family.

446. Are there cases when children should not obey their parents?

Yes, if a parent's order is: 1. Opposed to natural law, or the commandments of God or His Church; 2. Unreasonably opposed to a child's calling to the priesthood or religious life; 3. Manifestly contrary to right reason, including the good of the family or child. In such cases, children should continue to show esteem and respect for their parents, with prompt obedience in all other lawful matters.

447. How do we *assist* our parents?

By kindly helping them in their corporal and spiritual necessities. For, next to God, we are indebted to them for our very lives and countless benefits.

448. How may we sin against the duty of assisting our parents?

If we: 1. Abandon them in their time of need, in sickness or old age; 2. Neglect to secure the last sacraments for them; 3. Obstruct or fail to fulfill their reasonable final wishes.

449. What rewards have been promised to those practicing filial piety?

To show the great importance of the fourth commandment, a long and happy life was promised to those who kept it, and those who did not were deemed accursed (see Ecclus 3:1–16).

450. What are the duties of parents to their children?

They owe them the duties of life, love, and education.

451. How should parents give *life* to their children?

To give life to their bodies and souls, parents should: 1. Maintain a marriage disposed to accept the gift of children from God; 2. Provide food, shelter, and clothing suitable to their state in life; 3. Give them access to Mass, the sacraments, and other means of grace; 4. Teach the prayers and truths of the Catholic Faith from the earliest possible age; indeed, a Catholic mother should transmit the Faith to her children, as it were, "with the mother's milk."

452. How should parents *love* their children?

With: 1. Supernatural love, rooted in Christian charity, referring all to God and seeking holiness above all; 2. Ordered love, affectionate and dutiful, without over-indulgence, so that the children will always respect and obey them; 3. Impartial love, shared alike among all the children.

453. **How should parents *educate* their children?**
By providing instruction, vigilance, correction, and good example, such that the children may live as good Christians, with means suitable to their condition in life.

454. **What are the educational duties of parents?**
They must train their children first and most importantly in the truths and duties of religion, "the one thing necessary" (Lk 10:42*); after this, training their character, so that they will grow in virtue and attain mature adulthood. Lastly, helping them acquire the knowledge, skills, and means to secure their own future provision.

455. **What is the proper and immediate end of Christian education?**
"Christian education takes in the whole aggregate of human life, physical and spiritual, intellectual and moral, individual, domestic and social, not with a view of reducing it in any way, but in order to elevate, regulate, and perfect it, in accordance with the example and teaching of Christ."[20]

456. **May parents enlist the aid of tutors or schools in instructing their children?**
Yes. However, as the primary educators of their children, parents remain responsible before God to ensure the integrity of any and all instruction that their children receive.

457. **May parents utilize schools that will likely harm their children's faith or morals?**
No. It would be sinful to send a child to any school where he is likely to lose his faith or morals due to the curricula, teachers, or peers (see Mt 18:7). Government schools are almost universally problematic in this regard, and even many nominally Catholic schools pose the same difficulty today. Parents must therefore exercise great care, and "strain every nerve to ward off such an outrage [as unchristian education], and to strive manfully to have and to hold exclusive authority to direct the education of their offspring, as is fitting, in a Christian manner, and first and foremost to keep them away from schools where there is risk of their drinking in the poison of impiety."[21]

458. **Does the state have an absolute right over children's education?**
No, because children belong to the family before owing allegiance to the state. "Paternal authority can be neither abolished nor absorbed by the state; for it has the same source as human life itself. 'The child belongs to the father' (ST, II-II, q. 10, a. 12, c.) and is, as it were, the continuation of the father's personality; and speaking strictly, the child takes its place in civil society, not of its own right, but in its quality as member of the family in which it is born."[22]

459. **Why has the Church repeatedly condemned a universal moral code of education?**
Because it signifies "a withdrawal of education from every sort of dependence on the divine law, ... as if there existed no Decalogue, no Gospel law, no law even of nature stamped by God on the heart of man, promulgated by right reason, and codified in positive revelation by God Himself in the Ten Commandments."[23]

460. What are the dangers of naturalistic sex education?

Naturalistic, secular sex education is not merely "instructive," but also exposes and invites children to sexual experience, thus directly seducing to sin. The Church has warned against this: "A very grave danger is that fervor which nowadays invades the field of education in that most delicate matter of purity of morals. Far too common is the error of those who with dangerous assurance and under an ugly term propagate a so-called 'sex-education,' falsely imagining they can forearm youths against the dangers of sensuality by means purely natural, such as a foolhardy initiation and precautionary instruction for all indiscriminately, even in public; and, worse still, by exposing them at an early age to the occasions, in order to accustom them, so it is argued, and as it were to harden them against such dangers."[24]

461. What is the basic error of those advocating for a naturalistic sexual education?

They fail to recognize "the inborn weakness of human nature, and the law of which the Apostle speaks, 'fighting against the law of the mind' (Rom 7:23)"; furthermore, they ignore the fact that, "particularly in young people, evil practices are the effect not so much of ignorance of intellect as of weakness of a will exposed to dangerous occasions, and unsupported by the means of grace."[25]

462. How should parents transmit a true Catholic sexual education to their children?

"It is of the highest importance that a good father, while discussing with his son a matter so delicate, should be well on his guard and not descend to details, nor refer to the various ways in which this infernal hydra destroys with its poison so large a portion of the world; otherwise it may happen that instead of extinguishing this fire, he unwittingly stirs or kindles it in the simple and tender heart of the child."[26]

463. How might *coeducation* (educating the sexes together) be harmful?

"False also and harmful to Christian education is the so-called method of 'coeducation.'... The Creator has ordained and disposed perfect union of the sexes only in matrimony, and, with varying degrees of contact, in the family and in society. Besides there is not in nature itself, which fashions the two quite different in organism, in temperament, in abilities, anything to suggest that there can be or ought to be promiscuity, and much less equality, in the training of the two sexes. These, in keeping with the wonderful designs of the Creator, are destined to complement each other in the family and in society, precisely because of their differences, which therefore ought to be maintained and encouraged during their years of formation, with the necessary distinction and corresponding separation, according to age and circumstances."[27]

464. When should coeducation especially be avoided?

"Particularly in the most delicate and decisive period of formation, that, namely, of adolescence; and in gymnastic exercises and deportment, special care must be had of Christian modesty in young women and girls, which is so gravely impaired by any kind of exhibition in public."[28]

465. **Does homeschooling or similar education methods make children out of touch with reality?**
This is a risk in any educational setting, and with care to socialize their children well, parents can avoid it. "Vigilance does not demand that young people be removed from the society in which they must live and save their souls; but that today more than ever they should be forewarned and forearmed as Christians against the seductions and the errors of the world, which ... is all 'concupiscence of the flesh, concupiscence of the eyes, and pride of life' (1 Jn 2:16*). Let them be what Tertullian wrote of the first Christians, and what Christians of all times ought to be: 'sharers in the possession of the world, not of its error' (*De idololatria*, chap. 14)."[29]

466. **Should mothers stay at home, rather than enter the workforce?**
Yes. Unless truly necessary for the basic sustenance of the family, mothers "should love to remain at home"[30]—especially during the first six years of a child's life, which are most critical for nurturing them and shaping their Christian character.

467. **How must parents maintain vigilance over their children?**
They must watch over the souls of their children as a precious gift confided to them by God, keeping them "unstained from the world" (Jas 1:27) and protecting them from whatever could pervert or corrupt them; especially immoral forms of media and bad companions.

468. **Is unguarded access to digital communication technologies harmful to children?**
Yes. Such tools—especially "social media" and personal devices with internet access—are generally designed to foster vicious curiosity; they impair the development of critical thought, interfere with memory retention, develop addiction to superficial pleasures, encourage materialism and consumerism, and circumvent the loving protection of parental authority. In short, they expose the child to a near and constant occasion of sin.

469. **Is vigilance alone sufficient for the moral education of children?**
No. Parents must also add positive encouragement and direction, as well as loving discipline and correction where needed, to confirm their own authority and train their children in virtue.

470. **What is the principal duty of parents in educating their children?**
Parents must above all set a good example for them, striving constantly to serve as a patient and caring model of Christian virtue and holiness.

Duties in Church and State

471. **What are the duties of the faithful toward their ecclesiastical superiors?**
Because ecclesiastical superiors are like spiritual fathers in the Church, the faithful owe them a sincere love, respect, obedience, and assistance, analogous to that of earthly fathers.

472. **What are the duties of the Church's pastors to the faithful?**
1. To instruct them in their duties and the truths of religion; 2. To administer the sacraments to them; 3. To pray for them and teach them to pray; 4. To set a good example; 5. To correct them when necessary; 6. To combat abuse and scandal; 7. To assist them in their spiritual necessities.

473. **May we ever correct our pastors or other ecclesiastical superiors?**
Yes. Not in the punitive mode of a superior, but rather, "the fraternal correction which is an act of charity is within the competency of everyone in respect of any person toward whom he is bound by charity."[31] Thus, St. Paul corrected St. Peter, the first pope (see Gal 2:11).

474. **When may a subordinate correct a superior?**
Whenever: 1. The matter is sufficiently grave, e.g., posing a clear danger to souls; 2. There is reasonable hope that the superior will heed the correction, and not become worse; 3. The correction is done with charity, gentleness, and respect, avoiding impudence and harshness; 4. Secret sins are first corrected in private, whereas public or scandalous sins should be denounced in public.[32]

475. **What are the duties of citizens toward civil authorities?**
They must: 1. Love their country, and particularly their local community; 2. Respect all civil authority; 3. Pray for those in public office; 4. Obey all just laws; 5. Contribute to the taxes of the state; 6. Exercise political rights conscientiously.

476. **What are the duties of civil authorities to those whom they govern?**
1. Make and enforce laws protecting the rights of citizens at all stages of life, from conception to natural death; 2. Serve the greatness and material prosperity of the country; 3. Appoint honest and capable officials; 4. Safeguard public safety; 5. Protect and promote public morality; 6. Defend and facilitate the mission of the Church.

477. **May we ever refuse obedience to civil or ecclesiastical authorities?**
Yes. As with all unjust laws, we may refuse obedience to any superior when they demand something opposed to natural or divine law, as grasped by our properly formed conscience.

478. **Must we comply with the prohibition of traditional Catholic liturgical rites?**
No. "What earlier generations held as sacred, remains sacred and great for us too, and it cannot be all of a sudden entirely forbidden or even considered harmful. It behooves all of us to preserve the riches which have developed in the Church's faith and prayer, and to give them their proper place."[33] The rites of venerable antiquity form a sacred and constitutive part of the common patrimony of the Church, and not even the highest ecclesiastical authority has power to proscribe them.[34]

479. **May the civil power prohibit Catholic worship in the interest of public health?**
No. States have power to issue general sanitary measures, which should be observed unless unreasonable. However, a general prohibition of Catholic worship

would exceed the bounds of the civil power, and violate the divine rights of God and His Church.

480. **Must we comply with civil mandates to undergo objectionable medical procedures?**
No. "Public magistrates have no direct power over the bodies of their subjects," and because the state exists for the welfare of citizens, "where no crime has taken place, ... [it] can never directly harm or tamper with the integrity of the body."[35]

481. **What if such procedures are intended to protect the health of the general population?**
Praiseworthy intentions notwithstanding, such initiatives are a form of medical violence and thus of tyranny. They may be justly opposed by citizens as such.

Chapter 16: Fifth Commandment

THOU SHALT NOT KILL.

482. **What does the fifth commandment forbid?**
All acts of murder, which unjustly destroy the life of the body or the soul.

483. **What acts of bodily murder are forbidden by this commandment?**
Homicide, suicide, abortion, and euthanasia. In addition, acts of unjust violence to bodily health or integrity, including sterilization and mutilation, and any acts of wrath or dissension that lead to murder.

484. **What analogous acts of "spiritual murder" are forbidden by this commandment?**
1. Scandal, whereby we lead another to sin—a kind of spiritual homicide; 2. Any mortal sin, whereby we destroy the life of grace in our own soul—a kind of spiritual suicide.

485. **Is it "murder" for us to use or kill animals?**
No. Animals have no inherent rights in themselves, and man has the right to use animals for some good purpose, e.g., work, food, leather, and so on. Creation is given to man's responsible use (see Gn 1:28), and Christ both "declared all foods clean" (Mk 7:19), and personally ate meat and fish.[36]

Homicide and Suicide

486. **What is *homicide*, or murder in the proper sense?**
It is the voluntary and unjust killing of another man.

487. **How grave is the sin of murder?**
It is among the gravest of sins against our neighbor: it assails the rights of God, who is the sole master of human life; it does an irreparable injustice to the victim and his family; it harms entire communities and undermines the social order.

488. **What forms of legalized murder have become all too common in many societies?**
1. *Abortion*, which intentionally destroys a child in the womb by chemical, surgical, or other means; 2. *Contraception*, which poses some temporary or permanent sterilizing obstacle to the conception of new life, and often causes abortion as well; 3. *Euthanasia*, which ends the life of the sick, handicapped, or elderly; 4. *In vitro fertilization* (IVF) methods, which inevitably lead to the destruction of cryopreserved (frozen) embryos; 5. *Political vengeance*, in which political prisoners and so-called "enemies of the state" are put in camps and even executed without due process of just laws.

489. **What demonstrates the close connection between contraception and abortion?**
This connection "is being demonstrated in an alarming way by the development of chemical products, intrauterine devices, and vaccines which, distributed with the same ease as contraceptives, really act as abortifacients in the very early stages of the development of the life of the new human being."[37]

490. **Does the Church infallibly teach that direct abortion is intrinsically evil?**
Yes, as it has always been taught by the ordinary and universal Magisterium: "Given such unanimity in the doctrinal and disciplinary tradition of the Church, Paul VI was able to declare that this tradition is unchanged and unchangeable (see Encyclical *Humanae Vitae*, 14). Therefore, by the authority which Christ conferred upon Peter and his Successors, in communion with the bishops—who ... albeit dispersed throughout the world, have shown unanimous agreement concerning this doctrine—I declare that direct abortion, that is, abortion willed as an end or as a means, always constitutes a grave moral disorder, since it is the deliberate killing of an innocent human being. This doctrine is based upon the natural law and upon the written word of God, is transmitted by the Church's Tradition, and taught by the ordinary and universal Magisterium."[38]

491. **What of those who commit sins of murder while claiming good intentions?**
The desire to limit suffering and remove inconvenience is increasingly common in materialistic societies, which have lost sight of the redemptive value of suffering. Even so, no claim of good intentions can ever justify murder, and those who commit it—whether by direct action or omission—are guilty of grave sin. The end does not justify the means (see Rom 3:8).

492. **May the suffering have recourse to medically-administered painkillers?**
Yes. Painkillers may be used to alleviate suffering, provided they are not used as a means to cause death.

493. **May ordinary care of the sick ever be legitimately discontinued?**
No. Even if death appears imminent, ordinary means of care should always be given to the suffering in our midst. In principle, this includes the obligation to provide medically-assisted nutrition and hydration for those who cannot eat or drink by themselves.

494. **Then are we obliged to keep ourselves or our loved ones physically alive at all costs?**
No. We need not undertake medical interventions that are *extraordinary*, i.e., dangerous or disproportionately burdensome when compared to their expected benefit. In this, we do not cause death, but only resign ourselves to its inevitability.[39] Such decisions must be made by the patient, or in their best interest by one legally entitled to do so.

495. **May vital organs be removed from someone declared clinically "brain dead"?**
No. Brain function alone is insufficient to determine true death. Removing vital organs from someone in such a state constitutes vivisection and medical homicide.

496. **What of healthcare workers who cooperate in any form of legalized murder?**
Depending on the degree of their cooperation, they may also be guilty of the grave sin of murder. If so, they must sincerely repent, find other employment, and make serious reparation for their sin.

497. **What of politicians who advocate for any form of legalized murder?**
They are complicit in grave sin, and may be publicly opposed. If they profess to be Catholic, they should be admonished by the Church's pastors, suitably punished in canon law if obstinate and unrepentant, and not admitted to Holy Communion until they have repented and repaired the scandal.[40]

498. **What other actions are likewise forbidden with respect to our neighbor?**
1. Inflicting bodily harm beyond legitimate self-defense; 2. Terrorism and other unjust psychological harm; 3. Production and distribution of food, drinks, or medical products harmful to health.

499. **What about medical products using fetal stem cells in production and testing?**
The development of such products cooperates in the abominable crimes of child-murder and organ theft, which currently drive the abortion and fetal industries. The knowing use of such products—e.g., abortion-tainted vaccines—involves the grave omission of a firm and public protest against such evils, rendering our principled rejection of them ineffective and unconvincing in practice; and conscious consumption of the products of these inhuman "industries" gives the appearance of complicity in these evils.

500. **What is the central moral problem with such products?**
However remote the original abortion, the creation and use of such abortion-tainted products continues to instrumentalize the bodies of murdered children, through cell lines once belonging to them.

501. **What kinds of sins are committed in the creation or use of such products?**
1. *Past sins*: abortion, vivisection, torture, child abuse, organ theft, depriving an infant of baptism and supernatural life; 2. *Present sins*: commodification of the human person, marketing and sale of stolen body parts; 3. *Future sins*: supporting the growth of an industry that thrives on heinous evils, encouraging further child-murder and

human experimentation (deriving new fetal cell lines, grafting human organs onto animals, artificial embryo creation for exploitation).

502. **Can the principle of "material and remote cooperation in evil" justify the use of such products?**
No, because of the obvious and proximate connection between the conscious consumer and the fetal industry. Even if medicines or vaccines used fetal stem cells in the remote past, this does not justify their licit use in the present, as the fetal industry continues to flourish and benefit from such horrendous evils—placing consumers in the de facto situation of supporting it. The Catholic who uses such products causes scandal by participating in a kind of objective "conspiracy against life."

503. **What about the principle of "double effect"?**
The principle of *double effect*—foreseeing two simultaneous effects from the same act: one undesired evil and one intended good—requires that our action itself be good, or at least morally neutral. While medicating to protect one's health is a moral good in the abstract, using an *abortion-tainted product* to do so is wrong in itself, vitiated by the circumstance of its creation: it came directly from the abuse and murder of children, and may even contain remnants of their tiny bodies. Therefore, the principle does not apply.

504. **Has the Magisterium categorically and uncompromisingly condemned any use of fetal tissues of murdered unborn children?**
Yes. "The use of human embryos or fetuses as an object of experimentation constitutes a crime against their dignity as human beings who have a right to the same respect owed to a child once born, just as to every person. This moral condemnation also regards procedures that exploit living human embryos and fetuses—sometimes specifically 'produced' for this purpose by in vitro fertilization—either to be used as 'biological material' or as providers of organs or tissue for transplants in the treatment of certain diseases. The killing of innocent human creatures, even if carried out to help others, constitutes an absolutely unacceptable act."[41]

505. **What is *suicide*, or self-murder?**
The act by which a person voluntarily ends his own life.

506. **Is suicide a grave sin?**
Yes. It is as serious as murder, and for the same reasons.

507. **May we ever act in a way that could foreseeably lead to our own death?**
Yes, provided that our action is: 1. Not evil in itself; 2. Not intended to cause our own death; 3. Undertaken for a very grave reason—e.g., risking death by performing good works in times of plague, war, natural disaster, etc.

508. **Besides suicide, what other actions are forbidden with respect to ourselves?**
1. Amputation or mutilation of our bodies, unless deemed medically necessary to preserve our life; 2. Needless privation or excessive labor that leads to loss of health;

3. Mortification so excessive as to permanently and gravely harm our health, or render the performance of duties impossible.

509. **Is it permissible to undergo medical treatments designed to contradict our biological sex?**
No. Being contrary to natural and divine law, it is gravely sinful to alter one's body with chemicals or mutilation to express a different bodily sex than that which has been given by God.

510. **What of the felt need to "self-identify" as a different sex than that given by God?**
The causes of such feelings are many and complex, e.g., social conditioning, trauma, mental illness, etc., but ultimately represent a grave delusion. To act on them would signify a kind of revolt against the wise and God-given order of creation. Remedy may therefore be sought in counseling and other licit means that help accept and live the truth of our God-given sex as expressed in our natural body.

511. **Should the various movements of "sexual identity" innovation therefore be opposed?**
Yes. Any initiatives that assist or encourage men to "identify" as women or vice versa by chemicals, surgery, attire, or simple assertion — or that claim the civil authority has a right or duty to act as if this were possible or legitimate — must all be firmly rejected and consistently opposed at all levels of society.

512. **What do all such movements have in common?**
A brazen rebellion against reality and God's wise, creating will — a rejection of nature and nature's God, who has ordained the biological sex of each person and ordered it to complementarity and procreation. As such, these movements beget widespread confusion about reality itself, and pose a grave threat to the civil order of nations and the salvation of souls.

Legitimate Killing

513. **May a man ever kill legitimately, without being guilty of the sin of murder?**
Yes. Through his own voluntary actions, an individual may waive his right to life when: 1. The common good of *social order* is justly enforced by lawful authorities, as in the execution of criminals; 2. *Legitimate defense* is undertaken, as in just warfare or self-defense.

514. **When does society have the right to inflict the death penalty?**
The lawfully constituted public authority may put proven criminals to death for the most serious crimes when this is necessary to maintain social order in repairing injustice, protecting the innocent, deterring further crime, and summoning the criminal to true repentance and atonement.

515. From whom do public authorities hold the right to execute criminals?
From God Himself, the sole master of life and death, whose justice the public authorities represent in society: "The authority does not bear the sword in vain" (Rom 13:4).

516. What is *war*?
An ongoing conflict in which two or more nations or parties contend by violence to maintain their rights, acquire property and influence, or reestablish public order.

517. What conditions are necessary to render a war truly just?
The war must: 1. Be a last resort; 2. Be undertaken only in response to external aggression and to prevent certain, grave, and lasting damage; 3. Pose some prospect of success; 4. Not produce worse evils than those present.

518. What are the rights of individual soldiers under the fifth commandment?
In a just war, soldiers have the right to stop their foes with lethal force while sparing non-combatants. If the war is clearly unjust, they do not possess this right. If there is any doubt, one may defer to his superior officer as far as conscience permits.

519. May atomic weapons be justly used?
No, for the damage they cause is so extensive and indiscriminate, and with such long-term effects on the natural world, that it cannot avoid harming the innocent.

520. What are the rights of a private individual under the fifth commandment?
He may harm or kill an unjust aggressor in order to defend his life or that of his neighbor, provided he does not use force in excess of what is required to neutralize the threat.

521. What conditions are required for a person to protect himself with lethal force?
He must: 1. Believe that there is a clear and present danger of death; 2. Use deadly force only as a last resort.

522. Is it therefore morally permissible for individuals to make, keep, and use firearms?
Yes. Man has the right to own and use the tools of a legitimate self-defense, particularly in the face of disproportionate threats, e.g., mob violence, terrorism, etc.

523. Is everyone obliged to defend his neighbor against an unjust aggressor?
No. Although such defense may be praiseworthy, we are only obliged to do so if we have an express duty to protect the other's life (e.g., parents for their children, safety officers for their community); and not everyone is properly equipped or skilled to offer reasonable defense in the face of serious threats.

Chapter 17: Sixth and Ninth Commandments

Thou shalt not commit adultery.
Thou shalt not covet thy neighbor's wife.

524. What duty do these two commandments require?
They require the virtue of *chastity*, and forbid all sins opposed to this virtue.

525. What is chastity?
The moral virtue which leads us to abstain from disordered desire for sexual pleasure or disordered use of the sexual faculties. "Nothing is beautiful but what is pure,
and the purity of men is chastity. Chastity is called honesty and the possession of
it honor. It is also called integrity and its opposite corruption. In short, it has its
peculiar glory of being the fair, unspotted virtue of both soul and body."[42]

526. Is chastity an obligatory virtue?
Yes. As a natural virtue, it fosters self-mastery and subjects the passions to our reason
and will, which is necessary for being a mature, integrated, selfless, happy person,
and for the prosperity of the family and peace in society. As a supernatural virtue,
it maintains our dignity as adopted children of God, members of Jesus Christ, and
temples of the Holy Spirit.

527. What are the consequences of weakening the virtue of chastity?
Although all vice is a sort of slavery to sin ("everyone who commits sin is a slave to
sin" [Jn 8:34]), unchastity is a particularly powerful form of self-centered slavery. "To
the degree that a person weakens chastity, his or her love becomes more and more
selfish, that is, satisfying a desire for pleasure and no longer self-giving."[43]

528. What are the three forms of chastity?
1. *Conjugal* chastity, in which married couples use the sexual faculty according to
God's design; 2. Chastity of *widowhood*, in which complete abstinence from sexual
relations (also called *continence*) is practiced after the death of a spouse; 3. *Virginal*
chastity, or lifelong continence.

529. How is fidelity related to chastity?
Fidelity is the virtue by which a person remains faithful to the vows or promises
he has made, especially regarding the steadfast commitment of spousal chastity, or
religious vows by which a person is dedicated to a stable state of life blessed by God.

Sins against Chastity

530. How may we sin against chastity?
Exteriorly, by violating the sixth commandment; or *interiorly*, by violating the ninth.

531. What constitutes an exterior sin against chastity?
1. Lustful actions and touches, especially any use of the sexual faculties outside of
marriage; 2. Lustful speech or songs; 3. Lustful looks.

532. **What constitutes an interior sin against chastity?**
1. Any lustful thought, when we intentionally dwell on it and take pleasure in it;
2. The desire or determination to later engage in a lustful thought or act.

533. **What are the chief exterior sins against chastity?**
1. *Fornication*, sexual relations between the unmarried; 2. *Adultery*, sexual relations when one or both parties are married to someone else; 3. *Prostitution*, the sale of sexual acts as a commodity; 4. *Concubinage* or *cohabitation*, the quasi-regular arrangement of sexual intimacy among the unmarried; 5. *Rape*, the forced sexual violation of another; 6. *Pornography*, the creation, distribution, or use of materials designed to arouse lust; 7. Sexual acts *contrary to the natural order*, including: *Contraception*, any deliberate frustration of fertility in the conjugal act; *Sodomy*, sexual relations between persons of the same sex, also called homosexual or lesbian (between women) acts; *Masturbation*, erotic stimulation of one's own genital organs for sexual self-gratification; *Pederasty*, sexual relations between an adult man and a pubescent or adolescent boy; *Pedophilia*, sexual relations between an adult and a child (either boy or girl); *Bestiality*, sexual relations between a human being and an animal.

534. **Why is *contraception* contrary to nature and intrinsically evil?**
"No reason, however grave, may be put forward by which anything intrinsically against nature may become conformable to nature and morally good. Since, therefore, the conjugal act is destined primarily by nature for the begetting of children, those who in exercising it deliberately frustrate its natural power and purpose sin against nature and commit a deed which is shameful and intrinsically vicious."[44]

535. **Can contraceptive conjugal acts be justified as "lesser evils" within marriage?**
No. "It is not valid to argue, as a justification for sexual intercourse which is deliberately contraceptive, that a lesser evil is to be preferred to a greater one, or that such intercourse would merge with procreative acts of past and future to form a single entity, and so be qualified by exactly the same moral goodness as these. Though it is true that sometimes it is lawful to tolerate a lesser moral evil in order to avoid a greater evil or in order to promote a greater good, it is never lawful, even for the gravest reasons, to do evil that good may come of it (see Rom 3:8)—in other words, to intend directly something which of its very nature contradicts the moral order, and which must therefore be judged unworthy of man, even though the intention is to protect or promote the welfare of an individual, of a family or of society in general. Consequently, it is a serious error to think that a whole married life of otherwise normal relations can justify sexual intercourse which is deliberately contraceptive and so intrinsically wrong."[45]

536. **Is *masturbation* (also called "self-abuse" and "onanism") intrinsically evil?**
Yes. "Masturbation is an intrinsically and seriously disordered act. The main reason is that, whatever the motive for acting this way, the deliberate use of the sexual faculty outside normal conjugal relations essentially contradicts the finality of the faculty."[46]

537. **What are the main causes of the spread in practice of masturbation?**
"Linked with man's innate weakness following original sin," this practice is also due to "the loss of a sense of God, with the corruption of morals engendered by the commercialization of vice, with the unrestrained licentiousness of public entertainment and publications, as well as with the neglect of modesty, which is the guardian of chastity."[47]

538. **What are the specific evils of pornography?**
It induces creators, distributors, and consumers to use others as mere "objects" for selfish, lustful gratification, and teaches people who appear in pornographic images to commodify themselves, particularly in matters that should remain hidden by modesty and protected within marriage. Since pornography attacks sexual desire and the conjugal act itself, it wages war on marriage.

539. **Are all exterior acts against chastity gravely sinful in themselves?**
Yes. All are mortal sins, and those who commit them must repent if they wish to attain the eternal reward of heaven, for "nothing unclean will enter" (Apoc 21:27). "Neither the fornicators, ... nor adulterers, ... nor men who practice homosexuality ... will inherit the kingdom of God" (1 Cor 6:9–10*).

540. **What of Catholics who are publicly known to commit such sins?**
Catholics engaged in open adultery, cohabitation, pornography, homosexual lifestyle, or political activism for such causes (e.g., the so-called "LGBTQ+ agenda"), must be regarded as public sinners, and until they have repented and been reconciled to the Church, they must be denied Holy Communion by any minister of the sacrament (see Mt 18:17).[48]

541. **Isn't this discipline overly harsh toward sinners, whom Our Lord invites us to love?**
No. Authentic love is inseparable from truth, and the Church is obliged to honor Our Lord in the Eucharist and save the public sinner from eating and drinking judgment unto himself (see 1 Cor 11:29).

542. **What are the effects of sins against chastity on our intellect, will, and exterior behavior?**
Such sins: 1. *Darken the intellect*, impairing right reason, fostering dishonesty and dissipation; 2. *Weaken the will*, nurturing vanity, effeminacy, excessive attachment to earthly goods, inconstancy, and addiction; 3. *Beget violence*, e.g., predation, rape, human trafficking, and murder (especially of the unborn).[49]

543. **Do sins against chastity also cause uniquely grave disorder in the passions?**
Yes. Especially when such sins become habitual, the passions can become so unruly as to make the most shameful acts appear desirable. "God gave them up in the lusts of their hearts to impurity, ... because they exchanged the truth about God for a lie" (Rom 1:24–25).

Preserving Chastity

544. What are the principal means of preserving chastity?
Prayer, modesty, increased love for spiritual things, and vigilance, by which we remove the internal and external occasions of lust.

545. What helpful advice do we have for preserving chastity?
That of St. Francis de Sales: "Seek out good and pure men, read and ponder holy things; for the word of God is pure, and it will make those pure who study it: wherefore David likens it to gold and precious stones [see Ps 118:127*]. Always abide close to Jesus Christ Crucified, both spiritually in meditation and actually in Holy Communion; for ... if you rest your heart upon our dear Lord, the very Lamb, pure and immaculate, you will find that soon both heart and soul will be purified of all spot or stain."[50]

546. What are some external occasions of lust to be on special guard against?
1. Companions who hold impure conversation; 2. Gatherings of men with women in imprudent settings; 3. Contemporary film, music, videos, and other media that glorify sexual gratification; 4. Pornography; 5. Idle time spent on the internet or television.

547. Should we especially pray not to be led into temptation against chastity?
Yes. With much of contemporary civilization awash in sexual immorality of various kinds, such prayer is especially important in obtaining for us the graces necessary to remain chaste.

548. What forms of prayer are most advisable for maintaining chastity?
1. Eucharistic adoration, whereby our eyes are fixed on their proper divine object; 2. Devotion to Mary, Immaculate Queen of Virgins; 3. Regular practice of the presence of God; 4. Frequent and humble confession, which strengthens the virtues contrary to the sins confessed; 5. Frequent and devout reception of Holy Communion, which weakens the habit of evil and strengthens virtue; 6. The daily examination of conscience; 7. Corporal mortifications;[51] 8. Use of sacramentals like holy water and holy salt, to purify our house of tempting spirits.

Chapter 18: Seventh and Tenth Commandments

Thou shalt not steal.
Thou shalt not covet thy neighbor's goods.

549. What is the shared aim of these two commandments?
Both of them command a thorough respect for the property of others, and their right to possess it.

550. What does the seventh commandment require?
It forbids us from unjustly taking the property of others, and obliges us to repair any harm we have done.

551. What does the tenth commandment require?
It forbids us from harboring jealousy at the goods of our neighbor, and all unjust interior desire for the property of others.

552. Does man have a right to property?
Yes. The right to acquire, possess, and use things (also called *ownership*) is inscribed in nature and confirmed by revelation, and was maintained in the civil laws of all nations prior to the twentieth century.

553. Are political systems that deny the right to private property evil in themselves?
Yes. Be it named *socialism*, *communism*, or otherwise, any system that denies the basic right to property "is in opposition both to reason and to divine revelation"[52] and "intrinsically perverse."[53]

554. Where do such systems exist today?
Spreading first from the communist regime of the Soviet Union in 1917, several countries now employ socialist and neo-Marxist models of government.

555. Are Catholics permitted to collaborate with communism?
No. "No one who would save Christian civilization may collaborate with it in any undertaking whatsoever. Those who permit themselves to be deceived into lending their aid toward the triumph of communism in their own country, will be the first to fall victims of their error."[54]

556. Did the Church forbid Catholics to propagate communism?
Yes. Pope Pius XII decreed in 1949: "All those who profess the materialist and anti-Christian doctrine of communists, and particularly those who defend and propagate it freely and knowingly, incur ipso facto excommunication specially reserved for the Holy See."[55]

557. How may the ideals of communism and socialism be easily recognized?
They may be found anywhere there is advocacy for the dissolution of privacy, property rights, the natural family, physical currencies, and personal ownership of the means of production.

558. What principle of Catholic social doctrine is a sure safeguard against these false ideals?
Subsidiarity, or decision-making at the lowest and most local level possible. "Every social activity ought of its very nature to help the members of the body social, and never destroy or absorb them."[56]

559. What emerging geopolitical movements are especially opposed to subsidiarity?
1. *Globalism*, which advocates for open borders and the dissolution of individual states; 2. *Technocracy*, which would subjugate private rights and liberties through socioeconomic systems entirely dependent on technological gateways controlled by a small number.

Sins against Property

560. How may we sin against the seventh commandment?
We harm the property of others by: 1. Theft; 2. Unjust retention; 3. Unjust damage.

561. What is *theft* or *stealing*?
Unjustly taking something belonging to our neighbor, with the intention of depriving the rightful owner of it permanently.

562. What are the different kinds of theft?
Larceny, robbery, fraud, usurpation, usury, extortion, and embezzlement.

563. What is *larceny*?
Secret theft, accomplished by stealth or subterfuge; e.g., shoplifting, embezzlement, paid work done poorly.

564. What is *robbery*?
Open theft, accomplished by violence or abuse of power; e.g., brigandage, unjust confiscation.

565. What is *fraud* or *cheating*?
Theft by knowingly misrepresenting or concealing a fact so that our neighbor will act to his own detriment; e.g., selling defective or imaginary goods to believing customers.

566. What is *usurpation*?
Theft of another's position, office, or authority; e.g., seizing a civil or ecclesiastical position by fraud or force.

567. What is *usury*?
Theft by exacting interest on a loan without legitimate title, or in excess of just proportion.

568. Are all loans at interest usurious, and therefore evil in themselves?
No. A *loan* is a contract by which we deliver something to another, on the condition that the other will restore the thing or its equivalent. Interest may be justifiable in proportion to the resulting loss and risk undertaken.

569. **What is *extortion*?**
Theft by administrators or officials who use their authority to obtain some end outside of their proper authority by force or coercion; e.g., politicians who use blackmail to remain in power, or levy excessive taxes.

570. **What is *embezzlement*?**
Theft by fraudulently taking personal property with which one has been entrusted as a fiduciary; e.g., state officials taking public funds, or a caretaker taking money from an incapacitated or elderly person.

571. **What is *unjust retention*?**
Keeping the property of another without sufficient reason.

572. **How may we retain the property of another unjustly?**
If we: 1. Do not return something on loan, or keep stolen goods; 2. Keep something we found, without seeking its rightful owner; 3. Keep a thing after learning its rightful owner; 4. Knowingly profit by a computation error; 5. Render a false account of property we administer; 6. Do not comply with the clauses of a will; 7. Do not pay just wages; 8. Do not pay our debts in a timely manner; 9. Do not keep our promises.

573. **What is *unjust damage*?**
Causing the loss or injury of another's goods of body or soul through malice or culpable imprudence.

574. **How may we become guilty of unjust damage?**
If we: 1. Directly injure public or private property; 2. Allow another's property to be ruined when left in our care; 3. Damage another's reputation by spreading ill-founded or calumnious reports; 4. Fail to check violence or injustice while in public office; 5. Lose private or public goods through ignorance or negligence; 6. Compose or approve defective legal documents; 7. Knowingly risk the health of others through harmful medical practice or regulations.

Reparation for Theft

575. **What does the seventh commandment order us to do?**
It orders us to make *restitution*. We are obliged by natural and divine law to: 1. Return to another what belongs to him; 2. Repair the wrong that we have done to our neighbor.

576. **When should such restitution be made?**
As soon as possible. The longer we delay in making it, the heavier the loss we inflict upon the rightful owner, and the greater our risk of dying in the debt of sin.

577. **What are the causes that suspend or remove our duty to make restitution?**
1. Physical impossibility, as long as this persists; 2. Moral impossibility, as when full restitution would reduce us to extreme poverty or irreparable grave harm;

3. Alternative legal arrangement with the creditor; 4. Canceling of our debt by the creditor; 5. Secret compensation.

Covetousness

578. **What does the tenth commandment forbid?**
After having forbidden us by the seventh commandment to take and keep the property of others, God forbids us by the tenth commandment to *covet* or unjustly desire the same.

579. **Why do we say that coveting is an *unjust* desire?**
Because we may justly desire the property of others, as whenever our intended means for obtaining it is legitimate, e.g., fair sale or contract.

580. **How may we become guilty of covetousness?**
If we: 1. Intend to steal or cause some loss to our neighbor, even if we do not actually perform such acts; 2. Wish for the misfortune or death of another so as to inherit his property; 3. Desire the spread of social disorder in order to become rich.

581. **What sort of sin is committed by covetousness?**
A sin of the same gravity as the intended theft; except that there is no obligation to make restitution for covetousness if the desire has not been acted upon.

582. **What is *jealousy*?**
Whereas covetousness is an unjust desire for another's property, jealousy is an unjust desire for another's quality, skill, relationship, and so on; e.g., a person might be jealous of another's beauty, intelligence, or friendship.

583. **Is jealousy a sin?**
Yes. Although the goodness of another can rightly spur us to greater excellence by God's grace, we should be content with what talents, gifts, and graces are given to us, not striving to change what cannot be changed within God's providence.

Chapter 19: Eighth Commandment
THOU SHALT NOT BEAR FALSE WITNESS AGAINST THY NEIGHBOR.

584. **What does the eighth commandment require?**
It requires perfect respect for the truth. It directly forbids all lying, and indirectly forbids anything that could unjustly injure our neighbor's reputation or honor.

585. **Have sins against this commandment become very widespread in our time?**
Yes. Especially following the Second World War, the use of media to distort facts, sway public opinion, and impose false perceptions of reality (e.g., propaganda) has ensnared many in habitual sins against this commandment.

Lying

586. What is a *lie*?
An expression or outward sign by which we convey something contrary to what we think is true, for the purpose of deceiving our neighbor.

587. Is every kind of lie forbidden?
Yes, because every lie violates the natural purpose of speech. They are the off-spring of Satan, "the father of lies" (Jn 8:44), offensive to Christ, who is "the truth" (Jn 14:6), and contrary to the divine "Spirit of truth" (Jn 14:17).

588. May we tell a lie to defend our life, property, or some other good?
No. This is the error of *consequentialism*. We may never "do evil so that good may come" (Rom 3:8). However, we may "hide the truth prudently"[57] for a just cause, as in the use of mental reservation or equivocation.

589. What is mental reservation?
Wide mental reservation is saying what is true, but withholding part of what is in our mind, aware that the hearer could grasp our full meaning in the particular circumstances. *Strict mental reservation* is saying what is outwardly false, but true only by some unspoken (mental) qualification unknown to the hearer.

590. Is strict mental reservation forbidden?
Yes, because it is a lie: our words would not correspond to the truth, and it is done with the purpose to deceive.

591. What is *equivocation*?
Using words that have a double meaning.

592. How do wide mental reservations and equivocations differ from outright lies?
In these we tell no objective falsehood, the full truth is discoverable, and we do not directly intend to deceive; we merely permit our listener to deceive himself, particularly if he has no right to the truth, or if knowing it could cause foreseeable harm.

593. In what cases must reservation or equivocation never be used?
1. Whenever we are bound to profess our faith; 2. In sacramental confession; 3. In contracts.

594. What is *perjury* or a *false oath*?
A lie in which we call God to witness the truth of what we say, to more effectively deceive. Perjury is always a mortal sin.

595. What is *false testimony*?
A lie made in a court of law or before a notary.

596. Are we obliged to offer testimony in a court of law?
Yes; when required to do so by the proper authority, we are bound to tell the truth and answer simply according to our conscience.

597. **Who is exempt from giving testimony in a court of justice?**
1. Those bound to sacramental or professional secrecy, as priests under the seal of the confessional; 2. Immediate family of the accused; 3. Those under pledged secrecy, except in matters of serious crimes against the Church or state.

598. **Is false testimony a serious sin?**
Yes. It is a sin against: 1. Truth itself; 2. Justice; 3. Religion, for it usually includes perjury; 4. Charity; 5. Lawful obedience.

599. **What is a false witness bound to do?**
He must: 1. Retract his false testimony, even in spite of grave inconvenience; 2. Repair the injury caused by his crime.

Other Sins against Truth

600. **Is counterfeiting also a sin of false testimony?**
Yes. *Counterfeiting* or *forgery*, by which false legal documents are created or approved, is a sin of false testimony.

601. **What other sins are committed against the truth?**
1. *Hypocrisy*, when we adopt the appearance of virtue to win esteem; 2. *Flattery*, false or exaggerated praise; 3. *Boastfulness*, exaggerating qualities we have or claiming those we don't; 4. *Dissimulation*, concealing the truth for an evil end; 5. *Indiscretion*, the revelation of truths which should be kept secret.

602. **What is our *reputation*?**
The good opinion that the public has of us, which is among our most precious earthly possessions: "A good name is to be chosen rather than great riches" (Prv 22:1).

603. **How may we sin against the reputation of our neighbor?**
Exteriorly by defamation, and *interiorly* by rash judgment and suspicion.

604. **What is *defamation*?**
Malicious or groundless injury done to our neighbor's reputation, whether by calumny or detraction.

605. **What is *calumny* or *slander*?**
Maliciously misrepresenting our neighbor's words or actions, or accusing him of faults that he has not committed, in order to injure his reputation.

606. **What is a calumniator obliged to do?**
He must: 1. Retract his misrepresentations or lies, even though it is inconvenient; 2. Repair any losses his neighbor may have sustained because of the calumny.

607. **What is *detraction* or *backbiting*?**
Saying things about someone or something to make the person or thing seem less good than it actually is, or the unjust revelation of another's hidden sin or secret fault.

608. **What is a detractor obliged to do?**
He must: 1. Restore, as much as possible, the reputation that he has injured; 2. Repair any other harm occasioned by his remarks.

609. **May we ever justly reveal another's hidden sins or faults?**
Yes. Aside from cases protected by the seal of the confessional, we may be obliged to reveal secret faults when they endanger us, our neighbor, the local community, or the broader good of the Church or state. To reveal faults in these instances are not acts of detraction, but of justice and charity.

610. **What is *rash judgment*?**
An act of the mind by which we quickly condemn our neighbor's person or actions as evil, without sufficient reason or justification.

611. **What is *rash suspicion*?**
A general and groundless inclination to believe the worst about our neighbor.

612. **What is the safest course in forming an opinion about our neighbor?**
We must begin by judging only the external acts of our neighbor, weighing them against the truth and assuming the best about his actions, at least when there is no danger of harming a third party. We must leave the judgment of his intentions and the state of his soul to God, who alone "searches the heart" (Rom 8:27).

Chapter 20: First Precept of the Church

To assist at Mass on Sundays and holy days of obligation.

Assisting at Mass

613. **What does the first precept of the Church require of us?**
It orders all the faithful who have the use of reason and are not justly impeded, to assist at the Holy Sacrifice of the Mass on Sundays and holy days of obligation.

614. **Why does the Church order the faithful to attend Mass?**
In order to: 1. Determine the specific way we must observe the third commandment of worshipping God; 2. Ensure that we worship as a community, and not merely individually; 3. Further motivate the faithful to participate in the sacrifice of the Cross.

615. **Is assisting at Mass the greatest act of worship?**
Yes. There is no religious act more agreeable to God and no prayer more efficacious, for it is the divine sacrifice and prayer of Jesus Christ together with the Church, His Bride and Mystical Body.

616. **What is a *holy day of obligation*?**
A solemnity established by the Church for the purpose of celebrating the mysteries of religion or honoring the angels and saints.

617. **Why were holy days of obligation instituted?**
Primarily for the honor and glory of God; secondarily for the sanctification, edification, and instruction of the faithful.

618. **What are the different holy days of obligation?**
In addition to all Sundays (including Easter, Pentecost, and Trinity Sunday), the Church's current law obliges us to assist at the feasts of Christmas, Epiphany, Ascension, Corpus Christi, Mary the Mother of God, Immaculate Conception, Assumption, St. Joseph, Peter and Paul, and All Saints. The exact days may vary in a given country,[58] and even when a certain major feast is not obligatory, Catholics should do their utmost to attend Mass that day, to honor God and His holy ones.

619. **How should we sanctify holy days of obligation?**
In the same way as Sundays, by abstaining from servile work and attending Mass. It is also desirable to approach the sacraments on these days, practice additional prayer, and perform works of piety or charity.

Chapter 21: Second Precept of the Church

To fast and abstain on the days appointed.

Fasting and Abstinence

620. **What does the second precept of the Church require of us?**
It orders the faithful to fast and to abstain from flesh meat on certain days of the year.

621. **What is *fasting*?**
Denying ourselves by limiting the quantity of food we eat in a day, in imitation of the One who fasted at the beginning of His public mission on earth (see Mt 4:1–11). According to the ancient and constant tradition of the Church, fasting consists in taking only one meal per day; but it does not forbid that a little bit of food be taken in the morning and in the evening.[59]

622. **What is *abstinence*?**
Denying ourselves a certain kind of food—flesh meat—in imitation of the One who offered His flesh for us on the Cross. Non-canonical abstinence could involve the denial of other kinds of food, especially that which pleases us most.

623. **By the current law of the Church, who must fast and who must abstain?**
Fasting generally binds adults until their sixtieth year to eat only one full meal, with two additional *collations* (snacks) permitted.[60] *Abstinence* generally binds those fourteen and older to eat no flesh meat. The application of both laws can vary from region to region.

624. **What are the days of fasting and abstinence in the Church?**
According to the custom codified in 1917, *abstinence* was observed on every Friday of the year, and *fasting* on all days of Lent. Both *fasting and abstinence* were kept on Ash Wednesday, every Friday and Saturday of Lent, all Ember Days, and the vigils of Pentecost, Assumption, All Saints, and Christmas. In current law, fasting and abstinence are required at least on Ash Wednesday and Good Friday, with abstinence further required on all Fridays of the year (unless a solemnity occurs on a Friday).[61]

625. **Before 1917, how did the Church practice fasting and abstinence?**
Whenever fasting was observed, abstinence was as well. The Lenten fast included abstinence from all *lacticinia* (Latin "milk products"), which included butter, cheese, eggs,[62] and all animal products. Abstinence from lacticinia and animal products was even kept on Sundays of Lent, though fasting was not practiced on Sundays. Usually no food was eaten at all on Ash Wednesday or Good Friday, and the Wednesdays and Fridays of Advent were also fast days.

626. **What novelties were introduced in 1917?**
Eggs and lacticinia (and all animal products but flesh meat) became universally permitted on fasting days, and a holy day of obligation outside of Lent was made to overrule the requirement of Friday abstinence. Before 1917, the only day that would automatically abrogate the requirement of Friday abstinence was Christmas Day.

627. **Why does the Church order us to fast and abstain?**
In order to: 1. Determine, at least in some measure, the divine command to do penance (see Lk 13:3); 2. Further motivate the faithful to develop the virtue of holy temperance; 3. Manifest the communal character of penance—the entire Church Militant is fasting, just as God ordered communal fasting and penance in the Old Testament (see Jon 3:7–8).

628. **What is *Lent*?**
Also called *Quadragesima* (Latin "fortieth"), it is the season of fasting that lasts forty days (except Sundays), beginning on Ash Wednesday and ending after the Easter Vigil.

629. **Why was Lent established?**
Since the time of the apostles, Lent has been observed in one form or another: 1. To honor and imitate the fast of Our Lord; 2. To pay a tithe of our year to God; 3. To participate both spiritually and corporally in the sufferings of the Lord; 4. To prepare and be purified by penance for a worthy celebration of Easter, the greatest of all feasts.[63]

630. **What is the spiritual meaning of Lent and fasting?**
"The observance of Lent is the very badge of Christian warfare. By it we prove ourselves not to be enemies of Christ. By it we avert the scourges of divine justice.

By it we gain strength against the princes of darkness, for it shields us with heavenly help. Should men grow remiss in their observance of Lent, it would be a detriment to God's glory, a disgrace to the Catholic religion, and a danger to Christian souls. Neither can it be doubted that such negligence would become the source of misery to the world, of public calamity, and of private woe."[64]

631. **What other pious works are especially proper during Lent?**
Other penitential practices, almsgiving, the works of mercy, and prayer, e.g., the Stations of the Cross.

632. **Is it enough to merely practice external penance?**
No. If we wish to grow in sanctity, we must also adopt a Catholic *spirit of penance*, mortifying our senses and humbling ourselves interiorly before God.

633. **What causes can exempt us from the law of fasting or abstinence?**
Physical and moral impossibility exempts from this law. This generally includes the sick, pregnant and nursing mothers, and those prevented by duty or arduous labor.

634. **Who has the power to dispense from the law of fasting or abstinence?**
1. The pope, who can dispense the entire Church; 2. Bishops, who can dispense members of their diocese; 3. Parish priests, who can dispense members of their parish; 4. Religious superiors, who can dispense members of their institute.

635. **Are fasting and abstinence very beneficial for the soul?**
Yes, as they: 1. Expiate sin and appease God's justice; 2. Subdue unruly passions and keep us from sin; 3. Elevate the heart to God and supernatural realities; 4. Merit special graces; 5. Strengthen us to persevere in doing good; 6. Detach us from worldly things and inflame our love for heavenly things.

636. **Are fasting and abstinence also very beneficial for the body?**
Yes. They aid the function of bodily systems and ward off diseases caused by intemperance. Common scientific opinion further claims that they improve blood sugar control, decrease inflammation, and enhance heart health.

Chapter 22: Third and Fourth Precepts of the Church

To confess at least once a year.
To receive the Holy Eucharist at least once a year, at Easter time.

Yearly Confession

637. **What does the third precept of the Church require of us?**
It orders all the faithful who have the use of reason to confess their sins at least once a year, if they have mortal sins to confess. Of course, we should always confess mortal sins immediately, lest we die in this state.[65]

638. **At what age is a person obliged to go to confession?**
Whenever he has attained the use of reason, i.e., when he can distinguish between good and evil and freely choose between them.

639. **Should we only confess our sins once a year?**
No. If we wish to be saved, we must make a good confession immediately after falling into any grave sin, and it is desirable to confess even venial sins monthly, for the further health of our soul.

Easter Communion

640. **What does the fourth precept of the Church require of us?**
It orders all the faithful with the use of reason to receive Holy Communion at least once a year, at Easter time.

641. **Is this precept also a matter of divine law?**
Yes. Our Lord has ordered us to receive the Blessed Sacrament: "Unless you eat the flesh of the Son of Man and drink His blood, you have no life in you" (Jn 6:53).

642. **At what age is a person obliged to receive Holy Communion?**
Whenever he has attained some use of reason, being able to distinguish the Sacrament from common food, and has a sincere desire to receive the Lord.[66]

643. **What has the Church prescribed for giving First Communion to children?**
"The age of discretion for receiving Holy Communion is that at which the child knows the difference between the Eucharistic Bread and ordinary, material bread, and can therefore approach the altar with proper devotion. Perfect knowledge of the things of faith, therefore, is not required, for an elementary knowledge suffices—some knowledge (*aliqua cognitio*); similarly, full use of reason is not required, for a certain beginning of the use of reason, that is, some use of reason (*aliqualis usus rationis*) suffices."[67]

644. **Who can best judge a child's readiness to receive Holy Communion?**
"At what age children are to receive the holy mysteries no one can better judge than their father and the priest who is their confessor. For it is their duty to ascertain by questioning the children whether they have any understanding of this admirable Sacrament and if they have any desire for it."[68]

645. **Does giving Communion to infants, still observed in the Greek-Catholic churches, correspond to Catholic tradition?**
Yes. The Catholic Church "took care even from the beginning to bring the little ones to Christ through Eucharistic Communion, which was administered even to nursing infants. This, as was prescribed in almost all ancient ritual books, was done at baptism until the thirteenth century, and this custom prevailed in some places even later. It is still found in the Greek and Oriental Churches."[69]

646. **Has the Roman Church ever forbidden this ancient practice?**
No, as even the Council of Trent "in no way condemned the ancient practice of administering the Eucharist to children before they had attained the use of reason."[70]

647. **Should we only intend to receive Communion once a year, at Easter?**
No. The Church desires that we receive Communion frequently if possible, to be more closely conformed to Christ by the grace of this Most Holy Sacrament.

Chapter 23: Fifth and Sixth Precepts of the Church

To contribute to the support of the Church's pastors.
To observe the marriage laws of the Church.

Support of Pastors

648. **What does the fifth precept of the Church require of us?**
It orders us to support our pastors in proportion to their needs and our means, and to contribute to the work of the Church on earth.

649. **What is meant by our *pastors*?**
Those priests in whose districts we live, or the priests in whose churches we habitually attend Holy Mass and receive the sacraments, as well as the Holy See, i.e. the pope, particularly through the Peter's Pence.[71]

650. **How may we contribute to the extension of the Church's mission on earth?**
In funding the necessities of public worship, the care and preservation of ecclesiastical buildings, the building and equipping of schools, the support of works of charity, etc.

651. **Must we contribute to the support of wicked or heretical pastors?**
No. If we know our contributions are used for evil ends, we should instead oppose such bad pastors, while supporting the work of the Church in other ways; e.g., supporting parishes, religious communities, or seminaries where the integrity of Catholic faith, morals, and sacred liturgy are safeguarded. Only the laborer in the vineyard of the Lord is truly worth his hire (see Lk 10:7*).

Marriage in the Church

652. **What does the sixth precept of the Church require of us?**
It requires the faithful to contract marriage according to the form prescribed by the Church, and forbids us to marry within certain degrees of kinship, or—according to the traditional canonical practice—with full solemnity during certain times of the year.[72]

653. **Why are Catholics generally required to marry with the assistance of a competent Church official?**
In order to: 1. Safeguard the souls of the couple and the officiating priest by searching out any *impediments*, or causes that would prevent the validity of the sacrament; 2. Foster and secure the social order by recording proof of a true marriage; 3. Show that marriage affects the common good, especially that of the Church, and is not a mere private union.

654. **May we ever attend a marriage that we know is invalid?**
No. Such attendance implies agreement with the evil act, and offers objective scandal to others.

655. **May we ever undergo or attend a civil marriage of Catholics?**
Yes, provided that such a ceremony is required by local civil law, and is only in view of the subsequent canonical celebration of the marriage.

Section 4: Counsels and Beatitudes

Chapter 24: Evangelical Counsels

Nature of the Counsels

656. What is an *evangelical counsel*?
Some means of attaining perfection in holiness, which we find recommended in the Gospel.

657. What is the difference between a counsel and a precept?
1. Precepts come from an authority that commands, while counsels come from a desire that exhorts; 2. Precepts are obligatory, while counsels are optional.

658. What are the chief evangelical counsels?
They are: voluntary poverty, perpetual chastity, and perfect obedience.

659. What is *voluntary poverty*?
Depriving ourselves of material goods through love of the eternal good, which is God Himself. "The evangelical counsel of poverty in imitation of Christ who, although He was rich, was made poor for us, entails, besides a life which is poor in fact and in spirit and is to be led productively in moderation and foreign to earthly riches, a dependence and limitation in the use and disposition of goods."[1]

660. Is it therefore contrary to the Gospel to possess material wealth?
No. Neither material wealth nor material poverty is good or evil in itself; only the *use* of earthly riches has any moral value. As it is not money, but rather the inordinate *love* of money that is "the root of all evil" (1 Tm 6:10*), St. Paul teaches: "Those who make a purchase, [should behave] as if they had nothing; and those who use the things of this world, as if not dependent on them. For this world in its present form is passing away" (1 Cor 7:30–31*).

661. What of those who claim that Jesus desires all to be poor, calling them *blessed*?
We are not "blessed" by the simple fact of material poverty, any more than we are cursed by the fact of material wealth. The kingdom of heaven belongs to those who are *poor in spirit*, i.e., inwardly detached from earthly riches, with their hearts set on heaven.

662. Is renouncing wealth to embrace material poverty always a meritorious act?
No. Only those who embrace poverty out of *supernatural charity* merit grace (see Mt 19:29; 1 Cor 13:3), and many canonized saints from wealthy backgrounds have shown how great a blessing wealth can be, when used for the glory of God and salvation of souls.

663. **Is material wealth a sure sign of God's special favor, or poverty of His disfavor?**
No. As shown in the life of Our Lord Himself, and in countless saints throughout history, neither riches nor poverty are infallible indicators of God's favor.

664. **What is *perpetual chastity*?**
Also called *virginity* or *celibacy*, it is living in a state of perfect sexual continence, out of love for God and in service of His Church. "The evangelical counsel of chastity assumed for the sake of the kingdom of heaven, which is a sign of the world to come and a source of more abundant fruitfulness in an undivided heart, entails the obligation of perfect continence in celibacy."[2]

665. **What special glory belongs to perpetual chastity?**
It makes us more like the angels than other virtues, and conforms us more closely to the image of the virginal Christ.

666. **Why is perpetual chastity so hated and opposed in every age?**
Because it is one of the clearest signs of the Church's divine nature and directly opposes the work of Satan, who brings more souls to hell through sins of impurity than through any other kind of sin.[3]

667. **What is *perfect obedience*?**
"The evangelical counsel of obedience, undertaken in a spirit of faith and love in the following of Christ obedient unto death, requires the submission of the will to legitimate superiors, who stand in the place of God, when they command according to the proper constitutions."[4]

668. **Is perfect obedience the greatest of the evangelical counsels?**
Yes. By voluntary poverty, we offer God only our external goods; by chastity, we offer Him only our body; by obedience, we offer Him our very will and liberty.

669. **Does this counsel therefore require obedience in all things?**
No. Superiors are not to be obeyed when they command things contrary to a higher law, for "we must obey God rather than any human authority" (Acts 5:29); nor must they be obeyed in matters that fall outside the scope of their office or the constitutions of their religious institute.

670. **What is the purpose of the three evangelical counsels?**
To assure the triumph of charity in us, by healing the evil that paralyzes it and breaking the bonds that restrain it. "In order that the faithful of Christ may be capable of deriving more abundant fruit from this baptismal grace, he intends, by the profession of the evangelical counsels in the Church, to free himself from those obstacles, which might draw him away from the fervor of charity and the perfection of divine worship. By his profession of the evangelical counsels, then, he is more intimately consecrated to divine service."[5]

671. **What is the evil that paralyzes charity?**
The triple concupiscence: "Concupiscence of the eyes, concupiscence of the flesh, and the pride of life" (1 Jn 2:16*).

672. **How do the evangelical counsels remedy this evil?**
Poverty remedies concupiscence of the eyes, or greed for temporal goods; chastity remedies concupiscence of the flesh, or love of sensual pleasure; obedience remedies the pride of life, or the drive of self-assertion.

673. **What reward is reserved for those who practice the counsels?**
Contentment and joy in this life, and a higher degree of glory in the next, as Our Lord said: "Everyone who has left houses or brothers or sisters or father or mother or wife or children or fields for the sake of My name will receive a hundredfold and will inherit eternal life" (Mt 19:29*).

Religious Life

674. **What is the best form of practicing the evangelical counsels?**
It is to embrace the religious life, also called consecrated life.

675. **What is the *religious life*?**
Some form of life approved by the Church in which one professes the vows of poverty, chastity, and obedience (or their equivalent), according to a particular rule of life.

676. **Who lives the religious life?**
Those who live the vows in a shared rule of life including shared housing are generally called "religious," while those not living in common may be hermits, consecrated virgins, or otherwise.

677. **Who instituted the religious life?**
Its foundations are the counsels contained in the Gospel; its institution springs from the various charisms of the Holy Spirit dispensed within the Church; its regulation is from her hierarchy.

678. **Why was religious life instituted?**
To render perpetual homage to God on earth, and facilitate a form of life most conducive to spiritual perfection. Religious are "totally dedicated to God who is loved most of all, so that, having been dedicated by a new and special title to His honor, to the building up of the Church, and to the salvation of the world, they strive for the perfection of charity in the service of the Kingdom of God and, having been made an outstanding sign in the Church, foretell the heavenly glory."[6]

679. **Is the consecrated religious state superior to the state of marriage?**
Yes. Although holiness is attainable in both states, and marriage is also good and sacred, the religious state is already what the glorified life of heaven will be — it is therefore objectively superior to marriage.[7]

680. **According to St. Bernard of Clairvaux, what are the nine fruits of the religious life?**
The consecrated religious: 1. Spends his life in greater purity; 2. Falls more rarely; 3. Rises more promptly; 4. Walks more prudently; 5. Is refreshed with heavenly graces more frequently; 6. Rests more securely; 7. Dies more peacefully; 8. Is purified more quickly; 9. Is rewarded more abundantly.[8]

681. **What is required in one who aspires to the religious life?**
1. Right intention; 2. Health of body and mind; 3. Natural suitability for the life and works of the institute; 4. The grace of a vocation, confirmed by integrity of life; 5. Freedom from previous bonds, such as marriage.[9]

682. **What benefits flow from the religious life?**
1. It is a most powerful means of personal sanctification; 2. It makes the holiness of the Church shine forth more clearly, and gives her more effective workers in the Lord's vineyard; 3. It sustains society by intercessory prayer, exercises innumerable works of charity, and inspires the world with selfless example.

683. **What is the special mission and value of the strictly-cloistered religious life?**
"Since those who become the absolute property of God become God's gift to all, the life of [the cloistered] is truly a gift set at the heart of the mystery of ecclesial communion, accompanying the apostolic mission of those who exert themselves in proclaiming the Gospel."[10]

684. **Who have been the fiercest enemies of the strictly-cloistered religious life?**
The declared enemies of the Church itself, beginning with Martin Luther and later governors and even clergy inspired by the naturalistic, Freemasonic spirit, e.g., the Austrian Emperor Joseph II and the National Convention of revolutionary France — by whose orders the Discalced Carmelite Nuns of Compiègne were martyred in 1794, simply because of their uncompromising fidelity to the cloistered life.

685. **Has the Church always defended the strict and uncompromising character of the cloistered religious life?**
Yes, because the contemplative life is a "particular way of being the Church, of building the communion of the Church, of fulfilling a mission for the good of the whole Church. Cloistered contemplatives therefore are not asked to be involved in new forms of active presence, but to remain at the wellspring of Trinitarian communion, dwelling at the very heart of the Church."[11]

686. **In our day, why do some high-ranking clergy want to abolish or weaken the strictness of traditional forms of cloistered life?**

Because these churchmen are filled with a merely naturalistic spirit and the "heresy of action,"[12] whereas the radicalness and exclusivity of the cloistered and contemplative life powerfully demonstrates the primacy of the supernatural, of grace, and eternity. Such a form of life bothers these churchmen, because it is a rebuke to their naturalistic agenda that seeks to conform the Catholic Church to this world, transforming her into a kind of non-governmental humanitarian aid organization.

Chapter 25: The Beatitudes

Beatitude in General

687. **What is the end of all Christian morality?**

True *beatitude*, i.e., to make us reasonably happy in this life and eternally happy with God in the next.

688. **What is the epitome of all Christian morality?**

Those maxims given by Our Lord called the *evangelical Beatitudes*, which are the acts of certain virtues and gifts, communicated to our souls by the Holy Spirit.

689. **Why are they called *Beatitudes*?**

From the Latin *beatus* (blessed, happy), each begins with the word *blessed* and ends with some reward promised to the virtuous act it expresses.

The Christian Beatitudes

690. **How many Beatitudes are there?**

St. Matthew lists eight, which Our Lord proclaimed on a mountain in Galilee, near Capharnaum (see Mt 5:3–10). They are:

1. Blessed are the poor in spirit: for theirs is the kingdom of heaven.
2. Blessed are the meek: for they shall possess the land.
3. Blessed are they that mourn: for they shall be comforted.
4. Blessed are they that hunger and thirst after justice: for they shall have their fill.
5. Blessed are the merciful: for they shall obtain mercy.
6. Blessed are the clean of heart: for they shall see God.
7. Blessed are the peacemakers: for they shall be called children of God.
8. Blessed are they that suffer persecution for justice' sake: for theirs is the kingdom of heaven.

691. **What is meant by *the poor in spirit*?**

This refers "either to the contempt of riches, or to the contempt of honors, which results from humility."[13] This beatitude therefore concerns all who are: 1. Interiorly detached from the goods of this life; 2. Humble in the midst of material wealth, without ostentation or pride; 3. Patient in the midst of material poverty, without dejection or despair.

692. **In what way is the *kingdom of heaven* promised to the poor in spirit?**
In the present life this signifies the state of grace by which God reigns within us; in the life to come, it is eternal glory.

693. **What is true *meekness*?**
It consists in mastery of our passions and acting toward our neighbor with charity and humility, without sharpness, disdain, or impatience.

694. **What is *the land* promised to the meek?**
1. The land of our own hearts, of which we are always masters; 2. The land of others' hearts, which we conquer by amiability; 3. The land of the blessed, i.e., heaven.

695. **What are the mournful *tears* that Our Lord speaks of?**
Sorrows prompted by the Holy Spirit in the hearts of the faithful: tears of zeal, of repentance, of holy fear, of sadness, of compassion, and of hope.

696. **What is the *comfort* promised to those who weep?**
A spiritual joy in this life that surpasses all the pleasures of the world, and an everlasting consolation in the bliss of heaven.

697. **Who are they that *hunger and thirst after justice*?**
Those who seek supernatural merit through fasting; or who bring to their apostolate or daily duties the same zeal and fervor for God that a starving man would bring to the search for sustenance in the desert; or who have an extraordinary desire for holiness in their souls and in the world.

698. **How are these to be *filled*?**
Here they will enjoy full satisfaction of conscience, which will reproach them with nothing; and in the next life, the fullness of divine love will fill their hearts like an eternal fountain.

699. **Who are the *merciful*?**
Those who, moved by a neighbor's suffering, comfort him charitably in his corporal and spiritual necessities as far as one is able.

700. **What is the reward of the merciful?**
They will find mercy at the hands of the others, and will obtain it especially from God.

701. **What is *cleanness of heart*?**
Interior freedom from all affection for sin, especially sins against chastity.

702. **What is the reward given to a pure heart?**
Greater graces from God, uniquely heightened experiences of prayer in this life, and the perfect vision of God in the next.

703. **What are *peacemakers*?**
Those who love peace, laboring to establish it in themselves and all around them by opposing evil reports, enmities, estrangements, and indifference, and working to reconcile enemies.

704. **What reward will be given to peacemakers?**
The grace of inner peace in this life and the next, being called true children of the One who reconciled all things in Himself, "making peace through the blood of His Cross" (Col 1:20).

705. **Who are they that *suffer persecution for justice' sake*?**
Those who: 1. Are attacked because of their good works, prayer, charity, and zeal; 2. Bear their cross daily, constantly working to persecute their own evil inclinations.

706. **What is the reward of this beatitude?**
The same reward given to poverty of spirit, as true poverty of spirit naturally brings persecution upon it.

707. **What order do the Beatitudes follow?**
The first three remove the obstacles posed by a false conception of happiness. The next two point out the duties to merit true happiness. The sixth and seventh teach us the nature of true happiness, and the eighth sums up the others.

708. **What is the greatest anticipation of heavenly beatitude here on earth?**
Life in the state of grace and imitation of Christ, which is exercised chiefly in Christian prayer and in acts of supernatural love, whereby man communes with God in the depths of his soul and continuously advances in holiness and perfection.

709. **How can we best maintain this life of grace?**
By a true *lex orandi* (law and rule of prayer), making use of the means of grace that God has provided to us.

PART III — Worship: Being Holy
Lex Orandi

Sanctification in General

1. **What is *sanctification*?**
From the Latin *sanctus* (holy), sanctification is the process of becoming holy by participation in the inner life of God, through His free gift of grace.

2. **What is *worship*?**
In its broadest sense, worship is the act by which reverence is given to God on account of His excellence.[1] Acts of worship include all the means of sanctification; i.e., all the ways in which we honor God and become holy.

3. **What are these means?**
Prayer, the sacraments, and the public worship of the Church.

4. **How can we divide this portion of Christian doctrine?**
Into four considerations: 1. *Grace*, without which we cannot please God or become holy; 2. *Prayer*, by which we commune with God and ask His grace; 3. *Sacraments*, which signify and produce this grace; 4. *Liturgy*, which regulates the Church's public prayer and sacraments.

Section 1: Grace and Merit

Chapter 1: Grace

Grace in General

5. **What is *grace*?**
A supernatural gift which God freely bestows on us, through the merits of Jesus Christ, for our salvation or to accomplish some task.

6. **Why is grace called a *supernatural* gift?**
Because it is not something natural to us, but rather comes from God to lift us above the level of our human nature, and enjoy friendship and communion with Him.

7. **Why is grace said to be a *free* gift?**
Because we have no right to it, and God is perfectly free to refuse it; yet He grants it through His unbounded goodness and love for us.

8. **What is the cause of grace and why is it given *through the merits of Jesus Christ*?**
"As *a principal agent* it belongs to God alone to pour grace into the members of the Church; and *instrumentally* it is the humanity of Christ, that also is the cause of that in-pouring of grace.... Just as iron burns because of the fire joined to it, the actions of Christ's humanity were salutary because of the divinity united to it, of which the humanity was like an instrument."[1] It is, therefore, in consideration of the merits of Our Lord Jesus Christ that God has restored to man the graces of which he had been deprived by sin.

9. **Why is grace given to us *for our salvation or to accomplish some task*?**
Because the purpose of some grace is to enable us to live the life of holiness, and to merit life everlasting; the purpose of other graces is to help us accomplish some task, such as to prophesy, as was the case for the pagan Balaam (see Nm 22–24; and Jude 11) and the high priest Caiaphas (see Jn 11:51).

10. **Can grace be increased in the soul?**
Yes. "Grow in the grace and knowledge of Our Lord and Savior Jesus Christ" (2 Pt 3:18).

11. **What are two general errors about divine grace?**
1. So exalting the natural powers of man as to make divine grace unnecessary, as *Pelagianism* and *naturalism*; 2. So exalting divine grace as to make man's free cooperation unnecessary or impossible, as *Lutheranism, Calvinism, Baianism,* and *Jansenism.*

12. **What is *naturalism*?**
An exclusion, and sometimes a negation, of the entire supernatural order. Naturalism ultimately leads to a complete Anti-Christianity, because it holds man and nature as self-sufficient.

13. **How does the Magisterium of the Church describe naturalism?**
    "The fundamental doctrine of the naturalists, which they sufficiently make known by their very name, is that human nature and human reason ought in all things to be mistress and guide…. They deny that anything has been taught by God; they allow no dogma of religion or truth which cannot be understood by the human intelligence, nor any teacher who ought to be believed by reason of his authority."[2]

14. **Conversely, what errors exalt divine grace to the detriment of our cooperation?**
    In addition to those of Luther and Calvin, the Church condemned the errors of Belgian theologian Michael Baius (+1589), Dutch bishop Cornelius Jansen (+1638), and French Jansenist theologian Paschal Quesnel (+1719), including the notions that "free will, without the help of God's grace, is valid only to sin,"[3] and that the fallen soul has "a general impotence for labor, for prayer, and for every good work."[4]

15. **What is the most common error about divine grace today?**
    Neo-Pelagianism, the notion that men will be saved merely by their morally good deeds, apart from cooperation with divine grace and saving faith.

16. **Does mere human existence enable man to reach perfection?**
    No. Man must become Christian, because he needs the help of God's grace for his: 1. Reason to understand the essential truths of faith without admixture of error; 2. Will to act rightly toward eternal life, his true perfection; 3. Passions to be well-ordered and in harmony with reason.

17. **What are the two kinds of grace?**
    Grace may be divided into two kinds: *actual* grace and *sanctifying* grace.

Actual Grace

18. **What is *actual* grace?**
    A temporary assistance of God, whereby God moves us to will and to act in order to help us become holy or cooperate in the justification of another.[5]

19. **Why is this grace called *actual*?**
    Because it does not abide in us habitually, but actively prompts us to perform a passing *act*, whether exterior or interior.

20. **What is *exterior* grace?**
    Anything outside of us that God uses to act upon our souls: e.g., the preaching of the Gospel, charitable advice, miracles, good example, pious reading, trials and adversity, etc.

21. **Are the so-called "charismatic gifts" examples of actual grace?**
    Yes. Authentic *charisms* like prophecy, healing, discernment, etc. are graces given for building up the Church. They are not indicators of personal holiness, and must always be carefully discerned, as St. John the Apostle relates: "Do not believe every

spirit, but test the spirits to see whether they are of God" (1 Jn 4:1). This kind of grace, also called *gratuitous* grace (*gratia gratis data*), does not of itself sanctify the one who has it. Rather, it is given to one person for the sake of facilitating the sanctification of others.[6]

22. **What is *interior* grace?**
An act by which God inwardly enlightens the mind or strengthens the will to shun evil and do good. It is further divided into sufficient grace and efficacious grace.

23. **What is *sufficient* grace?**
All grace that helps us do what is necessary in our life circumstances to reach heaven; it may be rendered useless by our culpable resistance to it.

24. **What is *efficacious* grace?**
All grace that produces its effect; it is all grace with which we cooperate, achieving the good for which it was given by God.

25. **Can we do anything without the help of actual grace?**
We can do nothing in the *supernatural* order without actual grace; that is, nothing in the way of our eternal salvation.

26. **Is actual grace necessary for the beginning of saving faith, and for persevering in it?**
Yes; God always takes the initiative in our sanctification. By actual grace, God moves a person who is in a state of sin to perform acts, such as prayer, that can lead to *saving faith*: that grace which enables us to begin to believe, and then accompanies and follows us so that we may persevere in faith and holiness to the end of our life.

27. **Why is the special assistance of grace necessary to persevere in holiness?**
Because of our ignorance, concupiscence, moral weakness, imperfection, and the limitations of nature, we lack the strength to attain heaven on our own efforts alone.

28. **Can we resist the grace of God?**
Yes. As a creature capable of free choice, man is able to abuse his freedom and reject the graces God gives him which are sufficient for his salvation.

29. **What happens when we are faithful to grace from moment to moment?**
Our fidelity to grace brings joy to those in heaven, helps us accomplish the tasks God gives us, and draws down new graces upon us.

30. **What are the consequences of infidelity to grace?**
Infidelity to grace may diminish the frequency and power of graces given to us. "Draw near to God and He will draw near to you" (Jas 4:8).

31. **Does God give everyone sufficient grace to be saved?**
Yes. No one can be saved without grace, and God desires all to be saved—therefore, God gives every man sufficient grace to avoid evil and do good. Whether or not we correspond to this divine gift is a matter of our free decision.

Sanctifying Grace

32. What is sanctifying grace?
Sanctifying grace—also called *habitual* grace, *justifying* grace, and the *state of grace*—is a supernatural gift that inheres in the soul, making us just, holy, and pleasing to God, "partakers of the divine nature" (2 Pt 1:4).

33. Why is this grace also called *habitual*?
Because it is a permanent disposition that remains in the soul, unless it is severed and banished by mortal sin.

34. Why is this grace also called *justifying*?
Because it rescues us from our exile and estrangement from God, and sets us in right relationship with Him, i.e., "His justice" (Lk 12:31*). It is a transmutation whereby we are changed by the remission of sins from the state of ungodliness to the state of justice or righteousness.[7]

35. Why is being in possession of *justifying* grace called the *state* of grace?
Because by this grace, God delivers the soul from the dominion of darkness, and transfers it into "the kingdom of His beloved Son" (Col 1:13).

36. How does this grace *inhere* in the soul?
It is a quality that directly and stably conforms the very substance of the soul to the divine goodness.

37. How does sanctifying grace make us just, holy, and pleasing to God?
It makes us partakers of the divine nature, because "God's love has been poured into our hearts through the Holy Spirit who has been given to us" (Rom 5:5). It calls forth in the soul a spiritual reflection of the uncreated beauty of God, which is not to be compared with the soul's natural likeness to God.

38. How does sanctifying grace differ from actual grace?
Sanctifying grace: 1. Is not temporary, but abides in the soul unless it is lost through mortal sin; 2. Is not discernible by the senses, but exists in the depths of the soul; 3. If lost, can only be regained with the assistance of actual grace.

39. How important is sanctifying grace?
After God Himself, whose greatest gift it is, it holds the most important place in our lives. 1. The sacraments were instituted to give, strengthen, preserve, or repair it; 2. The commandments were given to defend and nourish it; 3. The mission of the Church is to extend it to all mankind; 4. The aim of the demons is to deprive souls of it at any cost.

40. What are the effects of sanctifying grace in our soul?
1. It gives us supernatural life, enabling us to participate in God's very own life; 2. It incorporates us into the inner life of the most Holy Trinity, so that God dwells personally in us, and we in Him; 3. It informs and sustains our spiritual life, as the soul informs and sustains our body.

41. **What supernatural gifts are infused in the soul along with sanctifying grace?**
The three theological virtues, the four moral virtues, and the gifts of the Holy Spirit, which better dispose us to know and do God's will with ease and excellence.

42. **What should be our response to the possession of sanctifying grace?**
We should: 1. Give thanks for this precious gift, which assures us of heaven if we die with it; 2. Be faithful to it by obeying the laws of God and His Church; 3. Pray for this fidelity daily; 4. Use the established means to increase it, especially the sacraments.

43. **What is a common error about sanctifying grace today?**
The notion that this grace is already present in all souls, and need only be discerned, believed in, and celebrated.

44. **What does sanctifying grace enable us to do?**
It enables us to perform truly holy actions, directed to God and with His help, and thereby merit grace and salvation. As branches grafted onto the divine vine, we bear this fruit in Christ: "I am the vine, you are the branches. He who abides in Me, and I in him, he it is that bears much fruit, for apart from Me you can do nothing" (Jn 15:5).

Chapter 2: Justification and Merit

Justification

45. **What is *justification*?**
It is the term used to describe our passage from the state of sin to the state of grace:[8] "A translation from that state wherein man is born a child of the first Adam to the state of grace, and of the adoption of the sons of God, through the Second Adam, Jesus Christ, our Savior; and this translation, since the promulgation of the Gospel, cannot be effected without the laver of regeneration, or the desire thereof, as it is written: 'Unless a man be born again of water and the Holy Ghost, he cannot enter into the Kingdom of God' (Jn 3:5*)."[9]

46. **What wondrous effects are produced in the soul by justification?**
1. Our sins are truly remitted, effaced, and destroyed; 2. We are renewed interiorly, and become a new creature in Christ. Those who are thus reborn in grace are referred to as *the just* (see Mt 13:49*). "In that new birth, there is bestowed upon them, through the merit of His Passion, the grace whereby they are made just."[10]

47. **Is justification a very great miracle?**
Yes. The raising of sinful man to the state of divine grace is a greater miracle than the raising of the dead to life; indeed, it is a greater miracle than the creation of the material universe.

48. **Can anyone be certain of his justification?**
    Although the faithful may have reasonable hope of being in the state of grace, only a unique revelation from God could give someone certainty of this. "No one can know with a certainty of faith, which cannot be subject to error, that he has obtained the grace of God,"[11] and the Church infallibly declares: "If anyone saith, that it is necessary for every one, for obtaining the remission of sins, that he believes for certain, and without any wavering arising from his own infirmity and disposition, that his sins are forgiven him; let him be anathema."[12]

49. **What signs may give us reasonable hope of our justification?**
    If we: 1. Keep God's commandments; 2. Think of Him; 3. Are glad to hear Him spoken of; 4. Seek spiritual things over earthly things; 5. Practice works of mercy; 6. Delight in the Church's public worship; 7. Retain a clear conscience; 8. Frequently speak to God and the saints with love.

50. **Is sanctifying grace possessed in equal degree by all the just?**
    No. This grace can be increased in the soul through good works, and so the degree of justice varies among souls, just as the stars shine with different degrees of splendor.

51. **May the grace of justification be lost?**
    Yes. It is immediately lost by any mortal sin, but no exterior power can make us lose it: "Neither death, nor life, nor angels, nor principalities, nor things present, nor things to come, nor powers, nor height, nor depth, nor anything else in all creation, will be able to separate us from the love of God in Christ Jesus Our Lord" (Rom 8:38–39).

52. **If we lose this justice through mortal sin, can it ever be recovered?**
    Yes. God, who is infinitely good, restores His friendship to those who return to Him with a contrite heart.

53. **How does God give sanctifying grace again, once it has been lost?**
    Ordinarily, through the sacrament of penance, which He instituted for this purpose. When this is not available, we may yet receive sanctifying grace through an act of perfect contrition with the intention to go to the sacrament as soon as possible.

54. **What danger should we carefully avoid here?**
    We must not delay our conversion or risk new sins, taking God's mercy for granted. "God is not mocked. For what things a man shall sow, those also shall he reap" (Gal 6:7–8*).

Merit

55. What is *merit*?
The quality of a good act which gives us a right to some reward.

56. Strictly speaking, do we have a true "right" to any merit?
No. "With regard to God, there is no strict right to any merit on the part of man. Between God and us there is an immeasurable inequality, for we have received everything from Him, our Creator."[13]

57. What are the two principal kinds of merit?
1. *Natural* merit, when some temporal reward is justly bestowed on a morally good act in the natural order; 2. *Supernatural* merit, when a measure of divine grace is given as the reward for supernaturally good works, i.e., actions performed in the state of grace.

58. What is this supernatural power and the source of meriting founded upon?
The infinite mercy of God and the merits of His Son, as grace unites us in love to Jesus Christ and makes our acts supernatural and meritorious in Him.

59. How have the saints regarded their own merits?
"They do not glory in their own merits, for they attribute no good to themselves but all to Me, because out of My infinite charity I gave all to them."[14] As St. Thérèse of Lisieux maintains: "In the evening of this life, I shall appear before You with empty hands, for I do not ask You, Lord, to count my works. All our justice is blemished in Your eyes. I wish, then, to be clothed in Your own justice and to receive from Your love the eternal possession of Yourself."[15]

60. Are we able to gain merit if we are not in the state of grace?
No. The sinner cannot merit any grace whatsoever, but can only respond to God's invitation to grace. By cooperating with this divine initiative, he may then receive justification.

61. What graces are the just then able to merit?
For himself, the just can merit an increase of sanctifying grace, actual graces for further good works, and eternal glory in heaven. For sinners, he can merit the first graces of conversion and faith.

62. What determines the greatness of supernatural merit given for our good acts?
This depends on: 1. Our personal holiness; 2. The dignity of our act; 3. The purity of our intention; 4. The intensity of our charity.

63. Are our acquired merits permanent?
They are as permanent as sanctifying grace, of which they are the fruits. We lose them by losing this grace, and we recover them by recovering this grace.

Section 2: Christian Prayer

Chapter 3: Prayer in General

Nature of Prayer

64. **What is *prayer*?**
A lifting of the mind and heart to God, in order to adore Him, thank Him, ask His pardon, and seek His grace.

65. **Why should we adore God?**
Because He is the first principle, the sovereign master, and the last end of all things. "I am Alpha and Omega, the beginning and the end … Who is, and who was, and who is to come, the Almighty" (Apoc 1:8*).

66. **What should we thank God for?**
The many gifts He has lavished upon us, whether in the natural or supernatural order.

67. **What should we ask His pardon for?**
Our various sins and failings, and those defects of character that we struggle with.

68. **What is the animating principle of our prayer?**
The principle of all true prayer is the Holy Spirit, the third Person of the Blessed Trinity, who lives in the souls of the just and is called the "Spirit of grace, and of prayers" (Zac 12:10*).

69. **Why is the Holy Spirit the living principle of all true prayer?**
As our prayer is a personal relationship with the Blessed Trinity, God Himself must take the initiative in this loving communion within our souls. "For we do not know how to pray as we ought, but the Spirit Himself intercedes for us" (Rom 8:26).

70. **Is it possible to grow in the grace of prayer?**
Yes. Our earthly life is one of constant growth in our relationship with God through prayer, often simply called "the interior life."

71. **What should we do to grow in the grace of prayer?**
1. Obey the commandments; 2. Carefully avoid all that might be an obstacle to prayer, e.g., habitual distraction of mind, vain curiosity, pride and egotism, etc.; 3. Take steps to attract the Spirit of prayer, e.g., interior recollection, control of the senses, self-discipline, frequent invocation of the Holy Spirit, and correspondence to His inspirations; 4. Frequent the sacraments; 5. Enter deeply into the public worship of the Church.

72. **Is prayer very necessary?**
Yes. We are created for profound and personal relationship with God, upon whom we depend at every moment. This relationship is expressed and deepened through prayer, as St. Alphonsus says: "He who prays is certainly saved. He who prays not is certainly damned. All the blessed (except infants) have been saved by prayer. All the damned have been lost through not praying; if they had prayed, they would not have been lost."[1]

73. **How may the necessity of prayer be demonstrated?**
1. The example and instructions of Our Lord; 2. The teaching of Scripture and Tradition; 3. Our inability to achieve any supernatural good on our own; 4. The order of divine providence.

74. **How did Our Lord show the necessity of prayer?**
As frequently recorded in the Gospel, He prayed constantly Himself (see Mk 1:35; and Lk 6:12), and exhorted his followers to the same: "Watch and pray" (Mt 26:41).

75. **How does our inability to achieve any supernatural good show the necessity of prayer?**
We may perform morally good works in the natural order, but we can do nothing supernaturally good without the help of God's grace, which must be sought by prayer: "Apart from Me you can do nothing" (Jn 15:5), but "everyone who asks receives" (Mt 7:8).

76. **How does the order of providence show the necessity of prayer?**
God gives fertility to the fields, but wills us to till and tend them; He gives us intellectual powers, but requires us to study. Similarly, God wills our salvation—but on condition that we also will it, and cooperate with His grace through prayer.

Circumstances of Prayer

77. **When should we pray?**
"We ought always to pray" (Lk 18:1*), and "pray without ceasing" (1 Thes 5:17*).

78. **Why should we pray without ceasing?**
Because we are: 1. God's creatures by nature, who acknowledge His supreme authority by prayer; 2. His children by grace, who thank Him and seek His blessing by prayer; 3. His "fellow workers," the willing instruments of His work in the world (see 1 Cor 3:9), made effective by prayer.

79. **When are we obliged to pray?**
As soon as we have attained the use of reason, we are bound to pray regularly, praising God and living in His presence, and especially whenever we: 1. Receive God's natural and supernatural gifts, thanking Him; 2. Are strongly tempted against some virtue, asking God's efficacious help; 3. Have fallen into sin, humbly and confidently asking God's pardon; 4. Are in danger of death, asking God's special protection.

80. **How do good Christians practice daily prayer?**
They pray frequently, but especially every morning and evening, before and after meals, at the beginning of their more important actions, and in dangers, trials, and temptations.

81. **Why should we pray every morning and evening?**
Every *morning* we give ourselves to God and ask His blessing on our day. Every *evening* we thank God for His gifts, ask pardon for our faults, and beg grace to pass the night worthily.

82. **Why should we pray before and after meals?**
To ask God to bless the food we are about to eat, and thank Him for giving it to us.

83. **Why should we pray at the beginning of important actions, and amid various dangers?**
We refer all our works to God, whom we hope to love and serve in all our actions, and beg Him to bless our work, protect us from danger, and console us in our trials.

84. **To whom may we address our prayers?**
We may address our prayers directly to God, as well as to the Blessed Virgin Mary, and to His angels and saints.

85. **For whom should we pray?**
Firstly for our parents, our relations, benefactors, friends, and even enemies; for our priests, bishop, pope, and the whole Church; for all those in civil authority, those in need, and especially the sick and the dying; for all those who have not yet believed in Jesus Christ or entered His Church, for the conversion of sinners, and for the souls in purgatory.

Chapter 4: Life of Prayer

Qualities of Prayer

86. **What should we seek in prayer?**
Whatever tends to the glory of God and the salvation of our soul and that of our neighbor.

87. **When we pray, what should we desire first?**
Eternal life, and the supernatural charity that leads to it. All other goods we should desire only as means for gaining heaven: "Seek first His kingdom and His righteousness, and all these things shall be yours as well" (Mt 6:33).

88. **Is it lawful to ask for temporal blessings from God?**
Yes. We may entreat Him for all our needs: health, food, clothing, protection from evils and accidents, the preservation of our loved ones, success in good undertakings, peace in our homeland, victory over enemies, etc.

89. **How should we ask for these temporal things?**
We should always ask for them: 1. *Conditionally*, i.e., provided that they are not obstacles to our salvation; 2. *Humbly*, with perfect submission to the will of God.

90. **Does God hear our prayers for such temporal goods?**
Yes. "If you then, who are evil, know how to give good gifts to your children, how much more will your Father who is in heaven give good things to those who ask Him!" (Mt 7:11).

91. **How should we make our prayer?**
We must pray: 1. In the name of Our Lord Jesus Christ; 2. With attention; 3. With humility; 4. With faith; 5. With confidence; 6. With fervor; 7. With perseverance.

92. **What is meant by praying *in the name* of Jesus Christ?**
Praying to God *through* Christ, *with* Christ, and *in* Christ: 1. Relying solely on His merits; 2. Uniting ourselves to His prayer and sacrifice; 3. Asking those blessings that He has merited for us; 4. Being deeply convinced that He Himself prays within us.

93. **How do we pray with attention?**
By focusing our mind upon: 1. The words we pronounce; 2. Our meaning or intention; 3. The presence of God Himself, or some other holy theme.

94. **What is the most perfect of these three kinds of attention?**
The third. It does not end with the words or their meaning, but moves to the very purpose of prayer: God Himself, and our being in personal and conscious relationship with Him.

95. **What are the obstacles to attention in prayer?**
1. *Interior distractions*, irrelevant thoughts or frivolous images that arise in the mind and disturb this holy action; 2. *Exterior distractions*, things that draw away our attention, such as intruding noises and conditions unsuitable for prayer.

96. **What should we do when distractions arise in prayer?**
1. Turn the mind away from them, and gently drive them off; 2. Be humble and patient with ourselves, not discouraged or downcast. God is full of love and patience, and turns all our efforts at prayerful attention to a greater good.

97. **Are distractions sinful in themselves?**
No. We are not culpable for involuntary distractions; indeed, if we combat distractions in our prayer, it renders greater glory to God and gains us even greater merit.

98. **How do we pray with humility?**
By praying with a deep conviction of our extreme need, powerlessness, and dependence on God.

99. **How do we pray with faith?**
By praying with the certainty that God can grant us all that we ask of Him.

100. **How do we pray with confidence?**
By praying with the firm hope that God will hear us, and grant us what we need.

101. **How do we pray with fervor?**
By praying with an ardent love for God, and the desire to obtain what we ask.

102. **Does fervor consist in sensible affection or intense emotions?**
No. It is essentially a quality in the will, whereby we cling to God above all.

103. **Then Christian prayer is not always filled with consolation or pleasant feelings?**
No. Christian prayer is also united to Christ in the desert and upon the Cross. At times, we must endure periods of dryness or distaste with perseverance: "Watch and pray.... The spirit indeed is willing, but the flesh is weak" (Mk 14:38).

104. **How do we pray with perseverance?**
By refusing to give in to weariness or difficulty in our prayer, and never abandoning our daily commitment to prayer.

105. **What should we do if God refuses our prayer, or delays in granting it?**
Then we have either asked for the wrong thing, or in the wrong way, or else God is inviting us to persevere in asking while His providence prepares some greater good. In such instances, we should ask the Spirit of God to enlighten us as to how He wishes us to pray.

Kinds of Prayer

106. **What are the different kinds of prayer?**
They may be divided according to their particular ends or means of expression.

107. **What are the four kinds of prayer, divided according to their end?**
1. *Adoration*, praising the greatness of God and expressing our love for Him; 2. *Thanksgiving*, showing our gratitude for His gifts; 3. *Atonement*, seeking to make reparation for our sins and defects; 4. *Petition*, asking for His gifts.

108. **May prayers of petition be made on behalf of others?**
Yes. Seeking graces and favors on behalf of others is a form of petition called *intercession*.

109. **What are the two kinds of prayer, divided according to their means?**
1. *Vocal* prayer, which may be either private or public; 2. *Mental* prayer, which may be either meditation or contemplation.

110. **What is vocal prayer?**
Prayer expressed by word of mouth, voicing the thoughts of the mind and interior sentiments of the heart.

111. **What is private prayer?**
Prayer that we offer as private individuals, either alone or in common with several others, e.g., in a family.

112. **What is the public prayer of the Church?**
Also called *liturgy*, it is prayer offered by the ministers of the Church, with or without the faithful assembled, in the name of the Church and according to her prescribed forms.

113. **Is public prayer the most excellent of prayers?**
Yes. "Liturgical prayer, being the public supplication of the illustrious Spouse of Jesus Christ, is superior in excellence to private prayers."[2] It is objectively more efficacious in bringing sanctifying grace, although God may sometimes allow private prayer to be more efficacious for other graces.

114. **How may the faithful take part in this public prayer of the Church?**
By devout participation in the various liturgical offices, e.g., Holy Mass, Benediction, Vespers, processions, etc.

115. **What is mental prayer?**
Interior prayer, in which the mind and heart are applied to divine things, with or without words.

116. **What is meditation?**
From the Latin *meditatio* (thinking over), it is mental prayer in which the mind reflects on some spiritual theme in God's presence and stirs the will to make practical resolutions.

117. **Is meditation very useful?**
Yes. By meditation we absorb the truths of faith with our intellect, and make acts of repentance and love with our will, renewing good resolutions, strengthening against vice, and growing in virtue.

118. **What subjects of meditation should we prefer?**
The mysteries of Our Lord's life and Passion, as presented in the Gospels.

119. **What can help focus our attention for meditation?**
1. *Sacred reading (lectio divina)*, dwelling on the texts of scripture or the liturgy; 2. *Devotional reading* of the works of Catholic saints and spiritual masters; 3. *Sacred art*, in the Church's various visual and musical traditions.

120. **What are the most advisable methods for meditation?**
There are many classical approaches to Christian meditation, e.g., *lectio divina*, the Rosary, Ignatian exercises, Teresian imaginative prayer, etc. Even so, the goal of all true prayer is union with God, which cannot be "mastered" by any technique.

121. **What is contemplation?**
From the Latin *contemplatio* (looking at), it is mental prayer in which the mind and heart are lifted and absorbed in God's presence, engaged in the simple gaze and wordless act of loving communion.

122. **How does contemplation differ from meditation?**
Meditation is chiefly *discursive*, as our reason and intellectual efforts predominate; it is ordered to contemplation, which is chiefly *affective*, as the loving sentiments of the heart and will predominate. Contemplation may also be characterized by the predominance of the divine initiative, as God draws the soul into deeper union with Him and the soul abides with Him: "Behold I will allure her ... and I will speak to her heart" (Os 2:14*), "and We will come to them and make Our home with them" (Jn 14:23).

123. **Are there erroneous forms of prayer that must be avoided?**
Yes. Any path of prayer that seeks union with God apart from the sacred humanity of Jesus Christ, the Incarnate Word, is incomplete and deceptive: "No one comes to the Father, but by Me" (Jn 14:6).

124. **May we practice "Christianized" forms of Yoga, Zen, or other pagan prayer forms?**
No. Forms of prayer that are foreign to Christianity may not be safely practiced, as these are inherently linked to false worship and the deceptions of the devil. "What agreement hath the temple of God with idols?" (2 Cor 6:16*).

Efficacy of Prayer

125. **What are the effects of Christian prayer?**
Union with God, refreshment of soul, answered petitions, and merit.

126. **How does our prayer bring us into union with God?**
"Because when we pray we ought principally to ask to be united to God, according to Psalm 26:4*, 'One thing I have asked of the Lord, this will I seek after, that I may dwell in the house of the Lord all the days of my life.'"[3]

127. **How does our prayer bring refreshment to the soul?**
The very presence of God brings peace, and God often nourishes the soul with pious thoughts, holy affections, and interior foretastes of heavenly joy.

128. **When does our prayer yield fulfilled petitions?**
God fulfills our requests whenever: 1. We seek our last end or something necessary to attain it; 2. Our prayer has all the necessary qualities; 3. We pray for ourselves, or for someone who poses no obstacle to our petition.

129. **How does our prayer produce merit?**
Because God desires that we pray, it is a good work in itself; obtaining for us an increase of spiritual riches, especially the gifts of the Holy Spirit and infused virtues.

130. **Why is prayer infallible under these conditions?**

Because God has promised it, and He is faithful to all His promises. "Whatever you ask in My name, I will do it, that the Father may be glorified in the Son" (Jn 14:13).

Chapter 5: Principal Prayers

Pater Noster

131. **What form of vocal prayer was taught to us directly by God?**

Jesus Christ taught us the Pater Noster or "Our Father," also called the *Lord's Prayer*:

Pater noster, qui es in caelis,
sanctificetur nomen tuum.
Adveniat regnum tuum.
Fiat voluntas tua, sicut in caelo et in terra.
Panem nostrum quotidianum da nobis hodie,
et dimitte nobis debita nostra
sicut et nos dimittimus debitoribus nostris.
Et ne nos inducas in tentationem,
sed libera nos a malo. Amen.

Our Father, who art in heaven,
hallowed be Thy name.
Thy kingdom come.
Thy will be done on earth as it is in heaven.
Give us this day our daily bread,
and forgive us our trespasses
as we forgive those who trespass against us.
And lead us not into temptation,
but deliver us from evil. Amen.

132. **Is the Lord's Prayer the most excellent of all simple prayers?**

Yes. It has been revealed directly by Jesus Christ Our Lord, and includes everything we should pray for.

133. **Why do we call God our *Father*?**

Because He gives us natural life by creating and sustaining us in being, and gives us supernatural life by imparting grace to our souls and adopting us as His children.

134. **Why do Christians say *our* Father, and not *my* Father?**

To remind us that we: 1. Are brethren by being incorporated into Jesus Christ; 2. Ought to live in peace and unity; 3. Should pray for one another, as St. Cyprian explained: "The Teacher of peace and the Master of unity would not have prayer to be made singly and individually, ... and when we pray, we pray not for one, but for the whole people, because we, the whole people, are one."[4]

135. **Why do we say:** *Who art in heaven?*
Although God is everywhere, He is properly and especially in heaven, the place where He finally gathers His children together and manifests Himself to them in eternal joy.

136. **What do we ask with the words:** *Hallowed be Thy name?*
That the name of God, which is holy in itself, may be known, loved, and glorified by all men.

137. **What do we ask with the words:** *Thy kingdom come?*
That all nations would submit to God's loving dominion on earth, that He might reign in the hearts of all men through grace, and that His final victory over evil would be realized.

138. **What do we ask with the words:** *Thy will be done on earth as it is in heaven?*
That all men would fulfill God's holy will as faithfully as the angels do.

139. **What do we ask with the words:** *Give us this day our daily bread?*
For everything necessary to sustain our body and soul. For the body, we ask God for earthly food and all that pertains to our physical life; for the soul, we ask for heavenly nourishment on the word of God, and all graces of the spiritual life. Above all, we ask for the Holy Eucharist.

140. **What do we ask with the words:** *Forgive us our trespasses as we forgive those who trespass against us?*
That God would forgive all our sins and failings, promising to deal mercifully with those who have offended us in turn.

141. **What do we ask with the words:** *Lead us not into temptation?*
That, in view of our weakness, God would keep us from temptations that cannot be overcome by ordinary virtue, and that in all others He would give us strength to be victorious over them.

142. **What do we ask with the words:** *But deliver us from evil?*
To be delivered from: 1. Past, present, and future evils, i.e., all sins that we have committed, all that leads us to sin, and all consequences and penalties of sin; 2. Attacks of the devil and of other enemies of the Church; 3. All effects of concupiscence, which inclines us toward evil.

143. **What is the meaning of the word** *Amen,* **concluding the Lord's Prayer?**
An ancient Semitic word meaning "yes, it is true, so be it," *amen* expresses our assent to all that has been said, and our desire that our prayer be heard by our loving Father in heaven.

Ave Maria

144. After the Lord's Prayer, what is the Christian's most common formulaic prayer?
It is the Ave Maria or "Hail Mary," also called the *Angelic Salutation*:

Ave Maria, gratia plena, Dominus tecum.
Benedicta tu in mulieribus,
et benedictus fructus ventris tui, Jesus.
Sancta Maria, Mater Dei,
ora pro nobis peccatoribus,
nunc, et in hora mortis nostrae. Amen.

Hail Mary, full of grace, the Lord is with thee.
Blessed art thou amongst women,
and blessed is the fruit of thy womb, Jesus.
Holy Mary, Mother of God,
pray for us sinners,
now, and at the hour of our death. Amen.

145. Why is this prayer called the *Angelic Salutation*?
Because it begins with the words of the angel Gabriel, who announced to Our Lady the mystery of the Incarnation, which was about to be accomplished in her.

146. Why is this prayer so frequently recited by Christians?
Because of its heavenly origin, and the greatness of her to whom the prayer is addressed: the Mother of God, the perfect model of Christian prayer, and our most powerful intercessor with God.

147. What are the three parts of this prayer?
The words of: 1. The angel Gabriel; 2. St. Elizabeth; 3. The invocation added by the Church.

148. What does the word *Hail* express?
1. Our profoundly respectful greeting to the humble Virgin, chosen by God to be Mother of His Son; 2. Our joy at the mystery of the Incarnation, which God achieved in her.

149. What is the meaning of the words: *Full of grace*?
They remind us of Mary's Immaculate Conception and that superabundance of grace which Our Lord bestowed on her in view of her exalted mission as Mother of God.

150. What is the meaning of the words: *The Lord is with thee*?
They show that within the soul of the Blessed Virgin, the Father, Son, and Holy Spirit dwell in an exceptional manner.

151. **What is the meaning of the words:** *Blessed art thou amongst women?*
They show that the Blessed Virgin is highly favored among women, and indeed blessed with divine grace above all other creatures.

152. **What is the meaning of the words:** *Blessed is the fruit of thy womb?*
They confirm that Mary is blessed because she is the Mother of Him who is blessed above all, and the very Author of all blessedness. The graces lavished upon Mary come from Jesus Christ, and refer to Jesus Christ, who assumed her flesh in the Incarnation.

153. **What petition has the Church added to this preamble of praise?**
At the Council of Ephesus in 431, the Church introduced the words: "Holy Mary, Mother of God, pray for us," to which tradition has further added: "sinners, now and at the hour of our death."

154. **Why were these words of invocation added?**
To remind us of the holiness and dignity of Mary, inspire us with great confidence in her intercession, and encourage us to often seek her prayers on our behalf, especially when eternal life draws near.

155. **How should we recite the Angelic Salutation?**
With respect and admiration for the Blessed Virgin, faith in the truths it expresses, and confidence in the maternal goodness of Our Lady.

Gloria Patri

156. **What is the brief prayer of praise used by Christians throughout the world?**
It is the Gloria Patri or "Glory Be," also called the *Minor Doxology*.

Gloria Patri, et Filio, et Spiritui Sancto.
Sicut erat in principio, et nunc, et semper,
et in saecula saeculorum. Amen.

Glory be to the Father, and to the Son, and to the Holy Spirit.
As it was in the beginning, is now, and ever shall be,
world without end. Amen.

157. **Why is this prayer called the Minor Doxology?**
From the Greek *doxa* (glory), it is a prayer of adoration and praise of the Blessed Trinity. It is called "minor" to denote its brevity and distinguish it from the longer *Gloria in excelsis Deo* or Major Doxology, which is sung during Holy Mass.

158. **Is this prayer very ancient?**
Yes. Similar expressions of praise may be found in Scripture and the early Church Fathers, with its Trinitarian form becoming fixed in the Church by the time of the Arian crisis in the fourth century.

PART III — WORSHIP: BEING HOLY

159. **Why was this prayer so well suited to the early centuries of the Church?**
   Because it is a brief, clear, and jubilant confession of the Trinity: a dogma that was fiercely attacked in those days.

160. **Is this prayer often used in the official prayer of the Church?**
   Yes; it is used as a concluding prayer throughout her liturgical rites, as well as in many classical Catholic devotions, such as the Rosary.

Section 3: The Sacraments

Chapter 6: Sacraments in General

Nature of the Sacraments

161. **What is the meaning of the word** *sacrament*?
From the Latin *sacramentum* (oath), the term denotes a binding thing, with some sacred or secret content.

162. **What is a** *sacrament*?
An outward sign, instituted by Christ, to give grace; with the sign both signifying and effecting grace.

163. **How are the sacraments** *outward* **signs?**
Because they include sensible realities like bread, water, oil, actions, and words: things that outwardly signify the interior and immaterial graces which they confer.

164. **What is the source of the sacraments' efficacy?**
The Passion of Christ. "A sacrament is a sign that is both a reminder of the past, i.e. the Passion of Christ; and an indication of that which is effected in us by Christ's Passion, i.e., grace; and a prognostic, that is, a foretelling of future glory."[1]

165. **How do we know that the sacraments were instituted by Jesus Christ?**
From the Holy Scripture and the constant teaching of the Church from the earliest centuries.

166. **Why did Our Lord institute the sacraments?**
To continue His presence among us until the end of time, and extend the redeeming efficacy of His sacred humanity. The sacramental signs are therefore like Our Lord's humanity, and the graces conveyed by them are like the Godhead concealed beneath it: "What was visible in our Savior has passed over into His mysteries."[2]

167. **Why are the sacraments such fitting means for our sanctification?**
"The first reason is taken from the condition of human nature ... led by things corporeal and sensible to things spiritual and intelligible. The second reason is taken from the state of man who in sinning subjected himself by his affections to corporeal things. Now the healing remedy should be given to a man so as to reach the part affected by disease. The third reason is taken from the fact that man is prone to direct his activity chiefly toward material things.... Bodily exercise is [therefore] offered to him in the sacraments, by which he might be trained to avoid superstitious practices, consisting in the worship of demons, and all manner of harmful action."[3]

168. **How do the sacraments produce grace?**
Each sacrament is a unique divine invention, producing grace in the soul according to each sacrament's intended purpose, provided that the recipient poses no obstacle to it.

169. **Is there an absolute necessity of the sacraments for salvation?**
No. Whereas Christ's redeeming work is absolutely necessary for salvation, God Himself is not bound by His sacraments: He could give salvation in an *extraordinary* way, known only to Him, while always in virtue of Christ's Passion. However, in the *ordinary* way, God has bound eternal salvation to the sacrament of baptism.

170. **Then sacraments are ordinarily necessary for salvation?**
Yes, particularly the sacraments of baptism and penance.[4] The Lord Himself affirms the necessity of baptism (see Jn 3:5), and penance is necessary to all who have sinned mortally after baptism—being called a kind of "second baptism" in the first centuries. "Penance is called the second plank after the shipwreck, as baptism is the first."[5]

171. **How many sacraments are there?**
These seven: baptism, confirmation, Eucharist, penance, extreme unction, holy orders, and matrimony.[6]

172. **Why is it especially fitting to have seven sacraments?**
Because they reflect in the spiritual order the various needs of our bodily life.

173. **How are the needs of our bodily life reflected in the seven sacraments?**
We are born, grow in size and strength, eat, need medicine when sick, and must prepare for death; as social creatures, we must also be governed by superiors and help foster our own society. So it is in the supernatural life: we are born to the life of grace by baptism, made strong in this grace by confirmation, fed with the glorious Eucharist, healed (or resurrected, if our soul is dead through mortal sin) by penance, and prepared for death by extreme unction; we are governed in the spiritual society of the Church by men in holy orders, and foster it by the sacrament of matrimony.

174. **How may the sacraments be divided according to their kind?**
In four ways: 1. The first five sacraments especially perfect the *individual*, while the last two perfect *society*; 2. The *sacraments of the dead* (baptism and penance) give grace to anyone spiritually dead through original or mortal sin, while the *sacraments of the living* (confirmation, Eucharist, extreme unction, holy orders, matrimony) increase grace in those who are already in the state of grace; 3. Christ is present in every sacrament by His *power and action*, but in the Eucharist also by His *permanent and substantial presence*;[7] 4. Three sacraments *imprint an indelible character* (baptism, confirmation, holy orders) upon the soul and so may only be received once, while the others do not imprint a character and may be received more than once.

175. **What is required for a sacrament to exist?**
All true sacraments require the presence of the proper matter, form, minister, and intention. If these are rightly observed, the sacrament is *valid*; i.e., it truly exists and produces grace. If any element is lacking, the sacrament is *invalid*; i.e., it does not exist or produce grace.[8]

176. **If we *believe* a sacrament to be valid when it is really invalid, does it then produce grace?**
No. Grace is given by the sacrament itself, not merely from our faith in it. However, if we are not at fault for the invalidity, God will see our good faith and respond to our desire for His grace in some other way.

177. **Would one's desire for a sacrament (*votum sacramenti*) produce its effects in the soul?**
Only in the case of: 1. Baptism, through explicit desire for it and the dispositions of so-called "baptism of desire" or "baptism of blood"; 2. Penance, through desire for God's forgiveness with an act of perfect contrition, in view of receiving the sacrament when possible; 3. Eucharist, through spiritual communion.

Matter and Form

178. **What makes up the sensible part of the sacraments?**
Two components: matter and form.

179. **What is the *matter* of a sacrament?**
Sacramental matter is the physical element and exterior act that Jesus Christ has designated for the purpose, such as washing with water or anointing with oil.

180. **What is the *form* of a sacrament?**
Sacramental form is the formula of words that the minister pronounces at the moment of applying the matter, such as: "I baptize you …," "I absolve you …," etc.

181. **Must the form and matter be united to produce each sacrament?**
Yes. Just as man is composed of body and soul, so every sacrament forms a moral whole, composed of matter and form. The sacramental form determines the matter, ordering it to clearly signify and produce the effect of grace.

182. **What if the sacramental matter or form are not properly observed?**
If either matter or form are substantially altered, missing, or separated, then the sacrament is invalid and confers no sacramental grace.

183. **What would be an example of such a substantial change?**
Attempting baptism with words other than the Trinitarian formula (invalid form), or with a liquid other than natural water (invalid matter).

184. **What if the minister violates the essential matter or form in innocent ignorance, or with good intentions?**
Such a sacrament would still be invalid, because Jesus Christ has established the order for every sacrament, and the Church has clarified exactly what this order consists of. No sacrament is conferred unless this essential order is followed.

Minister and Intention

185. **What is meant by the *minister* of a sacrament?**
From the Latin *ministerium* (office), the minister is the one who has the power to validly confer a sacrament.

186. **How many kinds of ministers are there?**
Two: 1. The *ordinary* minister confers a sacrament by right of his ordained office (excepting matrimony, where the only ministers are the spouses); 2. The *extraordinary* minister may confer it by special privilege or delegated power due to some pressing necessity.

187. **May anyone be a minister of sacraments?**
With the exception of baptism and matrimony, only validly ordained men are able to confer sacraments. Otherwise, the sacraments are invalid.

188. **What intention must the minister have to validly confer a sacrament?**
The minister must at least have the *intention of doing what the Church does*, for he acts in her name, and with the power of Christ who is head of the Church.

189. **Why must the minister have this intention?**
Because, otherwise, the minister would be acting in his own name and authority, rather than that of God acting through His Church. This would render the sacrament invalid and even profane, for the Church, in Christ's name, is the dispensatrix of all His sacraments.

190. **Must a minister be in the state of grace or have the true faith, for their sacraments to be valid?**
No, this was the error of the *Donatists*. Rather, the sacraments give grace by their own power. A minister may therefore confer a sacrament even while in the state of mortal sin or without holding the true faith, provided he has the intention to do what the Church does in celebrating the sacrament.

Receiving the Sacraments

191. **Who may receive the sacraments?**
Anyone still living on earth, provided they have the necessary dispositions.

192. **What are the necessary dispositions?**
1. For adult baptism and penance, we must have faith, hope, sorrow for sin, and a beginning of the love of God; 2. For the other sacraments of the living, the state of grace is either necessary (as for the Eucharist), or highly desirable for a fruitful reception; 3. The intention to receive the sacrament and its effects.

193. **What two general effects do the sacraments produce?**
1. *Grace*, which is produced by all the sacraments; 2. *Character*, which is only imprinted in the soul by some of the sacraments.

194. **What kinds of grace do the sacraments produce?**
1. *Sanctifying* grace, common to all of them; 2. *Sacramental* grace, differing with each sacrament.

195. **Do all receive equal grace from the same sacrament?**
No. The grace communicated to each will vary with our dispositions; it is more abundant in those who have more perfect dispositions.

196. **What is the *sacramental character*?**
An indelible spiritual mark, imprinted in the soul of one who receives baptism, confirmation, or holy orders. It is a certain participation in Christ's priesthood, as "the whole rite of the Christian religion is derived from Christ's priesthood. Consequently, it is clear that the sacramental character is specially the character of Christ, to whose priesthood the faithful are likened by reason of the sacramental characters, which are nothing else than certain participations of Christ's priesthood, flowing from Christ Himself."[9]

197. **What does this character achieve in the soul?**
Baptism incorporates man into the Church, the Mystical Body of Jesus Christ; confirmation enrolls him in the army of Jesus Christ; holy orders makes him the true minister of Jesus Christ.

Sacramental Ceremonies

198. **What is meant by the *ceremonies* of the sacraments?**
All those external acts of religion by which the Church administers the sacraments with due respect and dignity.

199. **What are the different kinds of ceremonies?**
Words, music, gestures, and postures, as well as sacred times, places, and objects. Ceremonies surrounding and ennobling the celebration of a sacrament may vary, whereas the essential ceremonies (matter and form) must be the same everywhere.

200. **What are the ceremonies surrounding a sacramental action for?**
1. Glorifying God by fittingly proclaiming the divine mysteries they signify; 2. Raising the mind and heart in the worship of God; 3. Instructing the faithful about the effects and obligations of the sacraments.

201. **May these ceremonies be changed at will, to suit contemporary circumstances?**
No. "If anyone says that the received and approved rites of the Catholic Church, that are customarily used in the solemn administration of the sacraments, may be despised, or without sin omitted at pleasure by the ministers, or be changed by any pastor of the churches into other new ones, let him be anathema."[10]

Errors about the Sacraments

202. **What heretics have especially attacked the sacraments?**
Chiefly the Protestants of the sixteenth century, and Modernists of the twentieth and the twenty-first century.

203. **What were some particular errors of the Protestants?**
The notions that: 1. Sacraments do not produce grace, but are only signs which excite our faith; 2. The number of the sacraments should be diminished; 3. Any person can confer the sacraments; 4. No sacraments imprint a character; 5. The sacramental ceremonies of the Catholic Church are entirely man-made, ridiculous, and contemptible.

204. **Has the Church clearly refuted and condemned these errors?**
Yes. These and many other related errors were condemned at the Council of Trent.

205. **What are some particular errors of the Modernists?**
The notions that: 1. Sacraments do not confer grace, but only affirm or celebrate the grace people already possess; 2. Sacraments are not the ordinary means of grace and salvation, because God intends for all to be saved, even without them; 3. Any manner of celebrating the sacraments is pleasing to God, so long as it arises from the local community.

Chapter 7: Baptism

Baptism in General

206. **What is *baptism*?**
A sacrament instituted by Christ to cleanse us from original sin and actual sin, and which makes us children of God and members of His Church.

207. **When did Jesus Christ institute the sacrament of baptism?**
According to common teaching, it was when Our Lord Himself was baptized in the Jordan River by St. John the Baptist, later commanding His disciples to baptize (see Mt 28:19).

208. **What is the meaning of the word *baptism*?**
From the Greek *baptizo* (plunge), it signifies immersion, bath, ablution, washing.

209. **What is the outward sign of the sacrament of baptism?**
The external washing of the body with water, along with the express invocation of the three Persons of the Blessed Trinity: Father, Son, and Holy Spirit.

210. **What is the meaning of this sign?**
It signifies spiritual regeneration, rebirth in Christ Jesus to a new creation, and spiritual resurrection to new life in Him (see 2 Cor 5:17; Jas 1:18; and Col 2:12).

211. **What is the sacramental matter of baptism?**
It is natural water; applied such that it flows directly on the body of him who is receiving baptism, at least on the head.

212. **How may this washing be validly performed?**
By: 1. *Infusion*, pouring water on the candidate; 2. *Immersion*, plunging the body of the candidate into the water; 3. *Aspersion*, sprinkling water on the body of the candidate (although the Church no longer recommends this rite).[11]

213. **What is the essential sacramental form of baptism?**
These exact words: "I baptize you in the name of the Father, and of the Son, and of the Holy Spirit."

214. **How are matter and form united in baptism?**
The one who is baptizing applies the water while pronouncing the words of the form.

215. **When is baptism invalid?**
Whenever: 1. A fluid other than natural water is used; 2. The water does not flow directly on the body or at least on the head; 3. The correct and entire form is not pronounced; 4. The form is not pronounced at the time of applying the water; 5. The form is not pronounced by the person pouring the water; 6. The recipient has already been baptized; 7. The person baptizing does not intend what the Church intends, as in the case of Mormon baptism.

216. **What should we do if we are in doubt about the validity of our baptism?**
Seek out a lawful minister of the Church to confer baptism conditionally, using the form: "If you are not baptized, I baptize you in the name of the Father, and of the Son, and of the Holy Spirit."

217. **Is baptism of very great importance?**
Yes. No other sacrament can be received before baptism, it cannot be repeated, and no one can be saved without receiving its sanctifying effects.

218. **What obligation therefore rests on all parents?**
All parents must seek baptism for their children as soon as possible, as it is a serious sin to risk the loss of a child's soul.

219. **Why can infants be baptized, if they do not have a personal faith?**
Infants have been baptized from apostolic times, in view of the supplied faith of the Church, represented by their godparents.

220. **Is sacramental baptism in water absolutely necessary for salvation?**
No. The justifying effect of baptism may also be supplied apart from its ordinary sacramental sign, through perfect love of God (so-called "baptism of desire") or martyrdom for the true faith (so-called "baptism of blood").

221. **Does "baptism of desire" produce all the effects of sacramental baptism?**
No. The common theological opinion holds that it does not imprint a character, confer sacramental grace, or remit the temporal punishment due to sin, unless one's charity is intense enough to merit this remission.

222. **Does "baptism of blood" produce all the effects of sacramental baptism?**
No. It imprints no character in the soul, because it is not a sacrament.

Administration of Baptism

223. **Who is the minister of baptism?**
The *ordinary* minister is a bishop or a priest; the *extraordinary* minister is a deacon delegated for the purpose, or, in danger of death, anyone may baptize.

224. **Why can anyone baptize in danger of death?**
Because God wishes all men to be saved (see 1 Tm 2:4), He has mercifully decreed that the most necessary means of salvation may be administered by all.

225. **Is it a grave obligation to baptize in such a case of necessity?**
Yes. It is a most serious obligation of charity.

226. **How is baptism administered in case of necessity?**
The person baptizing takes natural water and pours it (customarily in the form of a cross), on the head of the candidate (or some other part of the body if necessary), while at the same time pronouncing the words: "I baptize you in the name of the Father, and of the Son, and of the Holy Spirit."

227. **May parents baptize their children?**

Yes, in extraordinary circumstances when there is no ordinary minister available. After such a private baptism, the ceremonies of solemn baptism may later be supplied by the ordinary minister of the Church.

228. **What dispositions should adults bring to the reception of baptism?**

To receive baptism *validly*, they must intend to be baptized, believing in Jesus Christ the Redeemer and the Holy Trinity as Rewarder (see Heb 11:6). To receive it most *profitably*, they should hope in God and begin to love Him, with sorrow for their sins and resolution to avoid sin in the future.

229. **What ceremonies accompany the solemn baptism of infants?**

Solemn baptism, performed in the Church according to her traditional rites, is replete with special ceremonies: exorcisms, exsufflations, imposition of blessed salt, etc.

230. **Must the candidate for baptism be given a sponsor?**

The Church's norms say that insofar as possible there should be *sponsors*, also called *godparents*, in the administration of solemn baptism.[12] At times, however, finding a suitable godparent may be morally impossible.

231. **Why has the Church made this obligation?**

So that the newly baptized may have: 1. A witness of their entrance into the Church; 2. Someone to vouch for his good dispositions if he is an adult, or be surety for his good will if he is an infant; 3. An intercessor and helper in living according to our baptismal vows.

232. **How many sponsors may there be at baptism?**

One godfather or godmother, or both. They may assist at the baptism either in person or by proxy.

233. **What qualities are necessary in a baptismal sponsor?**

They must be capable, worthy, and intending to fulfill the role. As such, the Church excludes from the role of sponsor: 1. Heretics, schismatics, and excommunicates; 2. Public sinners, i.e., those living in open violation of God's commandments (whether or not they believe this to be sinful); 3. Those ignorant of the fundamentals of the Faith, or who have not yet been baptized and confirmed; 4. Normally, anyone under age sixteen.[13]

Effects of Baptism

234. **What are the effects of baptism?**

1. It gives sanctifying grace, which regenerates us in Christ Jesus; 2. It gives a new birth in the Holy Spirit, making us adopted children of God the Father; 3. It makes us members of the Church; 4. It washes away all sin; 5. It imparts a sacramental character, indelibly imprinted on the soul.

235. **How is baptism a spiritual regeneration?**
"It signifies and actually brings about the birth of water and the Spirit without which no one 'can enter the Kingdom of God' (Jn 3:5)."[14]

236. **How does baptism cleanse the soul completely?**
It washes away original sin and any actual sins that were committed before baptism, and remits any punishment still due to sin.

237. **How does baptism make the soul truly pleasing to God?**
It makes us a "new creature" (2 Cor 5:17) by communicating the grace of God to our soul and making it the temple of His divine indwelling. We become children of God, brothers and coheirs of Jesus Christ, and are filled with the gifts of the Holy Spirit and the infused virtues.

238. **What character is imprinted in the soul at baptism?**
The invisible seal or spiritual mark of Christ, distinguishing us from unbelievers and consecrating us to God forever. This indelible character sets us apart as members of the Church, qualifies us to receive the other sacraments, and enables us to offer God true and pleasing worship. "By the sacraments men are deputed to a spiritual service pertaining to the worship of God; it follows that by their means the faithful receive a certain spiritual character."[15]

239. **Does baptism return us to the state of justice and innocence once lost by Adam?**
Yes, although the defects in our fallen nature still remain, as a result of original sin: ignorance, concupiscence, suffering, and death.

240. **Why do these defects remain after baptism?**
Because our earthly life remains one of pilgrimage on the way to heaven, and these defects are opportunities to obtain greater merit and a higher degree of glory in the next life.

Baptismal Vows

241. **What is meant by baptismal *vows* or *promises*?**
The promises made by all candidates for baptism, or on their behalf if they are infants.

242. **What are these particular promises?**
They consist of three essential vows: 1. Renouncing Satan, his works and pomps; 2. Professing the true Catholic Faith; 3. Living by the teaching and example of Jesus Christ.

243. **What does it mean to *renounce Satan*?**
We entirely reject Satan and no longer wish to belong to him, obey him, or heed his perverse suggestions.

244. **What does it mean to renounce Satan's *pomps*?**
We reject the esteem of the world and its glittering rewards, which Satan uses as a powerful means of leading men astray.

245. **What does it mean to renounce Satan's *works*?**
We renounce all sin: every thought, desire, word, or deed contrary to the law of God.

246. **What are the second and third baptismal vows?**
We promise to take Jesus Christ as our only Lord, and ruler of all our thoughts and actions. Giving ourselves irrevocably to God, we bind ourselves to live for Him entirely.

247. **Are the promises of baptism very important?**
Yes. Our everlasting salvation depends on keeping them faithfully.

248. **Then merely being baptized is not sufficient for salvation?**
Baptism is sufficient for the salvation of infants and children before the age of reason, but adults must also faithfully perform the will of God (see Mt 7:21). "If they fail moreover to respond to [God's] grace in thought, word, and deed, not only shall they not be saved but they will be the more severely judged."[16]

249. **Is it useful to renew our baptismal promises?**
Yes. We would do well to renew them from time to time, particularly at our First Communion and on the yearly anniversary of our baptism.

Destiny of the Non-baptized

250. **What is the destiny of adults who die without sacramental baptism?**
They may not go automatically to hell, given the possibility of God's extraordinary providence, "since God will by no means suffer anyone to be punished with eternal torment who has not the guilt of deliberate sin."[17]

251. **Can the non-baptized avoid mortal sin and fulfill God's will without His grace?**
No. If anyone is saved, it is "by the operating power of divine light and grace."[18] The person who fulfills the natural law does so only with the help of this grace—which is then crowned with further graces enabling him to be saved. "It pertains to divine providence to furnish everyone with what is necessary for salvation, provided that on his part there is no hindrance."[19]

252. **Can we assume that there are many cases of extraordinary salvation for the non-baptized?**
No. Christ says that "the gate is narrow and the way is hard, that leads to life, and those who find it are few" (Mt 7:14); and, "in view of the fact that the Church stands plainly before the eyes of men like a city on a mountaintop, that the words of her ministers have gone forth to the ends of the earth, we do not venture to say that such cases as these are typical of large numbers."[20]

253. **Would the merits of Christ's redeeming sacrifice be the necessary cause of any such cases of extraordinary salvation?**
Yes. "There is salvation in no one else, for there is no other name under heaven given among men by which we must be saved" (Acts 4:12).

254. **If it is *possible* for the non-baptized to be saved, why must we evangelize?**
Because *possible* does not imply *likely*, and evangelizing is: 1. The explicit command of Christ; 2. Our duty in justice, as all men have a right to know God's revelation; 3. Our duty in charity, as Catholicism alone contains all of Christ's teachings and means of salvation; 4. Enabling others to reach a higher degree of eternal glory; 5. Sharing the peace and blessings of right faith on earth; 6. Rightly due to God, who desires to be known, loved, and served as He deserves, i.e., according to the truth.[21]

255. **Then the Church's missionary work is still most necessary?**
Yes. "Missionary activity derives its reason from the will of God, 'who wishes all men to be saved and to come to the knowledge of the truth. For there is one God, and one Mediator between God and men, Himself a man, Jesus Christ, who gave Himself as a ransom for all' (1 Tm 2:4–5*), 'neither is there salvation in any other' (Acts 4:12*). Therefore, all must be converted to Him, made known by the Church's preaching, and all must be incorporated into Him by baptism and into the Church which is His Body."[22]

256. **What heresies denied the necessity of baptism for infants?**
The Pelagian heresy denied the existence of original sin, and therefore asserted that infants do not need baptism; similarly, the Anabaptist heresy forbade baptism of children, saying that it was not necessary for salvation. But from the earliest times, the Church has baptized infants in order to confer grace, remove the effects of original sin, and ensure their salvation. The Council of Florence declared: "With regard to children, since the danger of death is often present and the only remedy available to them is the sacrament of baptism by which they are snatched away from the dominion of the devil and adopted as children of God, she admonishes that sacred baptism is not to be deferred."[23]

257. **Then what happens to infants who die without baptism?**
Having committed no personal sin, it seems unfitting that unbaptized infants should suffer the fate of those who are damned. A widespread theological opinion holds that their exclusion from the Beatific Vision may not necessarily entail pain and suffering; but rather, infants dying without baptism could be admitted to a peaceful eternity of purely natural goods—a kind of indirect or mediate vision of God.[24]

258. **How may this purely natural happiness be explained?**
St. Thomas Aquinas suggests: "It belongs to natural cognition that the soul knows that it is created for happiness, and that happiness consists of attainment of the perfect good. But that the perfect good for which human beings have been created is the glory that the saints possess is beyond natural knowledge. And so the Apostle

says in 1 Cor 2:9* that 'the eye has not seen, nor the ear heard, nor has it entered into the heart of human beings, what things God has prepared for those who love Him,' and then adds: 'and God has revealed them to us through His Spirit.' And this revelation indeed belongs to faith. And so the children's souls do not know that they are deprived of such a good, and they accordingly do not grieve. But those souls possess without anguish what they have by natural knowledge."[25]

259. **Would it be unjust to exclude unbaptized infants from the Beatific Vision?**
No, because human nature has no right to the Beatific Vision. We may ask God to grant these children the miracle of sanctifying grace on account of His infinite mercy, but their destiny ultimately remains a mystery which we entrust to the loving providence of God.

Chapter 8: Confirmation

Confirmation in General

260. **What is** *confirmation*?
A sacrament instituted by Christ to give us the Holy Spirit with the abundance of His gifts, and make us perfect Christians.

261. **What is the meaning of the word** *confirmation*?
It signifies the action of fortifying, strengthening, consolidating, completing, and perfecting; because it strengthens and completes the grace of baptism in our souls.

262. **How does confirmation differ from baptism?**
1. Baptism is a spiritual birth, while confirmation is an increase of spiritual life; 2. Baptism makes us members of Christ's Mystical Body, while confirmation enrolls us in His army of the Church Militant; 3. Baptism fills us with the gifts of the Holy Spirit, while confirmation gives them in even greater abundance. In a word, baptism makes us Christians, and confirmation empowers us to be perfect Christians.

263. **When did Jesus Christ institute the sacrament of confirmation?**
According to common opinion, on the night of the Last Supper: "Not by bestowing, but by promising it, according to John 16:7*: 'If I go not, the Paraclete will not come to you, but if I go, I will send Him to you.' And this was because in this sacrament the fullness of the Holy Ghost is bestowed, which was not to be given before Christ's Resurrection and Ascension, according to John 7:39*: 'As yet the Spirit was not given, because Jesus was not yet glorified.'"[26]

264. **What is the outward sign of confirmation?**
The imposition of the hands of the bishop, the anointing with sacred chrism, and the words that he pronounces at the same time.

265. **What invisible action is represented by this external sign?**
The descent of the Holy Spirit, with the abundance of His grace and gifts, into the soul of the person confirmed.

266. **What is the sacramental matter of confirmation?**
The imposition of hands and anointing with sacred *chrism*, which is a mixture of olive oil and balsam consecrated by the bishop every year, usually on Maundy Thursday.

267. **What is the traditional sacramental form of confirmation?**
The words: "I sign thee with the sign of the cross, I confirm thee with the chrism of salvation, in the name of the Father, and of the Son, and of the Holy Spirit." The Byzantine Catholic rite uses the words: "The seal of the gift of the Holy Spirit" (*signaculum doni Spiritus Sancti*),[27] to which corresponds the form used in the rite of Pope Paul VI: "Be sealed with the Gift of the Holy Spirit" (*accipe signaculum doni Spiritus Sancti*).

268. **Is the sacrament of confirmation necessary for salvation?**
Not absolutely; however, it is surpassingly useful for salvation, and to refuse or neglect to receive it through contempt is a grave offense to God, whose great gift it is.

269. **If we did not receive confirmation in our youth, should we receive it later?**
Yes. Christians need the help of this sacrament throughout their lives, and all the more so in times of trial and suffering.

Administration of Confirmation

270. **Who is the minister of confirmation?**
Only the bishop is the *ordinary* minister of confirmation. Any priest may be an *extraordinary* minister by proper delegation, using chrism consecrated by the bishop. In the Byzantine Catholic Church, any priest may confirm when he baptizes, but he must use chrism consecrated by the bishop.

271. **Who may receive confirmation?**
Any baptized Catholic.

272. **Why does confirmation presuppose baptism?**
Because confirmation is to baptism what maturity is to birth.

273. **At what age may confirmation be received?**
It may be received immediately after baptism, and thus can be administered even to infants (as usually done among Byzantine Catholics), although it is often delayed until the recipient is sufficiently instructed. Canon law prescribes that it be conferred at about the age of discretion (around 6 years).[28]

274. **What dispositions are required for adult confirmation?**
To receive the *character* imprinted by this sacrament, one must have the intention of being confirmed; to receive its other *effects*, one must be instructed in the principal truths of the Faith, and be in the state of grace.

275. **What of those who receive confirmation in the state of mortal sin?**
They commit sacrilege, and although their soul is imprinted with the sacramental character, they do not receive the Holy Spirit with all His graces and gifts; for, the Spirit of God cannot dwell in a soul that rejects Him through grave sin.

276. **What bodily dispositions are recommended for receiving confirmation?**
It is most proper to be: 1. Respectfully dressed; 2. Well groomed, with forehead washed and uncovered; 3. Fasting, if possible.

277. **What should we do to receive this sacrament profitably?**
We should prepare for it by prayer and retreat, remain in deep recollection while receiving it, and thank God for this great blessing after receiving it.

278. **What does each candidate do when he approaches the bishop for confirmation?**
Each one reveals his baptismal name, or the name of a special patron saint whom he has adopted for confirmation.

279. **How does the bishop confirm him?**
After pronouncing the candidate's name, he lays his hand on the candidate's head and anoints his forehead with chrism in the form of a cross, while pronouncing the form: "I sign thee," etc. He then adds a strike on the cheek while saying: "Peace be with thee."

280. **Why does the bishop anoint the forehead in the form of a cross?**
To show that confirmation draws its efficacy from the Cross of Jesus Christ, and that the cross is the standard of all His true soldiers. The sign is made on the forehead as the chief site of man's excellence: the intellect.

281. **Why does the bishop traditionally strike the candidate on the cheek?**
To teach the newly confirmed that this sacrament gives strength and courage to joyfully suffer insult and injury for the sake of Jesus Christ, as well as an interior patience and peace which the world cannot give.

Effects of Confirmation

282. **What are the effects of confirmation?**
1. An increase of sanctifying grace and more abundant outpouring of the gifts of the Holy Spirit; 2. A special sacramental grace; 3. An indelible character.

283. **Why does confirmation bring more abundant gifts of the Holy Spirit?**
Because confirmation is a kind of sacramental extension of Pentecost, whereby the Holy Spirit more richly empowers the faithful to undertake the spiritual combat and external witness of the Christian life.

284. **What is the sacramental grace proper to confirmation?**
A grace of strength, giving us a right to those actual graces necessary to confess Jesus Christ, in spite of trials and temptations.

285. **What character does confirmation imprint in the soul?**
It imprints the indelible character of a perfect Christian; a soldier and witness of Jesus Christ.

286. **What must we do to correspond with all the graces received in confirmation?**
We must keep faithfully the promises that we have made, follow the good lights and interior promptings of the Holy Spirit with docility, and boldly confess Jesus Christ.

287. **How should we confess Jesus Christ?**
We should confess Our Lord by our words and deeds.

288. **How do we confess Jesus Christ by *word*?**
By taking the side of truth and justice when these are attacked, defending the truths of the Gospel against those who speak against them, and professing our faith publicly when required.

289. **How may we confess Jesus Christ by *deed*?**
By making our actions reflect the example and teachings of Jesus Christ, above all by our truthfulness and charity. "By this all men will know that you are My disciples" (Jn 13:35).

290. **How do the confirmed grow in sanctification and personal holiness?**
By perfection in charity, i.e., loving God with our whole heart, soul, mind, and strength; and loving our neighbor as ourself (see Mt 22:37–40), and as Christ loves (see Jn 13:34; and 15:12). Such a life is only possible with the help of God's grace, by which the Holy Spirit moves the soul inwardly toward holiness.

291. **Are all Christians obliged to a life of personal holiness?**
Yes. Jesus Christ, "the divine Teacher and Model of all perfection, preached holiness of life to each and every one of His disciples of every condition. He Himself stands as the author and consumator of this holiness of life: 'Be you therefore perfect, even as your heavenly Father is perfect' (Mt 5:48*)," and those who follow Him must "conform themselves to His image seeking the will of the Father in all things. They must devote themselves with all their being to the glory of God and the service of their neighbor."[29]

292. **What does this way of holiness imply?**

Acceptance of the crosses in one's life, and Christian asceticism. "The way of perfection passes by way of the Cross. There is no holiness without renunciation and spiritual battle (see 2 Tm 4:7). Spiritual progress entails the ascesis and mortification that gradually lead to living in the peace and joy of the Beatitudes."[30]

293. **Are the various charisms reliable indicators of personal holiness?**

No. Whether humble or astounding, the charisms are not indicators of personal sanctity, but unique adornments and tools intended to help us fulfill our duties of state and build up the Church.

Pentecostalism

294. **What is *Pentecostalism*?**

Present in the so-called "Charismatic Movement" or "Renewal in the Spirit," it is a new phenomenon—in a sense, even a new religion—resembling heresies like Montanism that emphasize charismatic, demonstrative, sentimental, and irrational religious experience. It has penetrated many Christian communities and even non-Christian religions, and presents a real spiritual danger in our time.

295. **What are some reasons for this movement's growth, even among Catholics?**

1. Combining traditional practices (prayer, adoration, teachings, apostolate, religious enthusiasm) with novel "experiences" (emotional expression, promise of extraordinary charisms, etc.); 2. The allure of unusual phenomena and a felt sense of God's presence; 3. Seeking physical and mental wellness (in "healing services"), with the appearance of solving all difficulties in life; 4. Wide promotion and support from the secular media; 5. Occasional support from members of the Church's hierarchy, who see the movement as a supposed "New Springtime" of the Church or implementation of the "spirit" of Vatican II.

296. **What are the dangers inherent to these movements?**

They essentially equate religion with intuition, feeling, and irrational sentiment, ending in subjectivism and arbitrariness. Experience and emotion then become the measure of holiness and religious practice, also opening the door for demonic influence and deception. These movements often lack the reasonability and dignified disposition of awe that Catholics have always demonstrated before God's majesty.

297. **What is "baptism in the Holy Spirit"?**

According to its champions, this private experience is the very heart of the movement: a watershed moment of the spiritual life, a "personal Pentecost," a new and deeper experience of the presence of God.

298. **Does this practice belong to Catholic Tradition?**

No. This practice is unknown in the constant doctrine and discipline of the Catholic Church. As an essentially Protestant concept, it poses a serious threat to the Catholic identity of the faithful, as it undermines or attacks the nature and importance of the sacraments, especially baptism and confirmation.

299. **What did Our Lady and the apostles do, when moved by the Holy Spirit?**
At Pentecost, the Blessed Virgin Mary and the apostles did not practice *glossolalia*, speaking unintelligible and incoherent words, but spoke in a well-articulated way that everyone understood in their own language. They did not collapse and "rest in the spirit," they did not cry, clap their hands, jump, or dance, as characteristically happens in many of today's "Catholic charismatic" events and liturgies.

300. **Then what is the true Catholic expression of devotion to the Holy Spirit?**
The sacred liturgy uses the phrase *sobria ebrietas Spiritus*, the "sober inebriation" of the Holy Spirit. This means having an ardent heart while yet remaining sober and orderly, guided by reason, exterior dignity, supernatural wonder, and faith: our "reasonable and acceptable" offering of divine praise.[31]

301. **May we seek Church renewal in a new, so-called "Pre-Constantinian" Catholicism?**
No. Any authentic renewal must adhere faithfully to what Christ the Lord handed down to the apostles, and what has developed in the Church's constant teaching and prayer, without rupture, over two thousand years. It would be heretical to wish to erase the time from the Edict of Milan (313) to the beginning of Vatican II (1962), labeling the life of the Church during those seventeen centuries as "dark," "Constantinian," deprived of the guiding presence of the Holy Spirit.

302. **What is the path to true renewal in the Church?**
The Church, though always holy in itself, nevertheless needs constant renewal in its members, as we rise again and again from sin, repel temptation, tame vices, and multiply virtues, becoming more and more like Christ the Lord. The world also needs the renewal of conversion and repentance.

303. **What are the concrete characteristics of this authentic renewal?**
1. A theocentric attitude and "vertical view" of reality, faith, and liturgy; 2. True champions in the persons of saints; 3. Personal commitment to carrying the cross; 4. Firm grounding in the Sacrifice of the Mass, holy confession, and the mission to save souls; 5. Avoidance of spiritual sensationalism, exhibitionism, and celebrity worship (as often occurs in massive arena functions).

304. **What have the popes prescribed for authentic renewal of the Church?**
A return to the authentic and constant Catholic Tradition. "The true friends of the people are neither revolutionaries, nor innovators: they are traditionalists."[32] "We must use every means and exert all our energy to bring about the utter disappearance of the enormous and detestable wickedness, so characteristic of our time—the substitution of man for God; this done, it remains to restore to their ancient place of honor the most holy laws and counsels of the Gospel, … with no other aim than that Christ may be formed in all."[33]

Chapter 9: Eucharist

FIRST PART: EUCHARIST AS SACRAMENT

Eucharist in General

305. **What is the *Eucharist*?**
The sacrament that perpetuates the sacrifice of the Cross, in which Christ's immolated and glorified body and blood are really, truly, and substantially offered, present, contained, and received under the appearances of bread and wine.[34]

306. **Which three realities are signified in the Eucharist?**
1. The past sacrifice of the Cross, made present through this sacrament; 2. The present heavenly grace, imparted by this sacrament to nurture and preserve the soul; 3. The future joy and eternal glory, pledged in this sacrament.[35]

307. **What does the word *Eucharist* mean?**
Thanksgiving, because Jesus Christ gives perfect thanks to His Father in this sacrament, and offers us the means to offer pleasing worship to God. It also means *good grace*, because it contains Jesus Christ, the author and source of all grace.[36]

308. **What other names are given to this sacrament?**
With regard to the past: the Lord's *Sacrifice*. With regard to the present: the *Communion* or *Synaxis,* because we commune with Christ through it, partaking of His flesh and Godhead, and also because we commune with and are united to one another through it. With regard to the future: *Viaticum*, because it supplies the way to reach to heaven.

309. **When did Jesus Christ institute the sacrament of the Eucharist?**
On Holy Thursday, the night before His death, while gathered with His disciples at the Last Supper.

310. **How did God prepare for the institution of the Eucharist?**
It was prefigured in the Old Testament, above all in the sacrifices of Abel (see Gn 4:4), Abraham (see Gn 22:1–14), and Melchizedek (see Gn 14:18), the manna of the desert (see Ex 16:15), and especially in the sacrifice of the paschal lamb (see Ex 12:1–28). It was foretold particularly by the prophet Malachi: "From the rising of the sun to its setting My name is great among the nations, and in every place incense is offered to My name, and a pure offering; for My name is great among the nations, says the Lord of hosts" (Mal 1:11), and before instituting it, Christ Himself promised that "the bread which I shall give for the life of the world is My flesh" (Jn 6:51).

311. **What is the outward sign in the Eucharist?**
The sign is the *species*, or appearances, of bread and wine; i.e., whatever in these elements is detectable by the senses, such as size, color, odor, taste, etc.

PART III — WORSHIP: BEING HOLY

312. **What does this sign contain?**

No substance of bread or wine, but rather the substance of the very body and blood of Jesus Christ, joined by *natural concomitance* to His human soul, and to His divinity in virtue of the hypostatic union.

313. **What is the sacramental matter of the Eucharist?**

It is wheat bread, which serves for the consecration of the body of Our Lord; and grape wine mixed with a little water, which serves for the consecration of His blood. When the bread is pressed into wafer form, this is called a *host*.

314. **Must the bread necessarily be unleavened?**

No. The Latin Church must use unleavened bread, but Eastern Churches may use leavened bread, as the Council of Florence maintained: "The body of Christ is truly confected in both unleavened and leavened wheat bread, and priests should confect the body of Christ in either, that is, each priest according to the custom of his Western or Eastern Church."[37]

315. **Why did Our Lord choose bread and wine as the matter of this sacrament?**

1. To show that this sacrament is the true food of our souls, without which we "shall not have life" (Jn 6:54*); 2. To leave us a symbol of the close union which should exist among all members of His Church, who, "being many, are one bread, one body" (1 Cor 10:17*).

316. **How do the Church Fathers explain this symbolism of Church unity in the Eucharist?**

The first-century document *Didache* prays: "As this broken bread was scattered over the hills, and was gathered together and became one, so let Your Church be gathered together from the ends of the earth into Your kingdom";[38] and St. Cyprian teaches: "The body of the Lord cannot be flour alone or water alone, unless both should be united and joined together and compacted in the mass of one bread; in which very sacrament our people are shown to be made one, so that in like manner as many grains, collected, and ground, and mixed together into one mass, make one bread; so in Christ, who is the heavenly Bread, we may know that there is one body, with which our number is joined and united."[39]

317. **What is the form of the sacrament of the Eucharist?**

It consists in the words of *consecration* or solemn blessing, which are the very words of Jesus Christ: "This is My body ... This is the chalice of My blood," pronounced by His priest.

318. **What great miracle occurs when the priest speaks the words of consecration?**

When the priest pronounces these words, Our Lord Jesus Christ becomes instantly, really, truly, personally, and substantially present under the appearances of bread and wine.

The Real Presence

319. Can the presence of Christ in the Eucharist be outwardly observed by the senses?
No. His Eucharistic presence is properly known by faith alone. However, He sometimes works additional miracles to demonstrate this presence.

320. Where is the dogma of the Real Presence to be found?
It is illustrated in: 1. Holy Scripture; 2. Tradition; 3. The infallible teaching of the Church; 4. The life of the Church over two millennia; 5. Approved Eucharistic miracles.

321. How does Church teaching show the dogma of the Real Presence?
"In the august sacrament of the Holy Eucharist, after the consecration of the bread and wine, Our Lord Jesus Christ, true God and man, is truly, really, and substantially contained under the species of those sensible things,"[40] and, "if anyone says that He is only therein as in a sign, or in figure, or virtue; let him be anathema."[41]

322. How does Holy Scripture attest to the Real Presence?
In addition to many Old Testament preparations and foreshadowings, there are the remarkable accounts of its promise (see Jn 6:47–58), institution (see Mt 26:26–29; Mk 14:22–25; and Lk 22:15–20), and use (see 1 Cor 11:23–30) — texts that are clear and unequivocal.

323. How does Tradition bear witness to the Real Presence?
Since the days of the apostles, every Father and Doctor of the Church has held and taught the fact of Our Lord's Real Presence in the Eucharist and its sacrificial character.

324. How does Church history confirm this dogmatic fact?
We observe that even the schismatically separated Churches of the East still hold the Catholic Eucharistic dogma, as they always did before their separation.

325. Has this dogma also been confirmed by miracles?
Yes. Our Lord has at times made Himself known in this mystery by visible wonders, recorded throughout the world, as when sacred hosts have bled, levitated, been preserved from fire, etc. St. Thomas Aquinas asks: "Can anything be more marvelous than this sacrament?" and adds that the Eucharist is "the greatest of the miracles which Christ ever wrought (*miraculorum maximum*)."[42]

326. Does the Magisterium hold the Eucharist to be the greatest of miracles?
Yes. "This miracle, itself the very greatest of its kind, is accompanied by innumerable other miracles; for here all the laws of nature are suspended."[43]

327. How does Our Lord become truly present in the Holy Eucharist?
By the miracle of *transubstantiation*, the wondrous change of the whole substance of the bread into the body of Jesus Christ, and the whole substance of the wine into His blood.[44]

328. Is there any bread or wine remaining on the altar after the consecration?
No. After the consecration, the substances of bread and wine no longer exist—only their sensible species or *accidents* remain on the altar.

329. Is Jesus Christ, whole and entire, then present in the Eucharist?
Yes. Jesus Christ, whole and entire, is substantially present under the appearance of bread, as He is also wholly and entirely present under the appearance of wine.

330. How is Christ's human soul also present in the Eucharist?
"The soul is present under both kinds, by the force of that natural connection and concomitancy whereby the parts of Christ Our Lord, who hath now risen from the dead to die no more, are united together."[45]

331. How is Christ's divinity also present in the Eucharist?
"The divinity is present on account of the admirable hypostatical union thereof with His body and soul."[46]

332. How can we explain the mode of Christ's presence in the Eucharist?
It is a *sacramental* mode: His body is not present there *locally*, like a physical body that takes up dimensional space, for His living and risen body is properly in heaven. Rather, He is present *substantially*—within every particle of the sacred host, and every drop of the precious blood. In this way, He can be "present in many places in a sacramental manner at one and the same time, without external extension."[47]

333. Do the consecrated species still retain their natural properties?
Yes. The sacred species have the same properties as they did before transubstantiation (taste, appearance, etc.), and act as they would have acted when the bread and wine were present.

334. When does Christ cease to be present under the sacred species?
His presence departs when the sacramental species are irreparably altered or corrupted; e.g., the host is digested or decays, or the precious blood is diluted.

335. Should the Eucharist itself be worshipped?
Yes. "If anyone saith, that, in the Holy Sacrament of the Eucharist, Christ, the only-begotten Son of God, is not to be adored with the worship, even external of *latria*; and is, consequently, neither to be venerated with a special festive solemnity, nor to be solemnly borne about in processions, according to the laudable and universal rite and custom of holy Church; or, is not to be proposed publicly to the people to be adored, and that the adorers thereof are idolators; let him be anathema."[48]

336. Is the Eucharist the most excellent of all the sacraments?
Yes. For it contains Jesus Christ Himself, whereas the other sacraments have only an instrumental power derived from Him. We call the Eucharist the *Sacrament of sacraments* because it is "the end and consummation of all the sacraments."[49]

337. **Are the other sacraments in some way ordered to the Eucharist?**
Yes. Baptism makes us fit to receive the Eucharist; confirmation strengthens us to approach and defend it; penance and anointing of the sick dispose us to receive it worthily; holy orders furnishes ministers to consecrate it; matrimony stands as a sign of the Eucharistic communion between Christ and His Church.

338. **What are the principal errors about the dogma of Christ's Real Presence in the Eucharist?**
Those of: 1. *Berengarius* (+1088), who held that Christ is only figuratively present in the Eucharist; 2. Protestants like *Zwingli* (+1531) or *Calvin* (+1564), who denied the Real Presence entirely, while *Luther* (+1546) held it as only occurring during Holy Communion, and existing together with the substance of bread and wine (consubstantiation).

339. **Has God intervened to refute these errors?**
Yes, by: 1. Prompting St. Juliana of Mount-Cornillon to establish the feast of Corpus Christi; 2. Raising up St. Thomas Aquinas to admirably expound the Eucharistic dogma; 3. Multiplying Eucharistic miracles; 4. Prompting the infallible teaching of several councils, especially the Council of Trent; 5. Inspiring greater Eucharistic devotion throughout the Church, especially through Eucharistic Congresses and the devotion of perpetual adoration of the Blessed Sacrament; 6. Inspiring Eucharistic saints like St. Peter Julian Eymard (+1867) and the foundation of various religious congregations for the veneration of the Eucharist; 7. Strengthening many martyrs in confession of the Real Presence.

340. **Is the dogmatic formula of transubstantiation still understandable and relevant?**
Yes. The Tridentine formulation of this dogma is suitable for all men of all times, being a "perennially valid teaching of the Church"[50] and a divine truth that radically affects every aspect of life on earth: *Jesus Christ is truly with us.*

Administration of the Eucharist

341. **What two kinds of ministry pertain to the sacrament of the Eucharist?**
The ministry of *consecrating* the sacrament, and the ministry of *dispensing* it to the faithful in the form of Holy Communion.

342. **Who are the ministers for consecrating the Holy Eucharist?**
Only priests and bishops have power to consecrate the Eucharist, given to them when Christ commanded: "Do this for a commemoration of Me" (Lk 22:19*).

343. **What ministers most fittingly dispense the Eucharist in Holy Communion?**
The proper and fitting ministers of Holy Communion are bishops and priests: "To touch the sacred species and to distribute them with their own hands is a privilege of the ordained."[51]

344. **What is the role of deacons in dispensing Communion?**
In ancient times, deacons administered the chalice of the precious blood of Christ to communicants. Contrary to the Church's constant liturgical tradition of deacons being *extraordinary* ministers of Holy Communion,[52] the current Code of Canon Law admits them as ordinary ministers, together with bishops and priests.[53]

345. **May lay persons serve as extraordinary ministers of Holy Communion?**
This has sometimes been permitted in limited cases, e.g., during persecution or when there is insufficient clergy to visit the sick in remote areas, provided that there is no risk of loss of reverence. However, never in the history of the Church have lay persons distributed Communion at Holy Mass, as seen in some places today.

346. **Is it absolutely necessary to receive the Eucharist in order to be saved?**
No, as one may be saved by the grace of baptism. However, it is necessary for adults to receive the Eucharist in Holy Communion as a matter of precept: "Unless you eat the flesh of the Son of Man, and drink His blood, you shall not have life in you" (Jn 6:54*).

347. **When is the precept of Holy Communion binding?**
Our Lord did not personally determine the frequency of Holy Communion; He left this to His Church, which, while encouraging us to receive as often as we are properly disposed, requires us to do so at least once a year, usually at Eastertide.[54]

348. **Who may receive Holy Communion?**
Any baptized Catholic who has the use of reason and the proper dispositions.

349. **Why is it important to be properly disposed for Holy Communion?**
Every important action demands preparation, and the receiving of Jesus Christ, the Son of God, in Holy Communion is the most important action that man may perform on earth.

350. **What dispositions are required for receiving Holy Communion?**
There are two kinds: dispositions of soul and dispositions of body.

351. **What dispositions of *soul* are required for Holy Communion?**
1. Assent to all Catholic doctrine, including all of the Church's moral teachings;
2. The state of grace, i.e., being conscious of no unconfessed mortal sins. Being thus joined to Christ by faith and charity, we are ready to welcome Him into ourselves through the sacrament of His love.

352. **Is it necessary to confess even venial sins before receiving Holy Communion?**
It is not necessary, but very suitable. By purifying the soul, confession removes obstacles to certain actual graces and other precious benefits in Holy Communion, and intensifies our awareness of its dignity.

353. **What further dispositions of soul are most proper for Holy Communion?**
Detachment from all sin and worldly affections, with a desire of being united to Christ in faith, humility, confidence, and love.

354. **How may we suitably prepare for Holy Communion?**
1. Strive to be more recollected on the eve before our Communion; 2. Upon waking, think of the coming joy of receiving Our Lord; 3. When rising, remain recollected and prayerful before Mass; 4. During Mass, adore, thank, and petition God in interior union with the action of the priest; 5. At Communion, renew acts of faith, humility, contrition, and desire.

355. **What should we do after Holy Communion?**
Make a good thanksgiving, by: 1. Rejoicing immediately with deepest gratitude for Our Lord giving Himself to us; 2. Lavishing our faith, adoration, and love on Him; 3. Asking divine favors for ourselves and others.

356. **Should we limit our thanksgiving to the time just after Communion?**
It is best to prolong it, by: 1. Praying for some time after Mass is ended; 2. Leading a life in gratitude for the great grace of Communion we have received.

357. **What dispositions of *body* are required for Holy Communion?**
We must be fasting. Configuring our bodies to the image of the Virgin's womb, the unused tomb, and the inviolate tabernacle, we make ready to become a physical dwelling place for Our Lord.

358. **What does this bodily fast consist of?**
Foregoing all food and drink (except water) for at least one hour prior to Holy Communion.[55] To show still greater reverence for Our Lord, many choose to keep the more ancient discipline of fasting from midnight, or at least three hours before Communion.[56]

359. **Are there exemptions from this Eucharistic fast?**
Yes. Exception may be made for: 1. Water; 2. Medicine; 3. Priests offering more than one Mass in a day; 4. The sick, elderly, and their caretakers; 5. Cases where the Eucharist would otherwise be destroyed or profaned.

360. **What dispositions of body are most proper for Holy Communion?**
1. To be neatly and honorably dressed when approaching the altar, avoiding both ostentation and sloppiness; 2. To have a decent, modest, and recollected bearing.

361. **How should we approach to receive Holy Communion?**
We should not hurry, proceeding with hands folded and eyes downcast; we can also look up at a crucifix or other sacred image, to remain focused on divine things.

362. **How should we receive Holy Communion?**
While kneeling (if our physical condition allows it), and upon the tongue.

363. **Why have Christians received Holy Communion this way for so many centuries?**
To show that: 1. The Eucharist is no common food, but our very Lord and God; 2. The ordinary minister is no common man, but set apart by a special sacrament and anointed for this divine work; 3. We believe, adore, and submit to the ineffable divine Majesty hidden in the little host, allowing ourselves to be fed by the good God like little children, since this supernatural food is His alone to give, and we cannot earn it or be "equal" to it.

364. **Does it respect the Church's tradition to receive Holy Communion in the hand?**
No. The current practice of Communion in the hand is spiritually harmful and foreign to the Catholic liturgical patrimony, having been invented by Calvinists to signify their rejection of holy orders and transubstantiation.

365. **Why is Communion in the hand so spiritually harmful?**
It violates: 1. The rights of Christ, failing in the proper reverence due to His Eucharistic fragments, sacred vessels, and ordained ministers; 2. Catholic faith and piety, weakening belief in and witness to the Incarnation and transubstantiation; 3. The necessary custody of consecrated hosts, which are increasingly stolen and abused.

366. **Should the indult (special permission) for Communion in the hand be continued?**
No. There is no supposed "pastoral need" or alleged "right of the faithful" that can justify danger to faith or sacrilege, when Our Eucharistic Lord has a right to the greatest possible reverence.

367. **What ancient practice is sometimes invoked to defend Communion in the hand?**
In some places during the first centuries, Holy Communion was placed on the palm of the right hand, sometimes covered with a *dominicale* (white cloth), after which the faithful bowed to take the host directly by mouth. The hand was washed before and after to purify it, so that no fragment would be lost. There is no evidence that this practice was ever universal in the Church.[57]

368. **Why did the Church eventually prohibit Communion in the hand?**
An admirable consensus was already reached in East and West by the first millennium, when it was observed that conditions no longer existed to ensure the proper respect for the Eucharist, and the highest honors were increasingly and instinctively paid to this sacred mystery.

369. **Does the Church deny Holy Communion to public sinners?**
Yes. In her reverence for the Eucharist, care for the unity of her members, and concern for the sinner's salvation, the Church denies Communion to anyone in a public state of objectively grave sin; such as concubinage, adulterous cohabitation, public (especially political) support for abortion, same-sex civil unions, homosexual activity, etc.[58]

370. **May a public sinner nonetheless present himself for Communion?**
No. This is the damnable sin of *unworthy* Communion, "eating and drinking judgment" (cf. 1 Cor 11:29, 27). As St. John Chrysostom declared, "I too raise my voice, I beseech, beg, and implore that no one draw near to this sacred table with a sullied and corrupt conscience. Such an act, in fact, can never be called 'communion,' not even were we to touch the Lord's body a thousand times over, but 'condemnation,' 'torment,' and 'increase of punishment.'"[59]

371. **May the Eucharist be administered to Protestants or the Orthodox?**
No. As the sacrament of unity (see 1 Cor 10:17), the Eucharist "is properly the sacrament of those who are in full communion with the Church."[60] It may not be given to those who deny any truth of the Church's faith or her unity by formally adhering to any heretical or schismatic community. "It is the duty of all who heard Jesus Christ, if they wished for eternal salvation, not merely to accept His doctrine as a whole, but to assent with their entire mind to all and every point of it, since it is unlawful to withhold faith from God even in regard to one single point."[61]

Different Kinds of Communion

372. **How may the different kinds of communion be divided?**
1. By mode of reception: sacramental or spiritual; 2. By time and circumstance: First Communion, Easter Communion, Viaticum, and frequent Communion; 3. By our dispositions during reception: fervent, tepid, or unworthy.

373. **What is a *sacramental* Communion?**
Reception of the Eucharist in its visible species, the Blessed Sacrament of the Altar; this is what is normally meant by "receiving Holy Communion."

374. **What is *spiritual* communion?**
An act of pious desire to receive Jesus Christ into our souls, when we are in the state of grace but unable to communicate sacramentally.

375. **What is the theological explanation of *spiritual* communion?**
"The effect of the sacrament can be secured by every man if he receive it in desire, though not in reality. Consequently, just as some are baptized with the baptism of desire ... before being baptized in the baptism of water; so likewise some eat this sacrament spiritually before they receive it sacramentally."[62]

376. **When may spiritual communions be made?**
At any time and place, but especially at Mass and during visits to the Blessed Sacrament.

377. **Is the practice of making spiritual communions very profitable?**
Yes. Spiritual communions are most pleasing to Our Lord, and they merit grace for us and prepare us well for sacramental Communion.

378. **What is a suitable prayer to make a spiritual communion?**
My Jesus, I believe that You are present in the Most Holy Sacrament. I love You above all things, and I desire to receive You into my soul. Since I cannot at this moment receive You sacramentally, come at least spiritually into my heart. I embrace You as if You were already there and unite myself wholly to You. Never permit me to be separated from You. Amen.

379. **What is *First Communion*?**
A person's first sacramental Communion, typically occurring in childhood.

380. **What is Communion as *Viaticum*?**
Receiving Holy Communion in the probable danger of death: a duty for the faithful who are able to receive it.

381. **Who may receive Holy Communion away from a church, when not in danger of death?**
Those unable to attend Holy Mass; e.g., the sick, elderly, or imprisoned.

382. **What is *frequent* Communion?**
Receiving Holy Communion even more often than every Sunday; e.g., several times a week, or daily.

383. **What are the reasons to desire frequent Communion?**
1. The invitation of Our Lord; 2. The excellence of this sacrament; 3. The pious example of many saints; 4. The practice of early Christians; 5. Our constant need for growth in sanctification.

384. **What are the conditions for frequent Communion?**
The state of grace, and a right intention; not approaching "out of routine, or vainglory, or human respect, but [wishing] to please God, to be more closely united with Him by charity, and to have recourse to this divine remedy for [our] weakness and defects.... It is especially fitting that those who receive Communion frequently or daily should be free from venial sins, at least from such as are fully deliberate, and from any affection thereto; ... tak[ing] care that Holy Communion be preceded by careful preparation, and followed by an appropriate thanksgiving, according to each one's strength, circumstances, and duties."[63]

385. **What are the advantages of frequent Communion?**
St. Francis de Sales instructs us to communicate often, in order to learn how to love God, purify our sins, arise from miseries, console our afflictions, and strengthen ourselves against weakness.[64]

386. **What is *fervent* Communion?**
Sacramental Communion received when the soul has been well prepared: adorned with lively faith, firm hope, ardent charity, profound sentiments of adoration and humility, and a great desire for union with Christ.

387. **What is *tepid* Communion?**
Sacramental Communion received in the state of grace, but with voluntary distractions or lacking due preparation or any devotional effort.

388. **What is *unworthy* Communion?**
Sacramental Communion received when we are not in the state of grace, i.e., sacrilegious Communion.

389. **Does God punish unworthy Communions, even in this life?**
Yes. Besides blindness of mind and hardness of heart, such Communions may also be punished by loss of property, reputation, health, and life.

Effects of the Eucharist

390. **What are the various effects of the Holy Eucharist?**
1. Ineffable union with Jesus Christ; 2. Spiritual nourishment of the soul; 3. Intensification of charity and all virtues; 4. Forgiveness of venial sins and greater preservation from mortal sin; 5. Weakening of concupiscence; 6. Pledge of future glory.

391. **How does the Eucharist unite us intimately with Jesus Christ?**
Although natural food is absorbed by the body, we absorb and are absorbed by this divine food, being made one with Christ: "He who eats My flesh and drinks My blood abides in me, and I in him" (Jn 6:56).

392. **Can this ineffable union with Christ in Holy Communion be outwardly observed?**
No. Being a spiritual union, it cannot properly be detected by the senses. However, worthy Communions often produce sentiments of immense peace and joy in the soul.

393. **What is this spiritual nourishment of the soul?**
An increase of sanctifying grace, and the disposition of all actual graces necessary to preserve charity and union with Jesus Christ.

394. **How does the Eucharist intensify charity and all the virtues?**
By uniting us with Christ, God Incarnate, in the very "sacrament of love," the Eucharist elicits our greater love of God in the soul, and thereby strengthens all the other virtues.

395. **Why does the Eucharist remit venial sins?**
"This daily bread is taken 'as a remedy against daily infirmity.' The reality of this sacrament is charity, not only as to its habit, but also as to its act, which is kindled in this sacrament; and by this means venial sins are forgiven."[65]

396. **How does the Holy Eucharist preserve us from mortal sin?**
By: 1. Increasing sanctifying grace, which strengthens our soul for combat and renders us less susceptible to temptation; 2. Giving us a right to special graces; 3. Putting the devil to flight.

397. **How does the Eucharist weaken concupiscence?**
By increasing charity, as St. Augustine maintains: "Increase of charity is a lessening of licentious desires."[66]

398. **Is Eucharistic Communion especially valuable for preserving chastity?**
Yes, as St. Peter Julian Eymard explains: "The grace of purity comes only from Our Lord. Communion gives it, increases it, strengthens it, preserves and maintains it against all the assaults of hell, the world, and the flesh. You drink there the virginal blood of the spotless Lamb.... In His Eucharist, Jesus is the very essence of purity."[67]

399. **How is the Eucharist a pledge of future glory?**
It bears the infallible promise of a glorious resurrection for all who receive it worthily: "He who eats My flesh and drinks My blood has eternal life, and I will raise him up at the last day" (Jn 6:54).

Duties to the Eucharist

400. **How may we prove our love and devotion to Our Lord in the Blessed Sacrament?**
By: 1. Frequent Communion; 2. Visits to the Blessed Sacrament (e.g., holy hours of adoration); 3. Assisting regularly at Holy Mass; 4. Spiritual communions; 5. Reading reliable books on Eucharistic doctrine and spirituality; 6. Propagating Eucharistic devotion; 7. Often greeting the Lord spiritually in all the tabernacles of the world; 8. Practicing Eucharistic reparation; 9. Contributing to the decorum and maintenance of altars and sanctuaries where the Blessed Sacrament is reserved.

401. **What sign tells us that Jesus is truly present in a Catholic church?**
The red sanctuary lamp, which burns night and day before the tabernacle whenever the Holy Eucharist is reserved there.

402. **How may we outwardly show adoration to the Eucharist?**
1. Being reverent in any Catholic church, which is truly the house of God; 2. Genuflecting to the tabernacle where the Eucharist is reserved; 3. Kneeling on both knees or prostrating ourselves when the Eucharist is exposed to view for adoration.

SECOND PART: EUCHARIST AS SACRIFICE

Sacrifice in General

403. **What are the essential parts of a true sacrifice?**
1. *Immolation*, whereby some valuable thing is outwardly changed or destroyed; 2. *Oblation*, the (especially interior) act of offering the thing to God. "Hence every

sacrifice is an oblation, but not conversely. *Firstfruits* are oblations, because they were offered to God, according to Deuteronomy 26, but they are not a sacrifice, because nothing sacred was done to them."[68]

404. **Is the offering of sacrifice commanded by natural law?**
Yes. "It is a dictate of natural reason that man should use certain sensible things by offering them to God, in sign of the subjection and honor due to Him, like those who make certain offerings to their lord in recognition of his authority. Now this is what we mean by a sacrifice, and consequently the offering of sacrifice is of the natural law."[69]

405. **Is the offering of ritual sacrifice a universal practice?**
Yes. Since the Fall of man, some form of sacrifice was practiced in every religion until the emergence of Protestantism, which denied the need for ritual sacrifice.

406. **What kind of sacrifice does God demand?**
A sacrifice that is both interior and exterior, as we are creatures of body and soul. "A sacrifice is offered in order that something may be represented. Now the sacrifice that is offered outwardly represents the inward spiritual sacrifice, whereby the soul offers itself to God."[70]

407. **Can the true religion exist without a true sacrifice?**
No. The true religion must have a solemn, public, and external act by which men honor God and profess their absolute dependence on Him, in a ritual form that is pleasing to Him.

408. **Were the sacrifices of the primitive religion and the Mosaic Law pleasing to God?**
All sacrifices offered to God from the beginning of the world were agreeable to Him only insofar as they were figures and anticipations of the sacrifice of the Cross: the divine self-offering of His Son on Mount Calvary.

409. **How did Jesus prepare for the sacrifice of the Cross?**
By making His earthly life one long act of self-emptying love, offering it with the most perfect dispositions to the will of His Father.

Calvary and the Mass

410. **Was the sacrifice of the Cross a true sacrifice?**
Yes, as it was: 1. An external offering of a sensible thing (the human life of Jesus Christ); 2. Given to God; 3. Performed by a lawful minister (the Incarnate Son of God); 4. Destroyed, when Christ died on the Cross; 5. Offered to acknowledge God's sovereignty, and as atonement for the sins of Adam and all humanity.

411. **Is the sacrifice of the Cross the only true sacrifice of our Redemption?**
Yes. As the victim and the priest in this sacrifice are God Himself, it is the only true and perfect sacrifice, accomplished once and for all upon Calvary.

412. Did this sacrifice complete all the sacrifices God ever required?
Yes. At Mass, the Church prays: "O God, who in the one perfect sacrifice [of Christ] brought to completion the varied offerings of the Law; accept, we pray, this sacrifice from Your faithful servants and make it holy, as You blessed the gifts of Abel, so that what each has offered to the honor of Your Majesty may benefit the salvation of all."[71]

413. Does Our Lord continue this sacrifice upon earth?
Yes. Christ instituted a means to extend His perfect sacrifice throughout time and space, until the end of the world, as foretold by the prophet Malachi (see Mal 1:11).

414. What is the meaning of the title *Mass*?
The term *Mass* recalls the words spoken by the priest or deacon at the conclusion of the Eucharistic Sacrifice in the Roman liturgy: *Ite, missa est* (Go forth, you are sent).

415. What is the Sacrifice of the Mass?
It is the very sacrifice of the Cross, now really and truly re-presented and offered to God in an unbloody manner, under the external appearances of bread and wine.

416. How is the Mass truly the sacrifice of the Cross?
"We always offer the same Lamb, not one today and another tomorrow, but always the same one. For this reason the sacrifice is always only one.... Even now we offer that victim who was once offered and who will never be consumed."[72] Our Lord's same self-immolation is present, for, "this was His intention and desire at the Last Supper when He 'gave thanks.' He did not cease to do so when hanging upon the Cross, nor does He fail to do so in the august sacrifice of the altar."[73]

417. What does every valid Mass accomplish?
"The commemorative representation of [Christ's] death, which actually took place on Calvary, is repeated in every sacrifice of the altar, seeing that Jesus Christ is symbolically shown by separate symbols to be in a state of victimhood."[74] This truly "makes Christ's one, definitive, redemptive sacrifice always present in time."[75]

418. How does the Sacrifice of the Mass differ from that of the Cross?
The one and only difference is "the manner of offering";[76] 1. On the Cross, Christ really died—at Mass, His death is represented in a sacramental mode; 2. On the Cross, Christ offered Himself directly and visibly as High Priest—at Mass, He invisibly offers Himself through the hands of His priests; 3. On the Cross, Christ paid the debt of our sin and merited all grace—at Mass, He applies this satisfaction and merit to our souls.

419. Why is the Mass also called Christ's *Pascha* or Passover?
"Having celebrated the ancient Passover, which the multitude of the children of Israel immolated in memory of their going out of Egypt, He instituted the new Passover, namely, Himself to be immolated, under visible signs, by the Church through [her] priests, in memory of His own passage from this world unto the

Father, when by the effusion of His own blood He redeemed us, and delivered us from the power of darkness, and translated us into his kingdom."[77]

420. What is the essential sacrificial action of the Mass?

The separate consecration of the bread and wine achieves "the unbloody immolation of the divine Victim, which is made manifest in a mystical manner by the separation of the sacred species and by their oblation to the Eternal Father."[78] As "in Christ's Passion the blood was separated from the body,"[79] so the Mass "is an image representing Christ's Passion, which is His true immolation."[80]

421. Does this sacrifice depend on the faith of the assembly?

No. It is achieved at the moment of the double consecration, "when Christ is made present upon the altar in the state of a victim, ... performed by the priest and by him alone, as the representative of Christ and not as the representative of the faithful."[81]

422. Does every offering of Holy Mass have infinite value?

Yes, because it is an extension of the infinitely valuable sacrifice of Calvary: "As often as this commemorative sacrifice is offered, there is wrought the work of our Redemption."[82] The effects of each Mass within individual souls, however, are limited by our own dispositions.

423. How does the Mass glorify God and sanctify man?

1. It raises an abiding monument to God's glory, making the sacrifice of Christ present on earth for all time; 2. It gives all people a means to unite themselves to the only true and sacred sacrifice with which God is well pleased. "God Himself wishes that there should be a continuation of this sacrifice ... so that there may be no cessation of the hymn of praise and thanksgiving which man owes to God, seeing that he requires His help continually and has need of the blood of the Redeemer to remit sin."[83]

424. Is Holy Mass the most perfect of all prayers, and the center of the Church's worship?

Yes. It "represents and renews every day the principal mystery of our Redemption, Christ's sacrifice on the Cross," and all the sacraments "are most closely united with the Cross."[84] It perfectly fulfills the four ends of prayer: adoration, thanksgiving, atonement, and petition.

425. What are the major errors about the Sacrifice of the Mass?

Claims that it is: 1. Merely a spiritual offering of prayer and praise; 2. Merely a remembrance of Calvary; 3. A re-presentation of the Last Supper, not Christ's Passion; 4. A communal meal, not a true sacrifice; 5. Dependent for its validity or effectiveness on the participation of the congregation; 6. Not propitiatory for the living and the dead; 7. Able to be offered by someone other than an ordained priest; 8. Able to be offered with rubrics and ceremonies not determined by the universal Church.

Christ's Eternal Priesthood

426. Are Christ's sacrifice and His priesthood eternal?

Yes. "We have a great High Priest who has ascended into heaven" (Heb 4:14*) and "holds His priesthood permanently, because He continues forever. Consequently He is able for all time to save those who draw near to God through Him, since He always lives to make intercession for them" (Heb 7:24–25), having entered "not into a sanctuary made with hands, a copy of the true one, but into heaven itself, now to appear in the presence of God on our behalf" (Heb 9:24).

427. Does Christ still bear the marks of His sacrifice in heaven?

Yes. His self-offering is an eternal and glorious revelation of divine charity, and so He appears in the sight of God and all the angels and saints as "a Lamb standing, as though it had been slain" (Apoc 5:6).

428. Then Christ's eternal priesthood unites heaven and earth at every Mass?

Yes. At every Mass, the faithful come "to Mount Zion and to the city of the living God, the heavenly Jerusalem, and to innumerable angels in festal gathering, and to the assembly of the firstborn who are enrolled in heaven, and to a Judge who is God of all, and to the spirits of just men made perfect, and to Jesus, the Mediator of a new covenant, and to the sprinkled blood that speaks more graciously than the blood of Abel" (Heb 12:22–24).

429. Has the Church confirmed this link between the liturgies of heaven and earth?

Yes. "In the earthly liturgy we partake in anticipation of that heavenly liturgy … to which we are making pilgrimage."[85] "Who among the faithful could doubt that at the very hour of the sacrifice, at the word of the priest, the heavens are opened, that the angels are present at this mystery of Jesus Christ, the Most High itself united with the lowest, earth unites with heaven, visible and invisible become one?"[86]

430. Does the liturgy itself teach this truth?

Yes. In the Canon of Mass, the Church prays: "Humbly we beseech Thee, Almighty God, to command that these our offerings be carried by the hands of Thy holy angel to Thine altar on high, in the sight of Thy divine Majesty, so that those of us who shall receive the most sacred body and blood of Thy Son by partaking thereof from this altar may be filled with every grace and heavenly blessing: through the same Christ Our Lord."

431. Why does the priest make this solemn petition during Mass?

"In order to show the identity of the sacrifice of heaven, with the sacrifice of earth; … the identity of the Sacrifice of the Lamb, whether on the altar of heaven or that of earth."[87]

432. **Then Mass is truly a participation in the heavenly liturgy?**
Yes. Christ's one, all-sufficient sacrifice endures forever in glory; and we are called "to that great, heavenly, and all-sufficing supper, that is to the Pasch, or to Christ immolated, for Christ our Pasch is immolated."[88] "For behold in heaven we have a priest, in heaven we have a victim, in heaven we have a sacrifice."[89]

Offering Holy Mass

433. **To whom is the Sacrifice of the Mass offered?**
Being substantially the same sacrifice as the Cross, the Mass is offered to God alone, as an act of perfect adoration.

434. **Then what is meant by "Mass of the Blessed Virgin," "Mass of St. Peter," etc.?**
Various particular Masses are celebrated *in honor* of the Blessed Virgin, the angels and saints, etc.; but Mass is never offered *to* them as recipients of divine worship.

435. **Who offers the Sacrifice of the Mass?**
Christ Himself, the one High Priest (see Heb 4:14), through the ministry of the officiating priest, His earthly instrument.

436. **Is the sacrifice of the entire Church included in the Sacrifice of Mass?**
Yes. "In the sacrifice of the altar there is signified the general sacrifice by which the whole Mystical Body of Christ, that is, all the city of the redeemed, is offered up to God through Christ, the High Priest ... sacrific[ing] ourselves to the Eternal Father. For in the sacrament of the altar, as the same St. Augustine has it, the Church is made to see that in what she offers, she herself is offered (*De Civitate Dei*, bk. 10, chap. 6)."[90]

437. **Can the Church live without the Sacrifice of the Mass?**
No. The Mass is the very life of the Church, "the source and summit of the whole Christian life,"[91] and by it "the Church continually lives and grows."[92] The first Christians and martyrs left a luminous example of this truth, as many were martyred after declaring that it was not possible for them to live without the Lord's sacrifice: *Sine dominico non possumus.*[93]

438. **Why have the enemies of the Church always primarily attacked Holy Mass?**
"The Mass is the best and the most beautiful thing of the Church.... On this account the devil has always endeavored to abolish the Mass throughout the world by means of heretics, making them the precursors of Antichrist."[94]

439. **For whom is the Sacrifice of the Mass offered?**
It is offered for both the living and the dead.

440. **For whom among the living is Mass offered?**
For the faithful, whether they are just or sinners: that sinners may do penance, and that the just may increase in holiness.

441. **For whom among the dead is Mass offered?**
For those who died in the state of God's grace, yet still have sins to atone for in purgatory.

442. **Is the Mass also offered to beg God for temporal favors?**
Yes. The Church offers this sacrifice to obtain victory, peace, cure of disease, fruitful harvests, etc., insofar as these may help us in acquiring eternal life.

443. **When may Mass be offered?**
Every day of the year, except Good Friday: on this day, the host consecrated the day before is consumed by the priest, but no sacrifice is offered.

444. **Where should Mass take place?**
Mass should be celebrated only in blessed or consecrated churches or chapels.[95] By exception, it may be celebrated outside of a church, as in times of persecution or other objectively justified cases.

Assisting at Mass

445. **Is it advisable to assist often at Holy Mass?**
Yes. Devout assistance at Mass, also called "attending Mass," is the most grace-filled and exalted practice of the Christian life.

446. **How should we participate in the sacrifice of Christ at Mass?**
By uniting ourselves interiorly with the act of Christ's immolation, reproducing in our hearts "the likeness of the divine Redeemer through the mystery of the Cross, according to the words of the Apostle of the Gentiles, 'With Christ I am nailed to the Cross. I live, now not I, but Christ liveth in me' (Gal 2:19–20*). Thus we become a victim, as it were, along with Christ to increase the glory of the Eternal Father."[96]

447. **What do we achieve by assisting well at Holy Mass?**
We: 1. Offer to God a worship worthy of His greatness and love; 2. Satisfy divine justice; 3. Join ourselves more closely to Jesus; 4. Delight the Blessed Virgin Mary and the angels and saints; 5. Obtain contrition for our sins; 6. Rightly order our passions; 7. Grow in holiness; 8. Obtain divine favors for those for whom we intercede; 9. Comfort the souls in purgatory.

448. **To assist well at Mass, must we receive Holy Communion?**
No. As Mass exists first to glorify God, our assistance is primarily one of adoration, to which Holy Communion may be added if we are properly disposed. This is why we are bound to attend Mass at least once per week (on Sundays), but are bound to receive Communion only once per year.

449. **What is the best way to assist at Mass?**
There are many praiseworthy methods, but it is most advisable to attentively follow the action of the priest in the sanctuary, striving to unite our own interior sentiments

and intentions "to the High Priest and His earthly minister, at the time the consecration of the divine Victim is enacted, and at that time especially when those solemn words are pronounced, 'By Him and with Him and in Him is to Thee, God the Father Almighty, in the unity of the Holy Ghost, all honor and glory forever and ever'; to these words in fact the people answer, 'Amen.' Nor should Christians forget to offer themselves, their cares, their sorrows, their distress, and their necessities in union with their divine Savior upon the Cross."[97]

450. What should we do after Mass?
1. Thank God for the great honor of coming into His presence, and assisting at the Holy Sacrifice; 2. Ask His pardon for any lack of attention or devotion on our part; 3. Resolve to be faithful to our duties out of love for Him; 4. Make any petitions or intercessions that are of particular importance.

Chapter 10: Penance

Penance in General

451. What is the *virtue* of penance?
A supernatural habit moving us to have grief, shame, and hatred for our sins, with resolve to make reparation for them.[98]

452. What acts are contained within this virtue?
1. Breaking with our past life; 2. Detesting the sin we committed; 3. Confessing the sin to God; 4. Making a firm purpose to amend our life; 5. Making satisfaction for our sin.

453. Is penance a necessary virtue?
Yes. God can only forgive the repentant: "Repent and turn from all your transgressions, lest iniquity be your ruin" (Ez 18:30); for, "unless you repent you will all likewise perish" (Lk 13:5).

454. Are we forgiven because of our works of penance?
No amount of our own effort can remit our sins; only God can forgive the repentant. "This is not your own doing, it is the gift of God; not because of works, lest any man should boast" (Eph 2:8–9).

455. How is the virtue of penance different from the sacrament of penance?
The sacrament presupposes the virtue, and cannot exist without the proper acts of the virtue; but the virtue of penance can exist independently of the sacrament.

456. Then what is the *sacrament* of penance?
Also called *confession*, it is a sacrament instituted by Christ for the forgiveness of sins committed after baptism.

457. **Is the sacrament of penance necessary for salvation?**
It is necessary for those who commit mortal sin after baptism; however, as with baptism, those unable to access the sacrament of penance may still receive its effect through an earnest desire for it together with perfect contrition.

458. **When did Jesus Christ institute the sacrament of penance?**
After His Resurrection, when He breathed on His disciples and said: "Receive the Holy Spirit. If you forgive the sins of any, they are forgiven; if you retain the sins of any, they are retained" (Jn 20:22–23).

459. **What is the sacramental matter of penance?**
It consists of the sins of the penitent, together with his acts of contrition, confession, and satisfaction.

460. **What sins are necessary to confess in the sacrament of penance?**
All mortal sins that we have committed since baptism and not yet confessed. These sins must be confessed by number and species.[99]

461. **What does it mean to confess by *number* and *species*?**
We must tell the precise *nature* of any unconfessed mortal sin (i.e., the kind of act), along with *how many times* each was committed, as far as we can remember.

462. **Should we only confess mortal sins within the sacrament?**
No; we may also confess any venial sins, and it is most advisable to do so.

463. **What is the form of the sacrament of penance?**
It consists of the priest's words of absolution: "I absolve you from your sins, in the name of the Father, and of the Son, and of the Holy Spirit."

464. **What is *absolution*?**
The sentence of judgment which the priest (called a *confessor* in this sacrament) pronounces in the name and power of Jesus Christ, that remits the sins of a properly disposed penitent.

465. **May any sins be forgiven by this sacrament?**
Yes. No matter how grave our sins and failures, the love of God for us is infinitely greater, and those who truly repent and seek His forgiveness will always find it, "for He is gracious and merciful, slow to anger, and abounding in steadfast love" (Jl 2:13).

466. **May a confessor grant absolution without due examination of the penitent's acts?**
No. "Any practice which restricts confession to a generic accusation of sin or of only one or two sins judged to be more important is to be reproved."[100]

467. **How may a confessor be guilty of showing a false mercy?**
If he avoids the clear identification of a penitent's objectively grave sins; for it is not mercy to excuse or lie about sin, much less to leave penitents in the state of sin

because of a priest's refusal or failure to speak as an authoritative father and caring physician—tasks entrusted by Christ to every confessor.

468. **Does the confessor's role as judge, father, and spiritual physician imply clericalism or spiritual torture?**
No. "Confessors should always behave as just and merciful servants so that they may have 'regard for the divine honor and [for] the salvation of souls' (*Code of Canon Law*, can. 978, § 1)."[101] "The confessor is a pastor, a father, a master, teacher, a spiritual judge, and a physician who diagnoses and cures."[102]

469. **What is the *seal of confession*?**
The strict obligation imposed on priests to maintain inviolable secrecy about everything learned through sacramental confession. Matters discussed within this "tribunal of penance" must be known only to God, the priest as His representative, and the penitent who seeks His mercy.

470. **May a priest ever reveal something learned in the confessional?**
No. By divine law, the confessor may not violate the seal of the sacrament for any reason. No ecclesiastical authority has the power to dispense him from this seal, and no civil authority can oblige him to break it.

Administration of Penance

471. **Who can confer the sacrament of penance?**
Only an ordained priest with the proper faculty to hear confessions may grant absolution.[103]

472. **Can a priest without the faculty of hearing confessions ever absolve validly?**
Yes. In a state of a real and grave necessity, the Church automatically grants this faculty (jurisdiction) to any validly ordained priest—even one who is a heretic, schismatic, or excommunicate—so that no soul may be lost for lack of absolution.[104]

473. **Who may receive the sacrament of penance?**
Any baptized person who has committed sin after baptism.

474. **May a priest absolve someone who states his unwillingness to obey divine law?**
No. Even if this unwillingness only concerns a single grave matter—e.g., refusing to end an illicit sexual relationship or other voluntary and proximate occasion of sin—it is impossible for the unrepentant sinner to be absolved. "Return to Me, says the Lord of hosts, and I will return to you" (Zac 1:3).

Effects of Penance

475. **What are the effects of the sacrament of penance?**
This sacrament: 1. Remits all sins committed after baptism when these are confessed with contrition; 2. Remits all eternal punishment due to sin, and temporal

punishment in proportion to our dispositions; 3. Returns supernatural life to the sinner, and increases it in the just; 4. Restores our lost merits; 5. Confers specific graces for avoiding the sins confessed; 6. Often imparts a sensible peace and serenity of conscience.

476. **What should we do to receive the sacrament of penance worthily?**
We should make acts of contrition, confession, and satisfaction.

Acts of the Penitent

CONTRITION

477. **What is *contrition*?**
An interior sorrow and hatred of the sin we have committed, together with a firm purpose of amendment.

478. **What do we do in making an act of contrition?**
We look: 1. To the past with grief and regret, detesting the sins we committed; 2. To the future with determination, resolving to sin no more; 3. To God, with trust in His infinite mercy.

479. **Is contrition necessary?**
It is absolutely necessary for the remission of mortal sins, because without it, we show ourselves to be enemies of God, who cannot bestow His friendship upon us if we remain impenitent and obstinate in evil.

480. **What qualities should our contrition have?**
Our contrition should be: interior, supernatural, universal, and sovereign.

481. **How is our contrition *interior*?**
When sorrow really exists in our heart, and is not limited to words or exterior signs.

482. **Why must our contrition be interior?**
Because God sees our most hidden thoughts: "I the Lord search the mind and try the heart" (Jer 17:10); otherwise we would be hypocrites, and suffer the rebuke of Christ: "This people honors Me with their lips, but their heart is far from Me" (Mk 7:6).

483. **How is our contrition *supernatural*?**
When it is prompted by the Holy Spirit and springs from a supernatural motive.

484. **What are the principal supernatural motives?**
1. The infinite goodness of God, who is offended by sin; 2. The sufferings of Christ, borne for our sins; 3. The ugliness of sin itself; 4. The everlasting joy awaiting the friends of God, which is lost by sin.

485. **How is our contrition *universal*?**
When it extends to at least all mortal sins, without any exception or reserve.

486. **Why must contrition extend at least to all mortal sins?**
Because our contrition can only be sincere if we truly hate and repent of every mortal sin, any one of which is enough to separate us from God's friendship.

487. **How is our contrition *sovereign*?**
When it is experienced as the greatest of all sorrows, being the loss of all that we hold dearest and best in this world: "For what shall it profit a man, if he shall gain the whole world, and lose his own soul?" (Mk 8:36*).

488. **Why should our contrition be sovereign?**
Because it should reflect the sovereign good that we have lost by sin, and serve to realign our sentiments to those of God, who has a sovereign love for us and a perfect hatred for all that opposes our salvation.

489. **Is it necessary to weep or have feelings of deep sadness in our contrition?**
No. Although emotions of remorse are praiseworthy in contrition, it is sufficient if our reason looks upon sin as the greatest of evils, and our will detests and rejects it as such.

490. **What is a *firm purpose of amendment*?**
The absolutely necessary and entirely sincere resolution not to commit sin again.

491. **Why is this firm resolution necessary to receive absolution?**
Because we are not truly sorry for our sins unless we are personally resolved to avoid them in the future; without this resolve, we remain enemies of God, willing to sin again.

492. **Does fear of relapsing into sin prevent us from having a firm purpose of amendment?**
No. We may bravely resolve never to sin again, even in the face of fear of our own weakness.

493. **If the sinner relapses after confession, does this prove that his purpose was not firm?**
No. His sincerity is only questionable if he: 1. Relapses immediately and almost without resistance; 2. Takes no means to avoid the sin or its near occasion.

494. **How may we ensure the sincerity of our purpose of amendment?**
We should not only avoid sin, but also strive to correct our vices and shun the near occasions of sin.

495. **How may we correct our vices?**
We must pray, watch over ourselves, multiply acts of the opposite virtues, and often approach the sacraments of penance and Holy Eucharist.

496. **How may we avoid the near occasions of sin?**
By avoiding those particular places, persons, or situations that would ordinarily lead to sin on our part.

497. **What is *perfect* contrition?**
Sorrow for sin that springs from the motive of charity, as we regret offending God because He is our dearest Friend, infinitely good in Himself and worthy of all our love.

498. **What is the effect of perfect contrition?**
It has power to efface all sin even before absolution, provided that the penitent has the desire and intention to confess as soon as possible.

499. **What is *imperfect* contrition?**
Also called *attrition*, it is sorrow for sin that springs from fear, as we regret offending God because He is perfectly just, and our sins merit punishments that we are right to dread.

500. **Why is this contrition called *imperfect*?**
Because, although legitimate and praiseworthy in itself, attrition is inspired by the lesser motive of fear of God's just punishments, rather than the perfect motive of love for Him.

501. **How can we obtain true contrition for our sins?**
1. Humbly ask it of God, the only source of all grace; 2. Excite it within ourselves by considering His infinite goodness, His infinite love for us, and the fatal consequences of sin.

502. **What is the most effective meditation for exciting contrition within ourselves?**
Meditation on the Passion of Our Lord, who suffered and died out of love for sinful man.

CONFESSION

503. **What is sacramental *confession*?**
The act of accusing ourselves of our sins before the priest, for the purpose of receiving absolution from him.

504. **Why is confession an act of *accusing* ourselves?**
Because it is not a simple narration of events, a whispered secret, or an excuse; it is an avowal of guilt before God for every sin committed, whose priest wields divine power to bind or loose our sins.

505. **Why do we accuse ourselves *of our sins*?**
Because confession is not a counseling session or a gossip corner; we should speak only of sins, all of them, and only our own.

506. **When are we bound to confess our sins?**
Confession is binding by divine law from the moment that we lose God's grace in our soul through mortal sin; it is binding by ecclesiastical law at least once per year, and before receiving Communion if we are in mortal sin.[105] Liturgical law also recommends it before receiving the sacraments of marriage,[106] anointing of the sick, confirmation, and holy orders.

507. **What qualities should confession possess?**
It should be: humble, sincere, simple, prudent, and complete.

508. **When is confession *humble*?**
When we accuse ourselves of sin with the lowly attitude of a culprit who knows his guilt, and regrets having offended his loving Father.

509. **When is confession *sincere*?**
When we accuse ourselves of sins just as we know them, without augmenting, lessening, or excusing them.

510. **When is confession *simple*?**
When we accuse ourselves of sin frankly and directly, without being obscure or introducing unnecessary details.

511. **When is confession *prudent*?**
When we accuse ourselves without disclosing another's sin, unless this is necessary to clarify our own sin.

512. **When is confession *complete* and *integral*?**
When we accuse ourselves at least of every mortal sin that we can recall after a serious examination of conscience, together with the number and pertinent circumstances of each.

513. **What if we are unsure about the exact number of our sins?**
We should tell the number as nearly as possible; e.g., "As far as I remember, I committed such a sin about/approximately five times," or, "weekly," etc.

514. **What if we are unsure of whether a sin was mortal, or if we truly committed one?**
There is no obligation to confess such sin, although it is best to do so.

515. **Should we tell all the circumstances surrounding our sins?**
Great detail is unnecessary. We should only share relevant circumstances that affect the species or malice of the sin, or our culpability in it: e.g., stealing a ciborium involves two sins (theft and sacrilege).

516. **Is it a grave sin to willfully conceal a mortal sin in confession?**
Yes. This entails the added grave sin of sacrilege, and renders the confession itself invalid, nullifying the absolution of the priest.

517. **What must we do to secure integrity in our confession?**
We must: 1. Ask for light and insight from the Holy Spirit; 2. Examine our conscience carefully. Sometimes it is helpful to write down our sins, so as not to forget them.

518. **Why should we ask for insight from the Holy Spirit?**
Because He is sent to "convince the world of sin" (Jn 16:8), and by His grace we can make a good examination of conscience, know our sins well, and conceive true contrition for them.

519. **Is frequent confession very useful?**
Yes. It roots out vice, gives us greater purity of heart, renews our fervor, and promotes our advancement in spiritual perfection.

520. **What is a *general confession*?**
One that includes the confession of every past sin that we can recall, including those already confessed—whether for our entire life, or only during a particular period of time.

521. **When is a general confession necessary?**
Whenever the penitent is morally certain that some or all of his preceding confessions have been sacrilegious, owing to lack of contrition or integrity. He is then under a grave obligation to make a general confession, beginning with the first confession that he knows was null.

522. **When may a general confession be useful?**
If we are: 1. Preparing for First Communion; 2. Undertaking a new state in life (e.g., marriage, priesthood); 3. In doubt of the validity of a past confession; 4. Seeking a higher degree of prayer and interior union with God.

523. **Who should be forbidden to make a general confession?**
All scrupulous or excessively anxious persons, because of the serious harm that can result.

524. **How should we prepare for confession?**
We should keep ourselves in a state of recollection, examine our conscience, and above all, excite ourselves to contrition.

525. **What should we do when we enter the confessional?**
We should: 1. Kneel, make the sign of the cross, and say: "Bless me, Father, for I have sinned"; 2. Tell how long it has been since our last confession; 3. Accuse ourselves of our sins; 4. Conclude with: "For these and all the sins of my past life, I beg the mercy of God and ask you, Father, for penance and absolution"; 5. Listen to the advice of the confessor; 6. Make a good act of contrition.

526. **What is a suitable formula for an act of contrition?**
O my God, I am heartily sorry for having offended You, and I detest all my sins because I dread the loss of heaven and the pains of hell, but most of all because they offend You, my God, who are all good and deserving of all my love. I firmly resolve with the help of Your grace to sin no more and to avoid the near occasions of sin. Amen.

527. **Are we obliged to answer any clarifying questions asked by our confessor, or allowed to ask him clarifying questions?**
Yes, provided that they concern the matter of our confession.

528. **What should we do while the priest is giving us absolution?**
We should remain in spirit at the feet of Jesus crucified, whose blood is cleansing our soul at that moment.

529. **What should we do upon leaving the confessional?**
We should: 1. Thank God for His forgiveness; 2. Reflect seriously on the advice of our confessor; 3. Resolve to put it into practice; 4. Perform the penance imposed on us as soon as possible.

SATISFACTION

530. **What is *satisfaction*?**
Reparation of the insult which our sins have offered to God, or of the wrong which they have done to our neighbor.

531. **Why are we obliged to make satisfaction for our sins?**
We must not only repent of our sins; we must also repair the injustice and harm that our sins have caused in the very order of creation, by enduring the temporal punishment due to them. Thus, one may be sorry for breaking a window, and receive the owner's forgiveness—but this does not remove the obligation to repair or replace the broken window.

532. **When God forgives our sin, does He not also remit our punishment?**
God's forgiveness restores grace to the soul and remits the everlasting punishment due to mortal sin, but some temporal punishment often remains, which we must suffer either in this life or in purgatory.

533. **What are the two general kinds of satisfaction?**
1. *Sacramental* satisfaction, acts that the priest prescribes to the penitent during confession; 2. *Extra-sacramental* satisfaction, acts performed voluntarily by the penitent, beyond those imposed by the confessor and outside the sacrament of penance.

534. What are the three major works of satisfaction?
1. *Prayer*, including all acts of religion; 2. *Fasting*, including all voluntary privations and mortifications of body or mind; 3. *Almsgiving*, including all works of mercy to our neighbor.

535. How do we make satisfaction to our neighbor?
By repairing the wrong we have done to him, or being reconciled with him if we have given him offense.

536. Are we obliged to perform the proper penance imposed by the confessor?
Yes. Failing to perform it does not invalidate the sacrament, but it does make us guilty of a more or less grave sin of disobedience.

537. How should we perform our penance?
1. *Exactly*, just as prescribed; 2. *Promptly*, as soon as possible; 3. *Devoutly*, with all the care and attention that we should bring to an act of religion.

538. What if we forget what our penance was?
We ought to ask the confessor again. If the confessor has forgotten, we are not bound to repeat the confession; we can perform a penance we believe is honestly proportionate to the sins committed.

539. What if the priest assigns an unreasonable or overly burdensome penance?
Within the confessional, we should humbly tell the priest if we believe that the penance is unsuitable, especially if it will impose undue burdens or seems impossible to fulfill.

540. May works of satisfaction be performed in addition to that assigned by the confessor?
Yes. The devout follower of Christ makes such acts frequently throughout life. This is the *spirit of penance*, uniting ourselves to Jesus Christ in His atonement for sin.

541. What is the effect of the spirit of penance?
It makes everything contribute to paying our debt of punishment to God. The least privation, the slightest humiliation, the smallest alms, the least act of patience, kindness, or mortification, offered to God in union with Christ, is of great value in atonement for our sins.

Suffrages and Indulgences

542. What are *suffrages*?
Any acts by which we come to another's assistance by prayer and intercession, or by paying his debt of sin through our own satisfactory merits.

543. **Is there a community of shared suffrages in the Church?**
Yes. This is an aspect of the communion of saints, whereby the members of the Church Militant, Suffering, and Triumphant are able to pray and make satisfaction for one another.

544. **What is the *treasury of the Church*?**
It consists of the infinite supernatural merits of Christ Our Lord, and the prayers and good works of the Blessed Virgin, all the saints, and all the faithful.

545. **What is an *indulgence*?**
The remission in whole or in part of the temporal punishment due to actual sins whose guilt is already forgiven. This remission is made outside the tribunal of penance, by applying the spiritual treasury of the Church.

546. **What are the two kinds of indulgence?**
Considered according to its effect, an indulgence is either plenary or partial: 1. *Plenary* indulgences remit all temporal punishment due to sin; 2. *Partial* indulgences remits only some part of this punishment. "A plenary indulgence can be acquired only once in the course of a day; a partial indulgence can be acquired multiple times."[107]

547. **What is the most remarkable and solemn indulgence?**
The indulgence of the *Jubilee*, which is a plenary indulgence accompanied with certain privileges, granted by the pope to the universal Church for a certain length of time.

548. **Has the Church received this power to grant indulgences from Christ?**
Yes. "The power of conferring indulgences was granted by Christ to the Church; and she has, even in the most ancient times, used this power."[108]

549. **Who has power in the Church to grant indulgences?**
Only her pastors; i.e., the pope and bishops who, being established by the Holy Spirit to rule the Church of God, are therefore dispensers of its spiritual treasures.

550. **What general conditions are required to gain an indulgence?**
"A person must be baptized, not excommunicated, and in the state of grace at least at the end of the prescribed works."[109]

551. **What must we do to gain a plenary indulgence?**
We must be free from all attachment to sin, perform the indulgenced work (e.g., pray at a cemetery on All Souls Day), "and fulfill the following three conditions: sacramental confession, Eucharistic Communion, and prayer for the intention of the Sovereign Pontiff."[110]

552. **What if we cannot gain certain indulgences due to some inability or disability?**
Various exceptions and exemptions can be made by the Church's pastors in such cases.[111]

553. How may we apply indulgences to the souls in purgatory?
1. The indulgence must be applicable to the faithful departed; 2. We must have the intention of applying it in this way; 3. We must be in the state of grace while doing so.

554. How may we gain a plenary indulgence at the hour of death?
As death approaches, we should: 1. Receive the sacraments, or at least be contrite for our sins; 2. Invoke the holy name of Jesus at least in our heart; 3. Accept death with submission to God's will, and in atonement for our sins.[112]

Chapter 11: Anointing of the Sick

Anointing of the Sick in General

555. What is *anointing of the sick*?
A sacrament instituted by Christ that bestows spiritual healing and comfort to the sick, and potentially physical strength and healing.

556. Why is this sacrament called *anointing* of the sick, or *extreme unction*?
Because this holy *unction*, or "anointing" with blessed oil, is made upon the faithful in *extreme* cases, e.g., dangerous illness or possible death. Different names were used for this sacrament in the first millennium: *holy oil, the unction, unction of the sick, the blessing of consecrated oil, unction of God, the office of the unction,* etc. *Extreme unction* became general in the Latin Church from the twelfth century, and after the Council of Vatican II, it has commonly been called *anointing of the sick*.

557. Did Jesus Christ personally institute this sacrament?
Yes. "If anyone says that extreme unction is not truly and properly a sacrament instituted (see Mk 6:13) by Christ Our Lord and announced by the blessed apostle James (see Jas 5:14), but is only a rite received from the Fathers or a human invention, let him be anathema."[113]

558. What is the sacramental matter for anointing of the sick?
The anointing of the recipient with *oil of the sick*, which is olive oil previously blessed by the bishop, or in urgent cases by the priest,[114] and in the Byzantine Catholic Church ordinarily by the priest.

559. How are these unctions performed upon the recipient?
The holy oil is applied in the sign of the cross upon various parts of the body, depending on the rite in use and local custom. In the traditional Roman Rite, the five senses are anointed by way of the eyes, ears, nostrils, mouth, hands, feet, and (as appropriate) a man's loins. The Byzantine rite adds anointings of the forehead (seat of bad thoughts) and the chest (seat of the heart, from which "comes all evil" [Mt 15:19*]).

560. **Why are the five senses so often emphasized in this sacrament?**
Because these are the windows by which we perceive and respond to reality, for good or for evil. Each must therefore be sanctified as "instruments of righteousness" (Rom 6:13), that we might present our bodies as "a living sacrifice, holy and acceptable to God" (Rom 12:1).

561. **What is the sacramental form for anointing of the sick?**
The traditional form of immemorial use consists in the words pronounced by the priest at each anointing: "Through this holy unction and of His most tender mercy, may the Lord pardon thee whatsoever sins thou hast committed by thy (eyes, ears, nostrils, mouth, hands, feet, loins)."

562. **What is the sacramental form in the new rite of Pope Paul VI?**
"Through this holy anointing may the Lord in His love and mercy help you by the grace of the Holy Spirit, and may the Lord who frees you from sin, save you and raise you up."

563. **What is the sacramental form in the Byzantine rite?**
"Holy Father, Physician of souls and bodies, You sent your only-begotten Son, Our Lord Jesus Christ, to heal every infirmity and to deliver us from death. By this anointing heal your servant N. of the spiritual and bodily sickness which afflicts him (her), and restore his (her) health by the grace of Your Christ, through the prayers of our most holy Lady, the Mother of God and ever-Virgin Mary, and of all your saints. For You, our God, are the fountain of healing, and to You we give glory, together with Your only-begotten Son, and Your consubstantial Spirit, now and ever, and forever. Amen."

Administration of Anointing of the Sick

564. **Who may be the minister of anointing of the sick?**
Only a bishop or a priest can administer this sacrament.

565. **Can any priest administer this sacrament validly?**
Yes, as the power of jurisdiction is not necessary for this sacrament to be valid.

566. **What conditions are necessary for receiving this sacrament validly?**
The recipient must: 1. Be a Catholic; 2. Have at least the potential use of reason; 3. Begin to be in some danger from sickness or old age.

567. **Why must the recipient have the use of reason?**
Because "the form of this sacrament does not apply to children, since they have not sinned by sight and hearing, as expressed in the form. Therefore this sacrament should not be given to them."[115]

568. **Must we be in immediate danger of death to receive extreme unction?**
No; indeed, it would be a serious failure in charity to delay the sacrament until all hope of recovery is lost, or the person is approaching unconsciousness.

569. **May this sacrament be given to someone about to enter a dangerous situation?**
No. This sacrament is only for healing present evils originating in some bodily defect, as in illness or life-threatening injury. For potential and external evils or risks (going into battle, disaster relief, or childbirth), the faithful should have recourse to the sacraments of penance and the Holy Eucharist.

570. **Should large "healing services" be held, where anyone may receive this sacrament?**
No. Such a practice distorts the essential meaning of this sacrament, which presupposes a dangerous illness,[116] rather than serving to merely improve bodily health or emotional wellness. Since this sacrament also remits sins,[117] the faithful could be misled to neglect the frequent reception of the sacrament of penance.

571. **May anointing of the sick ever be repeated?**
Yes, as often as "danger [to life] has become more threatening."[118]

572. **What disposition is necessary for receiving this sacrament?**
The state of grace, as extreme unction is a sacrament of the living. If the sick person is aware of being in mortal sin, he is bound to confess or make an act of perfect contrition before receiving extreme unction.

573. **What further dispositions are advisable for receiving this sacrament?**
1. Great confidence and hope in God, relying on His power, goodness, and mercy; 2. Perfect submission to His holy will, as "all things work together unto good" (Rom 8:28*) for those who love Him; 3. Readiness to offer up our sickness and suffering to God, as penance for our sins and to gain merit.

574. **May this sacrament be given to someone while they are unconscious?**
Yes. It is reasonable to suppose that any Catholic would request this sacrament if they could.

575. **What items should we prepare when extreme unction will be given to a sick person?**
It is commendable to prepare a table, covered with a white linen cloth, and set out a crucifix, a plate with pieces of cotton or similar material (to wipe the anointed areas), some bread crumbs and a bowl of water for the priest to purify his hands, and a lit candle to hold near the priest as he anoints.

576. **How should the recipient conduct himself during this sacrament?**
As much as possible, he should unite his intention and sentiments to the prayers of the priest, confidently offering God the sacrifice of his life, if this be His will.

577. **Is anointing of the sick necessary as a means of salvation?**
No. We can be saved by penance, and this sacrament is only its complement.

Effects of Anointing of the Sick

578. **What are the effects of this sacrament?**
Some effects concern the soul, others have to do with the body.

579. **What effects concern the soul?**
This sacrament: 1. Confers sanctifying grace; 2. Remits sin; 3. Effaces all remains of sin; 4. Consoles and strengthens the soul, especially for its final struggle and judgment.

580. **What effects concern the body?**
As may be read in James 5:15, "the Lord shall raise him up." This sacrament can relieve the sufferings of the sick person, and may even restore bodily health if God judges this advantageous to his soul.

581. **What attitude should the sick person have after being anointed?**
1. Lively gratitude to God for all His benefits; 2. Filial abandonment to His will, especially the acceptance of sickness and suffering; 3. Loving desire to see His glory in heaven, in His good time.

582. **How should we assist a dying person in his last moments?**
We should pray with and for him, frequently offer him the crucifix to kiss, excite him to hope in God, suggest pious aspirations, repeat the blessed names of Jesus, Mary, and Joseph, and at his last moment, recite the prayers for recommending a departing soul.

583. **What is a suitable prayer for accepting one's death?**
O Lord God, with true contrition for having offended You, I accept from Your hands, with faith, hope, and love, this death with all its pains, anguish, and suffering, in reparation for my sins and for love of You and for Your greater glory, through Jesus Christ Our Lord. O Mary, my sweet heavenly Mother, St. Joseph, and my dear Guardian Angel be with me, protect me, and accompany me as I come before the face of God. Jesus, Mary, Joseph!

584. **What are *last rites*?**
This expression refers to the Church's entire office provided for the dying; i.e., confession, Viaticum, extreme unction, and several other prayers and psalms.

Chapter 12: Holy Orders

Holy Orders in General

585. **What is *holy orders*?**
A sacrament instituted by Christ that permanently changes the soul of a man to make him participate in Our Lord's divine priesthood, giving spiritual power and grace to discharge sacred duties worthily.

586. **When did Jesus Christ institute the sacrament of holy orders?**
Our Lord gradually advanced the apostles to all the functions of holy orders: 1. He placed them above the other disciples; 2. He gave them power to consecrate His body and blood;[119] 3. After the Resurrection, He gave them power and jurisdiction to remit sins, preach, baptize, and perform all other priestly duties (see Jn 20:22–23; and Mt 28:19–20).

587. **Do the laity also participate in Christ's priesthood?**
Yes, albeit in the *common* and not the *ministerial* priesthood: "It must be firmly held that the 'priesthood' common to all the faithful, high and reserved as it is, differs not only in degree, but in essence also, from priesthood fully and properly so-called, which lies in the power of offering the sacrifice of Christ Himself, since he bears the Person of Christ, the supreme High Priest."[120]

588. **How are the common and the ministerial priesthood related, yet distinct?**
"The ministerial priest, by the sacred power he enjoys, teaches and rules the priestly people; acting in the Person of Christ, he makes present the Eucharistic Sacrifice, and offers it to God in the name of all the people. But the faithful, in virtue of their royal priesthood [see 1 Pt 2:9], join in the offering of the Eucharist. They likewise exercise that priesthood in receiving the sacraments, in prayer and thanksgiving, in the witness of a holy life, and by self-denial and active charity."[121]

589. **What is the outward sign of holy orders?**
The imposition of the hands of the bishop, with the words of the sacramental form of each order, that signify the conferring of that particular order and the grace of the Holy Spirit.

590. **Are there many different orders?**
Yes, "from the times of the apostles."[122] "If anyone says that besides the priesthood there are not in the Catholic Church other orders, both major and minor, by which, as by certain steps, advance is made to the priesthood, let him be anathema."[123]

591. **Has the Roman Church always kept both major and minor orders?**
Yes. From at least the third century in the Roman Church, there have always been at least seven orders: porter, lector, exorcist, acolyte, subdeacon, deacon, and priest.[124]

592. How are these seven orders distinguished?

Four *minor* orders: porter, lector, exorcist, and acolyte. Three *major* orders: subdeacon, deacon, and priest. The priesthood comprises two degrees: that of the simple priest and the bishop.[125]

593. What orders properly constitute the *sacrament* of holy orders?

The diaconate (deacons), presbyterate (priests), and episcopate (bishops), according to the perennial teaching of the Church.[126] St. Ignatius of Antioch, a disciple of the apostles, thus affirmed: "Let all reverence the deacons as Jesus Christ, and the bishop as the image of the Father, and the presbyters as the council of God, and assembly of the apostles. Apart from these, one cannot speak of the Church."[127]

594. Who can act in the Person of Christ the Head (*in persona Christi capitis*)?

Only the bishop and the priest. The deacon, though a participant in the sacrament of holy orders, acts rather in service of Christ's Body, the Church.[128]

595. How do the ancient major and minor orders differ?

1. Minor orders and subdiaconate do not imprint a sacramental character; 2. Only major orders have been classically regarded as referring directly to divine worship and especially the Eucharist; 3. Major orders bind the recipient to lifelong continence (celibacy) and daily recitation of the Divine Office.

596. Should the law of priestly celibacy be maintained in the Church?

Yes. The priest represents Christ, who lived in perfect celibacy as the divine Bridegroom wedded to His spiritual Bride, the Church. The law of priestly celibacy belongs to immemorial and apostolic tradition, and must never be abolished or rendered optional in the Roman Church.

597. Has the law of priestly celibacy been opposed in the past?

Yes, and so it has been strongly defended as one of the ancient laws that "go back to the apostles and were established by the Fathers ... [despite] many who, ignoring the statutes of our forefathers, have violated the chastity of the Church by their presumption and have followed the will of the people, not fearing the judgment of God."[129]

598. Haven't married men been admitted to the sacred priesthood in the past?

Yes, by way of exception. However, even in these cases, the apostolic norm and constant law of the Roman Church has been to observe perpetual continence after ordination, even for the married. This norm is still maintained in the Oriental Churches for unmarried candidates and priests who are widowers, although they unfortunately abandoned this apostolic practice for married priests by the time of the "Quinisext Council" of Constantinople in 692. This same Council, however, kept the law of continence for married bishops.[130]

PART III — WORSHIP: BEING HOLY

MATTER AND FORM

599. What are the matter and form of the diaconate?

"In the ordination to the diaconate, the matter is the one imposition of the hand of the bishop which occurs in the rite of that ordination. The form consists of the words: ... ['Send forth upon him the Holy Spirit, so that by the grace of His seven gifts he may be strengthened to carry out faithfully the work of Your ministry']."[131]

600. What are the matter and form of the presbyterate?

"In the ordination to the priesthood, the matter is the first imposition of hands of the bishop which is done in silence, but not the continuation of the same imposition through the extension of the right hand, nor the last imposition to which are attached the words: *Accipe Spiritum Sanctum: quorum remiseris peccata*, etc. The form consists of the words of the 'Preface,' of which the following are essential and therefore required for validity: ... ['We ask You, all-powerful Father, give this servant of Yours the dignity of the presbyterate. Renew the Spirit of holiness within him. By Your divine gift may he attain the second order in the hierarchy and exemplify right conduct in his life']."[132]

601. What are the matter and form of the episcopate?

"In the episcopal ordination or consecration, the matter is the imposition of hands which is done by the bishop consecrator. The form consists of the words of the 'Preface,' of which the following are essential and therefore required for validity: ... ['Perfect in Thy priest the fullness of Thy ministry and, clothing him in all the ornaments of spiritual glorification, sanctify him with the heavenly anointing']."[133]

602. Are the new rites of ordination introduced by Pope Paul VI valid?

Yes. The new rites for diaconal and presbyteral ordination remained the same as in the traditional Roman rite ordination.

603. What about the new formula for episcopal ordination?

Pope Paul VI established the formula: "Pour out upon this chosen one the power that is from You, the governing Spirit whom You gave to Your beloved Son, Jesus Christ, the Spirit given by Him to His holy apostles, who founded the Church in every place to be Your temple for the unceasing glory and praise of Your name." Being almost identical to a third-century text in the *Traditio Apostolica* and the form of episcopal ordination in the Catholic Coptic and West Syrian (Antiochene) or Maronite Rites, this new formula of Pope Paul VI is undoubtedly valid.

604. Were any well-known saints ordained in the Coptic, West Syrian, or Maronite rites?

Yes; e.g., Sts. Athanasius and Cyril of Alexandria ordained in the Coptic Rite, and Sts. John Chrysostom and Jerome, ordained priests at Antioch in the West Syrian Rites.

605. **What is the formula of the episcopal consecration in the Catholic Byzantine rite?**
"Strengthen this Your chosen one whom You had deemed worthy to come under the yoke of the Gospel and to the dignity of the episcopate through the imposition of my sinful hands and those of the concelebrant bishops here present by illumination and power and grace of the Holy Spirit, as You have strengthened Your holy apostles and prophets, as You have anointed kings, as You have consecrated Pontiffs." St. Josaphat and many other saintly bishops of the Byzantine Catholic Church were ordained with this rite.

606. **What would be the consequence, if the new form of episcopal ordination were invalid?**
The last two popes (Benedict XVI, Francis) and almost the entire Roman episcopate since 1968 were ordained in the new rite of Pope Paul VI. Were this rite invalid, the Roman Church would be consequently deprived of a functioning hierarchy and papacy, contrary to the promise of Christ that "the gates of hell shall not prevail against [the Church]" (Mt 16:18*).

RIGHTS AND POWERS

607. **What ceremony serves as a preparation for receiving orders?**
The ancient Roman Catholic ceremony of *tonsure*, consisting of cutting a little hair from the head of the man who is thereby admitted to the clerical state, allowed to wear clerical garb in public, and subject to the rights and responsibilities reserved to the clergy.

608. **What rights do the minor orders confer?**
The right and grace to perform certain lower functions in church, many of which are today delegated to laymen, except for: 1. The blessing of bread and firstfruits, reserved to ordained lectors; 2. Solemn exorcisms, reserved to the bishop or an ordained exorcist approved by him.

609. **Are the minor orders rooted in the diaconate?**
Yes. The principle of *auxiliary service in the liturgy* is fully contained and expressed by the sacramental diaconate, and divine wisdom has imprinted the character of divisibility in those liturgical functions which are not strictly priestly; leaving the Church free to distribute, in a non-sacramental way and according to needs and circumstances, the different aspects of the diaconate that are found in the lower or minor orders, especially the ministries of *lector* (reader) and *acolyte* (altar server).

610. **Are the services of lector and acolyte proper to the "common priesthood" of the laity?**
No. Already in the Old Testament, God established the principle that those who carry out any service in public worship—even a more humble one—must receive a stable or sacred designation; a principle preserved by the Church's designation of sacred ministers with special rites of *ordination*. The services of the lector and acolyte

have therefore never been understood as an exercise of the common priesthood of the laity.

611. **Has the Church maintained this principle of divine worship since the beginning?**
Yes. The apostles preserved this principle by establishing the order of deacons by divine revelation, analogous to the Old Testament Levites. The disciple of the apostles, Pope Clement I (+97) testifies to the same: "We must do everything in order, with regard to what the Lord has ordered to do according to the appointed times. He ordered the oblations and worship services to be performed not by chance or without order. By His sovereign decision, He Himself has determined where and by whom these services are to be performed, so that all things will be done in a holy manner according to His good pleasure and pleasing to His will. For the high priest has been assigned liturgical services reserved for him, priests have been given their own proper place, on the Levites devolve special ministrations (*diakoniai*), and the layman is bound by the laws that pertain to laymen."[134]

612. **Can a married layman ever receive minor orders?**
Yes, as already envisioned by the Council of Trent: "If there should not be unmarried clerks at hand to exercise the functions of the four minor orders, their place may be supplied by married men of approved life; provided they have not been twice married, be competent to discharge those duties, and wear the tonsure and the clerical dress in church."[135]

613. **What power and right does the order of subdeacon confer?**
The power to present the chalice at the altar, sing the Epistle during Solemn Mass, and wash the altar linens.

614. **What power and right does the order of deacon confer?**
As a ministry of service,[136] the diaconate gives power to assist the priest during Solemn Mass, sing the Gospel, preach the homily, carry the Eucharist to the sick, and canonically assist at marriages. The Church's constant tradition also regarded them as extraordinary ministers of solemn baptism,[137] and of Holy Communion during Mass in cases of necessity;[138] whereas the new Code of Canon Law regards the deacon as an ordinary minister of these,[139] as well as of the solemn Eucharistic blessing with the monstrance or ciborium.[140]

615. **What is the particular character of the diaconate?**
He is a living icon of Christ the Servant in the Church, "a minister who depends on the bishop and the priest,"[141] with a special grace and faculty to serve them in liturgy and apostolic action: "The deacon does not receive the spirit in which the priest participates, but the spirit to be under the authority of the bishop."[142]

616. **In which spiritual powers and offices (*munera*) of the priesthood does the deacon participate?**
As he is not a priest, the deacon does not participate in the sanctifying office (*munus sanctificandi*) in a proper sense; yet he participates more broadly in the teaching office (*munus docendi*), in that he can announce the Gospel and preach.[143] There is a difference between the nature of a bishop's or priest's sermon on the one hand, and that of the deacon on the other: as the deacon only preaches *per modum catechizantis*, "in the form of a catechesis (rudimentary instruction)," while the doctrinal exposition of the Gospel and of the Faith properly belongs to the bishop and the priest.[144] Similarly, the deacon participates in the governing office (*munus regendi*) as belonging to the Church's hierarchy, but only as cooperator of the bishop and the priest.

617. **Then the diaconate is substantially different from any service of the laity?**
Yes, because a deacon is not a layperson. "As it is a grade of holy orders, the diaconate imprints a character and communicates a specific sacramental grace. The diaconal character is the configurative and distinguishing sign indelibly impressed in the soul, which configures the one ordained to Christ, who made Himself the deacon or servant of all (see Mk 10:45; and Lk 22:27)."[145]

618. **What concrete governing powers do deacons exercise, that the laity cannot?**
Some limited powers of government or jurisdiction by reason of their ordination; e.g., to obtain posts requiring the power of order, to be appointed diocesan judges (even the only judge), and to confer certain dispensations.[146]

619. **What power and right does the order of priest confer?**
The priesthood gives power to celebrate the Sacrifice of the Mass, absolve the faithful from their sins, administer sacraments and sacramentals not reserved to bishops, preach, bless persons and objects, and preside over assemblies of the faithful.

620. **What powers and rights does consecration to the episcopate confer?**
The *episcopate* gives the fullness of priesthood,[147] with power to: 1. Confer the sacrament of holy orders; 2. Confer the sacrament of confirmation; 3. Be the teacher and judge of faith and morals for his diocese; 4. Assist at councils; 5. Bless abbots and abbesses; 6. Consecrate virgins; 7. Consecrate the holy oils, in first place the chrism, churches, altars, church bells, and sacred vessels; 8. Receive jurisdiction over local churches (dioceses), when lawfully appointed.

621. **Does the pope possess a power of order superior to that of a bishop?**
No. All bishops are equals to the pope in the episcopal character and powers, but the pope has an immediate and universal jurisdiction over the entire Church.

622. **How is the power of *jurisdiction* different from the power of *order*?**
1. The power of jurisdiction is conferred by a superior, but the power of order is conferred by the sacrament; 2. The power of jurisdiction may be limited or revoked, but the power of order adheres in the soul and cannot be lost; 3. The power of

jurisdiction confers the legal authority to rule over some portion of the baptized, but the power of order confers the spiritual ability to validly confect the sacraments.

Administration of Holy Orders

623. **Who is the minister of the sacrament of holy orders?**
The bishop is the only minister of this sacrament.

624. **Who may serve as an extraordinary minister of some minor orders?**
When delegated by the competent ecclesiastical authority, a priest may confer tonsure, minor orders, and probably subdiaconate. In the past, abbots also had the privilege of conferring tonsure and minor orders among their subjects.

625. **From what bishop may a candidate receive holy orders?**
He should receive them from his own local ordinary, unless he has written permission ("dismissorial letters") to be ordained by another bishop, or there is some state of objective and exceptional necessity, e.g., persecution or extraordinary crisis in the Church.

626. **What are the most important preconditions for receiving holy orders validly and licitly?**
The candidate must be: 1. A man; 2. Baptized and confirmed; 3. Of sufficient age;[148] 4. Able to exercise free will; 5. Free or exempt from irregularities and impediments; 6. Intent on serving the Church and saving souls; 7. Holding the integrity of the Catholic Faith, and the requisite philosophical and theological knowledge; 8. Of good reputation, with moral probity, proven virtue, and the other physical and psychological qualities appropriate to the order to be received;[149] 9. Free from proven homosexual tendencies.[150]

627. **What may prevent a man from receiving sacramental ordination?**
An *impediment*, or canonical hindrance that excludes him from receiving it validly; e.g., anyone who: 1. Suffers from mental or psychological illness; 2. Has previously committed heresy, apostasy, or schism; 3. Lives in a merely civil marriage; 4. Has committed voluntary homicide; 5. Has procured a completed abortion or positively cooperated in it; 6. Has attempted suicide; 7. Has voluntarily mutilated himself or another gravely; 8. Has simulated an act of orders reserved to priests or bishops.[151]

628. **What are the noteworthy non-sacramental ceremonies in priestly ordination?**
1. The bishop clothing the candidates with the proper vestments; 2. The consecration made of the fingers and palm of each hand with holy oil; 3. In the traditional rite, laying on hands with the words: "Receive the Holy Spirit; whose sins you shall forgive, they are forgiven them, and whose sins you shall retain, they are retained."

Effects of Holy Orders

629. What are the four effects of this sacrament?

The sacrament of holy orders: 1. Confers special spiritual powers; 2. Imprints an indelible character on the soul; 3. Increases sanctifying grace; 4. Confers a special sacramental grace, giving the right to those graces necessary for the functions and duties of each order.

630. What obligations are imposed by the sacrament of orders?

The recipient is obliged to lead a holy life, and those in the order of subdeacon or higher are obliged to recite daily the Divine Office (Liturgy of Hours) and observe perfect and perpetual continence.

631. Do Catholic lay people have duties toward the sacrament of holy orders?

Besides those of the fourth commandment, they should: 1. Respect the priestly dignity; 2. Support vocations by giving alms; 3. Never discourage vocations to sacred orders, nor encourage the unfit to pursue them; 4. Pray that God sends good and holy priests to His Church.

Impossibility of Female Priesthood

632. Is it possible for women to receive holy orders?

No. By the will of God and the irreformable constitution of the Church, only baptized men are able to receive sacramental orders, as it configures them to the eternal priesthood of the God-Man, Jesus Christ, the Bridegroom of the Church His Bride, and enables them to represent Him sacramentally as a spiritual father.

633. What of those who clamor for the ordination of women as Catholic clergy?

They: 1. Oppose the divinely established order of the two sexes, each with its own specific mission; 2. Reject the hierarchical constitution of the Church; 3. Denigrate the unique dignity of Christian womanhood, consisting principally in motherhood, both physical and spiritual.

634. Why can't a woman be ordained a priest?

Because this would be: 1. Contrary to both Scripture and Tradition, as this was never done in the Old Law, nor in the New; 2. Inconsistent with the spousal meaning of priesthood, whereby a man represents and extends the presence of Christ the Bridegroom of the Church; 3. Opposed to the right ordering of the sexes, whereby "the head of every man is Christ, the head of a woman is her husband" (1 Cor 11:3), and no woman is "to teach or to have authority over men" (1 Tm 2:12); 4. Impossible, given the Church's infallible teaching that women cannot be ordained.

635. Has the Magisterium definitively rejected all possibility of women's ordination?

Yes. "In order that all doubt may be removed regarding a matter of great importance, a matter which pertains to the Church's divine constitution itself, in virtue of my ministry of confirming the brethren (cf. Lk 22:32*), I declare that the Church has no authority whatsoever to confer priestly ordination on women and that this judgment is to be definitively held by all the Church's faithful."[152]

636. Can the Blessed Virgin Mary be called a "priest"?
No. The Church has even forbidden artistic works that could give such an impression: "After mature examination, the Eminent Cardinals, general inquisitors of the Holy Office, have decided that images of the Blessed Virgin Mary wearing priestly vestments are not approved."[153]

637. Then what is the true character of Our Lady's greatness?
Her dignity as Mother of God is incomparably higher than that of any other creature, human or angelic, making her also the Mother of the Church and unique cooperator in the loving sacrifice of her divine Son. She is therefore the most noble member of the common and royal priesthood of the Church, not of the ministerial priesthood.

638. May women nonetheless receive the order of deacon?
No. The sacrament of holy orders is one sacrament, conferred in three grades. The sacramental ordination of women as deacons would therefore contradict the whole Tradition of the universal Church, both Eastern and Western, and violate her God-given order, since the Council of Trent dogmatically defined: "The divinely established hierarchy is made up of bishops, priests, and ministers,"[154] i.e., at least also of *deacons*.

639. Weren't there "deaconesses" in the ancient Church?
For the first five centuries of the Church, there is no trace of "deaconesses" in the West; and although the term does appear in the East, these women clearly did not receive the sacrament of holy orders: "The deaconess does not bless, and she does not fulfill any of the things that priests and deacons do, but she looks after the doors and attends the priests during the baptism of women, for the sake of decency."[155] The "deaconess" was evidently not a woman exercising the office of deacon, but rather a completely different ecclesiastical function.

640. Who fulfilled this historical role of the so-called "deaconess"?
The woman in charge of a monastic community of women was also called sometimes a *deaconess*. So also were consecrated virgins who had taken the vow of chastity. In the early Middle Ages in Gaul, abbesses or wives of deacons were also called *diaconissae*, by analogy in the case of the wives of priests (*presbyterissae*) or even of bishops (*episcopissae*).[156] In the Middle Ages, the nursing and teaching religious orders of nuns also fulfilled the functions of the deaconess, as did women who were instituted as widows or abbesses, still without any ordination.

641. **Does the Church have any power to ordain women to the sacramental diaconate?**
No. The Church has no power to elevate or declare any non-sacramental ecclesiastical office (such as the historical "deaconess") to be part of the tripartite sacrament of holy orders.

642. **Did the Church Fathers contend against a sacramental diaconate of women?**
Yes. The most explicit example comes from the fourth century: "Because the apostle mentions women after the deacons [see 1 Tm 3:10–11], the Montanists seize the favorable opportunity for heresy and hold with vain arrogance that the deaconesses must also be ordained; and this despite knowing that the apostles chose seven men to be deacons. Was it not possible to find a suitable woman then, when we read that there were holy women with the twelve apostles [see Acts 1:14]? But the Apostle commands that in the official liturgical assembly of the Church women should be silent [see 1 Cor 14:34]."[157]

643. **Should women receive minor orders, or exercise the service of lector or acolyte?**
No. The unbroken and universal practice of the Church prohibited women from the liturgical service of lector and acolyte, and canon law likewise prohibited women from receiving minor orders or the ministry of reader and acolyte.

644. **What is the deeper theological reason that women should not receive minor orders, or exercise the service of lector and acolyte?**
The minor orders and functions of lector and acolyte are rooted in the *diaconate*, a constitutive part of the sacrament of holy orders, which is reserved to men. In the absence of minor ordination, only male faithful can fulfill the functions of lector ("reader") or acolyte ("altar server"), because the male sex is the last link joining the inferior liturgical or deputy ministers with the diaconate at the symbolic level: the male sex of inferior ministers reflects the Levitical or diaconal liturgical ministry, which in turn was strictly ordered and subordinated to the priesthood—reserved by God exclusively for men in the Old Covenant, and continuing in the New, as attested by the constant and universal canonical and liturgical Tradition of the entire Church.

645. **Has the Holy See recently sought to change this universal tradition?**
Yes. In a grave and manifest rupture with the uninterrupted liturgical tradition of the Eastern and Western Church, Pope Francis altered the Code of Canon Law in 2021 to admit women to the instituted ministry of lector and acolyte[158]—a rupture already tolerated in practice by his predecessors, Popes Paul VI, John Paul II, and Benedict XVI. In the future, the Holy See must undoubtedly rectify this unprecedented break with the universal practice of the Church.

646. **Whom do those fulfilling any liturgical role in the sanctuary represent?**
All the ministers of the Church represent Christ, signifying degrees of His service, priesthood, and headship, and their various services are therefore performed by ordained men—or, in their absence, by their deputies: male readers and altar servers.

647. **Whom do the other faithful represent during liturgical worship?**
They represent and express the common priesthood during the liturgy, and are therefore gathered outside the sanctuary, in the nave of the church.

648. **Did Our Lady ever perform liturgical functions in the primitive Church?**
Despite being most worthy for such a service, there is no record of the Blessed Virgin Mary ever doing so. "Marian participation" in the liturgy—one of intense charity and interior union with Christ—is therefore the most active and fruitful liturgical participation possible for the common priesthood, and especially women.

649. **Why would Our Lady refrain from official liturgical or canonical acts?**
"If it were ordained by God that women should offer sacrifice or have any canonical function in the Church, Mary herself, if anyone, should have functioned as a priest in the New Testament.... But it was not God's pleasure [that she be a priest]. She was not even entrusted with the administration of baptism—for Christ could have been baptized by her rather than by John."[159]

Chapter 13: Marriage

Marriage in General

650. **What is *marriage* in itself?**
The exclusive, lifelong, indissoluble conjugal union contracted between one man and one woman, ordered to procreation and the mutual assistance of the spouses.

651. **Is marriage simply a matter of human decision, able to take various different forms?**
No. As an institution rooted in natural law, marriage has only one immutable form, which is discernible by reason itself and confirmed by divine revelation (see Gn 2:24; Mk 10:7–9; and Eph 5:31–32).

652. **What are the two fundamental properties of marriage?**
1. *Unity*—this bond unites man and wife in a complete, complimentary, and exclusive way; 2. *Indissolubility*—this bond can only be broken by death.

653. **What are the advantages of the exclusivity of marriage?**
1. It fosters mutual fidelity, trust, and love between the husband and wife; 2. It helps ensure the parentage of children; 3. It elevates marriage above other friendships and relations in society.

654. **What are the advantages of the indissolubility of marriage?**
1. It symbolizes and participates in the indissolubility of Christ's union with the Church; 2. It helps the spouses strive for virtue; 3. It lessens the chance of strife and discord; 4. It fosters spousal reconciliation; 5. It establishes the family as a stable pillar of society.[160]

655. Was marriage instituted before sin?

Yes, when God created Adam and Eve, and established their conjugal union in "one flesh" (see Gn 2:22, 24). Marriage is therefore "not only for a remedy against sin, but is chiefly for an office of nature; and thus it was instituted before sin, not as intended for a remedy."[161]

656. What is the end (purpose) of marriage?

The primary end (*finis operis*) of marriage is *procreation*, the begetting and education of children. The secondary end (*finis operantis*) is *mutual assistance*, the shared love and cooperation of the spouses in fulfilling their duties.

657. Why are these ends sometimes listed in a different order?

Sometimes the secondary end occurs first in the spouses' minds, as they may feel love for the other before thinking explicitly of procreation. However, this subjective experience does not change or supplant the objective end of marriage itself, as has been declared by the constant Magisterium through the centuries.[162]

658. What is the "threefold good" of marriage?

"The first is the birth of children and the educating of them to the worship of God. The second is that fidelity which one must render to the other. And the third is that it is a sacrament, or, in other words, the indivisibility of matrimony which shows forth the indivisible union of Christ and His Church."[163]

659. What is the *sacrament of matrimony*, or *Christian* marriage?

A sacrament instituted by Jesus Christ to sanctify the marriage of the baptized, so that man and woman can procreate and educate children in a holy manner for the Kingdom of God, and to give the couple and the family the graces necessary for their common life.

660. Who instituted the sacrament of marriage?

God Himself first instituted marriage in the Garden of Eden, and the Incarnate Son of God, Jesus Christ, then raised it to the dignity of a sacrament.[164]

661. Why is Christian marriage an image of Christ's mystical union with the Church?

St. Paul declares this sign as most appropriate (see Eph 5:23, 32), because "of all human relations there is none that binds so closely as the marriage tie, and from the fact that husband and wife are bound to one another by the bonds of the greatest affection and love."[165]

662. When did Jesus Christ elevate marriage to be one of His sacraments?

According to some theologians, Our Lord instituted marriage as a sacrament during the wedding at Cana (see Jn 2:1–11); according to others, it was later in His public ministry, or during the forty days before His Ascension.

663. **What is the matter and form of the sacrament of marriage?**

The matter of this sacrament is the mutual consent of the man and woman to *give* themselves to each other for life. The form consists of their public vows of consent, made before the Church, to *take* each other as spouse.

664. **What is necessary for this vowed consent to be valid?**

It must be: 1. Exchanged between two persons *qualified* by law (no impediments); 2. *True* and *mutual* consent, since neither feigned nor unilateral consent can create a true marriage; 3. *Externally* and *legitimately manifested* (according to canonical form), otherwise it could not be known and accepted by each party; 4. *Referring to the present* rather than the future, to distinguish it from an engagement and exclude placing future conditions on the marriage; 5. *Free* and *deliberate*, as both parties must understand and accept the obligations of the married state.

665. **How are the marriage vows *consummated* (definitively sealed) by the spouses?**

Through the *marital act*, i.e., the conjugal union of the spouses—a physical act of sexual intercourse that is ordered to procreation, which expresses and definitively seals the total self-gift of the spouses to one another. "Now they are not two, but one flesh. What therefore God hath joined together, let no man put asunder" (Mt 19:6*).

666. **Why does marriage have these ends and properties?**

In His perfect wisdom, God created marriage to secure peace and union within families, safety and provision for children, and stability in human society, as well as to serve as a mystical sign of His own unfailing love for the Church.

Administration of Marriage

667. **Who is the minister of the sacrament of marriage?**

The man and woman who exchange consent are the ministers, as nothing but their mutual consent creates the bond of marriage.

668. **Who may receive the sacrament of marriage?**

Any sexually mature baptized person who is free from impediment.

669. **Must Christians marry?**

No. There is no law prescribing marriage for those who do not desire it and prefer to live the single life in continence.

670. **Is the state of vowed virginity or celibacy superior to that of marriage?**

Yes, as those in the state of consecrated virginity or celibacy realize in this life that which awaits the blessed in heaven (see Mt 22:30). "If anyone saith, that the marriage state is to be placed above the state of virginity, or of celibacy, and that it is not better and more blessed to remain in virginity, or in celibacy, than to be united in matrimony; let him be anathema."[166]

671. **What are the remote preparations for a worthy marriage?**
1. Readiness for the married state by years spent in a virtuous Christian life; 2. Prudence in the choice of spouse; 3. Purity of intention, desiring to please God and obtain sanctity within marriage; 4. The traditional ceremony of betrothal, which calls down graces on the couple preparing for marriage; 5. Instruction regarding the nature and basic duties of marriage and family life.

672. **Is the state of grace necessary for a fruitful reception of the sacrament?**
Yes, because matrimony is a sacrament of the living. Whoever receives it in the state of mortal sin deprives himself of sacramental grace until he is reconciled with God.

673. **How is marriage normally celebrated?**
The priest reminds the couple of the importance of marriage and their principal obligations. He then witnesses the exchange of their vows of consent, and declares them united in matrimony. In many different Catholic rites, this is also followed by a blessing and exchange of rings, after which several concluding prayers are offered.

674. **What is a *Nuptial Mass*?**
In the traditional Roman Rite, this is a special form of Holy Mass celebrated immediately after the exchange of marriage vows, which includes unique and ancient formulae of blessing for the spouses to maintain fidelity and strength in God's grace and provision.

675. **What is the best way to prepare for a Nuptial Mass?**
1. Arrange that the bride, bridegroom, and entire wedding party can go to confession beforehand; 2. Spend time in earnest prayer, such as a holy hour the day or evening before the wedding; 3. Practice and encourage reverence and modesty in the wedding service and any celebration that follows.

Impediments to Marriage

676. **What is meant by a *marriage impediment*?**
Any objective circumstance that presents some obstacle to marriage. Such obstacles either *invalidate* or completely nullify an attempted marriage (diriment impediments), or render the marriage *illicit* or unlawful (prohibitive impediments).

677. **Does the Church have power to establish impediments to marriage?**
Yes. Jesus gave His Church the power to regulate the administration of the sacraments, and to determine and apply the moral law.

678. **What is the aim of the Church in establishing these impediments?**
To protect souls, safeguard sound morals, and maintain the honor of marriage in a fallen world.

679. **Are civil governments able to establish nullifying impediments to marriage?**
The civil power has no right to legislate on the sacraments, so it cannot establish diriment impediments for Christians; however, it may do so for the unbaptized, since these do not belong to the Church.

680. **What right does the civil authority have in regard to marriage?**
It has power over the civil effects of marriage (e.g., settlement of property, taxation status), but it has no right to declare an invalid marriage to be valid, or vice versa—the Church alone can judge such matters.

681. **How should Christians respond to civil laws that concern marriage?**
When a law touching upon marriage is not opposed to faith or morals, it is proper to obey it for the cause of social order, and to secure the legal effects of marriage.

682. **What is a declaration of marriage *nullity*?**
An objective judgment of an ecclesiastical court when, after extensive investigation, the Church declares that a sacramental marriage was never validly contracted between two parties that were once presumed to be spouses.

683. **What are the chief diriment impediments, rendering a marriage null and void?**
1. *Lack of sufficient age*; 2. *Impotence* to have intercourse; 3. *Prior bond* of an existing marriage, holy orders, or solemn religious vow; 4. *Disparity of cult*, or marriage with a non-Catholic without a dispensation; 5. *Natural* or *legal relationship* within certain degrees; 6. *Affinity*, or "in-law" relationship within certain degrees.

684. **What are the main defects in *canonical form* that can render a marriage invalid?**
1. Lack of a proper official (Catholic priest or deacon); 2. Wrong minister: an officiant who is not in full communion with the Church; 3. Failure of the couple's action, as when couples invent their own vow formula; 4. Complete lack of form, such as a merely civil service.

685. **What are the main defects in *spousal consent* that can render a marriage invalid?**
1. Lack of sufficient reason and discretion; 2. Inability to assume essential obligations; 3. Ignorance of the basic ends, duties, and nature of marriage; 4. Fraud, by which one person deceptively hides a significant and relevant fact from the other, e.g., same-sex attraction; 5. Error of persons, as in cases of mistaken identity; 6. Simulation of marriage, e.g., holding an intention entirely against children or fidelity.

686. **Does the Church allow marriage between Catholics and non-Catholics?**
Called *mixed marriages* (Catholic with a baptized non-Catholic) or *disparity of cult* (Catholic with a non-baptized), such unions were once entirely forbidden, and may now only be contracted with serious reason and special permission. The Church discourages such marriages because of the grave spiritual danger it poses to the Catholic spouse and their children.

687. **What are the marriage *banns*?**
Local, public proclamations that a marriage will soon be contracted by two particular persons, made to help discover whether there are any impediments to the potential marriage.

688. **Can the Church dispense from marriage impediments?**
The Church may dispense from impediments of ecclesiastical law, but not from impediments of natural and divine law, such as error, violence, prior bond, etc.

689. **Who has the power to grant marriage dispensations in the Church?**
The pope can dispense from any ecclesiastical impediment in any case, and local ordinaries can dispense from certain impediments in their own diocese.

690. **What should a couple do if they discover an impediment after marrying?**
If the impediment is uncertain, they should approach their pastor for counsel. If certain, they should live in continence until they obtain a dispensation or *sanation* of their marriage from the competent authority.

Effects and Duties of Marriage

691. **What are the effects of the sacrament of marriage?**
1. Increase of sanctifying grace in those who receive it worthily; 2. Unique sacramental grace that helps spouses fulfill their duties of state; 3. Confirmation of the unity and indissolubility of the contracted marriage bond.

692. **What duties are imposed by the sacrament of marriage?**
Three kinds: 1. The mutual obligations of the spouses to one another; 2. The obligations proper to each spouse; 3. The obligations of the parents to their children.

693. **What are the mutual obligations of the spouses?**
They must love each other with a faithful, chaste, patient, self-giving, devoted, and supernatural love.

694. **What are the special duties of the husband?**
As head of the household, he must exercise prudent authority and leadership as a worthy image of the provident and sacrificial love of Christ (see Eph 5:25), treating his wife with gentleness and respect, and providing for all her legitimate needs.

695. **What are the special duties of the wife?**
As the heart of the home, she must submit to her husband as to the Lord in legitimate matters (see Eph 5:22), showing him affection and loving support, carrying out her domestic tasks with devotion and attention, remaining modest and reserved in behavior and attire.

696. What are the duties of the spouses to their children?
All those implied by the fourth commandment, and above all that they work for the Christian education of their children, mindful that they will have to give an account for them before God.

697. What are the special duties of a father toward his children?
1. To demonstrate the protection and providence of God by providing for their material needs and safety; 2. To share with them his Catholic faith, and encourage them in this faith; 3. To ensure that they receive adequate human and spiritual formation; 4. To strengthen their character and equip them for the difficulties they will face in life.

698. What are the special duties of a mother toward her children?
1. To nourish and provide for their well-being, especially in the early years of life; 2. To provide them with basic education in Catholic faith and virtue; 3. To demonstrate the love of God by showing tender care and well-ordered affection; 4. To collaborate with her husband in tending to their formational needs.

699. If one spouse requests the marital act, must the other grant this request?
Yes. "The husband should give to his wife her conjugal rights, and likewise the wife to her husband" (1 Cor 7:3). Because marriage is a complete and mutual gift of one's body and property, if either party asks reasonably and seriously for the conjugal act, the other is bound in justice to grant it. Justifiable reasons for refusal include manifest evil intentions, such as use of contraception or acts contrary to nature.

Errors about Marriage

700. Is parental approval required for a couple to contract a valid marriage?
No. However, it is most advisable to seek the counsel of loving parents and prudent friends when choosing a worthy spouse.

701. Can the Church ever permit spouses to live apart from one another?
Yes. For a just cause, a local ordinary can permit spousal separation for up to six months at a time.[167] For certain grave causes, spouses may also be permitted to suspend or cease conjugal relations (separation from "bed") and cohabitation (separation from "board"), although the bond of marriage still persists.

702. What reasons could justify such a separation from bed and board?
1. Mutual consent for a just cause, there being no further obligations to children (e.g., desire to enter religious life); 2. Grave danger to soul or body; 3. Certainty that one of the parties has committed adultery.

703. In such cases, may Christians also seek a divorce in civil law?
Yes, when this is the only means of adequate self-defense; e.g., maintaining legal protection and provision for the innocent spouse or children. However, such civil

action has no effect on the marriage bond, which is beyond the power of the state to dissolve.

704. **Can those who divorce and later "remarry" another in civil law grow in grace and charity?**
No. One who knowingly chooses to live as though married to a civil partner while their true spouse is still alive is a public adulterer, living in the state of mortal sin. They can receive neither sanctifying grace nor salvation until they repent and are reconciled to God.

705. **May spouses use contraception?**
No. The conjugal act is ordered to procreation and expresses total and mutual self-giving, for which reason it is called the *marital act*. To intentionally render this act infertile—whether by interruption, barrier, surgery, chemicals, or otherwise—corrupts its very nature, and changes it into an act against the order established by God the Creator.

706. **May spouses contracept in order to practice responsible parenthood?**
No. "Any action which either before, at the moment of, or after sexual intercourse is specifically intended to prevent procreation—whether as an end or as a means,"[168] is in itself "an offense against the law of God and of nature, and those who indulge in such are branded with the guilt of a grave sin."[169]

707. **May spouses agree to abstain from conjugal relations within marriage?**
Yes. Abstaining from the marital act by mutual consent—whether permanently or for a time—has been practiced since apostolic times (see 1 Cor 7:5).

708. **How is such periodic abstinence different from contraception?**
Unlike contraceptive intercourse, conjugal relations during the periods of female infertility are not contrary to nature, and it is morally licit to confine oneself to these periods when there are serious reasons.

709. **Is it possible to abuse this morally licit method of periodic abstinence?**
Yes. Anything that admits of a legitimate use can also be abused, and periodic abstinence may be turned into a cloak for selfishness. "If the sincere intention of letting the Creator do His work freely is lacking, human selfishness will always be able to find new sophisms and expedients to silence consciences, if possible, and perpetuate the abuses ... [that oppose] readiness to accept with joy and gratitude the priceless gifts of God, which are children, and in the number that pleases Him."[170]

710. **Then the method of periodic abstinence can even become sinful?**
Yes, when used with a *contraceptive mentality*, i.e., for selfish motives directed against the procreative end of marriage. "Taking advantage of the 'infertile periods' in conjugal coexistence can become a source of abuse.... By separating the natural method from the ethical dimension, one ceases to perceive the difference between it and

the other 'methods' (artificial means) ... as if it were only a question of a different form of contraception."[171]

711. **Is it advisable to use the expression "Natural Family Planning"?**
No. This sounds overly technical and bureaucratic, like an economic plan for grain production or cattle breeding. It is unworthy to apply the word *planning* to human persons, potential children of God and new citizens of heaven.

712. **May spouses use artificial insemination, in vitro fertilization, or surrogate motherhood?**
No. It is never permitted to separate human procreation from the conjugal union, and any action that divides the unitive and procreative end of the marital act is against the natural order established by God, and therefore, gravely sinful.

713. **If one spouse dies, may the survivor marry again?**
Yes. The marriage bond is dissolved by death: "A wife is bound to her husband as long as he lives. If the husband dies, she is free to be married to whom she wishes, only in the Lord" (1 Cor 7:39).

714. **Does the civil power have authority to redefine marriage in civil law?**
No. Changing the nature of marriage is beyond the scope of any human power, and its redefinition in law is one of the greatest social evils of our time. Such initiatives must be strongly opposed by clergy and faithful of every rank.

715. **Why is the redefinition of marriage in civil law such a great evil?**
Governments that enact such measures—particularly those granting legal recognition to same-sex unions—are complicit in sins crying to heaven for vengeance, and place their nation on the path of moral and physical destruction.

716. **May a so-called "same-sex marriage" in civil law ever be blessed by the Church?**
No. Any unions that have the name of marriage without the reality of it are not capable of receiving the blessing of the Church, as these are contrary to natural and divine law.

717. **May the Church nonetheless support so-called "civil unions" between persons of the same sex?**
No. Even if such arrangements do not receive the name of "marriage" in law, they plainly imitate it—thus encouraging grave sin and causing serious scandal, which the Church can never approve or appear to condone.

718. **Should persons in state-recognized same-sex unions be eligible to adopt children?**
No. Their public rejection of natural and divine law renders them habitually unholy, unstable, and unfit to care for children, and organizations permitting such adoptions are complicit in grave sin, enacting a real moral violence against children.

719. **May we ever attend the celebration of such unions?**
No. To do so would be a failure in charity and justice, and cause serious scandal. "Woe to those that call evil good" (Is 5:20*), for, "if you do not warn him ... the wicked man will die in his iniquity, and I will hold you responsible for his blood" (Ez 3:18*).

Family as Domestic Church

720. **Why is the Catholic family called a *domestic church*?**
From the early centuries of Christianity, the family was seen as the Church "in miniature."[172] "The family is, so to speak, the domestic church. In it parents should, by their word and example, be the first preachers of the Faith to their children; they should encourage them in the vocation which is proper to each of them, fostering with special care a vocation to a sacred state."[173]

721. **What is the most sublime goal of the Catholic family as a domestic church?**
The first and most holy goal and end of matrimony is to raise future citizens of heaven. "By the command of Christ, it not only looks to the propagation of the human race, but to the bringing forth of children for the Church ... so that a people might be born and brought up for the worship and religion of the true God and our Savior Jesus Christ."[174]

722. **Can we also call the Catholic family a kind of "first seminary"?**
Yes. Families "animated by the spirit of faith and love and by the sense of duty, become a kind of initial seminary."[175] The supernatural spirit of love and of self-sacrifice of both parents—and often especially of the mother or grandmother—is the very seedbed and foundation of future priestly and religious vocations.

723. **How can families truly live as the "domestic church" today?**
1. Pray daily as a family, e.g., at meal times and before bed; 2. Assist weekly at Holy Mass; 3. Transmit the Catholic Faith, studying and discussing matters of faith as a family; 4. Practice mutual forgiveness, love, and tenderness in family relationships; 5. Invite others to join in your family's prayer and catechesis.

The Blessing of Large Families

724. **Even in situations of hardship, is it laudable for Christian parents to have many children?**
Yes. "The inheritance of the Lord are children: the reward, the fruit of the womb" (Ps 126:3*). Large Christian families are among the greatest blessings granted by God in this life.

725. **Has the Church often praised large families?**
Yes. "Large families are the most splendid flower beds in the garden of the Church. ... Their youth never seems to fade away, as long as the sweet fragrance of a crib

remains in the home, as long as the walls of the house echo to the silvery voices of children and grandchildren.... Children in large families learn almost automatically to be careful of what they do and to assume responsibility for it, to have a respect for each other and help each other, to be openhearted and generous. For them, the family is a little proving ground, before they move into the world outside, which will be harder on them and more demanding."[176]

726. What is the unique spiritual beauty of a large family?
Its continuous chain of sacramental celebrations. "Even outwardly, a large well-ordered family is almost a visible sanctuary.... The youngest of the children has just placed the little white dress among the dearest memories of life, and here is the first wedding veil in bloom, which gathers parents, children, and new relatives at the foot of the altar. Other marriages, other baptisms, other First Communions will follow, like renewed springtimes, perpetuating, so to speak, the visits of God and His grace in the house."[177]

Chapter 14: Sacramentals

Nature of Sacramentals

727. What are *sacramentals*?
Sacred actions or things, established by Christ or His Church, to obtain various corporal or spiritual effects by the Church's prayer.

728. Why are these sacred signs called *sacramentals*?
Because they bear a certain resemblance to the sacraments, are in some way related to them, and are often used in their administration.

729. How do sacramentals resemble the sacraments?
1. Some were instituted by Christ (e.g., exorcism, foot washing); 2. They involve some outward sign; 3. They produce or are occasions of certain spiritual effects.

730. How do sacramentals differ from the sacraments?
1. Not all are of divine institution; 2. They do not produce grace directly of themselves, but in virtue of the faith and prayer of the Church and the dispositions of the user.

731. Who can administer sacramentals?
Only a cleric who has the requisite power may confer blessings; some are restricted to bishops, whereas others can be conferred by priests.

732. Why were the sacramentals instituted?
To further extend the Kingdom of Christ on earth by permeating the created order with His grace, and causing more material things to serve as instruments for man's sanctification.

Kinds of Sacramentals

733. What are the different kinds of sacramentals?

1. *Actions* that include prayers, blessings, and exorcisms; 2. *Objects* that include anything formally blessed or employed in the Church's worship.

734. What *prayers* are considered sacramentals?

Especially: 1. The Lord's Prayer, Hail Mary, Glory Be, Confiteor, and any prayer prescribed or approved by the Church; 2. Solemn religious processions of the clergy and faithful.

735. What is a *blessing*?

Any authoritative action of the Church in which her ministers communicate the grace and favor of God to a particular person, place, or thing.

736. How many kinds of blessing are there?

Two: 1. *Invocative* blessings, the Church formally asking God to bestow temporal or spiritual benefits upon someone or something, without changing its substantial quality; 2. *Constitutive* blessings, imparting some sacred character to persons or things in God's name by the Church's command, endowing them with some new and abiding quality of sanctity, so that the profanation of them entails the malice of sacrilege.

737. What is a *consecration*?

The most solemn form of constitutive blessing, whereby the blessed person or thing becomes enduringly sacred and dedicated to the public worship of God in some way; e.g., the blessing of abbots, virgins, churches, altars, chalices.

738. Why is the sign of the cross so often used in Catholic blessings?

Because the Cross of Jesus Christ is the conduit of all grace and blessing, being the chosen instrument of our Redemption.

739. What are *exorcisms*?

Broadly speaking, it is when a Catholic cleric authoritatively commands that some person, place, or thing be liberated from and protected against the power and influence of the devil.

740. Are there different kinds of exorcisms?

Yes. They may be of simple form, as contained within the rite of baptism, or more solemn, as in the rite of major exorcism.

741. Are solemn exorcisms still performed today?

Yes. The power and authority to cast out demons, first given to the apostles (see Mt 10:1; Mk 6:7; and Lk 9:1) and passed down to their successors, is still exercised by the Church's clergy at need.

742. Does a priest need authorization to perform a solemn exorcism?
Yes. "No one can perform exorcisms legitimately upon the possessed unless he has obtained special and express permission from the local ordinary."[178]

743. May even lay people use non-solemn forms of exorcism in their prayer?
Yes. Unlike solemn exorcism, such prayers are not performed over the possessed, but ask generally for the preservation of humanity, the Church, and God's chosen ones. Because baptism does not grant lay people spiritual authority over others, they may not command demons as exorcists do when authorized. An excellent example of such a prayer is the so-called "minor exorcism" of Pope Leo XIII,[179] the Prayer to St. Michael the Archangel:

> Saint Michael the Archangel, defend us in battle. Be our protection against the wickedness and snares of the devil; may God rebuke him, we humbly pray. And do thou, O Prince of the Heavenly Host, by the power of God, thrust into hell Satan and all evil spirits who wander through the world for the ruin of souls. Amen.

744. What are sacramental *objects*?
Blessed items that serve as special instruments of sanctification: holy water, blessed salt, oils, candles, rosaries, scapulars, vestments, holy images or icons, bread, herbs, etc.

745. Is holy water a very useful sacramental?
Yes. A mixture of salt and water exorcised and sanctified by the constitutive blessing of a priest, holy water has been used from the earliest Christian centuries, is employed in most other blessings, and should be regularly used by Christians.

746. How may we use holy water?
1. Assist at the Asperges (holy water sprinkling rite) on Sundays before the principal High Mass; 2. Use it to make the sign of the cross upon entering a church; 3. Keep some at home as protection against evil spirits; 4. Sign ourselves with it before leaving home or going to bed, saying: "By the sign of Thy Cross, deliver us from our enemies, O Lord," or: "By Thy precious blood and by this holy water, wash away my sins, O Lord"; 5. Sprinkle it with faith upon anyone subject to bodily or spiritual harm; 6. Sprinkle it generously in places subject to spiritual harm (hotel rooms, rentals, or any strange place where evils may have been committed); 7. Have a priest bless our home with holy water (e.g., during Epiphanytide).

747. How might sacramentals be abused?
Through sins of: 1. *Sacrilege*, treating them without sufficient reverence, or putting them to profane use; 2. *Superstition*, relying merely on their external use without any true and interior worship of God.

Effects of Sacramentals

748. **What are the effects of the sacramentals?**
They vary, depending on each sacramental. By the prayer of the Church, they may:
1. Obtain actual graces; 2. Remit venial sins for which we repent; 3. Remit the temporal punishment due to sins already forgiven; 4. Drive out demons; 5. Cure or relieve sickness; 6. End disasters, famine, disease, and war; 7. Improve the fertility of farms, efficiency of tools, etc.

749. **Do the sacramentals infallibly produce their effects?**
Only constitutive blessings (consecration of churches, altars, etc.) are infallibly effective, as the efficacy of sacramentals depends on the faith and prayer of the Church, which God alone knows and answers according to His wisdom and the dispositions of those who use them.

Section 4: The Liturgy

Chapter 15: Sacred Liturgy

Liturgy in General

750. **What is the *liturgy*?**
This term is used for the many official rites and ceremonies of the Church's public worship, through which she glorifies God and sanctifies man.

751. **How has the Church properly defined this term?**
"The sacred liturgy is ... the public worship which our Redeemer as Head of the Church renders to the Father, as well as the worship which the community of the faithful renders to its Founder, and through Him to the heavenly Father. It is, in short, the worship rendered by the Mystical Body of Christ in the entirety of its Head and members."[1]

752. **What name is given to the laws that govern the liturgy?**
Rubrics regulate the precise actions for conducting each rite in itself; other liturgical laws are juridical-disciplinary, designating the nature of liturgical acts and certain ceremonial aspects of their celebration, such as time, place, objects used, etc.

753. **What is the purpose of liturgical rubrics?**
They: 1. Instruct the celebrant to perform the liturgy properly; 2. Preserve the integrity of the true worship; 3. Reinforce Catholic dogma; 4. Manifest the Church's unity of faith, hope, and charity across space and time.

754. **Do the liturgical ceremonies and rubrics also have a spiritual meaning?**
Yes. "Every ceremony of the Holy Mass, however small or minimal, contains in itself a positive work, a real meaning, a distinct beauty. They are like the flowers of the field, which, if they are small compared to the sublime cedars, yet in their smallness and beauty they manifest the omnipotence and wisdom of the Creator."[2] For this reason, St. Teresa of Avila declared: "I would rather die a thousand times than violate the least ceremony of the Church."[3]

755. **Is the liturgy primarily for the instruction or edification of man?**
No. The liturgy is primarily for the glorification of God. In a connected but secondary way, it is also a source of instruction and sanctification for those who participate in it.[4]

756. **Why is the liturgy essential to the Church?**
Because the Church was established to offer right worship. It continues the work of Our Lord, the eternal High Priest, "prolong[ing] the priestly mission of Jesus Christ mainly by means of the sacred liturgy."[5]

757. **How else does the liturgy benefit the Church?**
It is a rule of faith, an official depository of Catholic dogma, according to the Catholic axiom: *lex orandi, lex credendi* ("the law of prayer is the law of belief"), a bond of unity, a most powerful means of sanctification, and the principal instrument of Sacred Tradition.

History of Liturgy

758. **What is the origin of the liturgy?**
It originates in the eternal exchange of divine charity between the three Persons of the Blessed Trinity, which in turn is the object of ceaseless adoration in heaven (see Is 6:1–3; and Apoc 4:8).

759. **What is the origin of the liturgy on earth?**
Like religion itself, earthly liturgy goes back to the dawn of human history, developing gradually under the careful providence of God.

760. **What were the main liturgical acts of the patriarchal religion?**
1. The offering of sacrifice; 2. The dedication of sacred places; 3. The erection of stone altars.

761. **What form did the liturgy take under the Mosaic Law?**
In anticipation of the coming Redeemer, God formed a chosen priesthood and gave precise directions for the sacrifices, feasts, and ceremonies of the Old Law (see Leviticus).

762. **Who perfected the essential form of this Mosaic liturgy?**
Jesus Christ. After fulfilling all the prescriptions of the Old Covenant, Our Lord abrogated its ceremonial law in establishing the Eucharistic Sacrifice as the new and central act of divine worship for all time.

763. **Is Our Lord Jesus Christ the perfect teacher and model of the true divine worship?**
Yes. "In His life, totally oriented 'toward the Father' and deeply united to Him, Jesus Christ is the model also of our prayer";[6] and "not only as a model to be imitated, but as a Master to whom we should listen readily, a Shepherd whom we should follow."[7] For, "Christ Jesus, High Priest of the New and Eternal Covenant, taking human nature, introduced into this earthly exile that hymn which is sung throughout all ages in the halls of heaven."[8]

764. **Who has ensured the integrity of Catholic liturgy across time and space?**
The entire body of the Church; but chiefly the apostles and their successors, whom Our Lord empowered to safeguard the liturgy and oversee its development with the guidance of the Holy Spirit.

765. **May the Catholic hierarchy therefore create novel liturgical forms at will?**
No. Liturgical continuity is an essential aspect of the Church's holiness and catholicity: "For our canons and our forms were not given to the churches at the present day, but were wisely and safely transmitted to us from our forefathers."[9]

766. **Isn't any form of worship inherently sacred?**
No. Only *traditional* rites enjoy this inherent sanctity—liturgical forms that have been received from antiquity and developed organically in the Church as one body, i.e., in accord with the authentic *sensus fidelium* and the *perennis sensus ecclesiae* (perennial sense of the Church), duly confirmed by the hierarchy.[10]

767. **Why is this link to antiquity so essential for the sanctity of right worship?**
God has revealed how He desires to be worshipped: therefore, this sanctity cannot be fabricated or decreed; it can only be humbly received, diligently protected, and reverently handed on. This is the guiding apostolic principle: *Tradidi quod accepi*, "I handed over to you, what I first received" (1 Cor 15:3*). "So then, brethren, stand firm and hold to the traditions which you were taught by us, either by word of mouth or by letter" (2 Thes 2:15).

768. **Is it possible for a pope or bishop to issue a deficient liturgical form?**
Yes. The disciplinary acts of the hierarchy are not infallible; and although such errors are historically rare, even a pope may promulgate a deficient liturgical form, as with the novel Breviary of Pope Paul III (1536)[11] that caused decades of controversy before being retracted by Pope Pius V in 1568.

769. **Is the pope obliged to faithfully maintain the Church's traditional liturgical rites?**
Yes. The early medieval Papal Oath affirms: "I promise to keep inviolate the discipline and the liturgy of the Church as I have found them and as they were transmitted by my holy Predecessors,"[12] and the Papal Oath decreed by the Council of Constance echoes: "I will follow and observe in every way the rite handed down of the ecclesiastical sacraments of the Catholic Church."[13]

770. **Have attempts at liturgical innovation ever been condemned by the Church?**
Yes. The Jansenist Synod of Pistoia (1786) sought to reduce the liturgy "'to a greater simplicity of rites, by expressing it in the vernacular language, by uttering it in a loud voice'; as if the present order of the liturgy, received and approved by the Church, had emanated in some part from the forgetfulness of the principles by which it should be regulated"—a notion condemned as "rash, offensive to pious ears, insulting to the Church, favorable to the charges of heretics against it."[14] Pope Benedict XVI similarly affirmed: "In the history of the liturgy there is growth and progress, but no rupture. What earlier generations held as sacred, remains sacred and great for us too, and it cannot be all of a sudden entirely forbidden or even considered harmful."[15]

771. **Can a pope abrogate a liturgical rite of immemorial custom in the Church?**

No. Just as a pope cannot forbid or abrogate the Apostles' Creed or Niceno-Constantinopolitan Creed or substitute a new formula for them, neither can he abrogate traditional, millennium-old rites of Mass and the sacraments or forbid their use. This applies as much to Eastern as to Western rites.

772. **Could the traditional Roman Rite ever be legitimately forbidden for the entire Church?**

No. It rests upon divine, apostolic, and ancient pontifical usage, and bears the canonical force of immemorial custom; it can never be abrogated or forbidden.[16]

773. **Doesn't the traditional Roman Rite hinder the Church's unity or evangelizing mission?**

No. The Church condemns such notions,[17] and they contradict the facts of history: traditional worship has always fostered the true unity of the Church, and many souls have been drawn to faith precisely by witnessing the doctrinal and ritual integrity, clarity, and beauty of her constant liturgical rites.

774. **Isn't this Rite "clericalist" for excluding laity from the sanctuary during Mass?**

No. True participation in the sacred liturgy does not require one's action as a minister. The laity in the nave have the right and duty to interiorly unite themselves to the offering of the Son of God to His Father at the hands of the priest; but in the manner proper to them, without the confusion or symbolic contradiction of their presence in the sanctuary among the ordained ministers. The laity's proper role is to be inwardly sanctified by the sacraments, and to bring all secular matters into subjection to the Kingship of Christ.

775. **Isn't this Rite "obscurantist" with its clerical roles, silence, and mysterious elements?**

No. All traditional liturgical rites assign varied roles, words, and actions as an image of the many-layered cosmos, visible and invisible, and of the heavenly hierarchies of angels and saints, with Christ at their head. The sacred mysteries, before which saints and angels cover their faces (see Job 40:4; Is 6:2; Apoc 7:11; and 8:1), are appropriately veiled behind a visual or sonic *iconostasis* or "holy screen," as part of the proper reverence God has commanded (see Ex 33:18–23; and 2 Cor 3:7–11).

Aspects of Liturgy

776. **Are there many different liturgies in the Church?**

Yes; they are divided into two classes: Eastern liturgies and Western liturgies.

777. **Besides the Roman Rite, what other liturgies have flourished in the Latin Church?**

The Roman Rite is not the only liturgical expression in the Western or Latin Church: there are also the Ambrosian Rite in Milan, the Mozarabic Rite in Spain, and several "uses" (variants) of the Roman Rite in particular places: Braga in Portugal,

Lyons in France, and those proper to the Dominican, Carmelite, Premonstratensian, Cistercian, and Carthusian Orders.

778. What are the principal Eastern liturgies?
1. The Byzantine Liturgy; 2. The Antiochene Liturgy, also called the West Syriac or Syro-Antiochian Rite, traceable to the rite of St. James as celebrated by the Maronites, Syrians, and Malankarese; 3. The East Syriac Liturgy or Chaldean Rite, based on the liturgical traditions of Sts. Addai and Mari, as celebrated among the Chaldeans and by the Malabarese; 4. The Alexandrian Liturgy, found among the Egyptians, Ethiopians, and Eritreans; 5. The Armenian Liturgy, based on the Greek Liturgy of St. Basil.

779. What are the principal books of the traditional Roman Liturgy?
The Missal, Lectionary (Epistolary, Evangeliary), Breviary, Ritual, Pontifical, Ceremonial of Bishops, and the Martyrology.

780. What does the *Missal* contain?
All the prayers and ceremonies (and traditionally, also the readings) of Holy Mass.

781. What does the *Breviary* contain?
The Divine Office, the daily regimen of prayers recited at fixed hours of the day or night, drawn chiefly from the book of Psalms, which priests and religious are obliged to recite or sing in the name of the Church.

782. Are the Psalms especially significant for the prayer of the Church?
Yes. St. Ambrose calls them "the benediction of the people, the praise of God, the praising of the multitude, the rejoicing of all, the speech of all, the voice of the Church, the resounding confession of faith, the full devotion of authority, the joy of liberty, the cry of gladness, the echo of joy";[18] and Pope Pius X maintains that "the book of Psalms, like a paradise containing in itself the fruits all the other [books of Scripture], gives forth songs, and with them also shows its own songs in psalmody."[19]

783. What does the *Ritual* contain?
The sacred rites to be observed in administering the sacraments, blessings, burials, and other Church functions.

784. What does the *Pontifical* contain?
The various ceremonies and sacred functions reserved to bishops, such as the administration of sacred orders, the blessing of holy oils, consecration of churches, etc.

785. What does the *Ceremonial of Bishops* contain?
Particular ceremonies to be observed in cathedrals and collegiate churches, and certain other episcopal functions.

786. What does the *Martyrology* contain?
The official list or canon of those saints whom the Church commemorates each day throughout the liturgical year.

787. **Why is the Latin language so well suited to liturgical prayer?**
Because of its: 1. *Sacrality*—removal from profane use reinforces the unique and sacred character of the liturgy; 2. *Antiquity*—emphasizing the unity and perpetuity of the Faith itself; 3. *Stability*—as a "dead" language, its fixed terms and meanings protect the liturgy from doctrinal corruption; 4. *Universality*—expressing and facilitating the unity of the Church's liturgical prayer worldwide.

788. **What is the most solemn and expressive form of liturgical prayer?**
When it is sung in the form of sacred chant: diverse rites have their own proper musical chant traditions.

789. **Is chanting in divine worship a very ancient custom?**
Yes. It has been used since Old Testament times, and in the Church's infancy, her chant was a basic psalmody with modes borrowed mainly from the Synagogue. It was later advanced and perfected, above all in the shaping of plainchant by Sts. Ambrose and Gregory the Great.

790. **What did St. Gregory the Great do for liturgical chant?**
Pope St. Gregory I assisted greatly in improving the ancient melodies in accord with the laws of harmony and requirements of divine worship, fathering that heavenly musical form that is the genius of the Roman liturgy: Gregorian chant.

791. **What does the Magisterium say about Gregorian chant?**
That it is "the chant proper to the Roman Church, the only chant she has inherited from the ancient Fathers, which she has jealously guarded for centuries in her liturgical codices, [and] which she directly proposes to the faithful as her own.... Gregorian chant has always been regarded as the supreme model for sacred music."[20]

792. **What are the characteristics of Gregorian chant?**
Often called *plainchant*, this musical form is simple, intuitive, serious, clear, and expressive of truly divine Latin prayers and readings: never obscuring or distorting the terms, profound, sweet, and majestic.

793. **What makes a musical form truly fitting for liturgical worship?**
"Sacred music should possess, in the highest degree, the qualities proper to the liturgy, and in particular sanctity and goodness of form, which will spontaneously produce the final quality of universality.... The more closely a composition for church approaches in its movement, inspiration, and savor the Gregorian form, the more sacred and liturgical it becomes; and the more out of harmony it is with that supreme model, the less worthy it is of the temple."[21]

Chapter 16: Sacred Space

Sacred Space in General

794. Are all places equally holy, since God is present everywhere?
No. Throughout time, God has manifested His presence in specific places, making them particularly holy. At first, the divine apparition directly sanctified a place, as the patriarch Jacob said: "Surely the Lord is in this place" (Gn 28:16); and Moses was told: "The place on which you are standing is holy ground" (Ex 3:5). With the establishment of the Old Law, the tabernacle and temple became the locus of holiness: "The glory of the Lord filled the house of the Lord" (3 Kgs 8:11).

795. Did Jesus abolish the consecration of places by extending divine worship beyond the Temple in Jerusalem (see Jn 4:21)?
No. By establishing the sacramental system, especially the Holy Sacrifice of the Mass, Jesus determined that God would be particularly worshipped wherever these sacred rites would be offered, which in turn would sanctify those places.

796. Then in the New Law, what is a *sacred place*?
Places such as churches, chapels, and shrines, designated for a holy purpose by consecration or blessing prescribed in the Church's approved liturgical books, especially for divine worship and burial of the faithful.

Churches

797. What is a church building?
A public edifice set apart for divine worship, in which the faithful assemble to offer sacrifice, receive the sacraments, and take part in other religious ceremonies.

798. Can a church or sacred space be used for any purpose the pastor or people choose?
No. In a sacred space, only activities that exercise or promote worship, piety, and religion are permitted. Anything out of harmony with the holiness of the place is forbidden.[22]

799. Have churches been used from the beginning of Christianity?
Yes. Although humbler and less prominent in the ages of persecution, designated places of assembly for sacred worship have been in use since the apostolic period, as St. Paul attests (see 1 Cor 11:18).

800. Must Holy Mass normally be celebrated in a sacred space?
Yes. However, a grave cause may necessitate the offering of Mass in a fitting place other than a consecrated church. From the early centuries, such use has been made of forests, caves, catacombs, prisons, public buildings, and private homes.

801. **What are oratories and chapels?**
An *oratory* is a place which, by permission of the local ordinary, is dedicated to divine worship for some community. A private *chapel* has a narrower scope, being set aside for divine worship for at least one person.

802. **What is a *shrine* or *sanctuary*?**
A church or other sacred place which, with the approval of the local ordinary, is frequented by pilgrims because of some special devotion (e.g., a particular relic or approved apparition), and in which a special indulgence may be received.

803. **Why is the church building so important?**
"Because a church is not a barber's shop, nor a perfumer's stall or merchant booth; it is the dwelling of angels and archangels, the Kingdom of God, heaven itself."[23]

804. **What was the design of the early Christian churches?**
Emperor Constantine gave fourth-century Christians several basilicas or *praetoria*, formerly civil court buildings, after which many churches were then modeled. These consisted of a rectangle ending in a semicircle opposite the entrance, to which a transept was added, giving the early basilicas the form of a cross.

805. **Is there any particular design required for churches today?**
They must abide by the objective laws of beauty (integrity, proportion, and clarity) in order to worthily shelter the Holy Sacrifice, and lift man's soul to God.

806. **What are the main architectural styles for Christian churches?**
1. *Byzantine*, adding domes and curves to the early basilica form; 2. *Romanesque*, characterized by wide columns and semicircular arches; 3. *Gothic*, with its pointed arches and tall windows. 4. *Renaissance*, a revival of ancient Roman forms featuring columns, rounded arches, domes; 5. *Baroque*, highly decorated, with curves, high contrast in light and color, twisting elements; 6. *Neoclassical*, with sharp symmetries and geometric form, hulking facades, columns, mixing past styles.

807. **Does the Church also bless and consecrate her houses of worship?**
Yes. With a solemn act of blessing, the Church sets them apart for the Sacrifice of the Mass, secures angelic protection for them, and reminds the faithful of how holy they must be in order to come into the presence of God, and go forth as living temples of Jesus Christ.

808. **How might a sacred place be wrongly used?**
Whenever gravely immoral or scandalous acts are done in them, such as: 1. Homicide; 2. Impious use, e.g., pagan rites; 3. Sordid use, e.g., immoral plays or performances; 4. Burial of non-Catholics or declared excommunicates;[24] 5. Use as a dining room (even for the poor, when there are other options).

Bells

809. How does the Church announce her solemn functions and call to worship?
She ordinarily makes use of ringing bells to call the faithful to divine worship; a custom introduced in the Church during the first millennium.

810. Do church bells still play an important role in the life of Christians?
Yes, as they are: 1. Considered fitting for every church; 2. Consecrated or blessed only by a bishop; 3. Ordinarily rung only for holy purposes.

811. How else were the faithful summoned in the past, e.g., during persecutions?
They were summoned by some prearranged signal or notice; e.g., three crowings of the cock (which later inspired the custom of mounting an iron rooster on the belltower), or the wooden clapper or *crotalus*, still used during Holy Week in the Roman Rite.

Cemeteries

812. Where are the bodies of the faithful placed after death?
In a plot of consecrated ground called the *cemetery*, considered to be an annex of the church.

813. What is the meaning of the word *cemetery*?
It signifies a place of sleep or rest, in expectation of the final resurrection.

814. Should the bodies of Christians be buried in sacred ground?
Yes. The body of the Christian is "a temple of the Holy Spirit" (1 Cor 6:19), and must be treated with the greatest respect.

815. What of *cremation*, the destruction of dead bodies by fire?
While not evil in itself, cremation is opposed to the constant practice of the Church, which has always opposed the pagan custom of cremation and esteems bodily burial as one of the chief works of mercy.

816. Why should we bury bodies intact, and avoid cremation?
1. In imitation of Christ, who was truly buried and not cremated; 2. In witness to the bodily resurrection that will occur at the end of time; 3. In witness to the dignity of the body, made in God's image and fashioned into His temple through baptism; 4. To avoid disrespecting and desecrating the body itself, as occurs when human remains are kept in a home or scattered abroad.

817. How did the first Christians bury their dead?
In the *catacombs*: burial places for the faithful and especially the martyrs, where the bodies of the apostles Peter and Paul were also buried. The murals in the catacombs were often of Old Testament scenes of salvation, illustrating the Christian hope of resurrection: youths in the fiery furnace, Daniel in the lions' den, Jonah in the whale.

818. **What have the Church Fathers said about worthy burial of the dead?**
St. Augustine teaches: "If a father's garment and ring and suchlike is the more dear to those whom they leave behind, the greater their affection is toward their parents, in no wise are the bodies themselves to be spurned.... For our bodies pertain not to ornament or aid applied from without, but to the very nature of man. Whence also the funerals of the just men of old were cared for with dutiful piety, and their obsequies celebrated, and sepulture provided."[25]

Chapter 17: Sacred Objects

Altars

819. **What are the principal sacred objects?**
All *liturgical objects*, especially those that are used in Holy Mass.

820. **What may be included under the heading of *liturgical objects*?**
1. The altar; 2. Liturgical vessels; 3. Chalice linens; 4. Liturgical substances; 5. Sacred vestments.

821. **What is an *altar*?**
In the strictly liturgical sense, it is a consecrated stone upon which the host and chalice are placed during the celebration of Holy Mass.

822. **How does a fixed altar differ from a portable altar?**
A *fixed* altar is a significant slab of stone (marble, granite, slate, etc.) secured to a support and attached to the floor, solemnly consecrated in its place by the bishop. A *portable* altar is a small stone tile called an *altar stone*, which is consecrated and then placed within or upon an altar table for Mass.

823. **Is there any substitute for a *portable* altar?**
Yes; a specially blessed corporal, into which is sewn the relics of martyrs, in the manner of the *antimins* (antimension) used in the Byzantine Rite.

824. **Why are our altars made of stone?**
1. God decreed that stone be used for the first altars of sacrifice (see Ex 20:25); 2. Stone first received the sacrifice of Our Lord's body and blood (see Mt 27:60; Mk 15:46; and Lk 23:53); 3. The Church has retained the unbroken use of stone altars from apostolic times.

825. **What should the altar contain?**
Relics of martyrs should be sealed within the interior of a fixed altar, or in the hollow carved into one side of the altar stone.

826. **Why are the relics of martyrs placed within the altar?**
Because of the martyrs' perfect conformity to the sacrifice of Calvary, and in continuation of the practice of the early centuries, when persecuted Christians gathered in

the Roman catacombs to celebrate Masses upon the tombs of the martyrs. This also evokes the heavenly worship, where "under the altar [are] the souls of those who had been slain for the word of God and for the testimony they had upheld" (Apoc 6:9*).

827. Who has the power to consecrate altars?
The bishop alone, although the Church may grant this power to priests at need; e.g., missionaries in areas where there are no bishops.

828. When does an altar lose its consecration?
Whenever: 1. The relics have been removed; 2. The seal of the relics has been broken; 3. The fixed altar slab has been separated from the body of the altar; 4. The slab or altar stone is broken.

829. What are the principal furnishings of the altar?
1. The crucifix; 2. The altar cloths; 3. The candles or lamps; 4. Reliquaries and images of saints.

830. What cloths should cover the altar?
Three hemp or linen cloths, blessed by a bishop or deputed priest; the outer cloth should be longer than the others and reach to the ground on each side.

831. Why does the Church require that the altar be covered with three cloths?
To: 1. Honor the Blessed Trinity; 2. Signify the linens in which the body of Our Lord was wrapped for burial; 3. Sufficiently absorb the precious blood, if it should be spilled.

832. What should be placed on the altar whenever the priest says Mass?
Since the altar is another Calvary on which Christ is immolated, the Church expressly orders that a *crucifix*—a cross with the figure of Christ upon it—be placed on or above the altar, at least during Mass.

833. What candles are used at the altar?
There must be at least two candles for Low Mass and traditionally at least six for High Mass, placed symmetrically at either end.

834. Are any other lights used in the sanctuary?
Yes. The *sanctuary lamp* is always kept burning in the sanctuary, whenever the Blessed Sacrament is present in the tabernacle. It symbolizes the presence of Christ, the light of the world whom the darkness cannot overcome (see Jn 1:4–5; and 8:12).

835. What is the *tabernacle*?
A kind of locked and secured cabinet or chest, made of enduring wood, marble, or metal, blessed by the bishop or a deputed priest, to contain the Holy Eucharist.

836. **Why must the tabernacle be central and visibly prominent in the church?**
Because a Catholic church is built to house the sanctuary, the sanctuary is for the altar, the altar for the tabernacle, the tabernacle for the ciborium, and the ciborium contains the Most Blessed Sacrament.

837. **Is it most appropriate that the altar and tabernacle be united?**
Yes. "The Person of the Lord must occupy the center of worship, for it is that which unifies the relations of the altar and the tabernacle and gives to them their meaning. It is first of all by the sacrifice of the altar that Our Lord makes Himself present. ... To separate the tabernacle and the altar is to separate two things which should remain united by their origin and their nature."[26] To stress this unity, the Church established the traditional norm: "On an altar where the most Holy Eucharist is reserved, the Sacrifice of the Mass is to be habitually celebrated."[27]

838. **How should the tabernacle be arranged?**
It should be a fitting repository for the body of the Son of God: the inside should be lined with white silk and contain a corporal on which the ciborium and lunette may rest; the outside should be covered with a veil, unless it is sculptured, gilded, or jeweled.

839. **Is it proper to adorn the altar with reliquaries and statues?**
Yes. Particularly on great festivals, it is most proper to surround the altar with reliquaries, statues of saints, and flowers, but not so that the tabernacle is obscured or the altar cluttered. When the Blessed Sacrament is exposed on the altar, reliquaries and statues should be removed or veiled.

Vessels

840. **What is meant by liturgical *vessels*?**
The vessels used in Holy Mass, some of which are consecrated or simply blessed.

841. **Which of these vessels are consecrated or blessed?**
The chalice, paten, ciborium, lunette, and monstrance.

842. **What is the *chalice*?**
The gilded cup dedicated to hold the wine for consecration into Our Lord's blood. At the start and end of Mass it is covered with an ornamented silk cloth called the *chalice veil*.

843. **What is the *paten*?**
A small, gilded plate that covers the mouth of the chalice, used to offer the bread for consecration into Our Lord's body.

844. **What should the chalice and paten be made of?**
Gold or silver. If of any lesser metal, they should be gilded (covered with gold).

845. **Who consecrates the chalice and paten?**
The bishop traditionally consecrates the chalice and paten with sacred chrism.

846. **When do chalices and patens lose their consecration?**
Whenever they are regilded, broken, notably deteriorated, used for indecorous purpose, or sold.

847. **What is the *ciborium*?**
A vessel used to hold the consecrated hosts, reserving them for distribution to the faithful in Holy Communion. It should be crowned by a small cross, and covered with a veil, preferably of white silk.

848. **What is the *lunette*?**
A small, moon-shaped case containing the sacred host, which fits into the monstrance.

849. **What is the *monstrance*?**
The sacred vessel in which the Blessed Sacrament is exposed for the adoration of the faithful. It should be surmounted with a cross.

850. **Should the ciborium, lunette, and monstrance be blessed?**
The first two should be blessed by the bishop or a deputed priest, and it is also fitting to have the monstrance blessed.

851. **Who may touch the sacred vessels?**
When they contain the consecrated species, no one but a priest or a deacon has the right to touch them, except in some urgent necessity. When empty, laymen may only touch them for a reasonable cause (e.g., necessary maintenance), traditionally while wearing gloves.[28]

852. **Has this discipline been observed throughout Church history?**
Yes. From at least the fifth century, this discipline has been universally observed.

853. **Why does the Church practice such reverence toward the sacred vessels?**
Because Jesus Christ entrusted the handling of His body and blood to the ordained clergy, whose hands are uniquely blessed for the purpose; the vessels that directly contact the Blessed Sacrament are likewise held in the highest veneration.

854. **What liturgical vessels are not typically blessed?**
The cruets, thurible, incense-boat, aspersorium, aspergillum, altar-bells, and ablution vessels.

Linens

855. **What are the names of the chalice *linens*?**
The chalice linens properly include: the corporal, pall, and purificator.

856. **What is the *corporal*?**
A square piece of linen or hemp spread upon the altar for Mass, upon which the priest places the host and chalice. It signifies the winding sheet in which the body of our Savior was buried.

857. **Where is the corporal kept when not spread out on the altar?**
It is kept in a square case, generally made of silk or silver cloth, called the *burse*.

858. **What is the *pall*?**
A piece of linen or hemp, used to cover the mouth of the chalice.

859. **What is the *purificator*?**
A piece of linen or hemp used to purify the chalice, as well as the lips and fingers of the priest after the ablutions.

860. **Who has the right to bless the chalice linens?**
The bishop or his delegate may bless corporals and palls, while an ordinary priest may bless purificators.

861. **What other cloth does the priest use at Mass?**
The *lavabo towel*, with which he dries his fingers at the Lavabo during the Offertory; it is not blessed.

Substances

862. **What are the principal liturgical *substances*?**
They are: wax, oil, balsam, water, salt, bread, wine, and incense.

863. **What is *incense*?**
From the Latin *incendere* (to burn), it is a perfumed, resinous material that is burned in certain liturgical ceremonies, producing a fragrant smoke.

864. **Is the use of incense very ancient?**
Yes. Required by God in the Old Law (see Ex 30:7; and 40:27), the burning of blessed incense has been a feature in Catholic worship from at least the fifth century.

865. **What is signified by incense?**
It is an emblem of: 1. *Adoration*, the divine worship paid to Jesus Christ in the Holy Eucharist; 2. *Prayer*, ascending to God like the clouds of fragrant smoke; 3. *Grace*, descending to diffuse in our souls like the sweet odor spread through the church; 4. *Exorcism*, driving evil out of the space it fills.

866. **Does the Church incense anything besides the Holy Eucharist?**
Yes: 1. Relics and images of saints, to honor Christ who is wondrous in them; 2. Sacred ministers, to honor Christ in their person; 3. The faithful, living and dead, to honor the Christian character they received in baptism.

Vestments

867. **What are *vestments*?**
Clothing unique to the sacred ministers of the Church, which may be divided into:
1. Ecclesiastical garb; 2. Sacred vestments.

868. **What are the principal pieces of *ecclesiastical garb*?**
For diocesan (secular) clergy, the *soutane* or *cassock*: a long-sleeved, front-fastening robe that reaches the feet. For priests and lower clergy, it is black; for bishops, violet; for cardinals, red; for the pope, white. Religious have ecclesiastical garb called *habits*, proper to their order or congregation.

869. **What other attire is proper to bishops?**
A violet zucchetto, mozzetta, and biretta, as well as a pectoral cross and a ring—the sign of his spiritual union with his local church.

870. **Why is red the color proper to cardinals?**
It signifies their readiness to shed their blood for the Faith.

871. **What other attire is proper to the pope?**
A white zucchetto and red hat, a red mozzetta trimmed with white ermine fur, red slippers embroidered with gold, a pectoral cross containing a relic of the True Cross, a red cappa magna with gold lace, and the Ring of the Fisherman.

872. **What are *sacred vestments*?**
The garments worn by clergy during the liturgy, which vary according to each ministerial function in divine worship and bear some spiritual meaning and symbolism.

873. **What are the traditional vestments of the priest?**
The amice, alb, cincture, maniple, stole, chasuble, veils, cope, surplice, and biretta.

874. **What is the *amice*?**
A rectangular piece of linen that goes over the head and is fastened about the neck and shoulders with long strings. It is a sign of supernatural protection, the "helmet of salvation" (Eph 6:17).

875. **What is the *alb*?**
A tunic of white linen covering the priest's body. It is an emblem of innocence.

876. **What is the *cincture*?**
Once called a *girdle*, it is a cord usually made of hemp, linen, or silk, fastening the alb in place about the waist of the priest. It recalls the cords that bound Our Lord in His Passion, and symbolizes the virtue of chastity necessary for the proclamation of truth.

877. **What is the *maniple*?**
A strip of cloth with three crosses matching the stole, worn on the left arm. It is a sign of sorrow, and an emblem of service which the priest has vowed to God.

878. **What is the *stole*?**
A band of cloth worn around the neck and reaching to the knees, adorned with three crosses. It is the sign of priestly power, and must be worn for every priestly function.

879. **What is the *chasuble*?**
The outermost robe or vest which the priest wears to celebrate the Holy Sacrifice. It symbolizes the yoke of the Lord, i.e., divine charity.

880. **Should the chasuble be worn outside of liturgical actions?**
No. This is why the sacred ministers remove them before meeting with the faithful after Holy Mass.

881. **What are the principal veils used in the sacred functions?**
1. The *humeral* veil, which the priest wears in processions and at Benediction of the Blessed Sacrament; 2. The *offertory* veil, which the subdeacon wears during part of solemn Mass.

882. **What is the *cope*?**
An outer cloak that may be used in certain processions and blessings, e.g., the Asperges before High Mass, solemn Benediction, Vespers, etc.

883. **What is the *surplice*?**
A shortened alb with sleeves, which may be worn by clerics as well as certain laymen. It is an emblem of purity and holiness of life.

884. **What is the *biretta*?**
A square cap with three corners rising from the crown, generally with a tassel attached in the center.

885. **Are certain colors prescribed for the various ornaments and vestments?**
Yes. Some must always be white, while others should be of the color required for the proper Office and Mass of that day.

886. **What are the different liturgical colors in the Roman Church?**
1. White, a symbol of innocence, joy, and glory (for feasts of Christmas, Epiphany, Easter, Eucharist, Our Lady, angels, and saints); 2. Red, an emblem of martyrdom and ardent charity (for feasts of the Holy Cross, Precious Blood, Pentecost, and martyrs); 3. Green, expressing an ever-springing hope (for Sundays after Epiphany and after Pentecost); 4. Violet, representing sadness and mortification (for Advent, Septuagesima, Lent, Ember and Rogation Days, and Vigils); 5. Black, a sign of mourning (for Good Friday and All Souls); 6. Rose, a sign of the joyful dawn of salvation and promised forgiveness (for Gaudete Sunday in Advent and Laetare Sunday in Lent); 7. Gold, a substitute for white, as a sign of the heavenly glory of the highest feasts; 8. Blue, permitted in certain regions in honor of Our Lady.

887. **Should the various sacred vestments and ornaments be blessed?**

Yes. They are customarily blessed by the bishop or delegated priest, and lose this blessing when it is morally impossible to use them any longer—at which point they should be retired by fire, to prevent any profane use.

Chapter 18: Sacred Time

Sacred Time in General

888. **Are all times equally holy, since God exists eternally beyond time?**

No. Since the beginning of creation, God has blessed some times more than others, commanding that servile labor be avoided on the Sabbath (see Ex 20:8–11) precisely because "God blessed the seventh day and made it holy" (Gn 2:3*).

889. **Aren't all times now equally holy, since Jesus Christ is the same forever (see Heb 13:8)?**

No. Christ Himself observed the Jewish Sabbath, though declaring Himself "Lord of the Sabbath" (Lk 6:5) and giving His apostles authority to transfer the sacred day of worship to Sunday (see Acts 20:7; and 1 Cor 16:2); in turn, they established the liturgical year to be celebrated with appropriate ceremonies.

890. **What is the *liturgical year*?**

The Church's annual cycle of feasts and fasts, unfolding "the whole mystery of Christ, from the Incarnation and Birth until the Ascension, the day of Pentecost, and the expectation of blessed hope and of the Coming of the Lord."[29] In summary, "the liturgical year is Christ always living in His Church."[30]

891. **What spiritual benefits come to us through the liturgical year?**

"Recalling the mysteries of Redemption, the Church opens to the faithful the riches of her Lord's powers and merits, so that these are in some way made present for all time, and the faithful are enabled to lay hold upon them and become filled with saving grace."[31]

892. **Is the liturgical year superior to the civic calendar year?**

Yes. In the liturgical year, time is marked according to divine revelation and the triumphs of God's grace, rather than the passing establishments of earthly governments.

893. **How does the structure of the liturgical year compare to the civic year?**

Like the civic year, the ecclesiastical year also comprises 365 days, divided into fifty-two weeks; but it begins with the First Sunday of Advent, and ends with the week following the Last Sunday after Pentecost.

Feasts in General

894. What are the different kinds of feasts?
1. *Civic* feasts, or public holidays celebrating some aspect of the political order, e.g., the founding of a nation; 2. *Religious* feasts, which pertain to divine worship, e.g., the feast of Christ the King.

895. What is the origin of religious feasts?
They originated in the very institution of public worship, and may be found in the history of all nations. In the Old Law, the Hebrew people divided the year into seasons with appropriate religious feasts and ceremonies.

896. Does the Church have power to establish feasts?
Yes. Jesus Christ endowed the Church with power to regulate divine worship on earth.

897. What do the faithful gain from celebrating religious feasts?
We: 1. Consecrate our time in the worship rightly due to the Blessed Trinity; 2. Manifest our love for Jesus Christ, especially in recalling the chief events of His sacred life; 3. Call upon the intercession of holy angels and saints; 4. Grow in unity, faith, and holy joy through our common, cyclical worship.

898. Do different feasts make different graces available to us?
Yes. As each feast makes different aspects of the heavenly mysteries manifest to the senses, they also make unique actual graces available at different times.

899. How are Christian feasts divided?
1. Into feasts of obligation or devotion; 2. Into feasts of greater or lesser rank; 3. Into feasts of the temporal or sanctoral cycle.

900. Whom do the various Christian feasts honor?
The Blessed Trinity, Our Lord Jesus Christ, the Blessed Virgin, the holy angels, and the other saints.

Temporal Cycle

901. What is the *temporal cycle* of the ecclesiastical year?
A yearly sequence of feasts and fasts, patterned on the earthly life of Our Lord. It consists mainly of Sundays and the days comprising the various liturgical seasons.

902. How is the temporal cycle divided into seasons?
It is divided into the following principal seasons: Advent, Christmas, Epiphany, Septuagesima, Lent, Easter, and Pentecost.

903. What is *Advent*?
The time of preparing to celebrate the coming of Jesus Christ: 1. In history, at the first Christmas; 2. In mystery, by His grace in our souls; 3. In glory, at the end of time.

904. **How long does Advent last?**
It begins with the Sunday nearest the feast of St. Andrew, and includes four Sundays.

905. **What is the spirit of the season of Advent?**
It is a season of: 1. Penance, to prepare the way of the Lord in our souls; 2. Holy longing, as we desire the grace to receive Him worthily; 3. Sanctified hope, as we look forward to the consummation of all things and our eternal communion with Christ in heaven.

906. **What is *Christmas*?**
The season beginning with its proper feast of December 25, and extending through the season of *Christmastide*, consecrated to celebrating the birth and childhood of our Savior.

907. **What is the spirit of Christmastide?**
One of joy and gladness at the love of the Divine Child for us, and of great piety toward the Holy Family.

908. **What privileges does the feast of Christmas enjoy?**
A priest may celebrate three Masses on this day, and even if Christmas falls on a day of abstinence, eating meat is permitted.

909. **What should we do to celebrate Christmastide worthily?**
We should express our profound adoration, love, and thanksgiving to the Christ Child, and learn of His humility, detachment, and mortification.

910. **What is *Epiphany*?**
A feast celebrated twelve days after Christmas, which extends through the season of *Epiphanytide*, during which we commemorate the adoration of the Magi, the baptism of Our Lord in the Jordan, and His first miracle at Cana.

911. **What is the season of *Septuagesima*?**
The interval falling between Epiphanytide and the beginning of Lent. It is often called "pre-Lent," as the faithful turn their minds toward penance in preparation for the holy fast of Lent.

912. **What is *Lent*?**
The season extending from Ash Wednesday to Holy Saturday, in which we honor the forty days of Our Lord's fast in the desert, and prepare for a worthy celebration of His Passion, death, and Resurrection.

913. **Why is the beginning of this season called *Ash Wednesday*?**
Because the faithful have ashes traced or sprinkled on their heads in the sign of a cross, reminding us of the dust from which we are made (and to which our bodies will return after death), and the ashes once imposed upon public penitents to prompt humility and contrition.

914. **How should we keep the season of Lent?**
By fasting, prayer, almsgiving, more frequent study of the word of God and various religious exercises, such as the Stations of the Cross; in sum, by greater mortification and holiness.

915. **What is *Passiontide*?**
The final two weeks of Lent: Passion Week and Holy Week, which commemorate the Passion and death of Our Lord. The images in the church are veiled in violet during this time, and various prayers are suppressed from the liturgy as an expression of sorrow and greater penitence.

916. **What is *Holy Thursday*?**
Thursday of Holy Week, commemorating Our Lord's Last Supper, in which He instituted the sacraments of holy orders and the Eucharist. The Mass of the Lord's Supper concludes with a procession commemorating Christ's going forth to the Garden of Gethsemane prior to his betrayal and Passion.

917. **How can we spiritually profit from Holy Thursday?**
1. Participate in the Mass of the Lord's Supper; 2. Give special thanks for the priesthood and pray for all clerics; 3. Make acts of spiritual communion with the Eucharistic Christ and adore Him in the tabernacle; 4. Meditate on Christ's "high priestly" prayer in John 17.

918. **What is *Good Friday*?**
Friday of Holy Week, commemorating Our Lord's Passion with special rites, traditionally called the "Mass of the Presanctified" (*Missa praesanctificatorum*), including the reading of St. John's Passion account, the veneration of the Cross, and Holy Communion (traditionally, by the priest alone) by the reception of previously-consecrated hosts.

919. **How can we spiritually profit from Good Friday?**
1. Keep a strong canonical fast and abstinence; 2. Participate prayerfully in the Good Friday service; 3. Maintain a spirit of silence and recollection; 4. Meditate on Our Lord's Passion and the price of our Redemption; 5. Embrace whatever crosses God has given us, in union with Christ.

920. **What is *Easter*?**
The greatest feast and solemnity of the Church year: the Sunday of Our Lord's Resurrection from the dead, which opens the glorious season of Paschaltide.

921. **Why is this season called *Paschaltide*?**
Foreshadowed by the *Pasch* or Passover of the Old Law, the Church now celebrates the true Paschal Lamb, commemorating His sacrificial passage from death to life.

922. **What resolutions should we make on Easter Sunday?**

We should renew our baptismal vows and resolve to die forever to sin, and to live henceforth for God alone with the help of the resurrected Christ.

923. **What is meant by the procession on St. Mark's Day?**

Also called the *Great Litany* or *Major Rogation*, this procession occurs on April 25, the feast of St. Mark the Evangelist, to beg God to turn away scourges and preserve the fruits of the earth.

924. **What are the other *Rogation Days*?**

As on St. Mark's Day, these "minor rogations" are days of public prayer and penance, offered in reparation to God's justice and to draw down His blessing, observed on the Monday, Tuesday, and Wednesday before the feast of Ascension.

925. **What is *Ascension Day*?**

The feast celebrating the triumph of Jesus forty days after His Resurrection, when He ascended to heaven in the sight of His disciples. For this reason it falls on a Thursday.

926. **How should we celebrate the feast of Ascension?**

1. Rejoice in the glory of Our Lord's humanity; 2. Thank Him for going to prepare a place for us and be our Mediator with God the Father; 3. Imitate the saints in detachment from earthly goods and longing for our heavenly home, seeking "the things that are above, where Christ is sitting at the right hand of God. Mind the things that are above, not the things that are upon the earth. For you are dead: and your life is hid with Christ in God" (Col 3:1–3*); 4. Rejoice in the continued presence of Christ in the sacraments, especially in the most Holy Eucharist.

927. **What is the feast of *Pentecost*?**

Also known as Whitsunday, it is the feast on the fiftieth day after Easter, celebrating the visible descent of the Holy Spirit upon the apostles and the Blessed Virgin Mary.

928. **How should we pray on the feast of Pentecost?**

We should thank the Spirit of truth for making known to us the law of the Gospel, first solemnly promulgated by His Church on this day; and we should pray that He enkindle and sustain the fire of His divine charity in our souls.

929. **Does Pentecost also have a season?**

Yes. The time after Pentecost lasts until Advent of the following liturgical year, representing the glorified life of Christ in heaven, and the militant life of the Church on earth. For this reason, the vestments of the season are green, the color of growth and hope.

930. **During this season, what prominent feasts are celebrated?**

Trinity Sunday, Corpus Christi, the Sacred Heart, the Precious Blood, the Transfiguration, and the Kingship of Christ.

931. **What is the feast of *Trinity Sunday*?**
A feast specially consecrated to honoring the mystery of one God in three divine and coequal Persons; the cornerstone of our religion and of all divine revelation.

932. **What is the feast of *Corpus Christi*?**
A feast specially consecrated to publicly honoring the Blessed Sacrament, for which reason it is called the feast of *Corpus Christi* (the Body of Christ).

933. **Why is there a Eucharistic procession on the feast of Corpus Christi?**
1. To celebrate Christ's victory over sin, death, and hell; 2. To publicly affirm the dogma of the Real Presence; 3. To atone for acts of sacrilege and indifference against Our Lord in this sacrament; 4. To call down God's special blessing upon the place where the procession is held.

934. **What is the feast of the *Sacred Heart*?**
A feast honoring, under the symbol of His divine heart, the boundless charity of Jesus Christ for men, and to repair insults offered to Him, particularly in the Holy Eucharist.

935. **What is the feast of the *Precious Blood*?**
A feast instituted to beg for divine mercy through the ransoming blood of Jesus Christ, protecting us from evils and enabling us to gain endless joy in heaven. "You were ransomed … with the precious blood of Christ, like that of a lamb without blemish or spot" (1 Pt 1:18, 19).

936. **What is the feast of the *Transfiguration*?**
A feast celebrating the great miracle on Mt. Tabor when Christ manifested the glory of His divinity in His very body, and to remind us that we must join in His sufferings if we are to share in His glory.

937. **What is the feast of the *Kingship of Christ*?**
A feast instituted to publicly recognize Jesus Christ as our universal Sovereign in time and eternity, and to remind all nations that the civic order must recognize and conform to His law and rule to enjoy true peace and prosperity.

Sanctoral Cycle

938. **What is the *sanctoral cycle* of the liturgical year?**
The yearly sequence of feasts that pay special honor to the Blessed Virgin Mary, the other saints, and the holy angels.

939. **What are the principal feasts of the Blessed Virgin?**
Her Immaculate Conception, Presentation, Purification (Presentation of the Lord), Annunciation, Visitation, Assumption, Nativity, Seven Sorrows, and Holy Rosary. The feasts of her Purification and Annunciation are also considered by liturgical tradition as feasts of the Lord.

940. **What is the feast of the *Immaculate Conception*?**
A feast on December 8, honoring that unique privilege of the Blessed Virgin Mary by which she was preserved free from every stain of original sin; it prompts us to honor her and beg God for the grace of a pure and holy life.

941. **What is the feast of the *Nativity of the Blessed Virgin*?**
A feast on September 8, commemorating the glorious birth of the Blessed Virgin Mary; it entreats especially the blessing of peace.

942. **What is the feast of the *Presentation of the Blessed Virgin*?**
A feast on November 21, recalling the day Mary was presented in the temple by her pious parents, to be brought up there in the fear and love of God; it exemplifies the primacy of prayer and devotion that all Christians should maintain.

943. **What is the feast of the *Annunciation*?**
A feast on March 25, celebrating Mary's acceptance of God's will to become the Mother of His Son, as announced by the angel Gabriel. It is also regarded as the beginning of Our Lord's redemptive work on earth.

944. **What is the feast of the *Visitation*?**
A feast traditionally on July 2, commemorating Mary's visit to her cousin Elizabeth before the birth of St. John the Baptist; it exhorts us to works of fraternal charity.

945. **What is the feast of the *Purification*, also called the *Presentation of the Lord*?**
A feast on February 2, celebrating the first presentation of Jesus in the temple. It honors the obedience and humility of Jesus and Mary in submitting to the Mosaic Law of ritual purification, although they were not obliged to do so. It is also called *Candlemas* after the blessing of candles on this day, to recall that Christ is the light of the world (see Jn 8:12) and Christians are also called to be "lights" in imitation of Him (see Mt 5:14).

946. **What is the feast of the *Seven Sorrows*?**
A feast on September 15, commemorating the chief sorrows endured by Mary in union with her divine Son, particularly: 1. The prophecy of Simeon; 2. The flight into Egypt; 3. The loss of Jesus in Jerusalem; 4. The carrying of the Cross; 5. The Crucifixion; 6. The deposition; 7. The burial.

947. **What is the feast of the *Assumption*?**
A feast on August 15, celebrating the conclusion of Mary's life on earth, when her body and soul were assumed into heavenly glory. It teaches us to rejoice in the privileges of Our Lady, and to be confident in her intercession for us.

948. **What is the feast of the *Holy Rosary*?**
A feast on October 7, also known as the feast of *Our Lady of Victory*, instituted after the triumph of the Christian forces at the Battle of Lepanto in 1571 — a victory

largely credited to devotion to the Rosary. It therefore honors the joyful, sorrowful, and glorious mysteries in the life of Our Lord and His Blessed Mother.

949. **What feasts does the Church celebrate in honor of the holy angels?**
Chiefly the feasts of: 1. St. Michael and all the angels (September 29); 2. The Guardian Angels (October 2); 3. The Apparition of St. Michael (May 8); 4. The Archangel Gabriel (March 24); 5. The Archangel Raphael (October 24).

950. **How should we celebrate the various feasts of the holy angels?**
1. Imitate their purity, love of God, and immovable fidelity, that we may share their glory and happiness in heaven; 2. Express our confidence and gratitude for their work on our behalf, especially that of our guardian angel; 3. Ask their assistance to worthily worship God; 4. Invoke their protection in our spiritual battle against the evil spirits.

951. **What saints of the Old Testament does the Church especially venerate?**
1. The patriarchs Abel, Melchizedek, Abraham, Isaac, Jacob, Joseph, Job, and Tobit; 2. The prophets Moses, Samuel, David, Elijah, Elisha, Isaiah, Jeremiah, Daniel, Ezekiel, Jonah, Obadiah, and Malachi; 3. The martyrs Eleazar, the mother of the Maccabees, and her seven sons; 4. The holy women Sara, Anna, Judith, and Susanna.

952. **What saints of the New Testament are most solemnly celebrated by the Church?**
Besides Our Lady, principally St. Joseph, St. John the Baptist, and the holy apostles.

953. **How should we celebrate the various feasts of the saints?**
By thanking God for the graces given to them, invoking their intercession, and resolving to imitate them.

954. **What do the feasts of St. Joseph especially signify?**
They remind us of: 1. His exemplary virtue as the greatest saint after Mary; 2. His glorious mission as Spouse of the Virgin; 3. His unsurpassed service as adoptive father and Guardian of the Redeemer; 4. His great influence in heaven with the One who was pleased to obey him on earth; 5. His strength as the Patron of the universal Church; 6. His kindness as special Patron of the Dying.

955. **How should we celebrate the feasts of St. Joseph?**
By resolving to imitate his humble, mortified, and laborious life of obedience to the law of God.

956. **Why does the Church pay such great honors to St. John the Baptist?**
Because he was the last and greatest of the Old Testament prophets, and Precursor of the Messiah.

957. **What feasts honor the apostles Peter and Paul?**
1. In honor of both, the feast of their martyrdom (June 29); 2. In honor of St. Peter, the feasts of his Chair at Rome (February 22), his Chair at Antioch (January 18),

and his Chains (August 1); 3. In honor of St. Paul, the feasts of his Conversion (January 25), and his Commemoration (June 30).

958. **After Peter and Paul, what Apostle is most highly honored in the liturgical year?**
St. John, Apostle and Evangelist, the beloved disciple of Our Lord, at whose death God's public revelation was complete.

959. **What is the feast of *All Saints*?**
Also called *All Saints Day*, this feast on November 1 sanctifies one day each year to the honor of all the elect in heaven, many of whose names remain unknown to us here on earth.

960. **What is *All Souls Day*?**
This commemoration on November 2 urges the members of the Church Militant to seek God's mercy on behalf of the poor souls in purgatory.

961. **Why is All Souls Day observed just after the feast of All Saints?**
To show the close union between the Church Triumphant, the Church Militant, and the Church Suffering.

962. **How should we keep All Souls Day?**
1. Pray with greater fervor for the faithful departed, begging God to grant them eternal rest in heaven; 2. Honor the graves of our departed family and friends; 3. Meditate on our own death and judgment; 4. Grow in horror for sin.

963. **Are there many other feasts of saints in the sanctoral cycle?**
Yes. There are too many to recall here, just as heaven will have "a great multitude ... standing before the throne" (Apoc 7:9).

Chapter 19: Devotions

Devotions in General

964. **What is meant by *devotions*?**
Religious practices approved by the custom and practice of the Church, with the aim of nourishing faith and growing in holiness. Often called "popular piety," they are not obligatory, but the Church often attaches indulgences to their external practice.

965. **What kinds of external devotional practices exist in the Church?**
These are very numerous, and may include wearing an exterior emblem, joining a particular association, particular regimens of prayers and observances, pilgrimages and other good works, etc.

966. **What is the practice of *pilgrimage*?**
Prayerful and sacrificial travel to holy sites in honor of God or the saints, usually to ask or thank God for some special favor.

967. **How should pilgrimages be made?**
Pilgrimages are not secular vacations; they must be distinguished by a spirit of prayer and penance, and works of piety.

968. **By what particular sign may true devotion be recognized?**
By attentive and perfect fulfillment of the duties of our state of life, strengthened by virtue and enlivened by overflowing divine charity.

969. **How are *associations* an expression of devotion?**
Every voluntary association of the faithful (e.g., third orders, confraternities, sodalities, societies) shares a common end of growing in Christian piety or charity. Such associations are often more effective in achieving this end when established and directed by ecclesiastical authority.

970. **What is a *third order*?**
A stable association of the faithful that follow a modified form of the rule of a particular religious order, so that more individuals may participate in the spiritual goods and works of that order.

971. **How may we divide the principal recommended devotions?**
They may be divided into three classes, as they refer to Our Lord Jesus Christ, the Blessed Virgin, or the saints.

Devotions to Christ

972. **What are the principal devotions to Our Lord?**
Over the centuries, these have remained prominent: 1. The Passion; 2. The Holy Childhood; 3. The Blessed Sacrament; 4. The Sacred Heart; 5. The Holy Face; 6. The Holy Name.

973. **What is devotion to the *Sacred Passion*?**
A universal Christian devotion to the sufferings of Our Lord, as every Friday of the year is consecrated to honoring Our Lord's sorrowful Passion. Its practice may include making the Stations of the Cross, and venerating images of the Crucified and the Five Wounds.

974. **What is devotion to the *Holy Childhood*?**
Devotion to the Infant Christ, designed to increase our love for Jesus by contemplating the divine charms of His infancy and childhood. Its practice may include establishment of a Nativity Scene, praying the Litany of the Infant Jesus, and pilgrimage to Bethlehem, the Infant of Prague, or other shrines in honor of the Child Jesus.

975. **What is devotion to the *Blessed Sacrament*?**
Devotion to Jesus Christ, truly present in the Holy Eucharist. Its practice may include frequent Communion, prayer before the tabernacle, solemn Benediction, holy hours, nocturnal adoration, Communions of reparation, and Eucharistic processions.

976. **What is devotion to the *Sacred Heart*?**
Devotion to the Person and superabundant charity of Jesus Christ, symbolized by His exposed heart. Its practice may include prayers of consecration, the practice of the First Fridays, household enthronement, chaplets, and holy hours of reparation.

977. **What is devotion to the *Holy Face*?**
Devotion to the face of Christ, disfigured in his Passion and venerated in sacred relics like the Shroud of Turin, Veronica's Veil, and the Manopello Image. It is especially practiced during the feast of the Holy Face of Jesus on the Tuesday before Ash Wednesday.

978. **What is devotion to the *Holy Name*?**
Devotion to the name *Jesus*, because the name of God deserves great reverence: "At the name of Jesus every knee should bend, of those in heaven and on earth and under the earth" (Phil 2:10*). It is a name that the evil spirits fear, and when invoked can cast out demons. This devotion also seeks to make reparation for irreverent use of God's name, and is practiced especially in the Litany to the Name of Jesus and the feast of the Most Holy Name of Jesus, traditionally held on January 2.

Devotions to Mary

979. **What is the nature of all Marian devotion?**
It consists in showing her our respect, confidence, obedience, and love. After devotion to Our Lord, there is no devotion more holy, consoling, and effective than devotion to His Blessed Mother.

980. **Why is this devotion so helpful for growing in sanctification?**
Because this devotion was given to the Church by Our Lord, who committed the Blessed Virgin Mary to every Christian at the foot of the Cross, in the person of St. John: "Behold, your Mother" (Jn 19:27).

981. **What are some practices of Marian devotion?**
We may: 1. Celebrate her feasts with special attention; 2. Honor her especially on Saturdays, and throughout May and October; 3. Keep the First Saturdays in honor of her Immaculate Heart; 4. Recite prayers in her honor, especially the Rosary and the Angelus; 5. Wear the brown scapular and miraculous medal; 6. Visit and pray at her shrines; 7. Enter an association established in her honor; 8. Consecrate ourselves to her, especially following the method of St. Louis Marie de Montfort; 9. Inspire others with devotion to her.

982. **What is the Rosary?**
The term *Rosary* may signify either a sequence of prayers, or the chain of blessed beads used for this prayer. Its classical form consists of three sets of five mysteries, each of which is meditated upon while reciting one Pater, ten Aves, and one Gloria Patri, after which is customarily added the Fatima Prayer: "O my Jesus, forgive us

our sins, save us from the fires of hell and lead all souls to heaven, especially those most in need of Thy mercy."

983. **Who established the Rosary?**
The pious custom of using beads to repeat the Ave Maria dates from the Middle Ages, mirroring the recitation of the 150 Psalms. Tradition relates that its modern form was given by Our Lady to St. Dominic (+1221), in order to spread the Faith and fight heresy.

984. **What are the traditional fifteen mysteries of the Holy Rosary?**
1. The *Joyful* mysteries: the Annunciation, the Visitation, the Nativity of Our Lord, the Presentation of Jesus in the Temple, and His Finding in the Temple. 2. The *Sorrowful* mysteries: the Agony in the Garden, the Scourging, the Crowning with Thorns, the Carrying of the Cross, and the Crucifixion. 3. The *Glorious* mysteries: the Resurrection of Our Lord, the Ascension, the Descent of the Holy Spirit, the Assumption of the Blessed Virgin, and her Coronation in Heaven.

985. **Is the daily Rosary the most recommended form of Marian devotion?**
Yes. Throughout the centuries, the daily rosary has been repeatedly recommended by saints and holy pontiffs, and granted many indulgences by the Church.

986. **Has the Blessed Virgin Mary also urgently recommended the Rosary?**
Yes. In her famous and approved apparition at Fatima, Portugal, Our Lady herself encouraged the prayer of the Rosary, and in her final appearance of October 13, 1917, declared: "I am the Queen of the Rosary."

987. **How important is it to pray the Rosary?**
Sr. Lucia of Fatima relates that "the most holy Virgin, in these last times in which we live, has given a new efficacy to the recitation of the Rosary. She has given this efficacy to such an extent that there is no problem, no matter how difficult it is, whether temporal or above all spiritual, in the personal life of each one of us, of our families, of the families of the world or of the religious communities, or even of the life of peoples and nations, that cannot be solved by the Rosary. There is no problem I tell you, no matter how difficult it is, that we cannot resolve by the prayer of the Holy Rosary. With the Holy Rosary we will save ourselves. We will sanctify ourselves. We will console Our Lord and obtain the salvation of many souls."[32]

Other Devotions

988. **Which saints should we especially honor?**
Our Lady, St. Joseph, the apostles Peter and Paul, our guardian angels, and our patron saints.

989. **Why should St. Joseph be held in special reverence?**
For the same reasons that his feasts are celebrated; yet all the more so since he "approached nearer than any to the eminent dignity by which the Mother of God

surpasses so nobly all created natures.... God appointed him to be not only her life's companion, the witness of her maidenhood, the protector of her honor, but also, by virtue of the conjugal tie, a participator in her sublime dignity."[33]

990. **How may we honor our patron saints?**

By celebrating their feasts with some added devotion, and commemorating the day of our baptism, confirmation, or profession of religious vows in which we took them as patron.

991. **Why is it important to foster devotion to the souls in purgatory?**

Because this devotion is very pleasing to God, useful to ourselves and our neighbor, comprises all the works of mercy, and assures all kinds of blessings.

992. **What is true devotion?**

"Devotion is the pleasure of pleasures, the queen of virtues, and the perfection of charity. If charity be milk, devotion is the cream; if charity be a plant, devotion is its flowers; if charity be a precious stone, devotion is its luster; if charity be a rich balm, devotion is its odor: yes, the odor of sweetness, which comforts men and rejoices angels."[34]

993. **What is the purpose of all devotion—indeed, of the entire Christian life?**

To gain many graces by the mercy of God and intercession of His saints, and to train ourselves toward spiritual perfection; that we may better know, love, and serve God in this life, so to be happy with Him forever in the next. "Fear God, and keep His commandments: for this is all" (Eccles 12:13*).

APPENDIX — The Great Creeds

The Apostles' Creed

I believe in God, the Father Almighty, Creator of heaven and earth, and in Jesus Christ, His only Son, Our Lord, who was conceived by the power of the Holy Spirit and born of the Virgin Mary, suffered under Pontius Pilate, was crucified, died, and was buried; He descended into hell; on the third day He rose again from the dead; He ascended into heaven and is seated at the right hand of God, the Father Almighty; from there He will come to judge the living and the dead. I believe in the Holy Spirit, the holy Catholic Church, the communion of saints, the forgiveness of sins, the resurrection of the body, and the life everlasting. Amen.

The Niceno-Constantinopolitan Creed

I believe in one God, the Father Almighty, Maker of heaven and earth, of all things visible and invisible. I believe in one Lord Jesus Christ, the only-begotten Son of God, born of the Father before all ages. God from God, Light from Light, true God from true God, begotten, not made, consubstantial with the Father; through Him all things were made. For us men and for our salvation, He came down from heaven, and by the Holy Spirit was incarnate of the Virgin Mary, and became man. For our sake He was crucified under Pontius Pilate, He suffered death and was buried, and rose again on the third day in accordance with the Scriptures. He ascended into heaven and is seated at the right hand of the Father. He will come again in glory to judge the living and the dead, and His kingdom will have no end. I believe in the Holy Spirit, the Lord, the Giver of life, who proceeds from the Father and the Son, who with the Father and the Son is adored and glorified, who has spoken through the prophets. And I believe in one, holy, catholic, and apostolic Church. I confess one baptism for the forgiveness of sins, and I look forward to the resurrection of the dead and the life of the world to come. Amen.

The Athanasian Creed

Whoever wishes to be saved must, above all, keep the Catholic Faith. For unless a person keeps this Faith whole and entire, he will undoubtedly be lost forever. This is what the Catholic Faith teaches: We worship one God in the Trinity and the Trinity in Unity. Neither confounding the Persons, nor dividing the substance. For there is one Person of the Father, another of the Son, another of the Holy Spirit. But the Father and the Son and the Holy Spirit have one divinity, equal glory, and coeternal majesty. What the Father is, the Son is, and the Holy Spirit is. The Father is uncreated, the Son is uncreated, and the Holy Spirit is uncreated. The Father is boundless, the Son is boundless, and the Holy Spirit is boundless. The Father is eternal, the Son is eternal, and the Holy Spirit is eternal. Nevertheless, there are not three eternal beings, but one eternal Being. So there are not three uncreated beings, nor three boundless beings, but one uncreated Being and one boundless Being. Likewise, the Father is omnipotent, the Son is omnipotent, the Holy Spirit is omnipotent. Yet there are not three omnipotent beings, but one omnipotent Being.

Thus the Father is God, the Son is God, and the Holy Spirit is God. However, there are not three gods, but one God. The Father is Lord, the Son is Lord, and the Holy Spirit is Lord. However, there are not three lords, but one Lord. For as we are obliged by Christian truth to acknowledge every Person singly to be God and Lord, so too are we forbidden by the Catholic religion to say that there are three gods or lords. The Father was not made, nor created, nor generated by anyone. The Son is not made, nor created, but begotten by the Father alone. The Holy Spirit is not made, nor created, nor generated, but proceeds from the Father and the Son.

There is, then, one Father, not three fathers; one Son, not three sons; one Holy Spirit, not three holy spirits. In this Trinity, there is nothing before or after, nothing greater or less. The entire three Persons are coeternal and coequal with one another. So that in all things, as it has been said above, the Unity is to be worshipped in Trinity and the Trinity in Unity. He, therefore, who wishes to be saved, must believe thus about the Trinity.

It is also necessary for eternal salvation that he believes steadfastly in the Incarnation of Our Lord Jesus Christ. Thus, the right faith is that we believe and confess that Our Lord Jesus Christ, the Son of God, is both God and man.

As God, He was begotten of the substance of the Father before time; as man, He was born in time of the substance of His Mother. He is perfect God; and He is perfect man, with a rational soul and human flesh. He is equal to the Father in His divinity, but inferior to the Father in His humanity. Although He is God and man, He is not two, but one Christ. And He is one, not because His divinity was changed into flesh, but because His humanity was assumed unto God. He is one, not by a mingling of substances, but by unity of Person. As a rational soul and flesh are one man, so God and man are one Christ. He died for our salvation, descended into hell, and rose from the dead on the third day. He ascended into heaven, sits at the right hand of God the Father Almighty. From there He shall come to judge the living and the dead. At His coming, all men are to arise with their own bodies; and they are to give an account of their own deeds. Those who have done good deeds will go into eternal life; those who have done evil will go into the everlasting fire. This is the Catholic Faith. Everyone must believe it, firmly and steadfastly; otherwise, He cannot be saved. Amen.

The Tridentine-Vatican Profession of Faith

First issued by Pope Pius IV in 1564, this Profession of Faith was used by all generations of priests, bishops, cardinals, and popes, including the Fathers of the Second Vatican Council, remaining in force until 1967, when Pope Paul VI substituted a shorter formula with more general wording; in 1989 Pope John Paul II issued a slightly improved formula that still retains more general wording.

I, N. ..., with a firm faith believe and profess each and everything which is contained in the Creed which the holy Roman Church maketh use of. To wit:

I believe in one God, the Father Almighty, Maker of heaven and earth, and of all things visible and invisible. And in one Lord, Jesus Christ, the only-begotten Son of God. Born of the Father before all ages. God of God, Light of Light, true God of true God. Begotten, not made, of one substance with the Father. By whom all things were made. Who for us men and for our salvation came down from heaven. And became incarnate by the Holy Spirit of the Virgin Mary, and was made man. He was also crucified for us, suffered under Pontius Pilate, and was buried. And on the third day He rose again according to the Scriptures. He ascended into heaven and sits at the right hand of the Father. He will come again in glory to judge the living and the dead, and His kingdom will have no end. And in the Holy Spirit, the Lord and Giver of life, who proceeds from the Father and the Son. Who together with the Father and the Son is adored and glorified, and who spoke through the prophets. And one, holy, catholic, and apostolic Church. I confess one baptism for the forgiveness of sins, and I await the resurrection of the dead and the life of the world to come. Amen.

The apostolic and ecclesiastical traditions and all other observances and constitutions of that same Church I firmly admit to and embrace.

I also accept the Holy Scripture according to that sense which holy mother the Church hath held, and doth hold, and to whom it belongeth to judge the true sense and interpretations of the Scriptures. Neither will I ever take and interpret them otherwise than according to the unanimous consent of the Fathers.

I also profess that there are truly and properly seven sacraments of the New Law, instituted by Jesus Christ Our Lord, and necessary for the salvation of mankind, though not all are necessary for everyone; to wit, baptism, confirmation, Eucharist, penance, extreme unction, holy orders, and matrimony; and that they confer grace; and that of these, baptism, confirmation, and holy orders cannot be repeated without sacrilege. I also accept and admit the received and approved rites of the Catholic Church in the solemn administration of the aforesaid sacraments.

I embrace and accept each and everything which has been defined and declared in the holy Council of Trent concerning original sin and justification.

I profess, likewise, that in the Mass there is offered to God a true, proper, and propitiatory sacrifice for the living and the dead; and that in the most Holy

Sacrament of the Eucharist there is truly, really, and substantially, the body and blood, together with the soul and divinity, of Our Lord Jesus Christ; and that a conversion takes place of the whole substance of the bread into the body, and of the whole substance of the wine into the blood, which conversion the Catholic Church calls transubstantiation. I also confess that under either species alone Christ is received whole and entire, and a true sacrament.

I steadfastly hold that there is a purgatory, and that the souls therein detained are helped by the suffrages of the faithful. Likewise, that the saints, reigning together with Christ, are to be honored and invoked, and that they offer prayers to God for us, and that their relics are to be venerated. I most firmly assert that the images of Christ, of the Mother of God, ever Virgin, and also of other saints, ought to be kept and retained, and that due honor and veneration is to be given them.

I also affirm that the power of indulgences was left by Christ in the Church, and that the use of them is most wholesome to Christian people.

I acknowledge the holy, catholic, apostolic, Roman Church as the mother and teacher of all churches; and I promise true obedience to the Bishop of Rome, Successor to St. Peter, Prince of the Apostles, and Vicar of Jesus Christ.

I likewise undoubtedly receive and profess all other things delivered, defined, and declared by the sacred canons and general councils, and particularly by the holy Council of Trent, and by the Ecumenical Council of the Vatican, particularly concerning the primacy of the Roman Pontiff and his infallible teaching. I condemn, reject, and anathematize all things contrary thereto, and all heresies which the Church hath condemned, rejected, and anathematized.

This true Catholic Faith, outside of which no one can be saved, which I now freely profess and to which I truly adhere, I do so profess and swear to maintain inviolate and with firm constancy with the help of God until the last breath of life. And I shall strive, as far as possible, that this same Faith shall be held, taught, and professed by all those over whom I have charge. I, N., do so pledge, promise, and swear, so help me God and these holy Gospels of God. Amen.

Credo of the People of God of Pope Paul VI

We believe in one only God, Father, Son, and Holy Spirit, Creator of things visible such as this world in which our transient life passes, of things invisible such as the pure spirits which are also called angels, and Creator in each man of his spiritual and immortal soul.

We believe that this only God is absolutely one in His infinitely holy essence, as also in all His perfections, in His omnipotence, His infinite knowledge, His providence, His will, and His love. He is He Who Is, as He revealed to Moses (see Ex 3:14); and He is Love, as the apostle John teaches us (see 1 Jn 4:8); so that these two names, Being and Love, express ineffably the same divine reality of Him who has wished to make Himself known to us, and who, "dwelling in light inaccessible" (1 Tm 6:16*), is in Himself above every name, above every thing, and above every created intellect. God alone can give us right and full knowledge of this reality by revealing Himself as Father, Son, and Holy Spirit, in whose eternal life we are by grace called to share, here below in the obscurity of faith and after death in eternal light. The mutual bonds which eternally constitute the three Persons, who are each one and the same divine Being, are the blessed inmost life of God thrice holy, infinitely beyond all that we can conceive in human measure. We give thanks, however, to the divine Goodness that very many believers can testify with us before men to the unity of God, even though they know not the mystery of the most Holy Trinity.

We believe then in the Father who eternally begets the Son; in the Son, the Word of God, who is eternally begotten; in the Holy Spirit, the uncreated Person who proceeds from the Father and the Son as their eternal Love. Thus in the three divine Persons, *coaeternae sibi et coaequales*, the life and beatitude of God, perfectly one, superabound and are consummated in the supreme excellence and glory proper to uncreated Being, and always "there should be venerated Unity in the Trinity and Trinity in the Unity."

We believe in Our Lord Jesus Christ, who is the Son of God. He is the Eternal Word, born of the Father before time began, and one in substance with the Father, *homoousios to Patri*, and through Him all things were made. He was incarnate of the Virgin Mary by the power of the Holy Spirit, and was made man: equal therefore to the Father according to His divinity, and inferior to the Father according to His humanity; and Himself one, not by some impossible confusion of His natures, but by the unity of His Person.

He dwelt among us, full of grace and truth. He proclaimed and established the Kingdom of God and made us know in Himself the Father. He gave us His new commandment to love one another as He loved us. He taught us the way of the Beatitudes of the Gospel: poverty in spirit, meekness, suffering borne with patience, thirst after justice, mercy, purity of heart, will for peace, persecution suffered for justice' sake. Under Pontius Pilate He suffered—the Lamb of God bearing on Himself the sins of the world, and He died for us on the Cross, saving us by His redeeming blood. He was buried, and, of His own power, rose on the third day, raising us by His Resurrection to that sharing in the divine life which is the life of grace. He ascended to heaven, and He will come again, this time in glory, to judge the living and the dead: each according to his merits — those who have responded to the love and piety of God going to eternal life, those who have refused them to the end going to the fire that is not extinguished. And His kingdom will have no end.

We believe in the Holy Spirit, who is Lord and Giver of life, who is adored and glorified together with the Father and the Son. He spoke to us by the prophets; He was sent by Christ after His Resurrection and His Ascension to the Father; He illuminates, vivifies, protects, and guides the Church; He purifies the Church's members if they do not shun His grace. His action, which penetrates to the inmost of the soul, enables man to respond to the call of Jesus: "Be perfect as your heavenly Father is perfect" (Mt 5:48).

We believe that Mary is the Mother, who remained ever a Virgin, of the Incarnate Word, our God and Savior Jesus Christ, and that by reason of this singular election, she was, in consideration of the merits of her Son, redeemed in a more eminent manner, preserved from all stain of original sin, and filled with the gift of grace more than all other creatures.

Joined by a close and indissoluble bond to the mysteries of the Incarnation and Redemption, the Blessed Virgin, the Immaculate, was at the end of her earthly life raised body and soul to heavenly glory, and likened to her risen Son in anticipation of the future lot of all the just; and we believe that the Blessed Mother of God, the New Eve, Mother of the Church, continues in heaven her maternal role with regard to Christ's members, cooperating with the birth and growth of divine life in the souls of the redeemed.

We believe that in Adam all have sinned, which means that the original offense committed by him caused human nature, common to all men, to fall to a state in which it bears the consequences of that offense, and which is not the state in which it was at first in our first parents — established as they were in holiness and justice, and in which man knew neither evil nor death. It is human nature so fallen, stripped of the grace that clothed it, injured in its own natural powers, and subjected to the dominion of death, that is transmitted to all men, and it is in this sense that every man is born in sin. We therefore hold, with the Council of Trent, that original sin is transmitted with human nature, "not by imitation, but by propagation" and that it is thus "proper to everyone."

We believe that Our Lord Jesus Christ, by the sacrifice of the Cross, redeemed us from original sin and all the personal sins committed by each one of us, so that, in accordance with the word of the Apostle, "where sin abounded, grace did more abound" (Rom 5:20*).

We believe in one baptism instituted by Our Lord Jesus Christ for the remission of sins. Baptism should be administered even to little children who have not yet been able to be guilty of any personal sin, in order that, though born deprived of supernatural grace, they may be reborn "of water and the Holy Spirit" (Jn 3:5*) to the divine life in Christ Jesus.

We believe in one, holy, catholic, and apostolic Church, built by Jesus Christ on that rock which is Peter. She is the Mystical Body of Christ; at the same time a visible society instituted with hierarchical organs, and a spiritual community; the Church on earth, the pilgrim People of God here below, and the Church filled with heavenly blessings; the germ and the firstfruits of the Kingdom of God, through which the work and the sufferings of Redemption are continued throughout human history, and which looks for its perfect accomplishment beyond time in glory. In the course of time, the Lord Jesus forms His Church by means of the sacraments emanating from His plenitude. By these she makes her members participants in the mystery of the death and Resurrection of Christ, in the grace of the Holy Spirit who gives her life and movement. She is therefore holy, though she has sinners in her bosom, because she herself has no other life but that of grace: it is by living by her life that her members are sanctified; it is by removing themselves from her life that they fall into sins and disorders that prevent the radiation of her sanctity. This is why she suffers and does penance for these offenses, of which she has the power to heal her children through the blood of Christ and the gift of the Holy Spirit.

Heiress of the divine promises and daughter of Abraham according to the Spirit, through that Israel whose Scriptures she lovingly guards, and whose patriarchs and prophets she venerates; founded upon the apostles and handing on from century to century their ever-living word and their powers as pastors in the Successor of Peter and the bishops in communion with him; perpetually assisted by the Holy Spirit, she has the charge of guarding, teaching, explaining, and spreading the truth which God revealed in a then-veiled manner by the prophets, and fully by the Lord Jesus. We believe all that is contained in the word of God, written or handed down, and that the Church proposes for belief as divinely revealed, whether by a solemn judgment or by the ordinary and universal Magisterium. We believe in the infallibility enjoyed by the Successor of Peter when he teaches *ex cathedra* as pastor and teacher of all the faithful, and which is assured also to the episcopal body when it exercises with him the supreme Magisterium.

We believe that the Church founded by Jesus Christ and for which He prayed is indefectibly one in faith, worship, and the bond of hierarchical communion. In the bosom of this Church, the rich variety of liturgical rites and the legitimate diversity of theological and spiritual heritages and special disciplines, far from injuring her unity, make it more manifest.

Recognizing also the existence, outside the organism of the Church of Christ, of numerous elements of truth and sanctification which belong to her as her own and tend to Catholic unity, and believing in the action of the Holy Spirit who stirs up in the heart of the disciples of Christ love of this unity, we entertain the hope that the Christians who are not yet in the full communion of the one only Church will one day be reunited in one flock with one only shepherd.

We believe that the Church is necessary for salvation, because Christ, who is the sole Mediator and Way of salvation, renders Himself present for us in His body which is the Church. But the divine design of salvation embraces all men; and those who without fault on their part do not know the Gospel of Christ and His Church, but seek God sincerely, and under the influence of grace endeavor to do His will as recognized through the promptings of their conscience, they, in a number known only to God, can obtain salvation.

We believe that the Mass, celebrated by the priest representing the Person of Christ by virtue of the power received through the sacrament of orders, and offered by him in the name of Christ and the members of His Mystical Body, is the sacrifice of Calvary rendered sacramentally present on our altars. We believe that as the bread and wine consecrated by the Lord at the Last Supper were changed into His body and His blood which were to be offered for us on the Cross, likewise the bread and wine consecrated by the priest are changed into the body and blood of Christ enthroned gloriously in heaven, and we believe that the mysterious presence of the Lord, under what continues to appear to our senses as before, is a true, real, and substantial presence.

Christ cannot be thus present in this sacrament except by the change into His body of the reality itself of the bread and the change into His blood of the reality itself of the wine, leaving unchanged only the properties of the bread and wine which our senses perceive. This mysterious change is very appropriately called by the Church transubstantiation. Every theological explanation which seeks some understanding of this mystery must, in order to be in accord with Catholic Faith, maintain that in the reality itself, independently of our mind, the bread and wine have ceased to exist after the consecration, so that it is the adorable body and blood of the Lord Jesus that from then on are really before us under the sacramental species of bread and wine, as the Lord willed it, in order to give Himself to us as food and to associate us with the unity of His Mystical Body.

The unique and indivisible existence of the Lord glorious in heaven is not multiplied, but is rendered present by the sacrament in the many places on earth where Mass is celebrated. And this existence remains present, after the sacrifice, in the Blessed Sacrament which is, in the tabernacle, the living heart of each of our churches. And it is our very sweet duty to honor and adore in the blessed host which our eyes see, the Incarnate Word whom they cannot see, and who, without leaving heaven, is made present before us.

We confess that the Kingdom of God begun here below in the Church of Christ is not of this world whose form is passing, and that its proper growth cannot be confounded with the progress of civilization, of science, or of human technology, but that it consists in an ever more profound knowledge of the unfathomable riches of Christ, an ever stronger hope in eternal blessings, an ever more ardent response to the love of God, and an ever more generous bestowal of grace and holiness among men. But it is this same love which induces the Church to concern herself constantly about the true temporal welfare of men. Without ceasing to recall to her children that they have not here a lasting dwelling, she also urges them to contribute, each according to his vocation and his means, to the welfare of their earthly city, to promote justice, peace, and brotherhood among men, to give their aid freely to their brothers, especially to the poorest and most unfortunate. The deep solicitude of the Church, the Spouse of Christ, for the needs of men, for their joys and hopes, their griefs and efforts, is therefore nothing other than her great desire to be present to them, in order to illuminate them with the light of Christ and to gather them all in Him, their only Savior. This solicitude can never mean that the Church conform herself to the things of this world, or that she lessen the ardor of her expectation of her Lord and of the eternal kingdom.

We believe in the life eternal. We believe that the souls of all those who die in the grace of Christ—whether they must still be purified in purgatory, or whether from the moment they leave their bodies Jesus takes them to paradise as He did for the Good Thief—are the People of God in the eternity beyond death, which will be finally conquered on the day of the resurrection when these souls will be reunited with their bodies.

We believe that the multitude of those gathered around Jesus and Mary in paradise forms the Church of heaven, where in eternal beatitude they see God as He is (see 1 Jn 3:2), and where they also, in different degrees, are associated with the holy angels in the divine rule exercised by Christ in glory, interceding for us and helping our weakness by their brotherly care.

We believe in the communion of all the faithful of Christ, those who are pilgrims on earth, the dead who are attaining their purification, and the blessed in heaven, all together forming one Church; and we believe that in this communion the merciful love of God and His saints is ever listening to our prayers, as Jesus told us: "Ask, and you will receive" (Jn 16:24; see Lk 11:9–10). Thus it is with faith and in hope that we look forward to the resurrection of the dead, and the life of the world to come. Amen.

APPENDIX — Select Prayers and Sacramentals

SIGN OF THE CROSS

IN nómine Patris, et Fílii, ✠ et Spíritus Sancti. Amen.

IN the name of the Father, and of the Son, ✠ and of the Holy Ghost. Amen.

Father,   Son,   Holy...   ...Ghost

OUR FATHER

PATER noster, qui es in caelis, sanctificétur nomen tuum. Advéniat regnum tuum. Fiat volúntas tua, sicut in caelo et in terra. Panem nostrum quotidiánum da nobis hódie, et dimítte nobis débita nostra sicut et nos dimíttimus debitóribus nostris. Et ne nos indúcas in tentatiónem, sed líbera nos a malo. Amen.

OUR Father, who art in heaven, hallowed be Thy name. Thy kingdom come. Thy will be done on earth as it is in heaven. Give us this day our daily bread, and forgive us our trespasses as we forgive those who trespass against us. And lead us not into temptation, but deliver us from evil. Amen.

HAIL MARY

AVE Maria, grátia plena, Dóminus tecum. Benedícta tu in muliéribus, et benedíctus fructus ventris tui, Jesus. Sancta María, Mater Dei, ora pro nobis peccatóribus, nunc, et in hora mortis nostrae. Amen.

HAIL Mary, full of grace, the Lord is with thee. Blessed art thou amongst women, and blessed is the fruit of thy womb, Jesus. Holy Mary, Mother of God, pray for us sinners, now, and at the hour of our death. Amen.

GLORY BE

GLÓRIA Patri, et Filio, et Spirítui Sancto. Sicut erat in princípio, et nunc, et semper, et in saecula saeculórum. Amen.

GLORY be to the Father, and to the Son, and to the Holy Ghost. As it was in the beginning, is now, and ever shall be, world without end. Amen.

CONFITEOR

CONFÍTEOR Deo omnipoténti, beátae Maríae semper Vírgini, beáto Michaéli Archángelo, beáto Joánni Baptístae, sanctis Apóstolis Petro et Paulo, ómnibus Sanctis, et tibi, pater, quia peccávi nimis cogitatióne, verbo et ópere: [Now strike your breast three times, saying:] mea culpa, mea culpa, mea máxima culpa. Ideo precor beátam Maríam semper Vírginem, beátum Michaélem Archángelum, beátum Joánnem Baptístam, sanctos Apóstolos Petrum et Paulum, omnes Sanctos, et te, pater, oráre pro me ad Dóminum Deum nostrum. Amen.

I CONFESS to Almighty God, to Blessed Mary ever Virgin, to blessed Michael the archangel, to blessed John the Baptist, to the holy apostles Peter and Paul, to all the saints, and to thee, Father, that I have sinned exceedingly in thought, word, and deed: [Now strike your breast three times, saying:] through my fault, through my fault, through my most grievous fault. Therefore I beseech the Blessed Mary ever Virgin, blessed Michael the archangel, blessed John the Baptist, the holy apostles Peter and Paul, all the saints, and thee, Father, to pray to the Lord our God for me. Amen.

ACT OF RENEWAL OF BAPTISMAL PROMISES

IN Your presence, O most Holy Trinity, I declare that I believe in all that You have revealed and the Church has unchangingly transmitted. I renounce Satan, sin, and the world, with all its pomp and its vanities. I am resolved never to offend You again. My Lord Christ Jesus, true God and true man, with You I am united, to You alone I cling, and You only will I follow, for in You I desire to live and die. In the name of the Father, and of the Son, and of the Holy Spirit. Amen.

ACT OF FAITH

MY God, I firmly believe that You are one God in three divine Persons, Father, Son, and Holy Spirit. I believe that Your divine Son became man and died for our sins and that He will come to judge the living and the dead. I believe these and all the truths which the holy Catholic Church teaches, because You have revealed them who are eternal Truth and Wisdom, who can neither deceive nor be deceived. In this faith, I intend to live and die. Amen.

ACT OF HOPE

MY God, relying on Your infinite goodness and promises, I hope to obtain pardon of my sins, the help of Your grace, and life everlasting, through the merits of Jesus Christ, my Lord and Redeemer. Amen.

ACT OF LOVE

MY God, I love You above all things, with my whole heart and soul, because You are all good and worthy of all my love. I love my neighbor as myself for love of You. I forgive all who have injured me, and ask pardon of all whom I have injured. Amen.

ACT OF CONTRITION

MY God, I am heartily sorry for having offended You, and I detest all my sins because I dread the loss of heaven and the pains of hell, but most of all because they offend You, my God, who are all good and deserving of all my love. I firmly resolve with the help of Your grace to sin no more and to avoid the near occasions of sin. Amen.

HEROIC ACT OF CHARITY FOR THE POOR SOULS

MY God, I place in Your hands and those of Our Lady all the meritorious works that I will do in life and those that others will do for me after my death, so that they may serve the souls in purgatory. I entrust myself to Your mercy. Amen.

ACT OF SPIRITUAL COMMUNION

MY Jesus, I believe that You are present in the Most Holy Sacrament. I love You above all things, and I desire to receive You into my soul. Since I cannot at this moment receive You sacramentally, come at least spiritually into my heart. I embrace You as if You were already there and unite myself wholly to You. Never permit me to be separated from You. Amen.

Altar & Furnishings

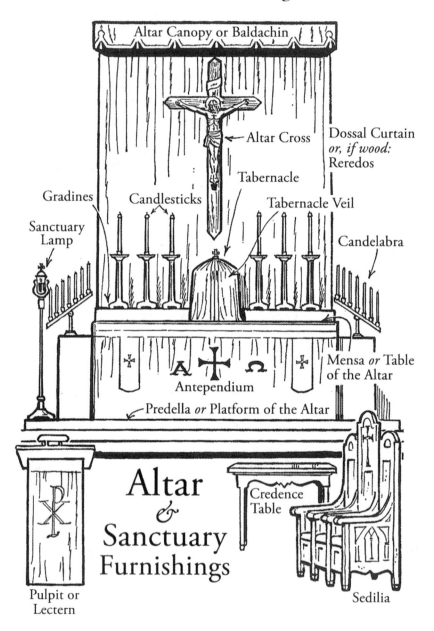

Altar Canopy or Baldachin

Altar Cross

Dossal Curtain
or, if wood:
Reredos

Tabernacle

Gradines

Candlesticks

Tabernacle Veil

Sanctuary
Lamp

Candelabra

Mensa *or* Table
of the Altar

Antependium

Predella *or* Platform of the Altar

Altar
&
Sanctuary
Furnishings

Credence
Table

Pulpit or
Lectern

Sedilia

Sacred Vessels

BURSE AND CORPORAL

VEILED CHALICE AND BURSE

MISSAL WITH STAND

CRUETS AND BELL

CHALICE WITH PURIFICATOR

CHALICE WITH PATEN

CHALICE WITH PALL

CHALICE WITH VEIL

Sacred Vestments

AMICE

ALB

CINCTURE

MANIPLE

STOLE

VESTED PRIEST

GOTHIC CHASUBLE

COPE & HUMERAL VEIL

CASSOCK

SURPLICE

COPE

Scripture Citation Abbreviations

1 Cor	1 Corinthians		Ez	Ezechiel (Ezekiel)
1 Esd	1 Esdras (Ezra)		Gal	Galatians
1 Jn	1 John		Gn	Genesis
1 Kgs	1 Kings (1 Samuel)		Hb	Habacuc (Habakkuk)
1 Mc	1 Machabees		Heb	Hebrews
1 Par	1 Paralipomenon (1 Chronicles)		Is	Isaias (Isaiah)
1 Pt	1 Peter		Jas	James
1 Thes	1 Thessalonians		Jer	Jeremias (Jeremiah)
1 Tm	1 Timothy		Jb	Job
2 Cor	2 Corinthians		Jl	Joel
2 Esd	2 Esdras (Nehemiah)		Jn	John (Gospel)
2 Jn	2 John		Jon	Jonas (Jonah)
2 Kgs	2 Kings (2 Samuel)		Jo	Josue (Joshua)
2 Mc	2 Machabees		Jude	Jude
2 Par	2 Paralipomenon (2 Chronicles)		Jgs	Judges
2 Pt	2 Peter		Jdt	Judith
2 Thes	2 Thessalonians		Lam	Lamentations
2 Tm	2 Timothy		Lv	Leviticus
3 Jn	3 John		Lk	Luke
3 Kgs	3 Kings (1 Kings)		Mal	Malachias (Malachi)
4 Kgs	4 Kings (2 Kings)		Mk	Mark
Abd	Abdias (Obadiah)		Mt	Matthew
Acts	Acts of the Apostles		Mi	Micheas (Micah)
Agg	Aggeus (Haggai)		Na	Nahum
Am	Amos		Nm	Numbers
Apoc	Apocalypse (Revelation)		Os	Osee (Hosea)
Bar	Baruch		Phlm	Philemon
Cant	Canticle of Canticles (Song of Songs)		Phil	Philippians
			Prv	Proverbs
Col	Colossians		Ps	Psalms
Dn	Daniel		Rom	Romans
Dt	Deuteronomy		Ru	Ruth
Eccles	Ecclesiastes		Soph	Sophonias (Zephaniah)
Ecclus	Ecclesiasticus (Sirach)		Ti	Titus
Eph	Ephesians		Tb	Tobias (Tobit)
Est	Esther		Ws	Wisdom
Ex	Exodus		Zac	Zacharias (Zechariah)

Endnotes

AUTHOR'S PREFACE

1. Council of Vatican II, Dogmatic Constitution *Lumen Gentium* (November 21, 1964), 23.
2. Roman Pontifical, *Ordination of Bishops*.

INTRODUCTION—CHRISTIAN DOCTRINE

1. St. Augustine, *In Ioann.* tr. 118, no. 5.
2. See Council of Vatican I, Dogmatic Constitution *Dei Filius* (April 24, 1870), chap. 3.
3. See Council of Vatican II, Dogmatic Constitution *Dei Verbum* (November 18, 1965), 10.
4. Council of Vatican II, *Dei Verbum*, 11. "God, who spoke first by the prophets, then by His own mouth, and lastly by the apostles, composed also the canonical Scriptures…, and that these are His own oracles and words—a Letter, written by our heavenly Father, and transmitted by the sacred writers to the human race in its pilgrimage so far from its heavenly country" (Pope Leo XIII, Encyclical *Providentissimus Deus* [November 18, 1893], 1).
5. Pope Pius XII, Encyclical *Divino Afflante Spiritu* (September 30, 1943), 37.
6. See *Ep. fest.* 39.
7. See *Tomus Damasi seu Confessio fidei ad Paulinum ep. Antioch.*, *De canone s. Scripturae*.
8. See Council of Carthage III, *De canone s. Scripturae*.
9. See Ecumenical Council of Trent, Session 4, *Decree on the Canonical Scriptures* (April 8, 1546). Before Luther, the Council of Florence confirmed the same canon (without dogmatic definition), see Pope Eugene IV, Bull of Union with the Copts *Cantate Domino* (February 4, 1442).
10. Council of Trent, Session 4, *Decree on the Canonical Scriptures*.
11. Council of Vatican I, Session 3, ch. 2.
12. See Encyclical *Spiritus Paraclitus* (September 15, 1920), 44.
13. From the prologue of his *Commentary on Isaiah*.
14. *The Story of a Soul*, Ms C, 36v–37r.
15. Pope Pius XII, *Divino Afflante Spiritu*, 24.
16. Pope Pius XII, *Divino Afflante*, 28.
17. *Panarion*, bk. 2, Anacephalaeosis IV, sect 61.
18. *De baptismo*, bk. 2, chap. 7, no. 12.
19. E.g., see Msgr. Gerard Van Noort, *Dogmatic Theology* (Westminster: Newman Press, 1961), 3:137–143.
20. See Council of Vatican II, *Dei Verbum*, 9.
21. Council of Vatican I, Dogmatic Constitution *Pastor Aeternus* (July 18, 1870).
22. Council of Vatican I, *Dei Filius*.

PART I—FAITH: BELIEVING TRULY

1. Each of these may be found at the back of this book.
2. Pope Leo XIII, Encyclical *Satis Cognitum* (June 29, 1896), 9.

SECTION 1: GOD THE FATHER AND CREATION

1. Council of Vatican I, *Dei Filius*, chap. 1.
2. Council of Vatican I, *Dei Filius*, chap. 4.

3. See these "Five Ways" according to St. Thomas Aquinas, in his *Summa Theologiae* [ST], I, q. 2, a. 3.
4. St. Ephraim the Syrian, *Nisibene Hymns*, Hymn III, no. 8.
5. Pope Eugene IV, Bull of Union with the Copts *Cantate Domino* (February 4, 1442).
6. *Contra sermonem Arianorum*, no. 16.
7. Pope St. Pius X, Motu Proprio *Doctoris Angelici* (June 29, 1914), 2.
8. See ST, I, q. 74, a. 2, c.
9. Regarding the truth of this sacred history, see Pontifical Biblical Commission, *Concerning the Historical Character of the First Three Chapters of Genesis* (June 30, 1909). See also Pope Pius XII, Encyclicals *Humani Generis* (August 12, 1950), 22 and *Divino Afflante Spiritu*, 1; Pope Leo XIII, *Providentissimus Deus*, 21; Pope St. Pius X, Encyclical *Lamentabili Sane* (July 3, 1907), 11; and Pope Benedict XV, *Spiritus Paraclitus*, 19.
10. The Council of Vatican II's document *Gaudium et Spes*, 24 made the ambiguous affirmation that "man is the only creature on earth that God has willed for its own sake."
11. St. Thomas Aquinas, ST, I, q. 19, a. 3, c.
12. Pope Leo XIII, Encyclical *Tametsi Futura Prospicientibus* (November 1, 1900), 6.
13. St. Irenaeus, *Adversus Haereses*, bk. 5, chap. 24, no. 3.
14. St. Thomas Aquinas, ST, I, q. 76, a. 1, c.
15. See Council of Vienne, Decree *De Summa Trinitate et Fide Catholica* (January 13, 1313).
16. "The intellectual principle which we call the mind or the intellect has an operation per se apart from the body. Now only that which subsists can have an operation per se.… [Therefore] the human soul, which is called the intellect or the mind, is something incorporeal and subsistent" (St. Thomas Aquinas, ST, I, q. 75, a. 2, c.).
17. Pope Pius IX, Apostolic Letter *Dolore Haud Mediocri* (April 30, 1860).
18. Pope Pius XII, Encyclical *Mystici Corporis Christi* (June 29, 1943), 75.
19. Pope Pius IX, Apostolic Constitution *Ineffabilis Deus* (December 8, 1854).
20. Congregation for the Doctrine of the Faith, Instruction *Donum Vitae* (February 22, 1987), I, 1.
21. See St. Thomas Aquinas, ST, I, q. 75, a. 2, c.
22. See Pope Leo X, Bull *Apostolici Regiminis* (December 19, 1513).
23. Pope Leo XIII, Encyclical *Arcanum Divinae* (February 10, 1880), 5.
24. See Council of Vienne, *De Summa Trinitate et Fide Catholica*.
25. Pope Pius XII, *Humani Generis*, 36.
26. Second-century Gnostics taught that man was formed in an imperfect state by seven preternatural archons, "yet was unable to stand erect … but wriggled on the ground like a worm. Then the power above taking pity

upon him, since he was made after his likeness, sent forth a spark of life, which gave man an erect posture, compacted his joints, and made him live" (St. Irenaeus, *Adv. Haer.*, bk. 1, chap. 24).

27 See also the Particular Council of Orange, can. 2; and Council of Trent, Session 5, *Decree on Original Sin*, can. 2 (June 17, 1546).

28 Pope Pius XII, *Humani Generis*, 37.

29 St. Thomas Aquinas gives the following explanation: "Man was so appointed in the state of innocence, that there was no rebellion of the flesh against the spirit. Wherefore it was not possible for the first inordinateness in the human appetite to result from his coveting a sensible good, to which the concupiscence of the flesh tends against the order of reason.… Hence it follows that man's first sin consisted in his coveting some spiritual good above his measure: and this pertains to pride. Therefore it is evident that man's first sin was pride" (ST, II-II, q. 163, a. 1, c).

30 The expression "in whom all have sinned" corresponds to the Latin Vulgate, whereas the Greek original reads "because in him." The Council of Trent used this translation of Rom 5:12 in its dogmatic canon on original sin: "death passed upon all men, in whom all have sinned" (Session 5).

31 See Council of Trent, Session 5, *Decree on Original Sin.*

32 Pope Pius IX, *Ineffabilis Deus.*

33 See St. Augustine, *De quantitate animae*, no. 80.

34 See St. Augustine, *Serm.* 341, chap. 9, no. 11; *De Civitate Dei*, bk. 18, chap. 51. Abraham saw the day of Christ and was glad, see Jn 8:56.

35 As the *Exsultet* of the ancient Roman Rite proclaims: *Nihil enim nobis nasci profuit, nisi redimi profuisset* (our birth would have been no gain, had we not been redeemed).

36 Pope Pius XI, Encyclical *Mortalium Animos* (January 6, 1928), 6.

37 Pope Pius XI, *Moralium Animos*, 11.

38 St. Thomas Aquinas, ST, I-II, q. 103, a. 4, rep. 1.

39 For this ambiguous affirmation, see Council of Vatican II, *Lumen Gentium*, 16.

40 Athanasian Creed, *Quicumque Vult.*

41 Known as the Declaration of God's Unity and *Al-Tawhid* (monotheism), this prayer of Surah 112 is counted among the most important chapters of the Quran and considered by Muslims worldwide to be equal in value to one-third of the entire Quran: "He is Allah, the one and only; Allah, the eternal, absolute; he begets not, nor is he begotten; and there is none like unto him."

42 See this misleading phrase in Council of Vatican II, *Lumen Gentium*, 16, and repeated in *Catechism of the Catholic Church*, 841.

43 Pope St. Gregory the Great says: "Abraham saw the day of the Lord when he received at his home the three angels of the most Holy Trinity: three guests whom he assuredly addressed as one, for even though the Perons of the Trinity are three in number, the nature of the deity is one" (*In Ev.*, Hom. 18, no. 3).

44 As found in the Council of Vatican II, Declaration *Nostra Aetate* (October 28, 1965), 2.

45 As stated in the Council of Vatican II, *Nostra Aetate*, 2.

46 *Praeambula fidei* (preambles of the Faith) are truths about God that can be known using natural reason. St. Thomas Aquinas says: "The existence of God and other like truths about God, which can be known by natural reason, are not articles of faith, but are preambles to the articles; for faith presupposes natural knowledge, even as grace presupposes nature, and perfection the perfectible" (ST, I, q. 2, a. 2, rep. 1).

47 As jointly affirmed by Pope Francis and Sheikh Ahmed Al-Tayeb, Grand Imam of Al-Azhar, in *A Document on Human Fraternity for World Peace and Living Together* (February 4, 2019).

48 Pope Leo XIII, *Providentissimus Deus*, 20.

49 For this confusing assertion, see Council of Vatican II, Decree *Unitatis Redintegratio* (November 21, 1964), 3; restated in *Catechism of the Catholic Church*, 819.

50 As with the case of the Ethiopian eunuch in Acts 8:26–40.

51 See especially Pope Pius IX, *Syllabus Errorum* (December 8, 1864).

52 A regrettable affirmation of the *Catechism of the Catholic Church*, 2212.

53 A confusing claim of the *Catechism of the Catholic Church*, 1676.

54 Council of Vatican I, *Dei Filius*, chap. 3, and can. 6.

55 Words of the famous French Freemason, the Marquis de La Tierce, in his introduction to the translation of Anderson's First Constitutions of Freemasonry, see: *Revue d'Histoire Moderne et Contemporaine* 1997/44-2, 197.

SECTION 2: GOD THE SON AND REDEMPTION

1 Pope St. Leo the Great, *Ep.* 28 (*Tomus ad Flavianum*).

2 Athanasian Creed, *Quicumque Vult.*

3 St. Augustine, *Serm.* 225, chap. 2.

4 Pope John Paul II, *General Audience* (August 21, 1996).

5 Pope Pius IX, *Ineffabilis Deus.*

6 Council of Ephesus, *Anathematismi Cyrilli Alexandrini* (431).

7 Pope Paul IV, Ordinance *Cum Quorundam* (August 7, 1555).

8 See Pope Pius XII, *Mystici Corporis Christi*, 11.

9 St. Thomas Aquinas, ST, III, q. 28, a. 2, c.

10 Pope Pius XII, Apostolic Constitution *Munificentissimus Deus* (November 1, 1950), 44.

11 Pope Pius XI, *Allocution to the Pilgrims of Vicenza* (November 30, 1933).

12 Pope Leo XIII, *Acta Sanctae Sedis*, vol. 28, yr. 1895–1896, pp. 130–131; see also Encyclical *Adiutricem Populi* (September 5, 1895), 8.

13 Pope John Paul II, Encyclical *Redemptoris Mater* (March 25, 1987), 39.

14 St. Bernard of Clairvaux, *Sermon for the Sunday within the Octave of the Annunciation.* St. Irenaeus likewise affirms: "Just as Eve, wife of Adam, yet still a virgin, became by her disobedience the cause of death for herself and the whole human race, so Mary, too, espoused yet a virgin, became

by her obedience the cause of salvation for herself and the whole human race." *Adv. Haer.* bk. 3, chap. 22.

15 Freed a man in the synagogue who was possessed by an impure spirit (see Mk 1:23–28), cured two demoniacs (see Mt 8:28–34), cured a demon-possessed man (see Mt 12:22), cured the demon-possessed daughter of a Canaanite woman (see Mt 15:22–28), cured a boy who was plagued by a demon (see Mt 17:14–21), cured a woman whom Satan had kept bound for eighteen years (see Lk 13:10–17).

16 Changing water into wine (see Jn 2:1–11), the great haul of fishes (see Jn 2:1–11), stilling the storm (see Mt 8:23–27), feeding at least five thousand people (see Mt 14:15–21), feeding at least four thousand people (see Mt 15:32–39), causing the fig tree to wither (see Mt 21:18–22), the second great haul of fishes (see Jn 21:1–14).

17 Curing the nobleman's son (see Jn 4:46–54), curing Peter's mother-in-law of a fever (see Mk 1:30–31), healing a leper (see Mk 1:40–45), healing the centurion's servant (see Mt 8:5–13), curing the paralytic (see Mt 9:1–8), curing a woman of an issue of bleeding (see Lk 8:43–48), opening the eyes of two blind men (see Mt 9:27–31), loosing the tongue of a mute man (see Mt 9:32–33), healing an invalid man at the pool called Bethesda (see Jn 5:1–9), restoring a withered hand (see Mt 12:10–13), curing a deaf and mute man (see Mk 7:31–37), opening the eyes of a blind man (see Mk 8:22–26), opening the eyes of a man born blind (see Jn 9:1–38), curing a man of dropsy (see Lk 14:1–4), cleansing ten lepers (see Lk 17:11–19), opening the eyes of two blind men (see Mt 20:30–34), restoring the ear of the high priest's servant (see Lk 22:50–51).

18 Raised the widow's son from the dead (see Lk 7:11–15), raised the daughter of a synagogue leader from the dead (see Mt 9:18–26), raised Lazarus from the dead (see Jn 11:1–46).

19 In addition to the general use of Latin, this Rite includes the *Amen, Alleluia, Hosanna,* and *Sabaoth* from Hebrew, and the great *Kyrie eleison* from Greek.

20 Fulton J. Sheen, *The Seven Last Words* (Garden City: Garden City Books, 1952), vii.

21 St. Augustine, *Serm.* 169.

22 Pope Pius IX, *Syllabus Errorum.*

23 These and many similar errors are condemned in the Council of Trent's famous *Decree on Justification* (Session 6 [January 13, 1547]).

24 Pope John Paul II, *General Audience* (May 21, 1997).

25 Pope Pius XI, Encyclical *Quas Primas* (December 11, 1925), 18.

26 Pope Pius XI, *Quas Primas,* 18.

27 Pope Pius XI, *Quas Primas,* 18.

28 Pope Pius XI, *Quas Primas,* 18.

29 According to St. Thomas Aquinas: "Elias was taken up into the atmospheric heaven, but not into the empyrean heaven, which is the abode of the saints: and likewise

Enoch was translated into the earthly paradise, where he is believed to live with Elias until the coming of Antichrist" (ST, III, a. 49, q. 5, rep. 2). Pope St. Gregory the Great says the same; see *In Ev.,* Hom. 29.

Section 3: God the Holy Spirit and Sanctification

1 St. Augustine, *De Civ.,* bk. 11, chap. 24.

2 Pope Leo XIII, Encyclical *Divinum Illud Munus* (May 9, 1897), 6.

3 See St. Thomas Aquinas, ST, I-II, q. 113, a. 9, c.

4 Pope St. Pius X, Motu Proprio *Sacrorum Antistitum, Oath against Modernism* (September 1, 1910).

5 See also Rom 12:4–5; Eph 1:22–23; 5:23; Col 1:18; and 2:19.

6 Pope Pius XII, *Mystici Corporis Christi,* 60.

7 Pope Pius XII, *Mystici Corporis Christi,* 63.

8 Pope Pius XII, *Mystici Corporis Christi,* 67, 86.

9 St. John Chrysostom, *On Eutropius,* Hom. 2, no. 15. "Christ is all to the child of His Church: both father and mother and tutor and nurse" (Clement of Alexandria, *Paedagogus,* bk. 1, chap. 6).

10 Pope Pius XII, *Mystici Corporis Christi,* 28.

11 Pope Leo XIII, *Divinum Illud Munus.*

12 Pope Pius XII, *Mystici Corporis Christi,* 26.

13 For this nebulous assertion, see Pope Francis, Encyclical *Fratelli Tutti* (October 3, 2020), 127, 276.

14 The *Catechism of the Catholic Church* ambiguously states: "Life in the Holy Spirit fulfills the vocation of man. This life is made up of divine charity and human solidarity" (1699).

15 Charles Journet, *The Church of the Word Incarnate* (London: Sheed and Ward, 1955), 148.

16 Council of Vatican II, *Dei Verbum,* 10.

17 Joseph Cardinal Ratzinger, *The Spirit of the Liturgy* (San Francisco: Ignatius Press, 2000), 165.

18 Joseph Cardinal Ratzinger, *Spirit of the Liturgy,* 165.

19 *Contra Iulianum, Against Julian,* bk. 2, chap. 10, no. 34.

20 See Pope Pius XII, *Mystici Corporis Christi.*

21 *De moribus Ecclesiae catholicae,* bk. 1, chap. 30, no. 62–63.

22 St. Cyprian, *Ep.* 73, no. 21; see St. Cyprian, *De unit.,* no. 6, 13; St. Fulgentius of Ruspe, *De Fide,* 37, 34; Council of Lateran IV, "Profession of Faith" (November 30, 1215); Pope Eugene IV, *Cantate Domino;* Pope Pius XII, *Mystici Corporis Christi,* 3.

23 Council of Vatican II, *Lumen Gentium,* 14; Decree *Ad Gentes* (December 7, 1965), 7.

24 St. Augustine, *Sermo ad Caesariensis Ecclesiae plebem,* no. 6.

25 St. Cyprian of Carthage, *De unit.,* no. 6.

26 Pope Pius IX, Allocution *Singulari Quadam* (December 9, 1854).

27 Pope Pius IX, Encyclical *Quanto Conficiamur Moerore* (August 10, 1863).

28 See St. Robert Bellarmine, *De Sacramento Baptismi,* bk. 1, chap. 6.

29 See St. Augustine, *De Civ.,* bk. 13, no. 7.

30 In 357, St. Athanasius refused to obey Pope Liberius, who commanded him to recognize the Arian bishops of

the Orient. Thereupon Pope Liberius excommunicated St. Athanasius.

31 Council of Vatican II, *Lumen Gentium*, 14.

32 St. Augustine, *De symbolo: Sermo ad catechumenos*, 14.

33 Council of Vatican II, *Lumen Gentium*, 25.

34 Journet, *Church of the Word*, 340–341.

35 Bishop Vinzenz Gasser, spokesman for the Theological Commission at Vatican I, see *Schema Primum de Ecclesia*, can. 9, Mansi 51, 552.

36 See St. Vincent of Lerins, *Commonitorium*, chap. 2, no. 6. The first use of the term "ordinary magisterium" in a papal document is found in Pope Pius IX, Letter *Tuas Libenter* (December 21, 1863), and Vatican I was the first council to speak of the college of bishops outside an ecumenical council as an ordinary and universal teaching authority, see *Dei Filius*.

37 *Code of Canon Law*, can. 749, §3.

38 Council of Vatican II, *Lumen Gentium*, 22.

39 Council of Vatican I, *Dei Filius*.

40 Council of Vatican II, *Lumen Gentium*, 12.

41 Pope Leo XIII, *Satis Cognitum*, 4.

42 Pope Pius XI, *Mortalium Animos*, 10.

43 Pope Pius XI, Encyclical *Rerum Ecclesiae* (February 28, 1926), 1.

44 Council of Vatican II, *Unitatis Redintegratio*, 3.

45 See *Serm.* 97, no. 2.

46 St. Augustine, *De Baptismo*, bk. 1, chap. 10, no. 14.

47 Regarding schismatics, St. Augustine said: "In many things they are with me, only in a few they are not with me; but because of these few points they have separated themselves from me, it doesn't mean anything that they be with me with all the rest" (*Enarr. in Ps.* 54, no. 19).

48 Pope Paul VI, Motu Proprio *Solemni Hac Liturgia* (June 30, 1968).

49 Fray Luis de Granada, *Obra Selecta* (Madrid: La Editorial Catolica, 1952), 309.

50 St. Augustine said, "In this world, in these evil days, not only from the time of the bodily presence of Christ and His apostles, but even from that of Abel, whom first his wicked brother slew because he was righteous, and thenceforth even to the end of this world, the Church has gone forward on pilgrimage amid the persecutions of the world and the consolations of God" (*De Civ.*, bk. 18, chap. 51). See also Mt 5:11; Jn 15:18–21; and Mt 10:16–39.

51 See *Code of Canon Law*, can. 588, §1.

52 This is the traditional name of the ordinary offices of the Roman Curia, presided over by a cardinal; since 2022 they have been called "Dicasteries."

53 See *Code of Canon Law*, can. 134, §1.

54 Council of Trent, Session 23, *Doctrine on the Sacrament of Holy Orders*, can. 2, 6 (July 15, 1563).

55 See Eusebius of Caesarea, *Hist. Eccl.*, bk. 6, chap. 43, no. 11.

56 *Code of Canon Law*, can. 750.

57 The bishops "proclaim Christ's doctrine infallibly whenever, even though dispersed through the world, but still maintaining the bond of communion among themselves and with the Successor of Peter, and authentically teaching matters of faith and morals, they are in agreement on one position as definitively to be held" (Council of Vatican II, *Lumen Gentium*, 25).

58 "Each and every thing which is proposed definitively by the Magisterium of the Church concerning the doctrine of faith and morals, that is, each and every thing which is required to safeguard reverently and to expound faithfully the same Deposit of Faith, is also to be firmly embraced and retained; therefore, one who rejects those propositions which are to be held definitively is opposed to the doctrine of the Catholic Church" (*Code of Canon Law*, can. 750, §2).

59 See Apostolic Letter *Ordinatio Sacerdotalis* (May 22, 1994), 4.

60 E.g., the assertion in *Lumen Gentium* 16 that says Muslims adore "together with us" Catholics the one God; or the assertion in *Dignitatis Humanae* 2 that says that the human person has a natural right to spread the religion of his choice (even if it were a false religion) without being impeded by civil law.

61 Opening Speech to the Council (October 11, 1962).

62 Opening Speech (October 11, 1962).

63 *General Audience* (January 12, 1966).

64 Dietrich von Hildebrand, *The Charitable Anathema* (Roman Catholic Books: 1993), 1. In the traditional Holy Friday Liturgy the Church also prays explicitly for heretics; unfortunately, the new Pauline Missal omits this prayer.

65 *Code of Canon Law*, can. 212, §3.

66 Congregation for the Doctrine of the Faith, Instruction *Donum Veritatis* (May 24, 1990), 30.

67 See Council of Vatican I, *Pastor Aeternus*, prooemium.

68 See Council of Vatican I, *Dei Filius* and *Pastor Aeternus*.

69 Council of Vatican I, *Pastor Aeternus*, chap. 4.

70 *Document on Human Fraternity for World Peace and Living Together*, signed by Pope Francis and Sheikh Ahmed Al-Tayeb, Grand Imam of Al-Azhar in Abu Dhabi (February 4, 2019).

71 Address to Participants in the Meeting promoted by the Pontifical Council for Promoting the New Evangelization (October 11, 2017). See also *Catechism of the Catholic Church* (2018 edition), 2267; Rescriptum "Ex Audientia Ss.mi" (May 11, 2018); and, Pontifical Council for the Promotion of the New Evangelization, *Directory for Catechesis* (Vatican City: Libreria Editrice Vaticana, 2020), 380.

72 These Jewish *Berekoth* prayers are taken from the fifth-century Babylonian version of the Talmud (T.B.).

73 Martin Luther especially despised the traditional Offertory Prayers as "an abomination": "That utter abomination follows which forces all that precedes in the mass into its service and is, therefore, called the offertory. From here on almost everything smacks and savors of sacrifice. ... Let us, therefore, repudiate everything that smacks of sacrifice, together with the entire canon" (*An Order of Mass and Communion for the Church at Wittenberg, 1523: Luther's*

Works. Volume 53. *Liturgy and Hymns.* Edited by Ulrich S. Leupold, Fortress Press/Philadelphia 1965, 25-26)

[74] In this, Pope Francis undermines the truth of the indissolubility of a valid and consummated marriage and, at the same time, the holiness of the two sacraments of the Eucharist and penance, which requires contrition and an intention not to sin against the divine commandments. Regarding the document of the Buenos Aires Bishops, Pope Francis maintained: "The document is very good and completely explains the meaning of chapter VIII of *Amoris Laetitia.* There are no other interpretations. And I am certain that it will do much good" (Letter of September 5, 2016). In his later audience with the Cardinal Secretary of State, "Ex audientia SS.mi" (June 5, 2017), the pope declared this approval of the norms of the Bishops of the Buenos Aires region to be "authentic Magisterium."

[75] See Council of Vatican I, *Pastor Aeternus.*

[76] A heresy propagated partly by the Council of Constance (1414–1418) and by the schismatic part of the Council of Basel (1431–1449), first explicitly condemned by Pope Pius II in 1460 with the Bull *Exsecrabilis.*

[77] Council of Vatican I, *Pastor Aeternus.*

[78] *Collegium (corpus, ordo).*

[79] Council of Vatican II, *Lumen Gentium,* Appendix, Preliminary Note of Explanation, 4.

[80] See *Code of Canon Law,* can. 337, §3. There can be cases when the pope "approves of or freely accepts the united action of the scattered bishops, so that it is thereby made a collegiate act" (Council of Vatican II, *Lumen Gentium,* 22).

[81] See Archbishop Dino Staffa, *Acta Synodalia Sacrosancti Concilii Oecumenici Vaticani Secundi,* vol. 3, per. 3, pt. 1, Congregationes Generales LXXX-LXXXII, Città del Vaticano 1973, 779.

[82] There were long periods in Church history where no general or ecumenical councils were held; e.g., from ca. 50–325 (nearly 300 years), from 870–1122 (252 years); 1563–1869 (306 years).

[83] Council of Vatican II, *Lumen Gentium,* 24.

[84] Council of Vatican II, *Lumen Gentium,* 24.

[85] Council of Vatican I, *Pastor Aeternus,* chap. 3.

[86] Pope Leo XIII, *Satis Cognitum,* 52.

[87] See *Code of Canon Law,* cann. 337–338.

[88] See *Code of Canon Law,* can. 439, §1.

[89] See *Code of Canon Law,* can. 440, §1. Can. 431 further states: "Neighboring particular Churches are to be grouped into ecclesiastical provinces, with a certain defined territory," and can. 435: "An ecclesiastical province is presided over by a Metropolitan, who is Archbishop in his own diocese."

[90] *Code of Canon Law,* cann. 460; 462, §1 and §2.

[91] *Code of Canon Law,* can. 466.

[92] Pope Pius XII, *Address to the Patriciate and the Roman Nobility* (January 8, 1947).

[93] Pope Pius XII, *Address to the to Participants in the Eighth International Congress of Administrative Sciences* (August 5, 1950).

[94] Pope Pius XII, *Address to Italian Catholic Jurists* (December 6, 1953).

[95] Pope Pius XII, *Address to the Tribunal of the Sacra Romana Rota* (October 2, 1945).

[96] Pope Leo XIII, Encyclical *Rerum Novarum* (May 15, 1891), 12.

[97] Pope Leo XIII, *Rerum Novarum,* 13.

[98] Pope Leo XIII, *Rerum Novarum,* 14.

[99] Pope Pius XII, *Address to the to Participants in the Eighth International Congress of Administrative Sciences.*

[100] Pope St. Pius X, Encyclical *Vehementer Nos* (February 11, 1906), 3.

[101] Pope Leo XIII, Encyclical *Immortale Dei* (November 1, 1885), 33.

[102] Pope Leo XIII, *Immortale Dei,* 14.

[103] See Pope Pius IX, *Syllabus Errorum.*

[104] Pope Leo XIII, *Immortale Dei,* 6–7.

[105] See Archbishop Federico Melendro Gutiérrez, *Acta Synodalia Sacrosancti Concilii Oecumenici Vaticani Secundi,* vol. 3, per. 3, pt. 2, Congregationes Generales LXXXIII-LXXXIX, Città del Vaticano 1974, 528.

[106] Pope Pius XII, *Mystici Corporis Christi,* 104.

[107] Pope Leo XIII, Encyclical *Libertas Praestantissimum* (June 20, 1888).

[108] "Those upon whom the penalty of excommunication or interdict has been imposed or declared, and others who obstinately persist in manifest grave sin, are not to be admitted to Holy Communion" (*Code of Canon Law,* can. 915).

[109] *Contra Auxentium,* no. 36.

[110] See Bishop Javier Miguel Ariz Huarte, *Acta Synodalia Sacrosancti Concilii Oecumenici Vaticani Secundi,* vol. 3, per. 3, pt. 2, Congregationes Generales LXXXIII-LXXXIX, Città del Vaticano 1974, 627.

[111] See Pope Leo XIII, *Libertas Praestantissimum.*

[112] As, e.g., in the following affirmations of Vatican II: "This [religious] freedom means that ... no one is to be forced to act in a manner contrary to his own beliefs, whether privately or publicly, whether alone or in association with others, within due limits. ... The right to this immunity continues to exist even in those who do not live up to their obligation of seeking the truth and adhering to it and the exercise of this right is not to be impeded, provided that just public order be observed" (*Dignitatis Humanae* [December 7, 1965], 2).

[113] Pope Leo XIII, *Libertas Praestantissimum,* 23.

[114] See Bishop Javier Miguel Ariz Huarte, *Acta Synodalia Sacrosancti Concilii Oecumenici Vaticani Secundi,* vol. 3, per. 3, pt. 2, Congregationes Generales LXXXIII-LXXXIX, Città del Vaticano 1974, 627.

[115] See Bishop Benigno Chiriboga, *Acta Synodalia Sacrosancti Concilii Oecumenici Vaticani Secundi,* vol. 3, per. 3, pt. 2, Congregationes Generales LXXXIII-LXXXIX, Città del Vaticano 1974, 647.

[116] See Pope Leo XIII, *Immortale Dei,* 32.

[117] *Syllabus Errorum,* proposition 15, repeating the

condemnation maid in the Apostolic Letter *Multiplices inter* (June 10, 1851) and in the Allocution *Maxima Quidem* (June 9, 1862).

118 *Syllabus Errorum*, proposition 16, repeating the condemnation maid in the Encyclical *Qui Pluribus* (November 9, 1846) and in the Encyclical *Singulari Quidem* (March 17, 1856).

119 Encyclical *Quanta Cura* (December 8, 1864), quoting Pope Gregory XVI, Encyclical *Mirari Vos* (August 15, 1832).

120 See Cardinal Alfredo Ottaviani, *Acta Synodalia Sacrosancti Concilii Oecumenici Vaticani Secundi*, vol. 3, per. 3, pt. 2, Congregationes Generales LXXXIII-LXXXIX, Città del Vaticano 1974, 377.

121 See Bishop Giuseppe Vairo, *Acta Synodalia Sacrosancti Concilii Oecumenici Vaticani Secundi*, vol. 3, per. 3, pt. 2, Congregationes Generales LXXXIII-LXXXIX, Città del Vaticano 1974, 749.

122 Tertullian, *Paen.*, chap. 10.

123 Ludwig Ott, *Fundamentals of Catholic Dogma*, 3rd ed. (London: Baronius Press, 2018), 333.

124 See St. Thomas Aquinas, ST, III, q. 49, a. 1, rep. 1.

125 St. Thomas Aquinas, ST, I-II, q. 113, a. 3, c.

126 See Council of Trent, Session 6, *Decree on Justification*, chap. 5.

127 See Council of Trent, Session 6, *Decree on Justification*, chap. 6.

128 Pope Pius XI, Encyclical *Miserentissimus Redemptor* (May 8, 1928), 7.

129 For these and other errors regarding the forgiveness of sins, see Council of Trent, Session 6, *Decree on Justification*.

130 An ambiguous phrase in Pope Francis, Apostolic Exhortation *Amoris Laetitia* (March 19, 2016), 297.

131 Fr. William Faber, *Sermon on the Fourth Sunday in Lent*, 1863.

132 St. Thomas Aquinas, "The Catechetical Instructions" in *Tradivox Catholic Catechism Index*, ed. Aaron Seng (Manchester: Sophia Institute Press, 2021), 6:82.

133 *Code of Canon Law*, can. 1176, §3.

134 St. Thomas Aquinas, ST, III-Sup., q. 88, a. 1, rep 3.

135 See Council of Trent, Session 6, *Decree on Justification* (especially can. 30), and Session 25, *Decree on Purgatory* (December 4, 1563).

136 *Ennar. in Ps.*, 37:3.

137 See St. Catherine of Genoa, *Treatise on Purgatory*, chap. 1.

138 Pope Benedict XII, Constitution *Benedictus Deus* (January 29, 1336).

139 Council of Vienne, Session 3, *Errors of the Beghards and Beguines Concerning the State of Perfection* (May 6, 1312).

140 Bull *Ex Omnibus Afflictionibus* (October 1, 1576).

141 *Humani Generis*, 26.

142 St. Augustine, *In Ioann.* tr. 67, no. 2.

143 Pope St. Gregory the Great, *Moralia in Job*, vol. I, bk. 4, no. 70.

144 Pope Vigilius, *Anathematismi contra Originem* (in 543), can. 9.

145 See Athanasian Creed, *Quicumque Vult*; Council of Lateran IV, "Profession of Faith" (November 30, 1215); Council of Lyons II, "Profession of Faith" (July 17, 1274); Pope Eugene IV, Bull of Union with the Greeks *Laetentur Caeli* (July 6, 1439); Council of Vatican II, *Lumen Gentium*, 48.

146 Msgr. Joseph Pohle, *Eschatology* (St. Louis: B. Herder Book Co., 1942), 60. "The majority of the Fathers, the Schoolmen, and the majority of modern theologians assume a physical fire, but stress the difference between this fire and ordinary fire. St. Thomas … explains the effect of physical fire on a purely spiritual essence as a binding of the spirits to material fire.… Through it the spirits are made subject to matter and hindered in their free movement" (Ott, *Fundamentals*, 509).

147 St. Thomas Aquinas, "The Catechetical Instructions" in *Tradivox Catholic Catechism Index*, ed. Aaron Seng (Manchester: Sophia Institute Press, 2021), 6:81–82.

148 Vision on July 13, 1917.

PART II — MORALS: ACTING RIGHTLY

1 St. Alphonsus Liguori, *Pratica di amar Gesù Cristo*, chap. 7, no. 3.

SECTION 1: GENERAL PRINCIPLES OF MORALITY

1 See Council of Trent, Session 5, *Decree on Original Sin*, can. 5.

2 Pope John Paul II, Encyclical *Veritatis Splendor* (August 6, 1993), 80.

3 Pope John Paul II condemned such *teleological* and *proportionalist* theories, which hold that it is impossible to qualify the deliberate choice of certain kinds of behavior or acts as "objectively evil," apart from a consideration of the intention for which the choice is made or the totality of the foreseeable consequences of that act (see *Veritatis Splendor*, 79).

4 These latter two errors have insinuated themselves even into recent papal documents regarding the case of couples living in adulterous unions; see Pope Francis, Apostolic Exhortation *Amoris Laetitia* (March 19, 2016), 295, 298, 301, and footnote 329.

5 St. Thomas Aquinas, ST, I, q. 79, a. 13, c.

6 St. John Henry Cardinal Newman, "Letter to the Duke of Norfolk" in *Certain Difficulties felt by Anglicans in Catholic Teaching* (London: Longmans, Green, and Co., 1900), 2:250.

7 St. Thomas Aquinas, ST, I-II, q. 91, a. 1, rep. 3.

8 See St. Thomas Aquinas, ST, I-II, q. 93, a. 1, c.

9 See St. Thomas Aquinas, ST, I-II, q. 91, a. 2, c.

10 See St. Thomas Aquinas, ST, I-II, q. 91, a. 5.

11 St. Thomas Aquinas, ST, I-II, q. 91, a. 4, c.

12 See St. Thomas Aquinas, ST, I-II, q. 90, a. 4, c.

13 See St. Thomas Aquinas, ST, I-II, q. 93, a. 3, rep. 2; q. 96, a. 4, rep. 2 and 3.

14 St. Thomas Aquinas, ST, II-II, q. 104, a. 5, rep. 2.

15 St. Thomas Aquinas, ST, II-II, q. 33, a. 4, rep. 2.

1 Council of Vatican I, *Dei Filius*, chap. 3.
2 Pope Benedict XV, Encyclical *Ad Beatissimi Apostolorum* (November 1, 1914).
3 Pope Stephan I, *Ep. Ad Cyprianum* (apud S. Cyprianum, *Ep.* 74).
4 *Commonitorium*, chap. 2, no. 5.
5 St. Vincent of Lerins, *Commonitorium*, chap. 23, no. 16.
6 Council of Vatican I, *Dei Filius*, chap. 4.
7 *Dei Verbum*, 10.
8 Pope Benedict XV, *Ad Beatissimi Apostolorum*, 25.
9 St. Robert Bellarmine, *De Romano Pontifice*, bk. 2, chap. 29.
10 St. John Henry Cardinal Newman, *The Arians of the Fourth Century* (London: Longmans, Green, and Co., 1908), 465–466.
11 See St. Thomas Aquinas, ST, II-II, q. 2, a. 8, c.
12 *Catechism of the Catholic Church*, 67.
13 For these episodes, see Exodus 7–9.
14 See Jordan Aumann, *Spiritual Theology* (London: Sheed & Ward, 1980), 412.
15 See Aumann, *Spiritual Theology*, 430.
16 See Fr. Peter Joseph, "Apparitions: Who is Behind It?" *Inside the Vatican*, March 2005, 32–39.
17 *Interior Castle*, mansion 6, chap. 9, no. 13.
18 *Ascent of Mount Carmel*, bk. 2, chap. 22, no. 5.
19 Pontifical Council for Culture, Pontifical Council for Inter-religious Dialogue, *Jesus Christ the Bearer of the Water of Life: A Christian Reflection on the "New Age"* (2003), 2.3.1.
20 Norberto Rivera Carrera, Arzobispo Primado de México, *Instrucción pastoral sobre el New Age* (January 6, 1996), 33. See also Congregation for the Doctrine of the Faith, *Letter to the Bishops of the Catholic Church on some Aspects of Christian Meditation* (October 15, 1989).
21 Committee on Doctrine of the United States Conference of Catholic Bishops, *Guidelines for Evaluating Reiki as an Alternative Therapy* (March 25, 2009), 11.
22 Pope John Paul II, *Crossing the Threshold of Hope* (New York: Random House, 1994), 90.
23 Pontifical Council for Culture, Pontifical Council for Interreligious Dialogue, *Jesus Christ the Bearer of the Water of Life*, 3.5.
24 Congregation for the Doctrine of the Faith, *Declaration on Masonic Associations* (November 27, 1983).
25 Giuliano Di Bernando, Grand Master of the Masonic lodge GLRI (Gran Loggia Regolare d'Italia) in the years 1990–1993, spoke these words on April 11, 2001, on RAI2 (Italian Television Media).
26 Between 1974 and 1976, Nicolas Aslan (1906–1980) published *Grande Dicionário Enciclopédico de Maçonaria e Symbologia* in four volumes in Rio de Janeiro (Brazil).
27 *Grande Dicionário*, 1:109.
28 *Grande Dicionário*, 2:525–526.
29 *Grande Dicionário*, 4:1020–1021.
30 *Grande Dicionário*, 2:604.
31 Pope Pius VIII, Encyclical *Traditi Humilitati Nostrae* (May 24, 1829).

32 Apostolic Letter *Praeclara Gratulationis Publicae* (June 20, 1894).
33 See Felix Sardà y Salvany, *Masonismo y Catolicismo* (Barcelona: Librería y Tipografía Católica, 1885), chap. 3.
34 Encyclical *Humanum Genus* (April 20, 1884), 7.
35 "Those who join a Masonic sect or other societies of the same sort, which plot against the Church or against legitimate civil authority, incur ipso facto an excommunication simply reserved to the Holy See" (can. 2335).
36 Congregation for the Doctrine of the Faith, *Declaration on Masonic Associations* (November 27, 1983).
37 Congregation for the Doctrine of the Faith, *Declaration on Masonic Associations*.
38 St. Thomas Aquinas, ST, I-II, q. 26, a. 4, c.
39 Words spoken to St. Jacinta in the hospital at Lisbon in 1920; see Fr. Andrew Apostoli, *Fatima for Today: The Urgent Marian Message of Hope* (San Francisco: Ignatius Press, 2010), 145.
40 See Apostoli, *Fatima for Today*, 145.
41 Council of Orange II (July 3, 529), can. 2.
42 *De servo arbitrio* (*The Bondage of the Will*).
43 Council of Trent, Session 6, *Decree on Justification*, can. 4.
44 St. John Henry Cardinal Newman, *Difficulties of Anglicans*, lecture 8.
45 St. Thomas Aquinas, ST, II-II, q. 14, a. 3, c.
46 St. Athanasius, *De virginitate*, no. 5.
47 St. John Chrysostom, as quoted by St. Thomas Aquinas in ST, II-II, q. 158, a. 8, sc.

1 Council of Trent, Session 6, *Decree on Justification*, can. 18.
2 Council of Vatican II, Constitution *Sacrosanctum Concilium* (December 4, 1963), 83.
3 St. Augustine, *De Civ.*, bk. 10, chap. 19.
4 See Council of Trent, Session 25, *Decree on the Invocation and Veneration of the Saints and Their Relics and Sacred Images* (December 4, 1563).
5 See Ecclus 44:14–15; 2 Mc 15:12–14; Heb 11; and Apoc 6:9.
6 See *Martyrium Polycarpi*; Tertullian, *De corona*, chap. 3; Origen, *De oratione*, chap. 11, no. 2; St. Cyprian, *Ep.* 39, no. 3; St. Augustine, *In Ioann.*, tr. 84, no. 1. See also sacred images in the catacombs.
7 See Council of Trent, Session 25; Council of Nicaea II, Session 7.
8 Council of Trent, Session 8, *Definition* (March 11, 1547). The Council refers here to St. Basil, *De Spir.*, chap. 18, no. 45.
9 St. Thomas Aquinas, ST, II-II, q. 92, a. 1, c.
10 Pope Pius IV, Bull *Iniunctum Nobis* (November 13, 1565); see also the Council of Trent, Session 7.
11 St. Ambrose of Milan, as quoted by St. Thomas Aquinas in ST, II-II, q. 93, a. 1, c.
12 St. Thomas Aquinas, ST, II-II, q. 81, a. 2, rep. 3.
13 *Sacrorum antistitum*.
14 See Apoc 1:10 and *Didache*, chap. 14.
15 St. Basil the Great, *De Spiritu Sancto*, 27:66.
16 Pope Leo XIII, *Rerum Novarum*.

[17] Pope John Paul II, Encyclical *Laborem Exercens* (September 14, 1981), 6.

[18] See Council of Vatican II, *Sacrosanctum Concilium*, 30.

[19] *Salus animarum suprema lex*, "the salvation of souls is the supreme law" (*Code of Canon Law*, can. 1752).

[20] Pope Pius XI, Encyclical *Divini Illius Magistri* (December 31, 1929), 95.

[21] Pope Leo XIII, Encyclical *Sapientiae Christianae* (January 10, 1890), 42.

[22] Pope Leo XIII, *Rerum Novarum*, 14.

[23] Pope Pius XI, *Divini Illius Magistri*, 62.

[24] Pope Pius XI, *Divini Illius Magistri*, 65.

[25] Pope Pius XI, *Divini Illius Magistri*, 66.

[26] Pope Pius XI, *Divini Illius Magistri*, 67.

[27] Pope Pius XI, *Divini Illius Magistri*, 68.

[28] Pope Pius XI, *Divini Illius Magistri*, 68.

[29] Pope Pius XI, *Divini Illius Magistri*, 92.

[30] Catechism of the Council of Trent, *Tradivox Catholic Catechism Index*, ed. Aaron Seng (Manchester: Sophia Institute Press, 2021), 7:375.

[31] St. Thomas Aquinas, ST, II-II, q. 33, a. 4, c.

[32] See also St. Thomas Aquinas, ST, II-II, q. 33, aa. 5–7.

[33] Pope Benedict XVI, Letter to the Bishops Accompanying the Apostolic Letter, "Summorum Pontificum" (July 7, 2007).

[34] As the medieval Papal Oath declared: "I shall keep inviolate the discipline and ritual of the Church, just as I found and received it handed down by my Predecessors."

[35] Pope Pius XI, Encyclical *Casti Connubii* (December 31, 1930).

[36] Several occasions are mentioned in the Gospels: see Mk 14:12–16; Lk 22:11–15; Jn 21:1–15; and Lk 24:42–43).

[37] Pope John Paul II, Encyclical *Evangelium Vitae* (March 25, 1995), 13.

[38] Pope John Paul II, *Evangelium Vitae*, 62.

[39] See Pope John Paul II, *Evangelium Vitae*, 65.

[40] See *Code of Canon Law*, can. 915.

[41] Pope John Paul II, *Evangelium Vitae*, 63.

[42] St. Francis de Sales, *Introduction to the Devout Life*, pt. 3, chap. 12.

[43] Pontifical Council for the Family, *The Truth and Meaning of Human Sexuality: Guidelines for Education within the Family* (December 8, 1995), II, 16.

[44] Pope Pius XI, *Casti Connubii*, 54. Pope Paul VI likewise declared: "Excluded is any action which either before, at the moment of, or after sexual intercourse, is specifically intended to prevent procreation — whether as an end or as a means" (Encyclical *Humanae Vitae* [July 25, 1968], 14).

[45] Pope Paul VI, *Humanae Vitae*, 14.

[46] Sacred Congregation for the Doctrine of the Faith, Declaration *Persona Humana* (December 29, 1975), 9.

[47] Sacred Congregation for the Doctrine of the Faith, *Persona Humana*, 9.

[48] See *Code of Canon Law*, can. 915.

[49] See St. Thomas Aquinas, *De malo*, q. 15, a. 3.

[50] *Introduction to the Devout Life*, pt. 3, chap. 13.

[51] Corporal mortifications can vary in form and intensity, depending on the persistence and vehemence of temptations against chastity, or depending on how regularly one succumbs to them. Such forms can include fasting, abstaining from alcohol, sleeping in a hard bed, flagellation, cold showers, etc.

[52] Pope Pius XI, Encyclical *Divini Redemptoris* (March 19, 1937), 14.

[53] Pope Pius XI, *Divini Redemptoris*, 58.

[54] Pope Pius XI, *Divini Redemptoris*, 58.

[55] See *Acta Apostolicae Sedis* 41, yr. 1949, p. 334.

[56] Pope Pius XI, Encyclical *Quadragesimo Anno* (May 15, 1931), 78.

[57] See St. Thomas Aquinas, ST, II-II, q. 110, a. 3, rep. 4.

[58] See *Code of Canon Law*, can. 1246, §2.

[59] See 1917 *Code of Canon Law*, can. 1251, §1. A full meal was taken usually at midday or after three o'clock in the afternoon, and a collation (snack) was allowed at night; the practice of an additional morning collation (snack) was introduced in the 19th century.

[60] The two smaller meals (collation, snacks) together must not equal to a full meal.

[61] See *Code of Canon Law*, cann. 1249–1253.

[62] From this tradition, Easter Eggs were introduced.

[63] As the Collect of the First Sunday of Lent affirms: "O God, Who dost purify Thy Church by the yearly observance of Lent."

[64] Pope Benedict XIV, Brief *Non Ambigimus* (May 30, 1741).

[65] As can. 719 of the *Codex Canonum Ecclesiarum Orientalium* (Code of Canons of the Eastern Churches) emphasizes: "Anyone who is aware of a grave sin is to receive the sacrament of penance as soon as possible."

[66] See St. Thomas Aquinas, ST, III, q. 80, a. 9, rep. 3.

[67] Sacred Congregation of the Discipline of the Sacraments, Decree *Quam Singulari* (August 8, 1910).

[68] Sacred Congregation of the Discipline of the Sacraments, *Quam Singulari*.

[69] Sacred Congregation of the Discipline of the Sacraments, *Quam Singulari*.

[70] Sacred Congregation of the Discipline of the Sacraments, *Quam Singulari*.

[71] *Peter's Pence* is the name given to the financial support offered by the faithful to the Holy Father as a sign of their sharing in the concern of the Successor of Peter for the many different needs of the universal Church and for the relief of those most in need.

[72] In the traditional practice of the Church, to solemnize marriage was to celebrate it with the solemn rites of the Church, such as the Nuptial Mass, ringing of bells, etc. Such solemnity was forbidden in the penitential seasons of Advent and Lent.

SECTION 4: COUNSELS AND BEATITUDES

[1] *Code of Canon Law*, can. 600.

[2] *Code of Canon Law*, can. 599.

³ This according to the words of Our Lady to Jacinta, while in the hospital in Lisbon in 1920, see: Fr. Andrew Apostoli, *Fatima for Today*, 145.

⁴ *Code of Canon Law*, can. 601.

⁵ Council of Vatican II, *Lumen Gentium*, 44.

⁶ *Code of Canon Law*, can. 573, §1.

⁷ See Council of Trent, Session 24, *Doctrine on the Sacrament of Matrimony* (November 11, 1563), can. 10.

⁸ See *Homilia in verba Matthaei*, chap. 13, v. 45; quoted in St. Alphonsus Liguori, *The True Spouse of Christ* (Dublin: John Coyne, 1835), 30.

⁹ See *Code of Canon Law*, can. 642.

¹⁰ Congregation for Institutes of Consecrated Life and for Societies of Apostolic Life, Instruction *Verbi Sponsa* (May 13, 1999), 7.

¹¹ Congregation for Institutes of Consecrated Life and for Societies of Apostolic Life, *Verbi Sponsa*, 6.

¹² The "heresy of action" or of "activism" was condemned by Pope Leo XIII in his Apostolic Letter *Testem Benevolentiae Nostrae* (January 22, 1899). In this letter, the pope refutes the error of clerics who, on the practical and theoretical level, give primacy to the temporal virtues and natural realities to the detriment of supernatural realities, i.e., grace, prayer, and penance. The "heresy of action" therefore substitutes (practically speaking) the primacy of man and his acts for the primacy of God's action.

¹³ St. Thomas Aquinas, ST, I-II, q. 69, a. 3, c.

PART III — WORSHIP: BEING HOLY

¹ See St. Thomas Aquinas, ST, II-II, q. 81, a. 3, rep. 2.

SECTION 1: GRACE AND MERIT

¹ St. Thomas Aquinas, *De Veritate*, q. 29, a. 4, c. 1.

² Pope Leo XIII, *Humanum Genus*, 12.

³ Pope St. Pius V, *Ex Omnibus Afflictionibus*.

⁴ Pope Clement XI, Dogmatic Constitution *Unigenitus* (September 8, 1713).

⁵ See St. Thomas Aquinas, ST, I-II, q. 111, a. 1.

⁶ See St. Thomas Aquinas, ST, I-II, q. 111, a. 1, c.

⁷ See St. Thomas Aquinas, ST, I-II, q. 113, a. 1, c.

⁸ "He saved us, not because of works done by us in righteousness, but according to his own mercy, by the washing of regeneration and renewal of the Holy Spirit, … so that being justified by his grace we might become heirs according to the hope of eternal life" (Ti 3:5, 7*).

⁹ Council of Trent, Session 6, *Decree on Justification*, chap. 4.

¹⁰ Council of Trent, Session 6, *Decree on Justification*, chap. 3.

¹¹ Council of Trent, Session 6, *Decree on Justification*, chap. 9.

¹² Council of Trent, Session 6, *Decree on Justification*, can. 13.

¹³ *Catechism of the Catholic Church*, 2007.

¹⁴ Thomas à Kempis, *Imitation of Christ*, bk. 3, chap. 58, no. 32.

¹⁵ *Acte d´offrande à l´Amour miséricordieux: Récréations pieuses – Prières*.

SECTION 2: CHRISTIAN PRAYER

¹ *The Great Means of Salvation and of Perfection*, chap. 1, conclusion.

² Pope Pius XII, Encyclical *Mediator Dei* (November 20, 1947), 37.

³ St. Thomas Aquinas, ST, II-II, q. 83, a. 1, rep. 2.

⁴ *De Oratione Dominica*, no. 8.

SECTION 3: THE SACRAMENTS

¹ St. Thomas Aquinas, ST, III, q. 60, a. 3, c.

² Pope St. Leo the Great, *Serm.* 74, no. 2.

³ St. Thomas Aquinas, ST, III, q. 61, a. 1, c.

⁴ See St. Thomas Aquinas, ST, III, q. 84, a. 5, c.

⁵ St. Thomas Aquinas, *Sent.* IV, d. 22, q. 2, a. 1, qa. 3, sc.

⁶ See Council of Florence, Session 8; Council of Trent, Session 7.

⁷ See St. Thomas Aquinas, ST, III, q. 65, a. 3, c.

⁸ See Pope Eugene IV, Bull of Union with the Armenians *Exsultate Deo* (November 22, 1439).

⁹ St. Thomas Aquinas, ST, III, q. 63, a. 3, c.

¹⁰ Council of Trent, Session 7, *On the Sacraments in General* (March 3, 1547), can. 13.

¹¹ See *Code of Canon Law*, can. 854.

¹² See *Code of Canon Law*, can. 872.

¹³ See *Code of Canon Law*, can. 874, §1.

¹⁴ *Catechism of the Catholic Church*, 1215.

¹⁵ St. Thomas Aquinas, ST, III, q. 63, a. 1, c.

¹⁶ Council of Vatican II, *Lumen Gentium*, 14.

¹⁷ Pope Pius IX, *Quanto Conficiamur Moerore*, 7.

¹⁸ Pope Pius IX, *Quanto Conficiamur Moerore*, 7.

¹⁹ St. Thomas Aquinas, *De Veritate*, q. 14, a. 11, rep. 1.

²⁰ Archbishop Michael Sheehan, *Apologetics and Catholic Doctrine* (Sydney: Baronius Press, 2019), 175. St. Thomas Aquinas taught similarly: "Those who are saved are in the minority" (ST, I, q. 23, a. 7, rep. 3).

²¹ See Archbishop Michael Sheehan, *Apologetics and Catholic Doctrine*, 175-176.

²² Council of Vatican II, *Ad Gentes*, 7.

²³ Bull of Union with the Copts *Cantate Domino*.

²⁴ See St. Thomas Aquinas, *De malo*, q. 5, a. 5; *Sent.*, II, d. 33, q. 2, a. 1, 2.

²⁵ *De malo*, q. 5, a. 3.

²⁶ St. Thomas Aquinas, ST, III, q. 72, a. 1, rep. 1.

²⁷ Council of Constantinople I, can. 7.

²⁸ Can. 891.

²⁹ Council of Vatican II, *Lumen Gentium*, 40.

³⁰ *Catechism of the Catholic Church*, 2015.

³¹ As prayed in the *Quam oblationem* prayer of the ancient Roman Canon of Mass.

³² Pope St. Pius X, Encyclical *Notre Charge Apostolique* (August 25, 1910).

³³ Pope St. Pius X, Encyclical *E Supremi* (October 4, 1903), 9.

³⁴ See Council of Trent, Session 13, *Decree on the Eucharist* (October 11, 1551), chap. 3.

³⁵ See "Catechism of the Council of Trent" in *Tradivox Catholic Catechism Index*, ed. Aaron Seng (Manchester: Sophia Institute Press, 2021), 7:240–285.

³⁶ See St. Thomas Aquinas, ST, III, q. 73, a. 4, c.

³⁷ Session 6.

³⁸ Chap. 9.

39 *Ep.* 62, no. 13.

40 Council of Trent, Session 13, *Decree on the Eucharist,* chap. 1.

41 Council of Trent, Session 13, *Decree on the Eucharist,* can. 1.

42 *Opusculum 57, in festo Corporis Christi,* lect. 1–4.

43 Pope Leo XIII, Encyclical *Mirae Caritatis* (May 28, 1902), 7.

44 The Council of Trent taught: "Christ, whole and entire, exists under the species of bread and under any part of that species, and similarly the whole Christ exists under the species of wine and its parts.... If anyone denies that in the venerable sacrament of the Eucharist the whole Christ is contained under each species and under each part of either species when separated, let him be anathema" (Session 13, *Decree on the Eucharist,* chap. 3 and can. 3).

45 Council of Trent, Session 13, *Decree on the Eucharist,* chap. 3.

46 Council of Trent, Session 13, *Decree on the Eucharist,* chap. 3.

47 Ott, *Fundamentals,* 414.

48 Council of Trent, Session 13, *Decree on the Eucharist,* can. 6.

49 See St. Thomas Aquinas, ST, III, q. 73, a. 3, c.

50 Pope John Paul II, Encyclical *Ecclesia de Eucharistia* (April 17, 2003), 15.

51 Pope John Paul II, Letter *Dominicae Cenae* (February 24, 1980), 11.

52 See *Code of Canon Law* [1917], can. 845 §1.

53 See can. 910, §1.

54 See *Code of Canon Law,* can. 920, §2.

55 See *Code of Canon Law,* can. 919, § 1.

56 As established by Pope Pius XII, see Apostolic Constitution *Christus Dominus* (January 6, 1953).

57 St. Cyril of Jerusalem's observation (see *Cat. Myst.* 5, no. 21) that the faithful would touch the consecrated blood of Christ to their eyes was a bizarre instance, and not representative of the general Catholic practice. The views and practices of an individual Father of the Church are not infallible, and may diverge from the common tradition and practice of the universal Church.

58 See *Code of Canon Law,* can. 915.

59 *In Isaiam,* Hom. 6, no. 3, quoted in Pope John Paul II, *Ecclesia de Eucharistia,* 36.

60 *Catechism of the Catholic Church,* 1395.

61 Pope Leo XIII, Encyclical *Satis Cognitum* (June 29, 1896).

62 St. Thomas Aquinas, ST, III, q. 80, a. 1, rep. 3.

63 Sacred Congregation of the Council, Decree *Sacra Tridentina Synodus* (December 20, 1905).

64 See *Introduction to the Devout Life,* pt. 2, chaps. 19–20.

65 St. Thomas Aquinas, ST, III, q. 79, a. 4, c.

66 *Serm.* 40 [on Mt 22:2 etc. against the Donatists].

67 *The Divine Eucharist: Fourth Series* (New York: Fathers of the Blessed Sacrament, 1912), 117–118.

68 St. Thomas Aquinas, ST, II-II, q. 85, a. 3, rep. 3.

69 St. Thomas Aquinas, ST, II-II, q. 85, a. 1, c.

70 St. Thomas Aquinas, ST, II-II, q. 85, a. 2, c.

71 Secret for the Seventh Sunday after Pentecost (traditional rite), and Prayer over the Offerings for the Sixteenth Sunday in Ordinary Time (new rite of Pope Paul VI).

72 St. John Chrysostom, *In Epistolam ad Hebraeos Homiliae,* Hom. 17, no. 3.

73 Pope Pius XII, *Mediator Dei,* 72.

74 Pope Pius XII, *Mediator Dei,* 70.

75 Pope John Paul II, *Ecclesia de Eucharistia,* 12.

76 Council of Trent, Session 22, *Doctrine on the Sacrifice of the Mass* (September 17, 1572), chap. 2.

77 Council of Trent, Session 22, *Doctrine on the Sacrifice of the Mass,* chap. 1.

78 Pope Pius XII, *Mediator Dei,* 115.

79 St. Thomas Aquinas, ST, III, q. 74, a. 1, c.

80 St. Thomas Aquinas, ST, III, q. 83, a. 1, c.

81 Pope Pius XII, *Mediator Dei,* 92.

82 Pope Pius XII, *Mediator Dei,* 79.

83 Pope Pius XII, *Mediator Dei,* 79.

84 Pope Pius XII, *Mediator Dei,* 164.

85 Council of Vatican II, *Sacrosanctum Concilium,* 8.

86 Pope St. Gregory the Great, *Dialogi,* bk. 4, chap. 58.

87 Dom Prosper Gueranger, *The Traditional Latin Mass Explained* (Brooklyn: Angelico Press, 2017), 83.

88 St. Athanasius, *Ep. heortastica,* Ep. 42.

89 St. John Chrysostom, *In Hebr.,* hom. 13, no. 3.

90 Pope Pius XII, *Mediator Dei,* 103.

91 Council of Vatican II, *Lumen Gentium,* 11.

92 Council of Vatican II, *Lumen Gentium,* 26.

93 *Martyrium Saturnini, Dativi et aliorum plurimorum,* 7, 9, 10.

94 St. Alphonsus of Liguori, *La Messa e l'Officio strapazzati,* pt. I, original ed.

95 See *Code of Canon Law,* can. 932.

96 Pope Pius XII, *Mediator Dei,* 102.

97 Pope Pius XII, *Mediator Dei,* 104.

98 See St. Thomas Aquinas, ST, III, q. 85, a. 1.

99 See Council of Trent, Session 14, *On the Most Holy Sacrament of Penance* (November 25, 1551), can. 7.

100 Pope John Paul II, Motu Proprio *Misericordia Dei* (April 7, 2002), 3.

101 Congregation for the Clergy, *The Priest, Minister of Divine Mercy: An Aid for Confessors and Spiritual Directors* (March 9, 2011), 44.

102 Congregation for the Clergy, *The Priest, Minister of Divine Mercy: An Aid for Confessors and Spiritual Directors,* 59.

103 See *Code of Canon Law,* can. 966, §1.

104 See *Code of Canon Law,* can. 976. This is an example of the principle of *supplet ecclesia* (the Church supplies), as further explained in can. 144.

105 See *Code of Canon Law,* can. 916.

106 See *Code of Canon Law,* can. 1065, § 2.

107 Apostolic Penitentiary, *Manual of Indulgences: Norms and Grants,* 1999 ed., 18, §1.

108 Council of Trent, Session 25.

109 *Code of Canon Law,* can. 996, §1.

110 Apostolic Penitentiary, *Manual of Indulgences,* 20, §1.

111 See Apostolic Penitentiary, *Manual of Indulgences,* 24–26.

112 For further explanation of this indulgence, see Apostolic Penitentiary, *Manual of Indulgences,* 12.

113 Council of Trent, Session 14, *On the Sacrament of Extreme Unction* (November 25, 1551), can. 1.

114 See *Code of Canon Law,* can. 999.2: "Any presbyter in

a case of necessity, but only in the actual celebration of the sacrament."

115 St. Thomas Aquinas, ST, III–Sup., q. 32, a. 4, sc. See also ST, III-Sup., q. 30, a. 1, c.

116 See *Code of Canon Law*, can. 998.

117 The *Catechism of the Catholic Church* specifies: "If the sick person was not able to obtain it through the sacrament of penance" (1532).

118 *Code of Canon Law*, can. 1004, §2.

119 See Council of Trent, Session 22, *Doctrine on the Sacrifice of the Mass*, chap. 1.

120 Pope Pius XII, Allocution *Magnificate Dominum* (November 2, 1954).

121 Council of Vatican II, *Lumen Gentium*, 10.

122 Council of Trent, Session 23, *Decree of Reformation* (July 15, 1563), chap. 17.

123 Council of Trent, Session 23, *Doctrine on the Sacrament of Holy Orders*, can. 2.

124 See Letter from Pope Cornelius to Bishop Fabian of Antioch from 251.

125 See Council of Trent, Session 23.

126 See Pope Pius XII, Apostolic Constitution *Sacramentum Ordinis* (November 30, 1947); Council of Vatican II, *Lumen Gentium*, 29 (for diaconate) and *Lumen Gentium*, 22 (for the episcopate). For the diaconate see also Congregation for Catholic Education, *Ratio Fundamentalis Institutionis Diaconorum Permanentium* (February 22, 1998), 7. See also *Code of Canon Law*, can. 1009, §1; *Catechism of the Catholic Church*, 1554.

127 *Ad Trallianos*, chap. 3; see also *Ad Magnesios*, chap. 6.

128 To clarify this aspect Pope Benedict XVI changed the wording of canons 1008 and 1009 of the *Code of Canon Law*, adding the following: "Those who are constituted in the order of the episcopate or the presbyterate receive the mission and capacity to act in the Person of Christ the Head, whereas deacons are empowered to serve the People of God in the ministries of the liturgy, the word, and charity" (*Code of Canon Law*, can. 1009, §3, revised per Motu Proprio *Omnium in Mentem* [October 26, 2009]).

129 Pope Siricius, Decretal *Cum in unum* (in 385), can. 1.

130 In the Russian Orthodox Church, since the nineteenth century at least, there has been a custom that is not contained in written sources, but is widespread. During the ordination to the priesthood, the bishop removes the wedding ring from the finger of the married candidate and places it on the altar. The newly ordained priest no longer has the right to wear the wedding ring. The explanation of this tradition lies in the rite of the sacrament of ordination and marriage. When the sacrament of marriage is performed, the husband and wife are led three times around the analogion, which is a lectern on which icons or the Gospel book are placed. When the sacrament of the priesthood is performed, the candidate is as well led around the altar three times. At the same time, the same hymns are sung as in the rite of the sacrament of marriage. Therefore, before performing the sacrament of ordination,

the future priest takes off the wedding ring and places it on the altar as a sign that his life henceforth belongs only to God: he is now betrothed to the Church of Christ.

131 Pope Pius XII, *Sacramentum Ordinis*.

132 Pope Pius XII, *Sacramentum Ordinis*.

133 Pope Pius XII, *Sacramentum Ordinis*.

134 *Ad Corinthios*, Ep. 1, chap. 40.

135 Session 23, *Decree of Reformation*, chap. 17.

136 See *Traditio Apostolica*, no. 8; *Didascalia Apostolorum*, chap. 2; and, Council of Vatican II, *Lumen Gentium*, 29.

137 See *Code of Canon Law* [1917], can. 741.

138 See *Code of Canon Law* [1917], can. 845, §2.

139 See can. 861, §1 (baptism) and can. 910, §1 (Holy Communion).

140 See can. 943. However, according to the constant tradition of the Church, the minister of the Eucharistic blessing (with the monstrance or the ciborium, containing the Blessed Sacrament) was only a priest.

141 See International Theological Commission, *From the Diakonia of Christ to the Diakonia of the Apostles* (September 30, 2002), III, 2.

142 *Traditio Apostolica*, no. 8.

143 See *Code of Canon Law*, cann. 757; and 767, §1.

144 See St. Thomas Aquinas, ST, III, q. 67, a. 1, rep. 1.

145 Congregation for Catholic Education, *Ratio Fundamentalis institutionis diaconorum permanentium*, 7.

146 See *Code of Canon Law*, can. 89; 129, §1; 274, §1; 478, §1; 1079, §2; 1425, §1; and 1425, §4.

147 See *Code of Canon Law*, can. 835, §1.

148 The minimum age for the diaconate: 23 years; for the presbyterate: 25 years; and for the episcopate: 35 years (see *Code of Canon Law*, cann. 1031, §1; and 378, §1.3).

149 See *Code of Canon Law*, can. 1029.

150 Pope Benedict XVI approved this norm of the Congregation for Catholic Education, whereby the Church "cannot admit to the seminary or to holy orders those who practice homosexuality, present deep-seated homosexual tendencies, or support the so-called 'gay culture'" (Instruction *Concerning the Criteria for the Discernment of Vocations with regard to Persons with Homosexual Tendencies* [August 31, 2005], 2).

151 See *Code of Canon Law*, can. 1041.

152 Pope John Paul II, *Ordinatio Sacerdotalis*.

153 *Acta Apostolicae Sedis* 8, yr. 1916, p. 146.

154 Session 23, *Doctrine on the Sacrament of Holy Orders*, can. 6.

155 *Constitutiones Apostolorum*, bk. 8, chap. 28.

156 From apostolic times through the entire history of the Church, deacons, priests, and bishops have, from the moment of their ordination, lived in perfect sexual continence — even when married and still living with one's wife. Therefore, one of the conditions of the ordination of a married man was the consent of his wife, since they had to live thenceforth in continence. See the studies of Alfons Maria Cardinal Stickler, *The Case for Clerical Celibacy: Its Historical Development and Theological Foundations*, 2nd ed. (San Francisco: Ignatius Press, 2019).

[157] Ambrosiaster, *In 1 Tim.*, chap. 3, v. 11.

[158] See the Motu Proprio *Spiritus Domini* (January 10, 2021) in the revision of can. 230, § 1.

[159] St. Epiphanius of Salamis, *Panarion*, bk. 3, Anacephalae-osis VII, sect 79, no. 3.

[160] See "Catechism of the Council of Trent" in *Tradivox Catholic Catechism Index*, ed. Aaron Seng (Manchester: Sophia Institute Press, 2021), 7:360–378.

[161] St. Thomas Aquinas, ST, III-Sup., q. 42, a. 2, rep. 2.

[162] See Pope Benedict XIV, Apostolic Constitution *Dei Miseratione* (November 3, 1741), 1; Pope Leo XIII, *Arcanum Divinae*, 10, 26; Pope Pius XI, *Casti Conubii*, 8. "The primary end of marriage is the procreation and the education of children; the secondary [end] is mutual assistance and a remedy for concupiscence" (*Code of Canon Law* [1917], can. 1013, §1). Karol Wojtyła (later Pope John Paul II) recognized the same: "The Church, as already mentioned, teaches consistently that the primary end of marriage is *procreatio*, whereas the secondary end is what in the Latin terminology has been defined as *mutuum adiutorium*" (*Love and Responsibility*, trans. Grzegorz Ignatik [Boston: Pauline Media, 2013], 50).

[163] St. Thomas Aquinas, "The Catechetical Instructions" in *Tradivox Catholic Catechism Index*, ed. Aaron Seng (Manchester: Sophia Institute Press, 2021), 6:141.

[164] See Council of Trent, Session 24.

[165] "Catechism of the Council of Trent" in *Tradivox Catholic Catechism Index*, ed. Aaron Seng (Manchester: Sophia Institute Press, 2021), 7:368.

[166] Council of Trent, Session 24, *Doctrine on the Sacrament of Matrimony*, can. 10.

[167] See *Code of Canon Law*, cann. 1151–1155.

[168] Pope Paul VI, *Humanae Vitae*, 14.

[169] Pope Pius XI, *Casti Connubii*, 56.

[170] Pope Pius XII, *Address to the Directors of the Associations for Large Families of Rome and Italy* (January 20, 1958).

[171] Pope John Paul II, *General Audience* (September 5, 1984), 3–4.

[172] See St. Augustine, *De bono viduitatis*, no. 29; *Ep.* 188, no. 3; St. John Chrysostom, *On Ephesians*, Hom. 20.

[173] Council of Vatican II, *Lumen Gentium*, 11.

[174] Pope Leo XIII, *Arcanum Divinae*, 10.

[175] Council of Vatican II, Decree *Optatam Totius* (October 28, 1965), 2.

[176] Pope Pius XII, *Address to the Directors of the Associations for Large Families of Rome and Italy*.

[177] Pope Pius XII, *Address to the Directors of the Associations for Large Families of Rome and Italy*.

[178] *Code of Canon Law*, can. 1172, §1.

[179] First inserted in the *Rituale Romanum* (editio quarta, 1895), this prayer was translated into numerous languages, became particularly widespread at shrines to St. Michael the archangel, and was universally pre-scribed at the conclusion of Low Mass.

SECTION 4: THE LITURGY

[1] Pope Pius XII, *Mediator Dei*, 20.

[2] Giuseppe Maria Leone, *La vita interiore del sacerdote, modellata sulla vita di Gesù Cristo: Conferenze*, vol. 2 (Valle di Pompei: 1894), 208.

[3] *Life*, chap. 33.

[4] See Council of Trent, Session 22, *Decree on the Sacrifice of the Mass*, chap. 1.

[5] Pope Pius XII, *Mediator Dei*, 3.

[6] Pope John Paul II, *General Audience* (January 24, 1986).

[7] Pope Pius XII, *Mediator Dei*, 163.

[8] Council of Vatican II, *Sacrosanctum Concilium*, 83.

[9] St. Athanasius, *Litt. Encycl.*, no. 1.

[10] See the Tridentine Profession of Faith, below.

[11] Also called the "Breviary of Cardinal Quignonez."

[12] *Liber Diurnus Romanorum Pontificum*. This oath was in use from the eighth through the tenth century.

[13] Session 39 (October 9, 1417), ratified by Pope Martin V.

[14] Pope Pius VI, Apostolic Constitution *Auctorem Fidei* (August 28, 1794), prop. 33.

[15] Letter to the Bishops Accompanying "Summorum Pontificum."

[16] See Council of Trent, Session 22 (September 17, 1562) and Pope St. Pius V, Bull *Quo Primum* (July 14, 1570). See also Pope Benedict XVI, Motu Proprio *Summorum Pontificum* (July 7, 2007), art. 1.

[17] See Pope Pius VI, *Auctorem Fidei*, prop. 78; Pope Gregory XVI, Encyclical *Quo Graviora* (October 4, 1833), 4.

[18] *Enarr. in Ps.* 1, no. 9.

[19] Apostolic Constitution *Divino Afflatu* (November 1, 1911).

[20] Pope St. Pius X, Motu Proprio *Tra Le Sollecitudini* (November 22, 1903), 3; see also Council of Vatican II, *Sacrosanctum Concilium*, 116.

[21] Pope St. Pius X, *Tra Le Sollecitudini*, 2–3.

[22] See *Code of Canon Law*, can. 1210.

[23] St. John Chrysostom, *In I Cor.*, Hom. 36.

[24] See *Code of Canon Law*, can. 1211.

[25] *Cura mort.*, chap. 5.

[26] Pope Pius XII, *Allocution to the International Congress on Pastoral Liturgy in Assisi*.

[27] Sacred Congregation of Rites, Decree *Sanctissimam Eucharistiam* (June 1, 1957), 3.

[28] See *Code of Canon Law* [1917], can. 1306.

[29] Council of Vatican II, *Sacrosanctum Concilium*, 102.

[30] Pope Pius XII, *Mediator Dei*, 165.

[31] Council of Vatican II, *Sacrosanctum Concilium*, 102.

[32] Frère Michel de la Sainte Trinité, *The Whole Truth about Fatima*, vol. 3 (Buffalo: Immaculate Heart Publications, 1990), 337.

[33] Pope Leo XIII, Encyclical *Quamquam Pluries*, (August 15, 1889).

[34] St. Francis de Sales, *Introduction to the Devout Life*, pt. 1, chap. 2.

Index of Errors

This index refers the reader to certain false systems of philosophy, theology, and moral practice addressed in this *Compendium*.

Index of Subjects

128, 313, 325, 329; of the sacraments in general, 241–242

certainty of justification, 142–144, 223

chalice, 260, 292, 309, 321, 323–325, 356

character, sacramental (*see* sacramental character)

charism, 70, 81, 94, 132, 211, 219–220, 253

charity, 55; God is, 68, 70, 145, 345; supernatural (theological), 37, 61, 69, 71, 74, 106, 123, 131, 132, 144–149, 168, 227 264, 287, 353

chastity, 30, 71–72, 151–152, 160, 192–195, 214, 266, 296, 303, 326; as an evangelical counsel, 90, 192, 209–211, 300. *See also* call: to chastity; celibacy

children: admitted to Holy Communion, 206–207, 260, 264; as primary end of marriage (*see under* marriage); baptism of, 188, 244, 247, 248, 346–347; duties of (*see under* duty); duties toward (*see under* duty); dying without baptism, 248–249

choice. *See* free will

chrism, 2, 249–250, 251, 293, 324

Christ, Jesus. *See* Jesus Christ

Christian: name, 1, 133; symbol of the true, 2, 133. *See also under* Catholic Church

Christmas, 203–204, 327, 330

church: architecture, 318–319; Catholic (*see* Catholic Church); defined, 72; non–Catholic, 83–87, 96, 257

Church Fathers, 343; as locus of Tradition, 6, 235; faithful to Tradition, 6, 75–76; on Scripture, 5, 316; on Tradition, 6; teaching of, 21, 36, 46, 76, 77, 256, 289, 297, 321

ciborium, 279, 292, 323, 324

circumcision, 51, 128

circumstance(s), of a moral act, 125, 126, 279

citizens: duties of (*see under* duty); rights of (*see under* right[s])

clergy: attire of, 291, 292, 294, 326–328, 357; ranks of Catholic, 87–90, 289, 291–294

clerics. *See* clergy

clothing, 92, 171, 181, 227; modesty in, 148, 152, 183, 194, 261, 301, 303. *See also under* clergy

cohabitation, 193, 194, 262, 304

collaboration, 196, 304; for common good, 99–104; among clergy, 96–97, 99; of laity in Church's mission (*see* laity)

collegiality, 96–97, 99

command(s): of conscience, 126–127, 348; of God (*see under* obedience); of parents and superiors (*see under* obedience); of the Church (*see* obedience: to the Church; precepts of the Church). *See also* duty; obedience

common good, 93, 99–104, 129, 150, 179, 190, 208

communication: of spiritual goods, 78, 79, 106–108, 337 (*see also* censure; indulgence[s]; interdict); technologies, 152, 184; truthfulness in, 16, 132, 150, 157, 175, 200–202

communion, 255, 259–263, 331; between the divine Persons, 212 (*see also under* relation[s]); kinds of, 239, 263–265; norms for sacramental, 95, 206–207, 259–263, 264–265, 279; of saints, 11, 106–108, 283, 349; pope

Sophia Institute

Sophia Institute is a nonprofit institution that seeks to nurture the spiritual, moral, and cultural life of souls and to spread the Gospel of Christ in conformity with the authentic teachings of the Roman Catholic Church.

Sophia Institute Press fulfills this mission by offering translations, reprints, and new publications that afford readers a rich source of the enduring wisdom of mankind.

Sophia Institute also operates the popular online Catholic resource CatholicExchange.com. *Catholic Exchange* provides world news from a Catholic perspective as well as daily devotionals and articles that will help readers to grow in holiness and live a life consistent with the teachings of the Church.

In 2013, Sophia Institute launched Sophia Institute for Teachers to renew and rebuild Catholic culture through service to Catholic education. With the goal of nurturing the spiritual, moral, and cultural life of souls, and an abiding respect for the role and work of teachers, we strive to provide materials and programs that are at once enlightening to the mind and ennobling to the heart; faithful and complete, as well as useful and practical.

Sophia Institute gratefully recognizes the Solidarity Association for preserving and encouraging the growth of our apostolate over the course of many years. Without their generous and timely support, this book would not be in your hands.

www.SophiaInstitute.com
www.CatholicExchange.com
www.SophiaInstituteforTeachers.org

Sophia Institute Press° is a registered trademark of Sophia Institute.
Sophia Institute is a tax-exempt institution as defined by the
Internal Revenue Code, Section 501(c)(3). Tax I.D. 22-2548708.